Praise for *The Android™ Developer's Cookbook, Second Edition*

"*The Android™ Developer's Cookbook, Second Edition*, contains the recipes for developing and marketing a successful Android application. Each recipe in the book contains detailed explanations and examples of the right way to write your applications to become a featured app in the Google Play Store. From understanding the basic features of different versions of Android to designing and building a responsive UI, this cookbook gives you the recipes for success. You will learn to work with Android on every level—from hardware interfaces (like NFC and USB), to networking interfaces that will show you how to use mobile data efficiently, and even how to take advantage of Google's powerful billing interface. The authors do an incredible job of providing useful and real-life code examples for every concept in the book that can easily be built on and adapted to any situation and makes this book an essential resource for all Android developers."

—David Brown, information data manager and application developer, San Juan
School District

"Easy to read and easy to understand but not lacking features. This is one of the best books I have read on Android development. If you have the basics down, the recipes in the book will take you to mastery."

—Casey Doolittle, lead Java developer, Icon Health and Fitness

"*The Android™ Developer's Cookbook, Second Edition,* provides a fantastic foundation for Android development. It teaches core skills such as layouts, Android life cycle, and responsiveness via numerous multi-threading techniques, which you need to be a skilled Android chef."

—Kendell Fabricius, freelance Android developer

"This book has something for everyone. I've been programming Android since 1.0 and I learned some things that are completely new to me."

—Douglas Jones, senior software engineer, Fullpower Technologies

The Android™ Developer's Cookbook

Second Edition

The Android™ Developer's Cookbook

Building Applications with the Android SDK

Second Edition

Ronan Schwarz

Phil Dutson

James Steele

Nelson To

↟Addison-Wesley

Upper Saddle River, NJ • Boston • Indianapolis • San Francisco
New York • Toronto • Montreal • London • Munich • Paris • Madrid
Capetown • Sydney • Tokyo • Singapore • Mexico City

Many of the designations used by manufacturers and sellers to distinguish their products are claimed as trademarks. Where those designations appear in this book, and the publisher was aware of a trademark claim, the designations have been printed with initial capital letters or in all capitals.

The authors and publisher have taken care in the preparation of this book, but make no expressed or implied warranty of any kind and assume no responsibility for errors or omissions. No liability is assumed for incidental or consequential damages in connection with or arising out of the use of the information or programs contained herein.

The publisher offers excellent discounts on this book when ordered in quantity for bulk purchases or special sales, which may include electronic versions and/or custom covers and content particular to your business, training goals, marketing focus, and branding interests. For more information, please contact:

U.S. Corporate and Government Sales
(800) 382-3419
corpsales@pearsontechgroup.com

For sales outside the United States, please contact:

International Sales
international@pearsoned.com

Visit us on the Web: informit.com/aw

Library of Congress Cataloging-in-Publication Data

Ronan Schwarz,
    The Android developer's cookbook : building applications with the Android SDK / Ronan Schwarz, Phil Dutson, James Steele, Nelson To.—Second edition.
        pages cm
    Includes index.
    ISBN 978-0-321-89753-4 (pbk. : alk. paper)
    1. Application software—Development. 2. Android (Electronic resource) 3. Operating systems (Computers) I. Schwarz, Ronan. II. Dutson, Phil, 1981– III. To, Nelson, 1976– IV. Title.

    QA76.76.A65S743 2013
    004.1675—dc23   2013014476

ISBN-13: 978-0-321-89753-4
ISBN-10:   0-321-89753-6
Text printed in the United States on recycled paper at RR Donnelley in Crawfordsville, Indiana.
First printing, June 2013

Editor-in-Chief
Mark Taub

Executive Editor
Laura Lewin

Development Editor
Michael Thurston

Managing Editor
John Fuller

Project Editor
Elizabeth Ryan

Copy Editor
Barbara Wood

Indexer
Jack Lewis

Proofreader
Denise Wolber

Technical Reviewers
Casey Doolittle
Douglas Jones
James Steele

Editorial Assistant
Olivia Basegio

Cover Designer
Chuti Prasertsith

Compositor
Achorn International

❖

To my beloved wife Susan and the OpenIntents Community:
Thank you for your support
—Ronan

To Martin Simonnet and the Niantic Project for all the fun they have provided
—Phil

To Wei with love
—Jim

To my dear mom
—Nelson

❖

Contents at a Glance

Table of Contents

Preface

Android is the fastest growing mobile operating system (OS). With more than 800,000 applications available in the Google Play store, the Android ecosystem is growing as well. There is enough diversity in device features and wireless carriers to appeal to just about anyone.

Netbooks have always been a natural platform to adopt Android, but the liveliness behind Android has fed the growth further into tablets, televisions, and even automobiles. Many of the world's largest corporations—from banks to fast food chains to airlines—have established a presence in Android and offer compatible services. Android developers have many opportunities, and relevant apps reach more people than ever before, increasing the satisfaction of creating a relevant app.

Why an Android Cookbook?

The Android OS is simple to learn, and Google provides many libraries to make it easy to implement rich and complex applications. The only aspect lacking, as mentioned by many in the Android developer community, is clear and well-explained documentation. The fact that Android is open source means anyone can dive in and reverse engineer some documentation. Many developer bulletin boards have excellent examples that were deduced using exactly this method. Still, a book that has a consistent treatment across all areas of the OS is useful.

In addition, a clear working example is worth a thousand words of documentation. Developers faced with a problem usually prefer to do a form of extreme programming; that is, they find examples of working code that does something close to the solution and modify or extend it to meet their needs. The examples also serve as a way to see the coding style and help to shape other parts of the developer's code.

This Android cookbook fills a need by providing a variety of self-contained recipes. As each recipe is introduced, the main concepts of the Android OS are also explained.

Who Should Read This Book?

Users who are writing their own Android applications will get the most out of this cookbook. Basic familiarity with Java and the Eclipse development environment is assumed but not required for the majority of the book. Java is a modular language, and most (if not all) of the example recipes can be incorporated with minimal change into the reader's own Android project. The motivation and coverage of each topic in this book make it usable as an Android course supplement.

Using the Recipes

In general, the code recipes in this cookbook are self-contained and include all the information necessary to run a working application on an Android device. Chapters 1 and 2 give an introduction to the overall use of Android, but feel free to jump around and start using whatever is necessary.

This book is written first as a reference, providing knowledge mostly by example with the greatest benefits through implementation of the recipes of interest. The main technique introduced in each recipe is specified in the section heading. However, additional techniques are included in each recipe as needed to support the main recipe.

After reading this book, a developer should

- Be able to write an Android Application from scratch
- Be able to write code that works across multiple versions of Android
- Be able to use the various Application Programming Interfaces (APIs) provided in Android
- Have a large reference of code snippets to quickly assimilate into applications
- Appreciate the various ways to do the same task in Android and the benefits of each
- Understand the unique aspects of Android programming techniques

Book Structure

- Chapter 1, "Overview of Android," provides an introduction to all aspects of Android outside of the code itself. It is the only chapter that doesn't include recipes, but it provides useful background material.
- Chapter 2, "Application Basics: Activities and Intents," provides an overview of the four Android components and an explanation of how an Android project is organized. It also focuses on the activity as a main application building block.
- Chapter 3, "Threads, Services, Receivers, and Alerts," introduces background tasks such as threads, services, and receivers, as well as notification methods for these background tasks using alerts.
- Chapter 4, "Advanced Threading Techniques," covers using AsyncTasks and using loaders.
- Chapter 5, "User Interface Layout," covers the user interface screen layout and views.

- Chapter 6, "User Interface Events," covers user-initiated events such as touch events and gestures.
- Chapter 7, "Advanced User Interface Techniques," covers creating a custom view, using animation, offering accessibility options, and working with larger screens.
- Chapter 8, "Multimedia Techniques," covers multimedia manipulation and record and playback of audio and video.
- Chapter 9, "Hardware Interface," introduces the hardware APIs available on Android devices and how to use them.
- Chapter 10, "Networking," discusses interaction outside of the Android device with SMS, web browsing, and social networking.
- Chapter 11, "Data Storage Methods," covers various data storage techniques available in Android, including SQLite.
- Chapter 12, "Location-Based Services," focuses on accessing the location through various methods such as GPS and using services such as the Google Maps API.
- Chapter 13, "In-App Billing," provides an instruction set on including in-app billing in your application using Google Play services.
- Chapter 14, "Push Messages," covers how to use GCM for handling push messages with an application.
- Chapter 15, "Native Android Development," discusses the components and structure used for native development.
- Chapter 16, "Debugging," provides the testing and debugging framework useful throughout the development cycle.

Additional References

There are many online references for Android. A few essential ones are

- Android Source Code: http://source.android.com/
- Android Developer Pages: http://developer.android.com/
- Open Source Directory: http://osdir.com/
- Stack Overflow Discussion Threads: http://stackoverflow.com/
- Talk Android Developer Forums: www.talkandroid.com/android-forums/

About the Authors

Ronan "Zero" Schwarz is cofounder of OpenIntents, a Europe-based open source company specializing in Android development. Ronan has more than fifteen years of programing experience in a wide variety of fields such as augmented reality, web, robotics, and business systems, as well as different programing languages, including C, Java, and Assembler. He has been working on the Android Platform since 2007 and, among other things, has helped create SplashPlay and Droidspray, both top finalists of the Google Android Developer Challenge I and II.

Phil Dutson is the lead UX and mobile developer for ICON Health and Fitness. He has worked on projects and solutions for NordicTrack, ProForm, Freemotion, Sears, Costco, Sam's Club, and others. Through the years he has been using, tweaking, and writing programs for mobile devices from his first Palm Pilot 5000 to his current collection of iOS and Android devices. Phil has also authored *jQuery, JQuery UI, and jQuery Mobile*; *Sams Teach Yourself jQuery Mobile in 24 Hours*; and *Creating QR and Tag Codes*.

James Steele was doing postdoctoral work in physics at MIT when he decided to join a start-up in Silicon Valley. Fifteen years later he continues to innovate, bringing research projects to production in both the consumer and mobile markets. He actively presents at and participates in various Silicon Valley new technology groups. Jim is VP of Engineering at Sensor Platforms.

Nelson To has more than ten applications of his own in the Android Market. He has also worked on enterprise Android applications for Think Computer, Inc. (PayPhone), AOL (AIM), Stanford University (Education App), and Logitech (Google TV). He also assists in organizing the Silicon Valley Android Meetup Community and teaches Android classes in both the Bay Area and China.

Overview of Android

The Android operating system (OS) has come a long way since the announcement of the Open Handset Alliance in late 2007. The idea of an open source OS for embedded systems was not new, but Google's aggressive backing of it has definitely helped push Android to the forefront in just a few years.

Many wireless carriers in multiple countries across various communication protocols have one or more Android phones available. Other embedded devices, such as tablets, netbooks, televisions, set-top boxes, and even automobiles, have also adopted the Android OS.

This chapter discusses various general aspects of Android that are useful for developers. It provides a foundation for the creation of Android applications and a context for the recipes in the rest of this book.

The Evolution of Android

Google, seeing a large growth of Internet use and search with mobile devices, acquired Android, Inc., in 2005 to focus its development on a mobile device platform. Apple introduced the iPhone in 2007 with some groundbreaking ideas, including multitouch and an open market for applications. Android was quickly adapted to include these features and to offer definite distinctions, such as more control for developers and multitasking. In addition, Android incorporated enterprise requirements, such as exchange support, remote wipe, and virtual private network (VPN) support, to go after the enterprise market that Research In Motion had developed and held so well with its BlackBerry models.

Device diversity and quick adaptation have helped Android grow its user base, but such growth comes with potential challenges for developers. Applications need to support multiple screen sizes, resolution ratios, keyboards, hardware sensors, OS versions, wireless data rates, and system configurations. Each can lead to different and unpredictable behavior, but testing applications across all environments is an impossible task.

Android has therefore been constructed to ensure as uniform an experience across platforms as possible. By abstracting the hardware differences, Android OS tries to insulate applications from device-specific modifications while providing the flexibility to tune aspects as needed. Future-proofing applications to the introduction of new hardware platforms and OS updates is also a consideration. This mostly works as long as the developer is well aware of this systematic approach. The generic Application Programming Interfaces (APIs) that Android offers and how to ensure device and OS compatibility are main threads discussed throughout this book.

Still, as with any embedded platform, extensive testing of applications is required. Google provides assistance to third-party developers in many forms as Android Development Tools (ADT) plugins for Eclipse (also as stand-alone tools), including real-time logging capabilities, a realistic emulator that runs native ARM code, and in-field error reports from users to developers of Google Play applications.

The Dichotomy of Android

Android has some interesting dichotomies. Knowing about them up front is useful for understanding not only what Android is, but what it is not.

Android is an embedded OS that relies on the Linux kernel for core system services, but it is not embedded Linux. For example, standard Linux utilities such as X Windows and GNU C libraries are not supported. Android applications are written using the Java framework, but Android is not Java. Standard Java libraries such as Swing are not supported. Other libraries such as Timer are not preferred; they have been replaced by Android's own libraries, which are optimized for usage in a resource-constrained, embedded environment.

The Android OS is open source, which means developers can view and use any of the system source code, including the radio stack. This source code is one of the first resources for seeing examples of Android code in action, and it helps clarify the usage when documentation is lacking. This also means developers can use the system in the same way as any core application and can swap out system components for their own components. However, Android devices do contain some proprietary software that is inaccessible to developers (such as Global Positioning System (GPS) navigation).

Devices Running Android

Worldwide there are hundreds of Android devices on the market from many manufacturers, including phones, tablets, televisions, car stereos, exercise equipment, and accessories. Software can access information on the target device using the `android.os.Build` class, for example:

```
if(android.os.Build.MODEL.equals("Nexus+One")) { ... }
```

All Android-supported hardware shares some common features due to the nature of the operating system. The Android OS is organized into the following images:

- Bootloader—Initiates loading of the boot image during start-up
- Boot image—Kernel and RAMDisk
- System image—Android operating system platform and apps
- Data image—User data saved across power cycles
- Recovery image—Files used for rebuilding or updating the system
- Radio image—Files of the radio stack

These images are stored in nonvolatile flash memory, so they are protected when the device powers down. The flash memory is used like read-only memory (hence, some call it ROM), but it can be rewritten as necessary (for example, with over-the-air Android operating system updates).

On start-up, the microprocessor executes the bootloader to load the kernel and RAMDisk to RAM for quick access. The microprocessor then executes instructions and pages portions of the system and data images into RAM as needed. The radio image resides on the baseband processor, which connects to the radio hardware.

A comparison of some of the early and more recent smartphone models is shown in Table 1.1. It shows that the processing hardware architecture is similar across devices: a microprocessor unit (MPU), synchronous dynamic random access memory (SDRAM or RAM for short), and flash memory (called ROM for short). The screen size is given in pixels, but the dots per inch (dpi) vary depending on the physical screen size. For example, the HTC Magic has a 3.2-inch diagonal screen with 320×480 pixels. This equates to 180 pixels per inch but is classified as a medium-pixel-density device by Android (which averages 160 dpi). All smartphones also offer a CMOS image sensor camera, Bluetooth (BT), and Wi-Fi (802.11), although there are variations.

Other than improved capacity and performance on newer models, another main differentiator is additional features. Some devices offer 4G; some have FM or additional cellular radios, video output (through HDMI or micro-USB), and a front-facing camera. Knowing the differentiators helps a developer create great applications. In addition to the built-in hardware, many Android devices come with a Micro Secure Digital (microSD) card slot. A microSD card provides additional storage space for multimedia and extra application data. However, until Android 2.2, the apps themselves could be stored only on the internal ROM.

HTC Models

HTC is a Taiwanese company founded in 1997. The first commercially available hardware running Android was the HTC Dream (also known as the G1 where G stands for Google). It was released in October 2008. Since then, HTC has put out over 20 phones running Android, including Google's Nexus One, the EVO 3D, and the One X+.

The Nexus One was one of the first Android devices to use a 1GHz microprocessor, the Snapdragon platform from Qualcomm. Snapdragon includes Qualcomm's own core as opposed to an ARM core, and it contains circuitry to decode high-definition video at 720p. Most smartphones that have followed also use a 1GHz microprocessor.

Table 1.1 **Representative Android Smartphones***

Model	MPU	RAM/ROM	Screen	Other Features
Galaxy Nexus (November 2011)	1.2GHz dual-core Samsung	1024MB/16GB or 32GB	HD Super AMOLED 720×1280 xhdpi	GSM/UMTS/HSPA+/HSUPA/CDMA/1xEV-DO/ LTE BT3.0 with A2DP, MHL through Micro-USB 2.0, 802.11b/g/n, 5MP camera 1.3MP front-facing camera, geotagging, Wi-Fi hotspot, AGPS, NFC
Droid RAZR MAXX (May 2012)	1.2GHz dual-core ARM Corex-A9 SoC	1024MB/16GB	Super AMOLED 540×960 QHD hdpi	GSM/CDMA/HSDPA/1xEV-DO/LTE BT4.0 with A2DP and EDR + LE, 802.11b/g/n, HDMI, Wi-Fi hotspot, 8MP camera 1.3MP front-facing camera, geotagging, DLNA, AGPS, HD 1080p video recording
Google Nexus 4 (November 2012)	1.5GHz Quad-core Qualcomm Snapdragon	2GB/8GB or 16GB	TrueHD-IPS Plus LCD 786×1280 xhdpi	GSM/UMTS/HSDPA,HSUPA,HSPA+ BT4.0 with A2DP and LE, 802.11b/g/n, Wi-Fi hotspot, Wi-Fi Direct, DLNA, HDMI, AGPS, SGPS, GLONASS, 8MP camera, 1.3 front-facing camera, geotagging, HD 1080p video recording
Galaxy Note 2 (November 2012)	1.6GHz Samsung Exynos 4 Quad 4412	2GB/32GB	Super AMOLED 720×1280	GSM/UMTS/HSDPA, HSUPA, HSPA+ BT4.0, 802.11a/b/g/n, GPS, AGPS, Geotagging, 8MP camera, 1.9MP front-facing camera, 1080p video recording, NFC
HTC One (March 2013)	1.7GHz Qualcomm Snapdragon 600 APQ8064T	2GB/32 or 64GB	Super LCD 3 1080×1920	GSM/UMTS/HSDPA, HSUPA, HSPA+ BT4.0, 802.11a/b/g/n, GPS, AGPS, QuickGPS, Geotagging, 4.3MP camera, 2.1MP front-facing camera, 1080p video recording, NFC

*Data from http://en.wikipedia.org/wiki/Comparison_of_Android_devices and http://pdadb.net/

Other distinctions of the Nexus One are the use of two microphones to cancel background noise during phone conversations and a backlit trackball that lights up in different colors based on the notification.

The HTC EVO 4G released in June 2010 produced quite a sensation as the first commercially available phone that supports WiMAX (802.16e-2005). HTC also released the EVO 3D in August 2011. It is similar to the EVO 4G but has the distinction of packing a 3D display that does not require the use of 3D glasses to view, as well as two rear-facing cameras that can record 720p HD videos in 3D.

Motorola Models

Motorola has put out close to ten additional phone brands running Android. The Motorola Droid X has capabilities similar to the HTC Droid Incredible, including HD video capture. In 2011 Google acquired Motorola Mobility in the hope of strengthening Android in the marketplace, giving a boost in innovation, and to protect the Android ecosystem through the use of Motorola Mobility's patent portfolio.

The Droid RAZR MAXX and RAZR MAXX HD are two phones developed by Motorola that have an exceptionally long battery life while keeping a fairly slim form factor.

Samsung Models

Samsung has been a strong force in the mobile market and is currently the number-one Android device manufacturer, accounting for 42 percent of all Android devices shipped during the fourth quarter of 2012. The most popular Samsung phones available are the Galaxy Note 2 and the Galaxy S3. Both of these devices feature Bluetooth 4.0, near field communication (NFC), and Samsung specifics such as S Beam and AllShare support.

The Samsung Galaxy Nexus was the first Android 4.2 phone and one of the first phones to be released with NFC built in. Samsung was the first to introduce smartphones that attempt to bridge the gap between phones and tablets. Some refer to these phones as "phablets," as both the Galaxy Note and Galaxy Note 2 feature a screen that is larger than 5 inches.

Tablets

With Apple's introduction of the iPad, Android manufacturers were expected to introduce tablet computers of their own. A tablet computer is loosely defined as having a screen of 4.8 inches or larger and Wi-Fi connectivity. Because many have 3G wireless service, they tend to be more like smartphones with large screens.

Archos was one of the first to market an Android tablet in late 2009. The first model had a diagonal screen size of 4.8 inches and was called the Archos 5. Archos has since introduced new models with screens ranging in size from 7 to 10 inches. Some models come with an actual hard drive, while others use flash drives for memory. Samsung offers several Galaxy Tab models with a variety of screen sizes from 7 to 10.1 inches.

Amazon offers the Kindle Fire line of tablets in four varieties. The tablets range in size from 7 inches to 8.9 inches and have either single- or dual-core processors. Each of these runs on a modified Android system that is connected to the Amazon Appstore as well as Amazon MP3 and Amazon Video.

Google has also partnered with Asus to release the Nexus 7, a 7-inch tablet with Android 4.2.1. Shortly thereafter, Google partnered with Samsung to build the Nexus 10. The Nexus 10 is the first Android tablet to contain a resolution of 2560×1600, which matches the display of the "retina" MacBook Pro computers and newer full-size iPad devices. A comparison of some tablet computer models is shown in Table 1.2.

Other Devices

Given that Android is a generic embedded platform, it is expected to be used in many other applications beyond smartphones and tablets. The first Android-based automobile is the Roewe 350, which Shanghai Automotive Industry Corporation manufactures. Android is mainly used for GPS navigation but can also support web browsing.

Saab has also created an information and entertainment system named IQon that runs on the Android platform, giving drivers real-time feedback about engine workload, speed, torque, and similar mechanical data. It displays this information through a built-in 8-inch console that features a touchscreen with a 3G or 4G data connection. While some of this information could be obtained by installing an aftermarket part into the engine control unit (ECU) of the car, the idea of having Android baked directly into the ECU is an interesting and exciting idea.

Android has also migrated into some new and exciting platforms such as watches and the OUYA console. The Pebble watch was a Kickstarter project to build a watch that could communicate with Android and iOS devices. It allows for access from an Android device through use of its software development kit (SDK) and communicates by using Bluetooth to show caller ID, current time, incoming text messages, email reminders, and so on. The OUYA console is a terrific example of pushing the Android system to the extreme. It is a console (similar to a PlayStation or Xbox) that is devoted to Android gaming. While the project is new and at the time of this writing not available to the general public, OUYA has promised to release low-cost, cutting-edge hardware on a yearly basis.

Hardware Differences on Android Devices

The hardware available on each Android device varies, as seen in Table 1.1. In general, most of the differences are transparent to the developer and not covered further here. However, a few hardware differences are important to understand to assist in writing device-independent code. Screens, user input methods, and sensors are discussed here.

Table 1.2   **Representative Android Tablets**

Model	MPU	RAM/ROM	Screen	Other Features
Archos 80 G9 (September 2011)	1000MHz TI OMAP 4430	512MB/16GB	TFT LCD 8 inches, 1024×768	BT2.1 + EDR, 802.11b/g/n, 0.9MP camera
Archos Gen10 101 XS (September 2012)	1500MHz TI OMAP 4470	1GB/16GB	TFT LCD 10.1 inches, 1280×800	802.11b/g/n, Bluetooth 4.0, attachable QWERTY-type keyboard, 1.3MP camera, GPS
Samsung Galaxy Note 10.1 (February 2012)	1400MHz Samsung Exynos	2GB/32GB	TFT LCD 10.1 inches, 1280×800	BT4.0, 802.11a/b/g/n, GPS, geotagging, 5MP camera, 1.9MP front-facing camera
Nexus 7 32GB (November 2012)	1300MHz Quad-core Cortex-A9 T30L	1GB/32GB	IPS TFT LCD 7 inches, 1280×800	GSM/UMTS/GPRS/EDGE/ UMTS/HSDPA/HSUPDA/ HSPA+, BT3, 802.11a/b/ g/n, 1.2MP camera, GPS, geotagging
Nexus 10 32GB (November 2012)	1700MHz Exynos 5 Dual 5250	2GB/32GB	PLS LCD 10 inches, 2560×1600	BT4, 802.11b/g/n, 5MP camera, 1.9MP front-facing camera, GPS, geotagging

Screens

Two technologies used for displays are liquid crystal displays (LCDs) and light-emitting diodes (LEDs). The two specific choices in Android phones are thin-film transistor (TFT) LCDs and active-matrix organic LED (AMOLED) displays. A benefit of TFT displays is a longer lifetime. A benefit of AMOLED displays is no need for backlighting and therefore deeper blacks and lower power usage.

Overall, Android devices are categorized into small, normal, large, and extra-large screens and low, medium, high, and extra-high pixel density. Note that the actual pixel density may vary but will always be defaulted to low, medium, high, or extra-high. Table 1.3 shows the typical screen size, resolution, and name associated with different screen sizes.

User Input Methods

Touchscreens enable users to interact with the visual display. There are three types of touchscreen technology:

- Resistive—Two layers of resistive material sit on top of a glass screen. When a finger, stylus, or any object applies pressure, the two layers touch and the location of the touch can be determined. Resistive touchscreens are cost-effective, but

Table 1.3   Device Screens Supported by Android

Screen Type	Low-Density (~120ppi), ldpi	Medium-Density (~160ppi), mdpi	High-Density (~240ppi), hdpi	Extra-High-Density (~3200dpi), xhdpi
Small screen (426×320dp)	QVGA (240×320) ldpi		480×640 hdpi	
Normal screen (470×320dp)	WQVGA400 (240×400) ldpi, WQVGA432 (240×432) ldpi	HVGA (320×480) mdpi	WVGA800 (480×800) hdpi, WVGA (480×854) hdpi	640×960 xhdpi
Large screen (640×480dp)		600×1024 mdpi		
Xlarge screen (960×720dp)	1024×600 ldpi	WXGA (1280×800) mdpi, 1024×768 mdpi, 1280×768 mdpi	1536×1152 hdpi, 1920×1152 hdpi, 1920×1200 hdpi	2048×1536 xhdpi, 2560×1536 xhdpi, 2560×1600 xhdpi

only 75 percent of the light shows through, and until recently multitouch was not possible.

- Capacitive—A layer of charged material is overlaid on a glass screen. When a finger or any conductive object touches the layer, some charge is drawn off, changing the capacitance, which is measured to determine the location of the touch. Capacitive touchscreens allow as much as 90 percent of the light through, although accuracy can be less than that of resistive touchscreens.

- Surface acoustic wave—This uses a more advanced method that sends and receives ultrasonic waves. When a finger or any object touches the screen, the waves are absorbed and are measured to determine the location of the touch. It is the most durable solution, but more suitable for large-scale screens such as those on automatic bank tellers.

All Android devices use either resistive or capacitive touchscreen technology, and all support multitouch. In addition, each Android device may provide an alternative method to access the screen through one of the following methods:

- D-pad (directional pad)—An up-down-right-left type of joystick
- Trackball—A rolling ball acting as a pointing device that is similar to a mouse
- Trackpad—A special rectangular surface acting as a pointing device

Sensors

Smartphones are becoming sensor hubs in a way, opening a rich experience for users. Other than the microphone that every phone has, the first additional sensor introduced on phones was the camera. Different phone cameras have varying capabilities, and this is an important factor for people when selecting a device. The same type of diversity is now seen with the additional sensors.

Most smartphones have at least three additional basic sensors: a three-axis accelerometer to measure gravity, a three-axis magnetometer to measure the ambient magnetic field, and a temperature sensor to measure the ambient temperature. For example, the HTC Dream (G1) contains the following sensors (which can be displayed using getSensorList() as described further in Chapter 9, "Hardware Interface"):

- AK8976A three-axis accelerometer
- AK8976A three-axis magnetic field sensor
- AK8976A orientation sensor
- AK8976A temperature sensor

The AK8976A is a single package from Asahi Kasei Microsystems (AKM) that combines a piezoresistive accelerometer, Hall-effect magnetometer, and temperature sensor. All provide 8-bit precision data. The orientation sensor is a virtual sensor that uses the accelerometer and magnetometer to determine the orientation.

For comparison, the Motorola Droid contains the following sensors:

- LIS331DLH three-axis accelerometer
- AK8973 three-axis magnetic field sensor
- AK8973 temperature sensor
- SFH7743 proximity sensor
- Orientation sensor type
- LM3530 light sensor

The LIS331DLH is a 12-bit capacitive accelerometer from ST Microelectronics. It provides much more accurate data and can sample up to 1kHz. The AK8973 is an AKM package with an 8-bit Hall-effect magnetometer and temperature sensor.

In addition, the Droid contains two more sensors. The SFH7743 is an Opto Semiconductor's short-range proximity detector that turns the screen off when an object (such as the ear) is within about 40mm distance. The LM3530 is an LED driver with a programmable light sensor from National Semiconductor that detects ambient light and adjusts the screen backlight and LED flash appropriately.

One other example of sensors available on an Android device is the HTC EVO 4G, which has the following sensors:

- BMA150 three-axis accelerometer
- AK8973 three-axis magnetic field sensor
- AK8973 orientation sensor
- CM3602 proximity sensor
- CM3602 light sensor

The BMA150 is a Bosch Sensortec 10-bit accelerometer which can sample up to 1.5kHz. The CM3602 is a Capella Microsystems, Inc., short-distance proximity sensor and ambient light sensor combined into one.

Overall, it is important to understand that each Android model has different underlying hardware. These differences can lead to varying performance and accuracy of the sensors.

Features of Android

The detailed features of Android and how to take advantage of them provide a main theme throughout this book. On a broader level, some key features of Android are major selling points and differentiators. It is good to be aware of these strong points of Android and use them as much as possible.

Multiprocess and App Widgets

The Android OS does not restrict the processor to a single application at a time. The system manages priorities of applications and of threads within a single application. This has the benefit that background tasks can be run while a user engages the device in a foreground process. For example, while a user plays a game, a background process can check stock prices and trigger an alert as necessary.

App Widgets are mini applications that can be embedded in other applications (such as the home screen). They can process events, such as start a music stream or update the outside temperature, while other applications are running.

Multiprocessing has the benefit of a rich user experience. However, care must be taken to avoid power-hungry applications that drain the battery. Multiprocess features are discussed further in Chapter 3, "Threads, Services, Receivers, and Alerts."

Touch, Gestures, and Multitouch

The touchscreen is an intuitive user interface for a hand-held device. If used well, it can transcend the need for detailed instructions. After a finger touches the screen, drags and flings are natural ways to interact with graphics. Multitouch provides a way to track more than one finger touch at the same time. This is often used to zoom or rotate a view.

Some touch events are available transparently to the developer without the need to implement their detailed behaviors. Custom gestures can be defined as needed. It is important to try to maintain a consistent usage of touch events across applications. Touch events are discussed further in Chapter 6, "User Interface Events."

Hard and Soft Keyboards

One feature on a hand-held device that polarizes users is whether it should have a physical (also called hard) keyboard or a software (also called soft) keyboard. The tactile feedback and definite placement of keys provided by a hard keyboard tend to make typing much faster for some, whereas others prefer the sleek design and convenience offered by a software-only input device.

With the large variety of Android devices available, either type can be found. A side effect for developers is the need to support both. One downside of a soft keyboard is that a portion of the screen needs to be dedicated to the input. This needs to be considered and tested for any user interface (UI) layout.

Android Development

This book is focused on writing Android code, the main aspect of Android development. However, dedicating a few words to the other aspects of development, including design and distribution, is appropriate.

Designing Applications Well

Three elements are needed for an excellent application: a good idea, good coding, and good design. Often, the last element is paid the least attention because most developers work alone and are not graphic designers. Google must realize this because it has created a set of design guidelines: icon design, App Widget design, activity and task design, and menu design. These can be found at http://developer.android.com/guide /practices/ui_guidelines/. Google has also taken things a step further by creating a site specifically to demonstrate design principles and how they can be implemented in Android applications. This can be found at http://developer.android.com/design /index.html.

Good design cannot be stressed enough. It sets an application apart, increases user adoption, and builds user appreciation. Some of the most successful apps on the market are a result of the collaboration between a developer and a graphic designer. A significant portion of an app's development time should be dedicated to considering the best design for it.

Maintaining Forward Compatibility

New Android versions are generally additive and forward compatible at the API level. In fact, a device can be called an Android device only if it passes compatibility tests with the Android APIs. However, if an application makes changes to the underlying system, compatibility is not guaranteed. To ensure forward compatibility of an application when future Android updates are installed on devices, follow these rules suggested by Google:

- Do not use internal or unsupported APIs.
- Do not directly manipulate settings without asking the user. A future release might constrain settings for security reasons. For instance, it used to be possible for an app to turn on GPS or data roaming by itself, but this is no longer allowed.
- Do not go overboard with layouts. This is rare, but complicated layouts (more than ten deep or 30 total layouts) can cause crashes.

- Do not make bad hardware assumptions. Not all Android devices have all possible supported hardware. Be sure to check for the hardware needed, and if it does not exist, handle the exception.
- Ensure that device orientations do not disrupt the application or result in unpredictable behavior. Screen orientation can be locked, as described in Chapter 2, "Application Basics: Activities and Intents."

Note that backward compatibility is not guaranteed with Android. It is best to declare the minimum SDK version as described in Chapter 2, so the device can load the proper compatibility settings. Using other new features on older targets is also discussed in various places throughout the book.

Ensuring Robustness

In the same vein as compatibility support, applications should be designed and tested for robustness. Following are a few tips to help ensure robustness:

- Use the Android libraries before Java libraries. Android libraries are constructed specifically for embedded devices and cover many of the requirements of an application. For cases such as working with third-party plugins and application frameworks, Java libraries are included. However, in cases where either can be used, the Android library is better.
- Take care of memory allocation. Initialize variables. Try to reuse objects rather than reallocate. This speeds up application execution and avoids excessive use of garbage collection. Memory allocations can be tracked using the Dalvik Debug Monitor Server (DDMS) tool as discussed in Chapter 16, "Debugging."
- Use the LogCat tool for debugging and check for warnings or errors as also discussed in Chapter 16.
- Test thoroughly, including different environments and devices if possible.

Software Development Kit (SDK)

The Android SDK is composed of the platform, tools, sample code, and documentation needed to develop Android applications. It is built as an add-on to the Java Development Kit and has an integrated plugin for the Eclipse Integrated Development Environment (IDE).

Installing and Upgrading

Many places on the Internet have detailed step-by-step instructions for how to install the Android SDK. For example, all the necessary links can be found on the Google website http://developer.android.com/sdk/. Currently Google has bundled together all the necessary pieces of the SDK into one convenient download as the ADT Bundle. This bundle contains Eclipse with the ADT plugin installed, the Android SDK Tools, Android Platform tools, the latest Android Platform, and the latest Android system image for the emulator. It is available for Windows, Mac, and Linux systems.

As this bundle is a zip and preconfigured, all that really needs to be done is to unzip the bundle and start the Eclipse program. When launched, the application will ask where the workspace should be set up. Once that is determined, a screen appears to help with setting up a new project or learning more about developing with Android.

For developers who do not wish to download the entire bundle and would rather install just the pieces they need, the general procedure outlined here emphasizes the most common installation steps. These steps should be performed on a host computer used as the development environment.

1. Install the Java Development Kit (for example, install JDK 6.0 for use with Android 2.1 or above; JDK 5.0 is the minimum version needed for any earlier version of Android).

2. Install Eclipse Classic (for example, version 4.2.1). In the case of Windows, this just needs to be unzipped in place and is ready to use.

3. Install the Android SDK starter package (for example, version r21). In the case of Windows, this just needs to be unzipped in place and is ready to use.

4. Start Eclipse and select **Help → Install New Software**. . . , and then type **https://dl-ssl.google.com/android/eclipse/** and install the Android DDMS and Android Development Tools.

5. In Eclipse, select **Window → Preferences**. . . (on a Mac, select **Eclipse → Preferences**) and select **Android**. Browse to the location where the SDK was unzipped and apply.

6. In Eclipse, select **Window → Android SDK and AVD Manager → Available Packages**, and then choose the necessary APIs to install (for example, Documentation for Android SDK, SDK Platform, Google APIs, API 17).

7. From the same Android SDK and AVD Manager menu, create an Android virtual device to run the emulator, or install USB drivers to run applications on a plugged-in phone.

8. In Eclipse, select **Run → Run Configurations**. . . and create a new run configuration to be used with each Android application (or similar for a debug configuration). Android JUnit tests can be configured here, too.

Now the environment should be configured to easily develop any Android application and run on the emulator or an actual Android device. Upgrading to a new version of the SDK is simply a matter of selecting **Help → Software Updates**. . . in Eclipse and choosing the appropriate version.

Software Features and API Level

The Android OS periodically rolls out new features, enhancements such as improved efficiency, and bug fixes. A main driver in OS improvement is the increased capability of hardware on new devices. In fact, major releases of the OS are generally coordinated with new hardware rollouts (such as Eclair's release with Droid).

Some legacy Android devices cannot support the new version requirements and are not updated with new OS releases. This leads to a user base with a variety of possible experiences. The developer is left with the task of checking for device capability or at least warning of required features. This can be done through a check of a single number: the API level. For a list of Android versions and the changes made in each version, see Appendix D.

Android currently follows a release schedule of six to nine months. Although possible, the over-the-air updates are logistically tricky and carriers prefer to avoid them. Hardware manufacturers also appreciate some stability, which does not mean the first devices in stores need an immediate update. However, when a release is made, the additional features are worthwhile for developers to use.

Emulator and Android Device Debug

The emulator launches a window on the development computer that looks like an Android phone and runs actual ARM instructions. Note that the initial start-up is slow, even on high-end computers. Although there are ways to configure the emulator to try to emulate many aspects of a real Android device such as incoming phone calls, limited data rate, and screen orientation change, some features (such as sensors and audio/video) are not the same. A recent addition to the emulator is the ability to use the host GPU. This has helped to speed up the visual effects and transitions displayed on the emulator. The emulator should be considered a useful way to validate basic functionality for devices not available to the user. For example, the tablet screen size can be tried without purchasing a tablet.

Note that a target virtual device must be created before the emulator can properly run. Eclipse provides a nice method to manage Android Virtual Devices (AVDs). A handy list of keyboard shortcuts for emulator functions is shown in Table 1.4.

In general, the first testing is best done with an Android phone. This ensures full functionality and identification of real-time issues that cannot be fully re-created with the emulator. To use an Android device as a developer platform, just hook it up to the USB using the USB cable that came with the phone and ensure that the USB driver is detected (this is automatic with a Mac; the drivers are included with the SDK for Windows; and see Google's web page for Linux).

Some settings on the Android device need to be changed to enable developer usage. From the home screen, select **MENU → Settings → Applications → Unknown sources** and **MENU → Settings → Applications → Development → USB debugging** to enable installation of applications through the USB cable. More details about Android debugging are provided in Chapter 16, "Debugging."

Table 1.4 **Android OS Emulator Controls**

Key	Emulated Function
Escape	Back key
Home	Home key
F2, PageUp	Menu key
Shift-F2, PageDown	Start key
F3	Call/Dial key
F4	Hangup/EndCall key
F5	Search key
F7	Power key
Ctrl-F3, Ctrl-KEYPAD_5	Camera key
Ctrl-F5, KEYPAD_PLUS	Volume up key
Ctrl-F6, KEYPAD_MINUS	Volume down key
KEYPAD_5	DPAD center
KEYPAD_4, KEYPAD_6	DPAD left, DPAD right
KEYPAD_8, KEYPAD_2	DPAD up, DPAD down
F8	Toggle cell network on/off
F9	Toggle code profiling (when -trace set)
Alt-ENTER	Toggle full-screen mode
Ctrl-T	Toggle trackball mode
Ctrl-F11, KEYPAD_7	Rotate screen orientation to previous layout
Ctrl-F12, KEYPAD_9	Rotate screen orientation to next layout

Using the Android Debug Bridge

It is often convenient to use the command line to access the Android device. This is possible when it is connected to a computer using the USB cable. The Android Debug Bridge (ADB), which comes with the SDK, can be used to access the Android device. For example, to log in to the Android device as if it were a Linux computer, type the following:

```
> adb shell
```

Then, many UNIX commands are usable on the device. Use exit to exit the shell. A single command can be appended to the shell command to be executed without needing to enter and exit the shell:

```
> adb shell mkdir /sdcard/app_bkup/
```

To copy files off the device, use `pull` and rename the files copied as needed:

```
> adb pull /system/app/VoiceSearchWithKeyboard.apk VSwithKeyboard.apk
```

To copy a file onto the device, use push:

```
> adb push VSwithKeyboard.apk /sdcard/app_bkup/
```

To delete an application, for example, com.dummy.game, from the device, type the following:

```
> adb uninstall com.dummy.game
```

These commands are the most commonly used, but more are available. Some additional commands are introduced in Chapter 16.

Signing and Publishing

For an application to be accepted on Google Play, it needs to be signed. To do this, a private key needs to be generated and kept in a secure place. Then, the app needs to be packaged in release mode and signed with the private key. When an application is upgraded, the same key needs to sign it to ensure a transparent update for the user.

Eclipse automatically does all of this. Just right-click on the project to be signed and select **Export. . . → Export Android Application** to initiate packaging. A password can be used to create a private key, which is saved for future applications and upgrades. Then, continue through the menu to the creation of an APK file. This is a packaged version of the Android project in release mode and signed with the private key. It is ready for upload to Google Play.

Google Play

After an application is designed, developed, tested, and signed, it is ready to be deployed into Google Play. To use Google Play, a Google Checkout account needs to be created. It is used not only to pay the initial developer fee of $25 but also for payments to the developer for any charged apps. Public exposure to a developer's creation is often exciting. Within hours of upload, an application can get hundreds of views, downloads, ratings, and reviews from around the world. A few considerations for publication of an app are provided here for reference.

End User License Agreement

Any original content distributed in a tangible form is automatically copyrighted in most of the world under the Berne Convention. Still, it is common practice to add a copyright line with a date of publication to the content, such as © 2013. The method for adding this symbol to an Android app is discussed in Chapter 5, "User Interface Layout."

This can be taken one step further in an end user license agreement (EULA), which is a contract between the developer (or company) and the customer (or end user) providing the developer a form of protection for publicly distributed software. Most EULAs contain sections such as "Grant of License," "Copyright," and "No Warranties." It is common practice to add a EULA to an application, especially if it is offered for sale. The method for adding a EULA to an Android app is discussed in Chapter 11, "Data Storage Methods."

Improving App Visibility

Users find applications in three different ways. Catering to these methods helps to increase visibility for an application.

Depending on the version of Play store users have on their devices, they may be able to find new apps by browsing "Just In" apps. Choose a good descriptive name for the application and place it in an appropriate category, such as "Games" or "Communication." Keep the description simple and to the point to get more views. The "Games" category is overladen with apps, so there are subcategories. If the app is fun but has no score or goal, consider the "Entertainment" category. Even so, with over 10,000 applications uploaded to the Android Market each month, an uploaded application is pushed off the "Just In" list within a day or two.

Google has a committee that reviews new Android applications and selects them to be shown prominently in various places of the "Apps" section of the Play store. The best way to get an application featured is to make sure that all screen resolutions and dpi levels are supported, there are well-articulated descriptions of the application, images and a video of the app in action are included, and the app includes no services that users perceive as a violation of privacy (such as reading system logs, sending SMS messages without stating why, and using fine location instead of coarse location unless absolutely required).

Another way users can find an app is by performing a keyword search. Determine the essential keywords users might choose and include those in either the title or the description of the app. Some users might speak a different language, so including appropriate international keywords can help.

The last way users find an app in the Play store is by looking in the category of "Top" apps; these apps get the highest ratings and the most downloads. To get in this category takes time and effort with possible updates to fix bugs. This points to the last consideration for app visibility: robustness. Ensure that the app does not contain major bugs, does not waste excessive battery life, and has a foolproof way to exit. Nothing turns off a potential customer more than seeing reviews that say, "This app uses all of my battery," or, "I can't uninstall this app." The "Top" apps are carved into "Free," "Paid," and "Trending."

One side note to mention: Almost all interactions between the developer and users take place through Google Play. Providing developer contact information or a supporting website is often superfluous, as people browsing the mobile market rarely use it.

Differentiating an App

Sometimes a developer creates an application only to find a similar variant already in the Android Market. This should be treated as an opportunity rather than a discouragement. Differentiating the app simply through better design, interface, or execution can quickly win over a user base. Basically, originality is nice, but it is not required. That being said, one must be careful to avoid using copyrighted material.

Charging for an App

Every time a new application or its update is uploaded to the Android Market, the developer must choose whether to provide it for free or charge for it. Following are the main options:

- Provide the app for free. Everyone who can access Google Play can see and install the app.
- Provide a free app, but include advertisements. In some cases, the developer negotiates sponsorship for an app. More often, the developer works with a third-party aggregator. Payouts are provided for clicked ads and less often for impressions (ad views). Figure 1.1 shows an example banner ad from AdMob (which is now part of Google). Such ads require the application to have permission to access the Internet and the location of the device. Consider using coarse location instead of fine location to avoid deterring some potential customers from installing the app.
- Provide the app for a charge. Google handles all transactions, including charges, but takes 30 percent of the proceeds and requires developers to have a merchant account set up through Google Wallet. Countries that are not set up for charges through Google Checkout cannot see or install an app for a charge. For these reasons, some developers turn to third-party app stores for distribution.
- Post a free limited version, but charge for a full version. This gives users the opportunity to try the app, and if they like it, they will have less resistance to purchasing the full version. For some apps, this is a natural model (such as a game with ten free levels), but not all apps can be partitioned this way.
- Sell virtual goods inside the app, or use in-app purchasing. Selling virtual items is familiar in pay-to-win apps that are free but require the user to make a purchase to increase inventory items, provide power-ups, or even to skip parts of the game. This is an important way Facebook apps work, and it is becoming a popular choice in the mobile world.

Free applications tend to get a lot of views. Even the most obscure and odd applications seem to be downloaded and viewed by at least 1,000 people in the first month the application is in the Play store. There are some developers who explicitly say, "This app is absolutely useless," and yet they get over 10,000 downloads and a four-

Figure 1.1   Example mobile banner ad from AdMob

star rating. Somewhat relevant free applications can get as many as 50,000 downloads, and extremely useful free applications have over 100,000 downloads. For most developers, such exposure is quite impressive.

Mobile advertisement is still in its infancy and usually does not entice enough users to click the ad to make the app profitable. For now, monetizing apps is best done by charging in the Play store or through in-app purchases. As long as the app is useful for some people, has a clear description, and has a good selection of positive reviews, users will purchase it. If an app is successful, it might make sense to raise its price.

Managing Reviews and Updates

If their apps are successful, most independent developers go through a process of releasing a version and adapting it based on user feedback. Users like to see a developer who is responsive. This leads to more people downloading an app, and as the number of downloads increases, the validity of the app increases.

In general, it seems about 1 in 200 people rate an application, and a small subset of those actually leave a review. If someone takes the time to type a review, it is usually worth paying attention to it, especially if the review comments are constructive, such as "Doesn't work on the HTC Hero," or "Nice app, just wish it did. . . ."

Updates that respond to user comments are seen in a positive light by new potential customers. In any case, the reason for the update should be clearly highlighted. Some users may get ten or more notifications a day of applications that have updates available. If they do not see a good reason to upgrade, they might not.

Alternatives to Google Play

Other independent Android app stores exist. They might not have as convenient access to Android devices as Google Play does, but they provide other benefits for developers such as better app visibility, more places to charge for apps, and taking no portion of the proceeds from an app. Also, some Android manufacturers create customized app stores that are accessible from their devices. For example, getting app visibility onto Motorola Android phones in the Chinese and Latin American markets can be done through the Motorola app market at http://developer.motorola.com/shop4apps.

Several third-party application stores also exist, which are given in the following list. Please note that some third-party stores pass around illegal, stolen, and/or cracked software. If you are absolutely determined to use a third-party store, make absolutely sure that you can trust it and do some research on it first.

- The Baidu App store (China)
  http://as.baidu.com/

- Amazon Apps
  www.amazon.com/appstore

- Opera Mobile Apps Store
  http://apps.opera.com/en_us/

- SlideMe
  http://slideme.org/

- Getjar
  www.getjar.com/

- AppBrain
  www.appbrain.com/

Application Basics: Activities and Intents

Each Android application is represented by a single Android project. An overview of the project structure, including a brief introduction to the basic building blocks of an application, is provided as useful background information for the recipes in this book. Then the focus of this chapter turns to activities and the intents that launch them.

Android Application Overview

An Android application consists of various functionalities. Some examples are editing a note, playing a music file, ringing an alarm, or opening a phone contact. These functionalities can be classified into four different Android components, shown in Table 2.1, each of which is specified by a Java base class.

Every application is made up of one or more of these components. They are instantiated by the Android OS as needed. Other applications are allowed to use them, too, within the specified permissions.

As multiple functionalities play out in the OS (some not even related to the intended application, such as an incoming phone call), each component goes through a lifecycle of getting created, focused, defocused, and destroyed. The default behavior can be overridden for a graceful operation, such as saving variables or restoring UI elements.

With the exception of ContentProvider, each component is activated by an asynchronous message called an Intent. The Intent can contain a Bundle of supporting information describing the component. This provides a method of passing information between components.

The rest of this chapter demonstrates the previous concepts using the most common component: the Activity. Because activities almost always specify an interaction with a user, a window is automatically created with each activity. Therefore, a short introduction to the UI is also included. Of the other components, Service and

Table 2.1   **Possible Components of an Android Application**

Functionality	Java Base Class	Examples
Focused thing a user can do	`Activity`	Edit a note, play a game
Background process	`Service`	Play music, update weather icon
Receive messages	`BroadcastReceiver`	Trigger alarm upon event
Store and retrieve data	`ContentProvider`	Open a phone contact

`BroadcastReceiver` are covered in Chapter 3, "Threads, Services, Receivers, and Alerts," and `ContentProvider` is covered in Chapter 11, "Data Storage Methods."

Recipe: Creating a Project and an Activity

A straightforward way to create an Android project or any of its components is to use the Eclipse IDE. This method ensures proper setup of the supporting files. The steps to create a new Android project are:

1. In Eclipse, choose **File → New → Android Application Project**. This displays a New Android Project creation screen.

2. Fill in the project name, such as **SimpleActivityExample**.

3. Fill in the application name, such as **Example of Basic Activity**.

4. Fill in the package name, such as **com.cookbook.simpleactivity**.

5. Select a minimum required SDK. This will be the lowest Android version the app can run on. Choosing at least API Level 8 or Android 2.2 is recommended.

6. Select a build target SDK from the choices provided. Choose the highest Android version that will be tested against.

7. Choose the SDK version the app will be compiled against. This should be the latest version available or the latest version required by the libraries.

8. Choose the base theme of the application. The theme can be edited or changed later if desired; this is just meant to be a good start.

9. Next, configure some more project defaults. Check **Create custom launcher icon** to replace the default icon now. To create the main activity in one of the next steps, be sure **Create Activity** is checked.

10. In the Configure Launcher Icon screen, choose among text, clip art from a small library, or an image from the hard drive. The resulting image will be created in all four standard resolutions.

11. To create the main activity in the same step, be sure **Create Activity** is checked and select **BlankActivity**. The use of fragments will be shown in a later recipe.

12. Fill in activity and layout names or leave them as is. To use one of the default navigation patterns, a minimum SDK version of 14 is required, as they rely on the ActionBar.

13. Press **Finish** to create the sample project.

All activities extend the abstract class `Activity` or one of its subclasses. The entry point to each activity is the `onCreate()` method. It is almost always overridden to initialize the activity, such as setting up the UI, creating button listeners, initializing parameters, and starting threads.

If the main activity is not created with the project or another activity needs to be added, the steps to create an activity are:

1. Create a class to extend `Activity`. In Eclipse, this can be done by right-clicking on the project, choosing **New** → **Class**, and then specifying `android.app.Activity` as the superclass.

2. Override the `onCreate()` function. In Eclipse, this can be done by right-clicking on the class file, choosing **Source** → **Override/Implement Methods...**, and then checking the `onCreate()` method. As with most overridden functions, the overwritten `onCreate()` method must invoke the superclass method, too; otherwise, an exception may be thrown at run-time. Here, `super.onCreate()` should be called first to properly initialize the activity, as shown in Listing 2.1.

Listing 2.1   **src/com/cookbook/simple_activity/SimpleActivity.java**

```
package com.cookbook.simple_activity;

import android.app.Activity;
import android.os.Bundle;

public class SimpleActivity extends Activity {

    @Override
    public void onCreate(Bundle savedInstanceState) {
        super.onCreate(savedInstanceState);
        setContentView(R.layout.main);
    }
}
```

3. If a UI is used, specify the layout in an XML file in the **res/layout/** directory. Here, it is called **main.xml**, as shown in Listing 2.2.

4. Set the layout of the activity using the `setContentView()` function and passing it the resource ID for the XML layout file. Here, it is `R.layout.main`, as shown in Listing 2.1.

Listing 2.2   res/layout/main.xml

```xml
<?xml version="1.0" encoding="utf-8"?>
<LinearLayout xmlns:android="http://schemas.android.com/apk/res/android"
    android:orientation="vertical"
    android:layout_width="match_parent"
    android:layout_height="match_parent"
    >
<TextView
    android:layout_width="match_parent"
    android:layout_height="wrap_content"
    android:text="@string/hello"
    />
</LinearLayout>
```

5. Declare the properties of the activity in the **AndroidManifest.xml** file. This is covered in more detail later in Listing 2.5.

Note that the string resources are defined in the **strings.xml** file in the **res/values/** folder, as shown in Listing 2.3. This provides a central place for all strings in case text needs to be changed or reused.

Listing 2.3   res/values/strings.xml

```xml
<?xml version="1.0" encoding="utf-8"?>
<resources>
    <string name="hello">Hello World, SimpleActivity!</string>
    <string name="app_name">SimpleActivity</string>
</resources>
```

Now the directory structure of this project and the additional autogenerated content are explored in more detail.

Directory Structure of Project and Autogenerated Content

The project structure is a mix of user-generated and autogenerated files. Figure 2.1 shows an example project structure, as seen from the Eclipse Package Explorer.

User-generated files include the following:

- **src/** contains the Java packages the developer writes or imports for the application. Each package can have multiple **.java** files representing different classes.
- **res/layout/** contains the XML files that specify the layout of each screen.
- **res/values/** contains the XML files used as references by other files.
- **res/values-v11/** contains the XML files for Honeycomb devices and above.
- **res/values-v14/** contains the XML files for Ice Cream Sandwich and above.

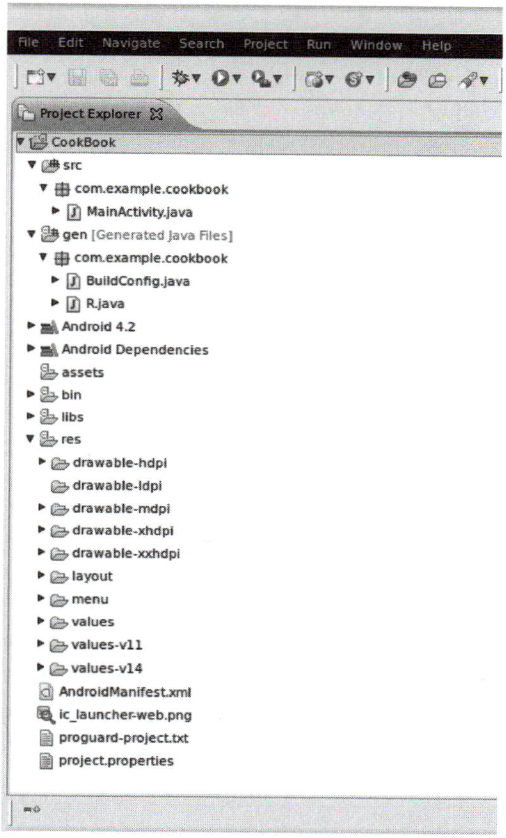

Figure 2.1   Android project directory structure, as seen in the Eclipse IDE

- **res/drawable–xhdpi/**, **res/drawable–hdpi/**, **res/drawable–mdpi/**, and **res/drawable–ldpi/** are directories that contain pictures the application uses. They have extra-large, high, medium, and low dots-per-inch resolution, respectively.

- **assets/** contains additional nonmedia files the application uses.

- **AndroidManifest.xml** specifies the project to the Android OS.

The **styles.xml** file is created in all of the **res/values-XX** folders. This is because the Android base theme changed to Holo starting with Honeycomb devices. It results in having different parent themes in an app theme.

Autogenerated files include these:

- **gen/** contains autogenerated code, including the generated class file **R.java**.

- **project.properties** contains project settings. Although autogenerated, it should be kept under revision control.

An application's resources include XML files describing the layout, XML files describing values such as strings, labels of UI elements, and additional supporting files such as pictures and sounds. At compile time, references to the resources are gathered into an autogenerated wrapper class called R.java. The Android Asset Packaging Tool (aapt) autogenerates this file. Listing 2.4 shows what it looks like for the "Creating a Project and an Activity" recipe.

Listing 2.4   **gen/com/cookbook/simple_activity/R.java**

```
/* AUTO-GENERATED FILE.  DO NOT MODIFY.
 *
 * This class was automatically generated by the
 * aapt tool from the resource data it found. It
 * should not be modified by hand.
 */

package com.cookbook.simple_activity;

public final class R {
    public static final class attr {
    }
    public static final class drawable {
        public static final int icon=0x7f020000;
    }
    public static final class layout {
        public static final int main=0x7f030000;
    }
    public static final class string {
        public static final int app_name=0x7f040001;
        public static final int hello=0x7f040000;
    }
}
```

Here, each resource is mapped to a unique integer value. In this way, the R.java class provides a way to reference external resources within Java code. For example, to reference the **main.xml** layout file in Java, the R.layout.main integer is used. To reference the same within XML files, the "@layout/main" string is used.

Referencing resources from within Java or XML files is demonstrated in Table 2.2. Note that to define a new button ID called home_button, the plus sign is added to the identifying string: @+id/home_button. More complete details on resources are given in Chapter 5, "User Interface Layout," but this suffices to cover the recipes in this chapter.

Android Package and Manifest File

The Android project, sometimes also referred to as an Android package, is a collection of Java packages. Different Android packages can have the same Java package names, whereas the Android package name must be unique across all applications installed on the Android device.

Table 2.2   **Resources in Java and XML Files**

Resource	Reference in Java	Reference in XML
res/layout/main.xml	`R.layout.main`	`@layout/main`
res/drawable-hdpi/icon.png	`R.drawable.icon`	`@drawable/icon`
@+id/home_button	`R.id.home_button`	`@id/home_button`
`<string name="hello">`	`R.string.hello`	`@string/hello`

For the OS to access them, each application must declare its available components in a single **AndroidManifest.xml** file. In addition, this file contains the required permissions and behavior for the application to run. Listing 2.5 shows what it looks like for the "Creating a Project and an Activity" recipe.

Listing 2.5   **AndroidManifest.xml**

```
<?xml version="1.0" encoding="utf-8"?>
<manifest xmlns:android="http://schemas.android.com/apk/res/android"
          package="com.cookbook.simple_activity"
          android:versionCode="1"
          android:versionName="1.0">
    <application android:icon="@drawable/icon"
                 android:label="@string/app_name">
        <activity android:name=".SimpleActivity"
                  android:label="@string/app_name">
            <intent-filter>
              <action android:name="android.intent.action.MAIN" />
              <category android:name="android.intent.category.LAUNCHER" />
            </intent-filter>
        </activity>
    </application>
    <uses-sdk android:minSdkVersion="8" />
</manifest>
```

The first line is required and standard across all XML files in Android to specify the encoding. The `manifest` element defines the Android package name and version. The `versionCode` is an integer that can be evaluated in programs to determine the upgrade or downgrade relationship. The `versionName` represents a human-readable format that can have major and minor revisions declared.

The `application` element defines the icon and label the user sees from the Android device menu. The label is a string and should be short enough to display under the icon on a user's device. Generally, the name can be up to two words of ten characters each without being cut off.

The `activity` element defines the main activity that is launched when the application is started and the name shown in the title bar when the activity is active. Here, the Java package name needs to be specified, which in this example is `com.`

`cookbook.simple_activity.SimpleActivity`. Because the Java package name is usually the same as the Android package name, the shorthand notation is often used: `.SimpleActivity`. However, it is best to remember that the Android package and the Java package are distinct.

The `intent-filter` element informs the Android system of the capabilities of the component. It can have multiple action, category, or data elements for this purpose. This element is used in different recipes in this book.

The `uses-sdk` element defines the API level required to run the application. In general, the API level is specified as follows:

```
<uses-sdk android:minSdkVersion="integer"
          android:targetSdkVersion="integer"
          android:maxSdkVersion="integer" />
```

Because the Android OS is constructed to be forward compatible, `maxSdkVersion` is highly discouraged and not even adhered to on devices with Android 2.0.1 or later. Google Play, however, continues to use this as a filter, so the application is not shown for download to devices running a higher SDK version.

Specifying `targetSdkVersion` is not required, but it allows devices of the same SDK version to disable compatibility settings that might speed up operation. `minSdkVersion` should always be specified to ensure that the application does not crash when run on a platform that does not support the required features in the application. Always choose the lowest API level possible when specifying this.

The **AndroidManifest.xml** file can also contain permission settings needed to run the application. More complete details about the options are provided in later chapters, but this suffices to cover the recipes in this chapter.

Recipe: Renaming Parts of an Application

Sometimes a portion of an Android project needs to be renamed. Maybe a file was copied manually into the project, such as from this book. Maybe the application name has changed during development, and the change needs to be reflected in the filesystem tree. Automatic tools help with this and ensure that cross-references are automatically updated. For example, in the Eclipse IDE, there are different ways to rename portions of an application:

- Rename the Android project, as follows:

    1. Right-click the project and **Refactor** → **Move** to a new directory in the filesystem.

    2. Right-click the project and **Refactor** → **Rename** the project.

- Rename the Android package, as follows:

    1. Right-click the package and **Refactor** → **Rename** the package.

    2. Edit the **AndroidManifest.xml** file to ensure that the new package name is reflected.

- Rename an Android class (such as the major components `Activity`, `Service`, `BroadcastReceiver`, `ContentProvider`) as follows:

  1. Right-click the **.java** file and **Refactor → Rename** the class.
  2. Edit the **AndroidManifest.xml** file to ensure that `android:name` has the new component name.

Note that renaming other files, such as XML files, usually requires manually changing the corresponding references in the Java code.

Recipe: Using a Library Project

Library projects allow the reuse of resources and code in other applications. They are also used for UI libraries that enable modern features on older devices. Library projects were introduced with release 14 of the SDK tools. Library projects are very similar to normal Android projects, as they too have source and resources folders and a manifest file. The main difference is that they cannot run on their own, and they cannot be compiled into an **.apk** file. To create a library project, do the following:

  1. In Eclipse, choose **File → New → Android Application Project**. This displays a New Android Project creation screen.
  2. Fill in the project name, such as **SimpleLibraryExample**.
  3. Fill in the application name, such as **Example of Basic Activity**.
  4. Fill in the package name, such as **com.cookbook.simplelibrary**.
  5. Select a build target from the choices provided. These choices are based on the SDK versions that are installed on the development computer.
  6. Uncheck **Create custom launcher icon**, as a library does not need one.
  7. Check **Mark this project as a Library**.
  8. To have activities in the library, check **Create Activity**. The created activity will be used in the main project; check this and select **BlankActivity** for now.
  9. Fill in an activity name or leave it as is.
  10. Change the layout name to **lib_activity_main**. As all resources are compiled into one R class in the end, it is best practice to give all resources of a library a prefix to avoid name conflicts.
  11. Press **Finish** to create the library project.

To use the library, a primary or main project is needed. Follow the "Creating a Project and an Activity" recipe to add one to the workspace, with a minor modification: Do not create an activity. Instead, use the activity from the library project.

To reference a library project from the main project, do the following:

  1. In Eclipse, right-click on the project and choose **Properties → Android**.

2. Scroll down to the library section and press **Add**.

3. The dialog will show all available library projects in the workspace. Select the **SimpleLibrary** project and press **OK**.

The project name and path reference are now shown in the Properties page. There is a green arrow indicating that the reference was checked as OK. If the referenced path cannot be found, a red cross will be shown instead.

After adding a library project, it is recommended to make a clean and full build of the workspace to make sure the changes worked as expected.

Internally, library references are saved in the **project.properties** file, which is used by both Eclipse and Ant. The resulting file should now look like this:

```
target=android-16
android.library.reference.1=../SimpleLibrary
```

Listing 2.6 adds the activity from the library to the **AndroidManifest.xml** file and makes it the default launcher activity.

Listing 2.6   AndroidManifest.xml of the Main Project

```
<manifest xmlns:android="http://schemas.android.com/apk/res/android"
    package="com.example.simpleproject"
    android:versionCode="1"
    android:versionName="1.0">

    <uses-sdk android:minSdkVersion="8" android:targetSdkVersion="15" />

    <application android:label="@string/app_name"
        android:icon="@drawable/ic_launcher"
        android:theme="@style/AppTheme">

        <activity
            android:name="com.cookbook.simplelibrary.LibMainActivity"
            android:label="@string/title_activity_activity_main" >
            <intent-filter>
                <action android:name="android.intent.action.MAIN" />

                <category android:name="android.intent.category.LAUNCHER" />
            </intent-filter>

        </activity>
    </application>
</manifest>
```

Note here that the package name of the application is completely different from the package name of the activity. Because the activity is loaded from the library project, its name must be set to a full qualified package and class name.

The project can now be run from within Eclipse; the activity from the library will come to the front.

There are many use cases for library projects, from white-label apps that set different themes in the main project but run on the same code base to using UI libraries like `ActionBarSherlock` to support a modern look and feel on older Android devices.

Activity Lifecycle

Each activity in an application goes through its own lifecycle. Once and only once when an activity is created is the `onCreate()` function executed. If the activity exits, the `onDestroy()` function is executed. In between, various events can lead to the activity being in multiple states, as illustrated in Figure 2.2. The next recipe provides an example of each of these functions.

Recipe: Using Activity Lifecycle Functions

This recipe provides a simple way to see the activity lifecycle in action. For illustration purposes, each overridden function is explicit, and a `Toast` command is added to show on screen when the function is entered (more detail on the `Toast` widget is provided in Chapter 3, "Threads, Services, Receivers, and Alerts"). The activity is shown in Listing 2.7. Run it on an Android device and try various cases. In particular, note the following:

- Changing the screen orientation destroys and re-creates the activity from scratch.
- Pressing the Home key pauses the activity but does not destroy it.
- Pressing the application icon might start a new instance of the activity, even if the old one was not destroyed.
- Letting the screen sleep pauses the activity, and the screen awakening resumes it. (This is similar to taking an incoming phone call.)

As seen here, various common user actions can cause the activity to be paused or killed, or can even launch multiple versions of the application. Before moving on, it is worth mentioning two additional simple recipes that can control this behavior.

Recipe: Forcing Single Task Mode

Navigating away from an application and launching it again can lead to multiple instances of an activity on the device. Eventually the redundant instance of the activity is killed to free up memory, but in the meantime it can lead to odd situations. To avoid these, the developer can control this behavior for each activity in the **AndroidManifest.xml** file.

To ensure that only one instance of the activity runs on the device, specify the following in an `activity` element that has the `MAIN` and `LAUNCHER` intent filters:

```
android:launchMode="singleInstance"
```

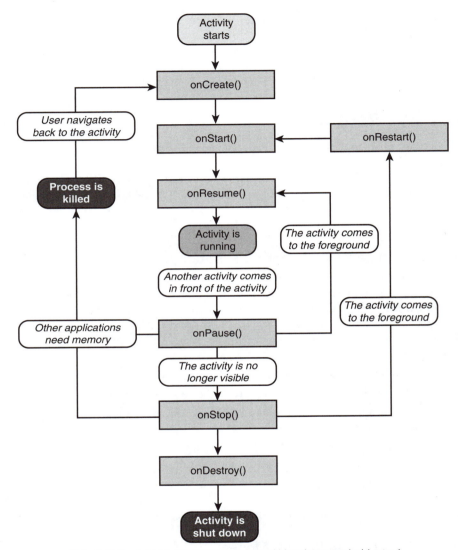

Figure 2.2 Activity lifecycle from http://developer.android.com/

This keeps a single instance of each activity in a task at all times. In addition, any child activity is launched as its own task. To further ensure that there is only a single task for all activities of an application, use the following:

```
android:launchMode="singleTask"
```

Listing 2.7   **src/com/cookbook/activity_lifecycle/ActivityLifecycle.java**

```java
package com.cookbook.activity_lifecycle;

import android.app.Activity;
import android.os.Bundle;
import android.widget.Toast;

public class ActivityLifecycle extends Activity {

    @Override
    public void onCreate(Bundle savedInstanceState) {
        super.onCreate(savedInstanceState);
        setContentView(R.layout.main);
        Toast.makeText(this, "onCreate", Toast.LENGTH_SHORT).show();
    }

    @Override
    protected void onStart() {
        super.onStart();
        Toast.makeText(this, "onStart", Toast.LENGTH_SHORT).show();
    }

    @Override
    protected void onResume() {
        super.onResume();
        Toast.makeText(this, "onResume", Toast.LENGTH_SHORT).show();
    }

    @Override
    protected void onRestart() {
        super.onRestart();
        Toast.makeText(this, "onRestart", Toast.LENGTH_SHORT).show();
    }

    @Override
    protected void onPause() {
        Toast.makeText(this, "onPause", Toast.LENGTH_SHORT).show();
        super.onPause();
    }

    @Override
    protected void onStop() {
        Toast.makeText(this, "onStop", Toast.LENGTH_SHORT).show();
        super.onStop();
    }

    @Override
    protected void onDestroy() {
        Toast.makeText(this, "onDestroy", Toast.LENGTH_SHORT).show();
        super.onDestroy();
    }
}
```

This allows the activities to share information easily as the same task.

In addition, it might be desirable to retain the task state, regardless of how a user navigates to the activity. For example, if a user leaves the application and relaunches it later, the default behavior often resets the task to its initial state. To ensure that the task is always in its last state when the user returns, specify the following in the activity element of the root activity of a task:

```
android:alwaysRetainTaskState="true"
```

Recipe: Forcing Screen Orientation

Any Android device with an accelerometer can determine which way is down. As the device is tilted from portrait to landscape mode, the default action is to rotate the application view accordingly. However, as seen in the "Using Activity Lifecycle Functions" recipe, the activity is destroyed and restarted upon screen orientation changes. When this happens, the current state of the activity might be lost, disrupting the user experience.

One option to handle screen orientation changes gracefully is to save state information before the change and restore information after the change. A simpler method that might be useful is to force the screen orientation to stay constant. For each activity in the **AndroidManifest.xml** file, the screenOrientation attribute can be specified. For example, to specify that the activity always stays in portrait mode, the following can be added to the activity element:

```
android:screenOrientation="portrait"
```

Similarly, landscape mode can be specified using the following:

```
android:screenOrientation="landscape"
```

However, this code still causes the activity to be destroyed and restarted when a hard keyboard is slid out. Therefore, a third method is possible: Tell the Android system that the application should handle orientation and keyboard slide-out events. This is done by adding the following attribute to the activity element:

```
android:configChanges="orientation|keyboardHidden"
```

This can be used alone or in combination with the screenOrientation attribute to specify the required behavior to the application.

Recipe: Saving and Restoring Activity Information

Whenever an activity is about to be killed, the onSaveInstanceState() function is called. Override this to save relevant information that should be retained. When the activity is then re-created, the onRestoreInstanceState() function is called. Override this function to retrieve the saved information. This allows for a seamless user experience when an application undergoes lifecycle changes. Note that most UI states do not need to be managed because they are, by default, taken care of by the system.

OnSaveInstanceState() is distinct from onPause(). For example, if another component is launched in front of the activity, the onPause() function is called. Later, if the activity is still paused when the OS needs to reclaim resources, it calls onSaveInstanceState() before killing the activity.

An example of saving and restoring the instance state consisting of a string and a float array is shown in Listing 2.8.

Listing 2.8   Example of onSaveInstanceState() and onRestoreInstanceState()

```
float[] localFloatArray = {3.14f, 2.718f, 0.577f};
String localUserName = "Euler";

@Override
protected void onSaveInstanceState(Bundle outState) {
        super.onSaveInstanceState(outState);
        //Save the relevant information
        outState.putString("name", localUserName);
        outState.putFloatArray("array", localFloatArray);
}

@Override
public void onRestoreInstanceState(Bundle savedInstanceState) {
        super.onRestoreInstanceState(savedInstanceState);
        //Restore the relevant information
        localUserName = savedInstanceState.getString("name");
        localFloatArray = savedInstanceState.getFloatArray("array");
}
```

Note that onCreate() also contains Bundle savedInstanceState. In the case of an activity reinitializing after previously being shut down, the bundle saved in onSaveInstanceState() is also passed to onCreate(). In all cases, the saved bundle is passed to the onRestoreInstanceState() function, so it is more natural to use this to restore states.

Recipe: Using Fragments

Fragments are the latest addition to the basic building blocks of an Android application. Fragments are smaller parts of an activity meant for the grouping of views and functionalities. The best analogy for them is to think of smaller building blocks that can be stacked on one another to fill the volume of a bigger block. The need for smaller blocks arose from the introduction of tablets and TV screens.

Fragments allow views to be bundled together and to be mixed and matched within one or two (or even more) activities as needed. The classic use case for this is going from landscape mode with a list and a detail view to portrait mode with a single list and a detail screen. In fact, this pattern has become so mainstream that it is now possible to create a skeleton app like this directly from the **Create New Project** dialog.

The steps to do this are similar to the ones described in the previous recipe:

1. In Eclipse, choose **File → New → Android Application Project**.
2. Fill in the project name, such as **SimpleFragmentExample**.
3. Fill in the application name, such as **Example of Basic Fragments**.
4. Fill in the package name, such as **com.cookbook.simplefragments**.
5. Select a minimum required SDK of API Level 11 or Android Honeycomb. Fragments can be used in lower API versions only if the support library extra is installed on the machine.
6. In the Create Activity screen, choose **MasterDetailFlow** as the start point.
7. Name the items used for demo purposes; for instance, **fruits**.
8. Press **Finish** to create the sample project.

Exploring the possibilities of this sample is left to the reader. Here, instead, a few important things about fragments are highlighted.

Fragments come with their own lifecycle, which is dependent on the hosting activities. As fragments can be added, shown, hidden, and removed at any time during the lifecycle of an activity, their existence is much more short-lived than that of other components. Similar to an activity, a fragment has onPause(), onResume(), onDestroy(), and onCreate() methods.

It is to be noted, however, that onCreate(Bundle) is the second method called on a fragment; the first one is onAttach(Activity), which signals that there is a connection to the hosting activity now. Methods can be called on the activity here; however, it is not guaranteed that the activity has been fully initialized itself. Only after onActivityCreated() is called is the activity passed through its own onCreate() method.

Given that fragments can be instantiated and added at much later times, the state of the activity in onAttach() should not be relied upon. The method used to initialize views and start most work is onCreateView(LayoutInflater, ViewGroup, Bundle). The Bundle class given here is the saved instance state, if the fragment is re-created.

Fragments use bundles also for serializing arguments. Every parcelable type of external information a fragment needs can be obtained from the hosting activity by calling setArguments() and can always be read in the fragments with the getArguments() call. This allows information coming from the starting intent of the activity to be passed directly to the fragment to be shown.

Multiple Activities

Even the simplest applications have more than one functionality. Hence, there is often a need to deal with multiple activities. For example, a game can have two activities: a high-scores screen and a game screen. A notepad can have three activities: view a list of notes, read a selected note, and edit a selected or new note.

The main activity, as defined in the **AndroidManifest.xml** file, is started when the application is started. This activity can launch another activity, usually after a trigger event. This causes the main activity to pause while the secondary activity is active. When the secondary activity ends, the main activity is brought to the foreground and resumed.

To activate a particular component of the application, an intent naming the component explicitly is used. If instead the requirements of an application can be specified by intent filters, an implicit intent can be used. The system then determines the best component or components to use, even if it is in a separate application or native to the OS. Note that unlike other activities, implicit intents that reside in other applications do not need to be declared in the current application's **AndroidManifest.xml** file.

Android uses implicit intents as often as possible, providing a powerful framework for modular functionality. When a new component is developed that meets the required implicit intent filter, it can be used in place of an Android internal intent. For example, say a new application for displaying phone contacts is loaded on an Android device. When a user selects a contact, the Android system finds all available activities with the proper intent filter for viewing contacts and asks the user to decide which one should be used.

Recipe: Using Buttons and TextView

To fully demonstrate multiple activities, it is useful to use a trigger event. A button press is introduced here for that purpose. The steps for adding a button to a given layout and assigning an action to a button press follow:

1. Put a button in the designated layout XML file:

```
<Button android:id="@+id/trigger"

    android:layout_width="100dip" android:layout_height="100dip"

    android:text="Press this button" />
```

2. Declare a button that points to the button ID in the layout file:

```
Button startButton = (Button) findViewById(R.id.trigger);
```

3. Specify a listener for when the button is clicked:

```
//Set up button listener

startButton.setOnClickListener(new View.OnClickListener() {

    //Insert onClick here

});
```

4. Override the onClick function for the listener to do the required action:

```
public void onClick(View view) {

    // Do something here

}
```

To show the result of an action, it is useful to change the text on the screen. The steps for defining a text field and changing it programmatically follow:

1. Put a text field in the designated layout XML file with an ID. It can also be initialized to some value (here, it can be initialized to the string named `hello` in the **strings.xml** file):

```
<TextView android:id="@+id/hello_text"

    android:layout_width="match_parent"

    android:layout_height="wrap_content"

    android:text="@string/hello"

/>
```

2. Declare a `TextView` that points to the `TextView` ID in the layout file:

```
private TextView tv = (TextView) findViewById(R.id.hello_text);
```

3. If the text needs to be changed, use the `setText` function:

```
tv.setText("new text string");
```

These two UI techniques are used in the subsequent recipes in this chapter. A more complete demonstration of UI techniques is covered in Chapter 5, "User Interface Layout."

Recipe: Launching a Second Activity from an Event

In this recipe, `MenuScreen` is the main activity, as shown in Listing 2.9. It launches the `PlayGame` activity. Here, the trigger event is implemented as a button click using the `Button` widget.

When a user clicks the button, the `startGame()` function runs and launches the `PlayGame` activity. When a user clicks the button in the `PlayGame` activity, it calls `finish()` to return control to the calling activity. Following are the steps for launching an activity:

1. Declare an intent that points to the activity to be launched.

2. Call `startActivity` on this intent.

3. Declare the additional activity in the **AndroidManifest.xml** file.

Listing 2.9   src/com/cookbook/launch_activity/MenuScreen.java

```
package com.cookbook.launch_activity;

import android.app.Activity;
import android.content.Intent;
import android.os.Bundle;
import android.view.View;
import android.widget.Button;
```

```
public class MenuScreen extends Activity {

    @Override
    public void onCreate(Bundle savedInstanceState) {
        super.onCreate(savedInstanceState);
        setContentView(R.layout.main);

        //Set up button listener
        Button startButton = (Button) findViewById(R.id.play_game);
        startButton.setOnClickListener(new View.OnClickListener() {
            public void onClick(View view) {
                startGame();
            }
        });
    }

    private void startGame() {
        Intent launchGame = new Intent(this, PlayGame.class);
        startActivity(launchGame);
    }
}
```

Providing Current Context in an Anonymous Inner Class

Note the additional consideration needed for launching an activity with a button press, as shown in Listing 2.9. The intent needs a context. However, using the `this` shortcut in the `onClick` function is not properly resolved. Following are different ways to provide current context in an anonymous inner class:

- Use `Context.this` instead of `this`.
- Use `getApplicationContext()` instead of `this`.
- Explicitly use the class name `MenuScreen.this`.
- Call a function that is declared at the right context level. This is what is used in Listing 2.8: `startGame()`.

These methods are usually interchangeable. Use the one that works best for the situation.

The `PlayGame` activity shown in Listing 2.10 is simply a button with an `onClick` listener that calls `finish()` to return control to the main activity. More functionality can be added as needed to this activity, and multiple branches of the code can lead to their own `finish()` calls.

Listing 2.10   src/com/cookbook/launch_activity/PlayGame.java

```
package com.cookbook.launch_activity;

import android.app.Activity;
import android.os.Bundle;
import android.view.View;
import android.widget.Button;
```

```
public class PlayGame extends Activity {

    public void onCreate(Bundle savedInstanceState) {
        super.onCreate(savedInstanceState);
        setContentView(R.layout.game);

        //Set up button listener
        Button startButton = (Button) findViewById(R.id.end_game);
        startButton.setOnClickListener(new View.OnClickListener() {
            public void onClick(View view) {
                finish();
            }
        });
    }
}
```

The button must be added to the main layout as shown in Listing 2.11, with the ID play_game to match what was declared in Listing 2.9. Here, the size of the button is also declared in device-independent pixels (dip), which are discussed more in Chapter 5, "User Interface Layout."

Listing 2.11   res/layout/main.xml

```
<?xml version="1.0" encoding="utf-8"?>
<LinearLayout xmlns:android="http://schemas.android.com/apk/res/android"
    android:orientation="vertical"
    android:layout_width="match_parent"
    android:layout_height="match_parent"
    >
<TextView
    android:layout_width="match_parent"
    android:layout_height="wrap_content"
    android:text="@string/hello"
    />
 <Button android:id="@+id/play_game"
    android:layout_width="100dip" android:layout_height="100dip"
      android:text="@string/play_game"
      />
</LinearLayout>
```

The PlayGame activity references its own button ID, end_game, in the R.layout.game layout resource that corresponds to the layout XML file **game.xml**, as shown in Listing 2.12.

Listing 2.12   res/layout/game.xml

```
<?xml version="1.0" encoding="utf-8"?>
<LinearLayout xmlns:android="http://schemas.android.com/apk/res/android"
    android:orientation="vertical"
    android:layout_width="match_parent"
    android:layout_height="match_parent"
```

```
        >
    <Button android:id="@+id/end_game"
        android:layout_width="100dip" android:layout_height="100dip"
        android:text="@string/end_game" android:layout_gravity="center"
        />
</LinearLayout>
```

Although the text can be written explicitly in each case, it is good coding practice to define variables for each string. In this recipe, the two string values `play_game` and `end_game` need to be declared in the string XML resource file, as shown in Listing 2.13.

Listing 2.13   res/values/strings.xml

```
<?xml version="1.0" encoding="utf-8"?>
<resources>
    <string name="hello">This is the Main Menu</string>
    <string name="app_name">LaunchActivity</string>
    <string name="play_game">Play game?</string>
    <string name="end_game">Done?</string>
</resources>
```

Finally, the **AndroidManifest.xml** file needs to register a default action to the new class `PlayGame`, as shown in Listing 2.14.

Listing 2.14   AndroidManifest.xml

```
<?xml version="1.0" encoding="utf-8"?>
<manifest xmlns:android="http://schemas.android.com/apk/res/android"
        android:versionCode="1"
        android:versionName="1.0" package="com.cookbook.launch_activity">
    <application android:icon="@drawable/icon"
                android:label="@string/app_name">
        <activity android:name=".MenuScreen"
                android:label="@string/app_name">
            <intent-filter>
                <action android:name="android.intent.action.MAIN" />
                <category android:name="android.intent.category.LAUNCHER" />
            </intent-filter>
        </activity>
        <activity android:name=".PlayGame"
                        android:label="@string/app_name">
                <intent-filter>
                    <action android:name="android.intent.action.VIEW" />
                    <category android:name="android.intent.category.DEFAULT" />
                </intent-filter>
        </activity>
    </application>
    <uses-sdk android:minSdkVersion="3" />
</manifest>
```

Recipe: Launching an Activity for a Result Using Speech to Text

In this recipe, launching an activity for a result is demonstrated. It also demonstrates how to use speech-to-text functionality from Google's `RecognizerIntent` activity and print the result to the screen. Here, the trigger event is a button press. It launches the `RecognizerIntent` activity, which does speech recognition on sound from the microphone and converts it into text. When finished, the text is passed back to the calling activity.

Upon return, the `onActivityResult()` function is first called with the returned data, and then the `onResume()` function is called to continue the activity normally. The calling activity can have a problem and not return properly. Therefore, `resultCode` should always be checked to ensure `RESULT_OK` before continuing to parse the returned data.

Note that in general any launched activity that returns data causes the same `onActivityResult()` function to be called. Therefore, a request code is customarily used to distinguish which activity is returning. When the launched activity finishes, it returns control to the calling activity and calls `onActivityResult()` with the same request code.

The steps for launching an activity for a result follow:

1. Call `startActivityForResult()` with an intent, defining the launched activity and an identifying `requestCode` variable.

2. Override the `onActivityResult()` function to check on the status of the result, check for the expected `requestCode`, and parse the returned data.

Following are the steps for using `RecognizerIntent`:

1. Declare an intent with action `ACTION_RECOGNIZE_SPEECH`.

2. Add any extras to the intent; at least `EXTRA_LANGUAGE_MODEL` is required. This can be set as either `LANGUAGE_MODEL_FREE_FORM` or `LANGUAGE_MODEL_WEB_SEARCH`.

3. The returned data bundle contains a list of strings with possible matches to the original text. Use `data.getStringArrayListExtra` to retrieve this data. This should be cast as an `ArrayList` for use later.

A `TextView` is used to display the returned text to the screen. The main activity is shown in Listing 2.15.

The additional supporting files needed are **main.xml** and **strings.xml**, which need to define a button and the `TextView` to hold the result. This is accomplished using Listings 2.11 and 2.13 in the "Launching a Second Activity from an Event" recipe. The **AndroidManifest.xml** file needs to declare only the main activity, which is the same as in the earlier "Creating a Project and an Activity" recipe. The `RecognizerIntent` activity is native to the Android system and does not need to be declared explicitly to be used.

Listing 2.15 **src/com/cookbook/launch_for_result/RecognizerIntent Example.java**

```java
package com.cookbook.launch_for_result;

import java.util.ArrayList;

import android.app.Activity;
import android.content.Intent;
import android.os.Bundle;
import android.speech.RecognizerIntent;
import android.view.View;
import android.widget.Button;
import android.widget.TextView;

public class RecognizerIntentExample extends Activity {
    private static final int RECOGNIZER_EXAMPLE = 1001;
    private TextView tv;

    protected void onCreate(Bundle savedInstanceState) {
        super.onCreate(savedInstanceState);
        setContentView(R.layout.main);

        tv = (TextView) findViewById(R.id.text_result);

        //Set up button listener
        Button startButton = (Button) findViewById(R.id.trigger);
        startButton.setOnClickListener(new View.OnClickListener() {
            public void onClick(View view) {
                // RecognizerIntent prompts for speech and returns text
                Intent intent =
                new Intent(RecognizerIntent. ACTION_RECOGNIZE_SPEECH);

                intent.putExtra(RecognizerIntent.EXTRA_LANGUAGE_MODEL,
                RecognizerIntent. LANGUAGE_MODEL_FREE_FORM);
                intent.putExtra(RecognizerIntent.EXTRA_PROMPT,
                "Say a word or phrase\nand it will show as text");
                startActivityForResult(intent, RECOGNIZER_EXAMPLE);
            }
        });
    }

    @Override
    protected void onActivityResult(int requestCode,
                                    int resultCode, Intent data) {
        //Use a switch statement for more than one request code check
        if (requestCode==RECOGNIZER_EXAMPLE && resultCode==RESULT_OK) {
                // Returned data is a list of matches to the speech input
                ArrayList<String> result =
                data.getStringArrayListExtra(RecognizerIntent.EXTRA_RESULTS);

            //Display on screen
            tv.setText(result.toString());
            }

        super.onActivityResult(requestCode, resultCode, data);
    }
}
```

Recipe: **Implementing a List of Choices**

A common situation in applications is to provide a user with a list of choices that can be selected by clicking them. This can be easily implemented using ListActivity, a subclass of Activity, and triggering an event based on what choice was made.

The steps for creating a list of choices follow:

1. Create a class that extends the ListActivity class instead of the Activity class:

```
public class ActivityExample extends ListActivity {

  //content here

}
```

2. Create a string array of labels for each choice:

```
static final String[] ACTIVITY_CHOICES = new String[] {

                "Action 1",

                "Action 2",

                "Action 3"

          };
```

3. Call setListAdapter() with the ArrayAdapter specifying this list and a layout:

```
setListAdapter(new ArrayAdapter<String>(this,

        android.R.layout.simple_list_item_1, ACTIVITY_CHOICES));

getListView().setChoiceMode(ListView.CHOICE_MODE_SINGLE);

getListView().setTextFilterEnabled(true);
```

4. Launch OnItemClickListener to determine which choice was selected and act accordingly:

```
getListView().setOnItemClickListener(new OnItemClickListener()

{

  @Override

  public void onItemClick(AdapterView<?> arg0, View arg1,

        int arg2, long arg3) {

    switch(arg2) {//Extend switch to as many as needed

    case 0:

        //code for action 1

        break;

    case 1:

        //code for action 2
```

```
            break;
        case 2:
            //code for action 3
            break;
        default: break;
        }
    }
});
```

This technique is used in the next recipe.

Recipe: Using Implicit Intents for Creating an Activity

Implicit intents do not specify an exact component to use. Instead, they specify the functionality required through a filter, and the Android system must determine the best component to use. An intent filter can be an action, data, or a category.

The most commonly used intent filter is an action, and the most common action is ACTION_VIEW. This mode requires a uniform resource identifier (URI) to be specified and then displays the data to the user. It does the most reasonable action for the given URI. For example, the implicit intents in cases 0, 1, and 2 in the following example have the same syntax but produce different results.

Following are the steps for launching an activity using an implicit intent:

1. Declare the intent with the appropriate filter specified (ACTION_VIEW, ACTION_WEB_SEARCH, and so on).

2. Attach any extra information to the intent required to run the activity.

3. Pass this intent to startActivity().

This is shown for multiple intents in Listing 2.16.

Listing 2.16   src/com/cookbook/implicit_intents/ListActivityExample.java

```
package com.cookbook.implicit_intents;

import android.app.ListActivity;
import android.app.SearchManager;
import android.content.Intent;
import android.net.Uri;
import android.os.Bundle;
import android.view.View;
import android.widget.AdapterView;
import android.widget.ArrayAdapter;
import android.widget.ListView;
import android.widget.AdapterView.OnItemClickListener;

public class ListActivityExample extends ListActivity {
```

```
    static final String[] ACTIVITY_CHOICES = new String[] {
        "Open Website Example",
        "Open Contacts",
        "Open Phone Dialer Example",
        "Search Google Example",
        "Start Voice Command"
    };
    final String searchTerms = "superman";

    protected void onCreate(Bundle savedInstanceState) {
        super.onCreate(savedInstanceState);

        setListAdapter(new ArrayAdapter<String>(this,
                android.R.layout.simple_list_item_1,
ACTIVITY_CHOICES));
        getListView().setChoiceMode(ListView.CHOICE_MODE_SINGLE);
        getListView().setTextFilterEnabled(true);
        getListView().setOnItemClickListener(new OnItemClickListener()
        {
            @Override
            public void onItemClick(AdapterView<?> arg0, View arg1,
                    int arg2, long arg3) {
                switch(arg2) {
                case 0: //opens web browser and navigates to given website
                    startActivity(new Intent(Intent.ACTION_VIEW,
                                    Uri.parse("http://www.android.com/")));
                    break;
                case 1: //opens contacts application to browse contacts
                    startActivity(new Intent(Intent.ACTION_VIEW,
                                    Uri.parse("content://contacts/people/")));
                    break;
                case 2: //opens phone dialer and fills in the given number
                    startActivity(new Intent(Intent.ACTION_VIEW,
                                    Uri.parse("tel:12125551212")));
                    break;
                case 3: //searches Google for the string
                    Intent intent= new Intent(Intent.ACTION_WEB_SEARCH);
                        intent.putExtra(SearchManager.QUERY, searchTerms);
                        startActivity(intent);
                    break;
                case 4: //starts the voice command
                    startActivity(new
                                    Intent(Intent.ACTION_VOICE_COMMAND));
                    break;
                default: break;
                }
            }
        });
    }
}
```

Recipe: Passing Primitive Data Types between Activities

Sometimes data needs to be passed to a launched activity. Sometimes a launched activity creates data that needs to be passed back to the calling activity. For example, the final score of a game needs to be returned to a high-scores screen. Following are different ways to pass information between activities:

- Declare the relevant variable in the calling activity (for example, `public int finalScore`) and set it in the launched activity (for example, `CallingActivity.finalScore=score`).
- Attach extras onto bundles (demonstrated in this recipe).
- Use Preferences to store data to be retrieved later (covered in Chapter 6, "User Interface Events").
- Use the SQLite database to store data to be retrieved later (covered in Chapter 11, "Data Storage Methods").

A `Bundle` is a mapping from string values to various parcelable types. It can be created by adding extras to an intent. This recipe shows data being passed from the main activity to the launched activity, where it is modified and passed back.

The variables (in this case, an `integer` and a `String`) are declared in the `StartScreen` activity. When the intent is created to call the `PlayGame` class, these variables are attached to the intent using the `putExtra` method. When the result is returned from the called activity, the variables can be read using the `getExtras` method. These calls are shown in Listing 2.17.

Listing 2.17   src/com/cookbook/passing_data_activities/StartScreen.java

```
package com.cookbook.passing_data_activities;

import android.app.Activity;
import android.content.Intent;
import android.os.Bundle;
import android.view.View;
import android.widget.Button;
import android.widget.TextView;

public class StartScreen extends Activity {
    private static final int PLAY_GAME = 1010;
    private TextView tv;
    private int meaningOfLife = 42;
    private String userName = "Douglas Adams";

    @Override
    public void onCreate(Bundle savedInstanceState) {
        super.onCreate(savedInstanceState);
        setContentView(R.layout.main);
        tv = (TextView) findViewById(R.id.startscreen_text);

        //Display initial values
        tv.setText(userName + ":" + meaningOfLife);

        //Set up button listener
        Button startButton = (Button) findViewById(R.id.play_game);
```

```
        startButton.setOnClickListener(new View.OnClickListener() {
            public void onClick(View view) {
                startGame();
            }
        });
    }

    @Override
    protected void onActivityResult(int requestCode,
            int resultCode, Intent data) {
        if (requestCode == PLAY_GAME && resultCode == RESULT_OK) {
            meaningOfLife = data.getExtras().getInt("returnInt");
            userName = data.getExtras().getString("returnStr");
            //Show it has changed
            tv.setText(userName + ":" + meaningOfLife);
        }
        super.onActivityResult(requestCode, resultCode, data);
    }

    private void startGame() {
        Intent launchGame = new Intent(this, PlayGame.class);

        //passing information to launched activity
        launchGame.putExtra("meaningOfLife", meaningOfLife);
        launchGame.putExtra("userName", userName);

        startActivityForResult(launchGame, PLAY_GAME);
    }
}
```

The variables passed into the PlayGame activity can be read using the getIntExtra
and getStringExtra methods. When the activity finishes and prepares an intent to
return, the putExtra method can be used to return data back to the calling activity.
These calls are shown in Listing 2.18.

Listing 2.18   src/com/cookbook/passing_data_activities/PlayGame.java

```
package com.cookbook.passing_data_activities;

import android.app.Activity;
import android.content.Intent;
import android.os.Bundle;
import android.view.View;
import android.widget.Button;
import android.widget.TextView;

public class PlayGame extends Activity {
    private TextView tv2;
    int answer;
    String author;
```

```
public void onCreate(Bundle savedInstanceState) {
    super.onCreate(savedInstanceState);
    setContentView(R.layout.game);

    tv2 = (TextView) findViewById(R.id.game_text);

    //reading information passed to this activity
    //Get the intent that started this activity
    Intent i = getIntent();
    //returns -1 if not initialized by calling activity
    answer = i.getIntExtra("meaningOfLife", -1);
    //returns [] if not initialized by calling activity
    author = i.getStringExtra("userName");

    tv2.setText(author + ":" + answer);

    //Change values for an example of return
    answer = answer - 41;
    author = author + " Jr.";

    //Set up button listener
    Button startButton = (Button) findViewById(R.id.end_game);
    startButton.setOnClickListener(new View.OnClickListener() {
        public void onClick(View view) {
            //Return information to calling activity
            Intent i = getIntent();
            i.putExtra("returnInt", answer);
            i.putExtra("returnStr", author);
            setResult(RESULT_OK, i);
            finish();
        }
    });
}
```

Threads, Services, Receivers, and Alerts

This chapter continues the introduction of the basic building blocks of an application. First, the explicit specification of threads is introduced as a method to separate tasks. Then, services and broadcast receivers are introduced. As shown in some recipes, services and broadcast receivers benefit from using threads. The application widget, which uses receivers, is then covered. This leads naturally to the discussion of various alerts available to the developer.

Threads

Every application by default runs a single process upon creation that contains all the tasks. To avoid hanging the user interface, time-consuming tasks, such as network downloads or computationally intensive calculations, should reside in a separate background thread. It is up to the developer to implement this properly, but then the Android OS prioritizes the threads accordingly.

Most applications can benefit from the use of threads. If such occasions are not detected in the software design phase, they quickly display during testing because the Android system provides an alert to the user when the UI hangs, as shown in Figure 3.1.

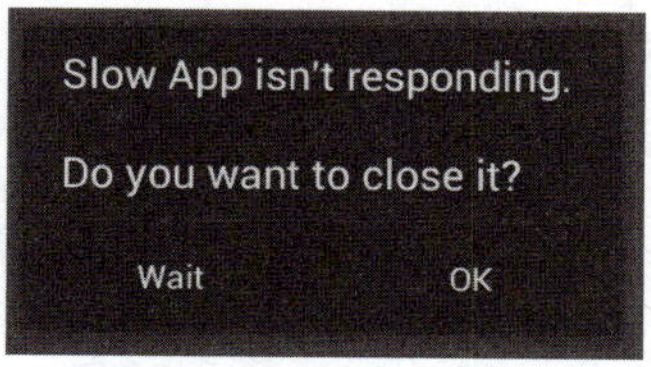

Figure 3.1   An example message that displays when a thread hangs

Recipe: Launching a Secondary Thread

In this recipe, a ringtone song is played when an on-screen button is pressed. This provides a simple illustration of how threads can be used with a time-consuming operation. In the following, calling the `play_music()` function without specifying a separate thread blocks the application during music playback:

```
Button startButton = (Button) findViewById(R.id.trigger);
startButton.setOnClickListener(new View.OnClickListener() {
    public void onClick(View view){
        // BAD USAGE: function call too time-consuming
        //   function causes main thread to hang
        play_music();
    }
});
```

This means that any user request such as navigating back to the home screen or multiple pushes of an on-screen button are not registered until the music is completely finished playing. The unresponsive UI might even cause the Android system to display an error such as the one shown in Figure 3.1.

This is resolved by launching a secondary thread to call the `play_music()` function as follows:

1. Create a new thread to hold a `Runnable` object:

   ```
   Thread initBkgdThread = new Thread(
       //Insert runnable object here
   );
   ```

2. Create a `Runnable` object that overrides the `run()` method to call the time-consuming task:

   ```
   new Runnable() {
     public void run() {
       play_music();
     }
   }
   ```

3. Start the thread, which then runs the task:

   ```
   initBkgdThread.start();
   ```

The setup of the secondary thread to contain the time-consuming task is quick, so the main thread can continue servicing other events.

Before the code for the full activity is shown, the supporting files are discussed. Media playback is covered more fully in Chapter 8, "Multimedia Techniques," but for illustration, the song is implemented here as a sequence of notes specified using ringtone text transfer language (RTTTL). For example, the following RTTTL code describes a quarter-note of the A (220Hz) just below middle C. Putting this in a single-line text file in the **res/raw/** directory registers it as the R.raw.a4 resource.

```
a4:d=4,o=5,b=250:a4
```

Then, a call in the activity to the media player plays this ringtone note:

```
m_mediaPlayer = MediaPlayer.create(this, R.raw.a4);
                 m_mediaPlayer.start();
```

This recipe uses four different notes in four separate RTTTL files: **g4.rtttl**, **a4.rtttl**, **b4.rtttl**, and **c5.rtttl**. These are just exact copies of the preceding example with the a4 changed in the file to reflect the new note in each case, but it can also be expanded to other notes or formats.

One aside is that MediaPlayer launches its own background thread to play the media. So, if this were a single longer file, it would be possible to avoid the use of an explicit thread as explained in Chapter 8, "Multimedia Techniques." That fact does not help when multiple files need to be played quickly, as here, but it is important to know that threads are not always necessary.

The trigger for starting the music is a button press. The Button widget needs to be specified in the main layout file (here called **main.xml**) and is identified with the name trigger, as shown in Listing 3.1.

Listing 3.1   res/layout/main.xml

```
<?xml version="1.0" encoding="utf-8"?>
<LinearLayout xmlns:android="http://schemas.android.com/apk/res/android"
    android:orientation="vertical"
    android:layout_width="match_parent"
    android:layout_height="match_parent"
    >
  <Button android:id="@+id/trigger"
    android:layout_width="100dip" android:layout_height="100dip"
    android:text="Press Me"
  />
</LinearLayout>
```

One side effect of launching a separate thread is that it still continues even if the main activity is paused. This is seen by implementing the background thread and navigating back to the home screen during music play. The music keeps playing until it is completed. If this is not the preferred behavior, the play_music() function can check a flag (here called paused), which is set during the main activity's onPause() function to stop music playback when the main thread is paused.

All the previous items are combined into the full activity PressAndPlay in Listing 3.2.

Listing 3.2   src/com/cookbook/launch_thread/PressAndPlay.java

```java
package com.cookbook.launch_thread;

import android.app.Activity;
import android.media.MediaPlayer;
import android.os.Bundle;
import android.view.View;
import android.widget.Button;

public class PressAndPlay extends Activity {

    @Override
    public void onCreate(Bundle savedInstanceState) {
        super.onCreate(savedInstanceState);
        setContentView(R.layout.main);

        Button startButton = (Button) findViewById(R.id.trigger);
        startButton.setOnClickListener(new View.OnClickListener() {
            public void onClick(View view){

                //Stand-alone play_music() function call causes
                //main thread to hang. Instead, create
                //separate thread for time-consuming task.
                Thread initBkgdThread = new Thread(new Runnable() {
                    public void run() {
                        play_music();
                    }
                });
                initBkgdThread.start();
            }
        });
    }

    int[] notes = {R.raw.c5, R.raw.b4, R.raw.a4, R.raw.g4};
    int NOTE_DURATION = 400; //millisec
    MediaPlayer m_mediaPlayer;
    private void play_music() {
        for(int ii=0; ii<12; ii++) {
            //Check to ensure main activity not paused
            if(!paused) {
                if(m_mediaPlayer != null) {m_mediaPlayer.release();}
                m_mediaPlayer = MediaPlayer.create(this, notes[ii%4]);
                m_mediaPlayer.start();
                try {
                    Thread.sleep(NOTE_DURATION);
                } catch (InterruptedException e) {
                    e.printStackTrace();
                }
            }
        }
    }

    boolean paused = false;
    @Override
    protected void onPause() {
```

```
        paused = true;
        super.onPause();
    }
    @Override
    protected void onResume() {
        super.onResume();
        paused = false;
    }
}
```

Note that the `Thread.sleep()` method pauses the thread for approximately the amount of time specified (in milliseconds). This is used to implement the note duration.

Also note the convention used in the lifecycle methods: Additional activity-specific logic is bracketed by the super methods. This is good practice to ensure proper completion of commands. So the internal pause flag is set to true before truly pausing the activity, and the activity is fully resumed before setting the internal pause flag to false.

Recipe: Creating a Runnable Activity

This recipe shows an activity that evaluates a computationally intensive function, such as edge detection in an image. Here, a dummy function called `detectEdges()` is run to emulate the actual image-processing algorithm.

If `detectEdges()` is called in `onCreate()` by itself, it hangs the main thread and does not display the UI layout until computation is done. Therefore, a separate thread needs to be created and started for the time-consuming function. Because the main purpose of the activity is this time-consuming operation, it is natural to have the activity itself implement `Runnable`. As shown in Listing 3.3, the background thread is declared in the `onCreate()` method. When the background thread is started, it calls the activity's `run()` method, which is overridden with the intended functionality.

The button is implemented exactly as in the previous "Launching a Secondary Thread" recipe. Pressing the button shows that the UI is still responsive when the background task `detectEdges()` runs.

Listing 3.3   **src/com/cookbook/runnable_activity/EdgeDetection.java**

```java
package com.cookbook.runnable_activity;

import android.app.Activity;
import android.os.Bundle;
import android.view.View;
import android.widget.Button;
import android.widget.TextView;

public class EdgeDetection extends Activity implements Runnable {
    int numberOfTimesPressed=0;

    @Override
    public void onCreate(Bundle savedInstanceState) {
```

```
super.onCreate(savedInstanceState);
setContentView(R.layout.main);
final TextView tv  = (TextView) findViewById(R.id.text);
//In-place function call causes main thread to hang:
/* detectEdges(); */
//Instead, create background thread for time-consuming task
Thread thread = new Thread(EdgeDetection.this);
thread.start();

Button startButton = (Button) findViewById(R.id.trigger);
startButton.setOnClickListener(new View.OnClickListener() {
    public void onClick(View view){

        tv.setText("Pressed button" + ++numberOfTimesPressed
            + " times\nAnd computation loop at "
            + "(" + xi + ", " + yi + ") pixels");
    }
});
}

@Override
public void run() {
    detectEdges();
}

//Edge Detection
int xi, yi;
private double detectEdges() {
    int x_pixels = 4000;
    int y_pixels = 3000;
    double image_transform=0;

    //Double loop over pixels for image processing
    //Meaningless hyperbolic cosine emulates time-consuming task
    for(xi=0; xi<x_pixels; xi++) {
        for(yi=0; yi<y_pixels; yi++) {
            image_transform = Math.cosh(xi*yi/x_pixels/y_pixels);
        }
    }
    return image_transform;
}
}
```

Recipe: Setting a Thread's Priority

The Android system handles thread priorities. By default, a new thread, myThread, gets a priority of 5. The developer can suggest a different priority by calling myThread.setPriority(priority) before myThread.start(). The priority cannot be set higher than Thread.MAX_PRIORITY (which is 10) or lower than Thread.MIN_PRIORITY (which is 1).

Android provides an alternative way to set threading priorities. With android. os.Process.setThreadPriority() a priority based on the "nice" Linux values between 20 and -20 can be requested. Both versions map to the same underlying system call, but android.os.Process.setThreadPriority() is more fine-grained.

Recipe: Canceling a Thread

Sometimes when a component is finished or killed, the developer wants the threads it spawns to also be killed. For example, take a thread defined in an activity:

```
private volatile Thread myThread;
```

The `myThread.stop()` method is deprecated because it might leave the application in an unpredictable state. Instead, use the following when needed, such as in the `onStop()` method of the parent component:

```
//Use to stop the thread myThread
if(myThread != null) {
    Thread dummy = myThread;
    myThread = null;
    dummy.interrupt();
}
```

At the application level, there is another way to do this: Declare all spawned threads as daemon threads using the `setDaemon(true)` method, as in the following example. This ensures that threads associated with that application are killed when the application's main thread is killed.

```
//Use when initially starting a thread
myThread.setDaemon(true);
myThread.start();
```

Finally, there is always the method of using a `while(stillRunning)` loop in the `run()` method and externally setting `stillRunning=false` to kill the thread. However, this might not provide sufficient control over the timing of when the thread stops.

Recipe: Sharing a Thread between Two Applications

The previous recipes motivated the use of multiple threads in a single application. The converse case is also sometimes useful, that is, use of multiple applications in a single thread. For example, if two applications need to communicate with each other, they can do so using binders rather than the more complicated inter-process communication (IPC) protocol. The steps for doing this follow:

- Make sure each application, when packaged for release, is signed with the same key for security reasons.
- Make sure each application is run with the same user ID. This is done by declaring the same attribute, `android:sharedUserId="my.shared.userid"`, in the **ActivityManifest.xml** file for each application.
- Declare each relevant activity or component to be run in the same process. This is done by declaring the same attribute, `android:process="my.shared.process-name"`, in the **ActivityManifest.xml** file for each component.

This ensures that the two components are run in the same thread and transparently share the same information. The more complex case where permissions cannot be shared is covered in the "Implementing a Remote Procedure Call" recipe in Chapter 4, "Advanced Threading Techniques."

Messages between Threads: Handlers

After multiple threads run concurrently, such as a main application thread and a background thread, there needs to be a way for them to communicate. Example use cases for such communication are:

- A main thread serves time-critical information and passes messages to the background time-consuming thread to update.
- A large computation completes and sends a message back to the calling thread with the result.

This can be accomplished with handlers, which are objects for sending messages between threads. Each handler is bound to a single thread, delivering messages to it and executing commands from it.

Recipe: Scheduling a Runnable Task from the Main Thread

This recipe implements a clock timer, which is often needed in applications. For example, it can be used in a game to keep track of how long a player takes to complete a level. This provides a simple way to handle user interaction while a background thread continues to run.

The timer is run in a background thread so it does not block the UI thread, but it needs to update the UI whenever the time changes. As shown in Listing 3.4, the TextView text starts with a welcome message and the button text with trigger ID starts with the value "Press Me".

Listing 3.4   res/layout/main.xml

```xml
<?xml version="1.0" encoding="utf-8"?>
<LinearLayout xmlns:android="http://schemas.android.com/apk/res/android"
    android:orientation="vertical"
    android:layout_width="match_parent"
    android:layout_height="match_parent"
    >
<TextView android:id="@+id/text"
    android:layout_width="match_parent"
    android:layout_height="wrap_content"
    android:text="@string/hello"
    />
<Button android:id="@+id/trigger"
    android:layout_width="100dip" android:layout_height="100dip"
```

```
        android:text="Press Me"
    />
</LinearLayout>
```

These text resources in the layout XML file are associated with `TextView` variables in the `BackgroundTimer` Java activity using the following initializers:

```
mTimeLabel = (TextView) findViewById(R.id.text);
mButtonLabel = (TextView) findViewById(R.id.trigger);
```

After being identified in Java, the text can be modified during run-time. When the application starts, `mUpdateTimeTask` starts a timer and overwrites the text `mTimeLabel` with the new time in minutes and seconds. When the button is pressed, its `onClick()` method overwrites the text `mButtonLabel` with the number of times the button was pressed.

The handler `mHandler` is created and used to queue the runnable object `mUpdateTimeTask`. It is first called in the `onCreate()` method, and then the recursive call in the task itself continues to update the time every 200ms. This is used more often than not to ensure a smooth time change each second without excessive overhead in task calls. The complete activity is shown in Listing 3.5.

Listing 3.5   src/com/cookbook/background_timer/BackgroundTimer.java

```java
package com.cookbook.background_timer;

import android.app.Activity;
import android.os.Bundle;
import android.os.Handler;
import android.os.SystemClock;
import android.view.View;
import android.widget.Button;
import android.widget.TextView;

public class BackgroundTimer extends Activity {
    //Keep track of button presses, a main thread task
    private int buttonPress=0;
    TextView mButtonLabel;

    //counter of time since app started, a background task
    private long mStartTime = 0L;
    private TextView mTimeLabel;

    //handler to handle the message to the timer task
    private Handler mHandler = new Handler();

    @Override
    public void onCreate(Bundle savedInstanceState) {
        super.onCreate(savedInstanceState);
        setContentView(R.layout.main);
```

```
        if (mStartTime == 0L) {
            mStartTime = SystemClock.uptimeMillis();
            mHandler.removeCallbacks(mUpdateTimeTask);
            mHandler.postDelayed(mUpdateTimeTask, 100);
        }

        mTimeLabel = (TextView) findViewById(R.id.text);
        mButtonLabel = (TextView) findViewById(R.id.trigger);

        Button startButton = (Button) findViewById(R.id.trigger);
        startButton.setOnClickListener(new View.OnClickListener() {
            public void onClick(View view){
                mButtonLabel.setText("Pressed " + ++buttonPress
                                                 + " times");
            }
        });
    }

    private Runnable mUpdateTimeTask = new Runnable() {
        public void run() {
            final long start = mStartTime;
            long millis = SystemClock.uptimeMillis() - start;
            int seconds = (int) (millis / 1000);
            int minutes = seconds / 60;
            seconds    = seconds % 60;

            mTimeLabel.setText("" + minutes + ":"
                                  + String.format("%02d",seconds));
            mHandler.postDelayed(this, 200);
        }
    };

    @Override
    protected void onPause() {
        mHandler.removeCallbacks(mUpdateTimeTask);
        super.onPause();
    }

    @Override
    protected void onResume() {
        super.onResume();
        mHandler.postDelayed(mUpdateTimeTask, 100);
    }
}
```

Recipe: Using a Countdown Timer

The previous recipe is an example of handlers and a functional timer. Another timer is provided with the built-in class CountDownTimer. This encapsulates the creation of a background thread and the handler queuing into a convenient class call.

The countdown timer takes two arguments: the number of milliseconds until the countdown is done and how often in milliseconds to process onTick() callbacks. The onTick() method is used to update the countdown text. Note that otherwise the recipe is identical to the previous recipe. The full activity is shown in Listing 3.6.

Listing 3.6   **src/com/cookbook/countdown/CountDownTimerExample.java**

```java
package com.cookbook.countdown;

import android.app.Activity;
import android.os.Bundle;
import android.os.CountDownTimer;
import android.view.View;
import android.widget.Button;
import android.widget.TextView;

public class CountDownTimerExample extends Activity {
    //Keep track of button presses, a main thread task
    private int buttonPress=0;
    TextView mButtonLabel;

    //countdown timer, a background task
    private TextView mTimeLabel;

    @Override
    public void onCreate(Bundle savedInstanceState) {
        super.onCreate(savedInstanceState);
        setContentView(R.layout.main);

        mTimeLabel = (TextView) findViewById(R.id.text);
        mButtonLabel = (TextView) findViewById(R.id.trigger);

        new CountDownTimer(30000, 1000) {
            public void onTick(long millisUntilFinished) {
                mTimeLabel.setText("seconds remaining: "
                        + millisUntilFinished / 1000);
            }
            public void onFinish() {
                mTimeLabel.setText("done!");
            }
        }.start();

        Button startButton = (Button) findViewById(R.id.trigger);
        startButton.setOnClickListener(new View.OnClickListener() {
            public void onClick(View view){
                mButtonLabel.setText("Pressed " + ++buttonPress + " times");
            }
        });
    }
}
```

Recipe: Handling a Time-Consuming Initialization

This recipe addresses a common case of needing to run a time-consuming initialization when an application starts. Initially, the layout is set to show a specific "Loading. . ." splash screen specified in the **loading.xml** file. In this example, it is a simple text message as shown in Listing 3.7, but it could be a company logo or introductory animation.

Listing 3.7   **res/layout/loading.xml**

```
<?xml version="1.0" encoding="utf-8"?>
<LinearLayout
  xmlns:android="http://schemas.android.com/apk/res/android"
  android:layout_width="wrap_content"
  android:layout_height="wrap_content">
  <TextView android:id="@+id/loading"
    android:layout_width="match_parent"
    android:layout_height="wrap_content"
    android:text="Loading..."
    />
</LinearLayout>
```

While this layout is being displayed, the function `initializeArrays()`, which takes time to complete, is launched in a background thread to avoid hanging the UI. The initialization uses static variables to ensure that a screen change or another instance of the activity does not require a recalculation of the data.

When the initialization is done, a message is sent to the handler `mHandler`. Since the act of sending a message is all the information needed, just an empty message is sent as `mHandler.sendEmptyMessage(0)`.

Upon receiving the message, the UI thread runs the `handleMessage()` method. It is overridden to continue with the activity after the starting initialization, here setting up the main screen specified in the **main.xml** layout file. The full activity is shown in Listing 3.8.

Listing 3.8   **src/com/cookbook/handle_message/HandleMessage.java**

```
package com.cookbook.handle_message;

import android.app.Activity;
import android.os.Bundle;
import android.os.Handler;
import android.os.Message;

public class HandleMessage extends Activity implements Runnable {

    @Override
    public void onCreate(Bundle savedInstanceState) {
        super.onCreate(savedInstanceState);
        setContentView(R.layout.loading);

        Thread thread = new Thread(this);
        thread.start();
    }

    private Handler mHandler = new Handler() {
        public void handleMessage(Message msg) {
            setContentView(R.layout.main);
        }
    };
```

```
    public void run(){
        initializeArrays();
        mHandler.sendEmptyMessage(0);
    }

    final static int NUM_SAMPS = 1000;
    static double[][] correlation;
    void initializeArrays() {
        if(correlation!=null) return;

        correlation = new double[NUM_SAMPS][NUM_SAMPS];
        //calculation
        for(int k=0; k<NUM_SAMPS; k++) {
            for(int m=0; m<NUM_SAMPS; m++) {
                correlation[k][m] = Math.cos(2*Math.PI*(k+m)/1000);
            }
        }
    }
}
```

Alerts

Alerts provide a quick message to the user outside of the application's main UI. An alert can be in an overlay window such as a toast or `AlertDialog` box. It can also be in the notification bar at the top of the screen. The toast alert provides a printed message to the screen with a single line of code. There is no need to work with the layout files. For this reason, it is also a handy debug tool, equivalent to the `printf` statement in C programs.

Recipe: Using Toast to Show a Brief Message on the Screen

The `Toast` method was introduced in the previous chapter in a compact form:

```
Toast.makeText(this, "text", Toast.LENGTH_SHORT).show();
```

It can also be written as a multiline command:

```
Toast tst = Toast.makeText(this, "text", Toast.LENGTH_SHORT);
        tst.show();
```

This form is useful when the text needs to be shown multiple times, as the instance in the first line can be reused.

Two other uses for the multiline `Toast` command are to reposition the text location or to add an image. To reposition the text location, or to center the toast in the screen display, use `setGravity` before calling the `show()` method:

```
tst.setGravity(Gravity.CENTER, tst.getXOffset() / 2,
                        tst.getYOffset() / 2);
```

To add an image to a toast, use the following:

```
Toast tst = Toast.makeText(this, "text", Toast.LENGTH_LONG);
```

```
ImageView view = new ImageView(this);
view.setImageResource(R.drawable.my_figure);
tst.setView(view);
tst.show();
```

Recipe: Using an AlertDialog Box

Providing a user with an alert and up to three buttons of possible actions can be done with the AlertDialog class. Some examples are:

- "Your final score was 90/100: Try this level again, advance to next level, or go back to the main menu."
- "The image file is corrupt. Choose another or cancel action."

This recipe takes the first example and shows how to provide an action on each choice depending on which button is clicked. The example code is shown in Listing 3.9.

AlertDialog is initialized using the create() method; the text is specified using the setMessage() method; the three possible button texts and corresponding actions are specified using the setButton() method; and finally, the dialog box is displayed to the screen using the show() method. Note that the logic in each of the onClick() callback functions is just an example to show how to specify button actions.

Listing 3.9   Providing Action Choices with AlertDialog

```
AlertDialog dialog = new AlertDialog.Builder(this).create();

dialog.setMessage("Your final score: " + mScore + "/" + PERFECT_SCORE);
dialog.setButton(DialogInterface.BUTTON_POSITIVE, "Try this level again",
        new DialogInterface.OnClickListener() {
            public void onClick(DialogInterface dialog, int which) {
                mScore = 0;
                start_level();
            }
        });
dialog.setButton(DialogInterface.BUTTON_NEGATIVE, "Advance to next level",
        new DialogInterface.OnClickListener() {
            public void onClick(DialogInterface dialog, int which) {
                mLevel++;
                start_level();
            }
        });
dialog.setButton(DialogInterface.BUTTON_NEUTRAL, "Back to the main menu",
        new DialogInterface.OnClickListener() {
            public void onClick(DialogInterface dialog, int which) {
                mLevel = 0;
                finish();
            }
        });
dialog.show();
```

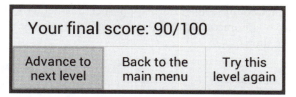

Figure 3.2   An alert dialog box with three options

This produces the pop-up dialog box shown in Figure 3.2. Note that the buttons are displayed in the order BUTTON_POSITIVE, BUTTON_NEUTRAL, and BUTTON_NEGATIVE. If a dialog box with two options or one option is needed, do not specify all three button choices.

Recipe: Showing Notification in the Status Bar

The status bar across the top of the device screen shows pending notifications for users to read whenever they choose. In general, because an activity mostly interacts with the user, services are more likely to use this feature. As a rule, notifications should be concise and minimal for the best user experience.

The steps for creating a status bar notification are:

1. Declare a notification and specify how it displays on the status bar:

```
String ns = Context.NOTIFICATION_SERVICE;

mNManager = (NotificationManager) getSystemService(ns);

final Notification msg = new Notification(R.drawable.icon,
        "New event of importance",
        System.currentTimeMillis());
```

2. Define how it looks when the status bar is expanded for details and the action taken when clicked (this future action is defined by a PendingIntent class):

```
Context context = getApplicationContext();

CharSequence contentTitle = "ShowNotification Example";

CharSequence contentText = "Browse Android Cookbook Site";

Intent msgIntent = new Intent(Intent.ACTION_VIEW,
                    Uri.parse("http://www.pearson.com"));

PendingIntent intent =
        PendingIntent.getActivity(ShowNotification.this,
            0, msgIntent,
            Intent.FLAG_ACTIVITY_NEW_TASK);
```

3. Add any further configurable information, such as whether to blink an LED, play a sound, or automatically cancel the notification after it is selected. The latter two are shown here:

```
msg.defaults |= Notification.DEFAULT_SOUND;

msg.flags |= Notification.FLAG_AUTO_CANCEL;
```

4. Set the information for the notification event to the system:

```
msg.setLatestEventInfo(context, contentTitle, contentText, intent);
```

5. When the event of interest happens in the application, trigger notification with a unique identifier:

```
mNManager.notify(NOTIFY_ID, msg);
```

6. Upon completion, clear notification as needed with the same identifier.

If any information gets changed, the notification should be updated rather than sending another notification. This can be done by updating the relevant information in step 2, and then calling `setLatestEventInfo` again. An example activity illustrating a notification is shown in Listing 3.10.

Listing 3.10   src/com/cookbook/show_notification/ShowNotification.java

```java
package com.cookbook.show_notification;

import android.app.Activity;
import android.app.Notification;
import android.app.NotificationManager;
import android.app.PendingIntent;
import android.content.Context;
import android.content.Intent;
import android.net.Uri;
import android.os.Bundle;
import android.view.View;
import android.view.View.OnClickListener;
import android.widget.Button;


public class ShowNotification extends Activity {

    private NotificationManager mNManager;
    private static final int NOTIFY_ID=1100;

    /** called when the activity is first created */
    @Override
    public void onCreate(Bundle savedInstanceState) {
        super.onCreate(savedInstanceState);
        setContentView(R.layout.main);

        String ns = Context.NOTIFICATION_SERVICE;
        mNManager = (NotificationManager) getSystemService(ns);
```

```
final Notification msg = new Notification(R.drawable.icon,
        "New event of importance",
        System.currentTimeMillis());

Button start = (Button)findViewById(R.id.start);
Button cancel = (Button)findViewById(R.id.cancel);

start.setOnClickListener(new OnClickListener() {
    public void onClick(View v) {
        Context context = getApplicationContext();
        CharSequence contentTitle = "ShowNotification Example";
        CharSequence contentText = "Browse Android Cookbook Site";
        Intent msgIntent = new Intent(Intent.ACTION_VIEW,
                Uri.parse("http://www.pearson.com"));
        PendingIntent intent =
            PendingIntent.getActivity(ShowNotification.this,
                    0, msgIntent,
                    Intent.FLAG_ACTIVITY_NEW_TASK);

        msg.defaults |= Notification.DEFAULT_SOUND;
        msg.flags |= Notification.FLAG_AUTO_CANCEL;

        msg.setLatestEventInfo(context,
                contentTitle, contentText, intent);
        mNManager.notify(NOTIFY_ID, msg);
    }
});

cancel.setOnClickListener(new OnClickListener() {
    public void onClick(View v) {
        mNManager.cancel(NOTIFY_ID);
    }
});
    }
}
```

With Android 4.1 came additional notification styles and an API based on a builder pattern to create them. The recommended way to use them is by using the NotificationCompat API, which requires the addition of **android-support-v4. jar** to the project's **/libs/** folder. The four new styles are big text, big picture, inbox style, and the ability to add a progress bar to a notification. All notifications still need to have a small icon, title, and content text. Big text and big picture are very similar (either a text or a bitmap object is added as content). The big-picture style is shown in Listing 3.11.

Listing 3.11 A Big-Picture-Style Notification

```
Button startBigPic = (Button)findViewById(R.id.startBigPic);
Button stopBigPic = (Button)findViewById(R.id.stopBigPic);

startBigPic.setOnClickListener(new OnClickListener() {
    public void onClick(View v) {
```

```
                    Context context = getApplicationContext();
                    CharSequence contentTitle = "Show Big Notification Example";
                    CharSequence contentText = "Browse Android Cookbook Site";

                    Intent msgIntent = new Intent(Intent.ACTION_VIEW,
                            Uri.parse("http://www.pearson.com"));
                    PendingIntent intent =
                        PendingIntent.getActivity(ShowNotification.this,
                                0, msgIntent,
                                Intent.FLAG_ACTIVITY_NEW_TASK);

                    NotificationCompat.Builder builder =
                        new NotificationCompat.Builder(context);
                    builder.setSmallIcon(R.drawable.icon);
                    builder.setContentTitle(contentTitle);
                    builder.setContentText(contentText);
                    builder.setContentIntent(intent);

                    NotificationCompat.BigPictureStyle pictureStyle = new
                        NotificationCompat.BigPictureStyle();
                    Bitmap bigPicture= BitmapFactory.decodeResource(getResources(),
                        R.drawable.bigpicture);
                    pictureStyle.bigPicture(bigPicture);

                    builder.setStyle(pictureStyle);


                    mNManager.notify(NOTIFY_ID+1,builder.build());
                }
            });
        stopBigPic.setOnClickListener(new OnClickListener() {
            public void onClick(View v) {
                mNManager.cancel(NOTIFY_ID+1);
            }
        });
```

Intent, title, and content text are the same as in the previous notification. A new builder instance is obtained and the mandatory information is set by calling builder.setSmallIcon(..) and builder.setContentXX(..) for text, title, and intent. The NotificationCompat.BigPictureStyle class needs to be given a bitmap object, which can be read from the drawable folder with BitmapFactory.decodeResource(getResources,R.drawable.bigpicture). A call to builder.setStyle(pictureStyle); will ensure that the image gets displayed, then the notification is shown.

The inbox style displays a list of text lines that resemble an email inbox. The steps to display this are the same, except that an instance of NotificationCompat.InboxStyle is given to the builder, and every line of text needs to be added to the style object by calling inboxStyle.addline(..) with a CharSequence argument. This is shown in Listing 3.12.

Listing 3.12 **Inbox-Style Notification**

```
Button startInbox = (Button)findViewById(R.id.startInbox);
Button stopInbox = (Button)findViewById(R.id.stopInbox);

startInbox.setOnClickListener(new OnClickListener() {
    public void onClick(View v) {


        Context context = getApplicationContext();
        CharSequence contentTitle = "Show Big Notification Example";
        CharSequence contentText = "Browse Android Cookbook Site";

        Intent msgIntent = new Intent(Intent.ACTION_VIEW,
                Uri.parse("http://www.pearson.com"));
        PendingIntent intent =
            PendingIntent.getActivity(ShowNotification.this,
                    0, msgIntent,
                    Intent.FLAG_ACTIVITY_NEW_TASK);

        NotificationCompat.Builder builder =
            new NotificationCompat.Builder(context);
        builder.setSmallIcon(R.drawable.icon);
        builder.setContentTitle(contentTitle);
        builder.setContentText(contentText);

        NotificationCompat.InboxStyle inboxStyle =
            new NotificationCompat.InboxStyle();

        for(int i=0;i<4;i++){
            inboxStyle.addLine("subevent #"+i);
        }

        builder.setStyle(inboxStyle);
        builder.setContentIntent(intent);

        mNManager.notify(NOTIFY_ID+2,builder.build());
    }
});
stopInbox.setOnClickListener(new OnClickListener() {
    public void onClick(View v) {
        mNManager.cancel(NOTIFY_ID+2);
    }
});
```

Services

A service is an Android component that runs in the background without any user interaction. It can be started and stopped by any component. While it is running, any
component can bind to it. A service can also stop itself. Some illustrative scenarios of a
service are:

- An activity provides the user a way to select a set of music files, which then starts a service to play back the files. During playback, a new activity starts and binds to the existing service to allow the user to change songs or stop playback.

- An activity starts a service to upload a set of pictures to a website. A new activity starts and binds to the existing service to determine which file is currently being uploaded and displays the picture to the screen.

- A broadcast receiver receives a message that a picture was taken and launches a service to upload the new picture to a website. The broadcast receiver then goes inactive and is eventually killed to reclaim memory, but the service continues until the picture is uploaded. Then, the service stops itself.

The general lifecycle of a service is illustrated in Figure 3.3.

As an aside on the third scenario, any background task within a component will be killed when the component is killed. Therefore, tasks that are meaningful to continue even after the component stops should be done by launching a service. This ensures that the operating system is aware that active work is still being done by the process.

All services extend the abstract class `Service` or one of its subclasses. Similar to an activity, the entry point to each service is the `onCreate()` method. There is no concept of pausing a service, but it can be stopped, which calls the `onDestroy()` method.

Recipe: Creating a Self-Contained Service

The steps to create a self-contained service associated with a single component are:

1. Create a class to extend `Service`. (In Eclipse, this can be done by right-clicking the project, choosing **New → Class**, and specifying `android.app.Service` as the superclass.)

2. Declare the service in the **AndroidManifest.xml** file by adding a variation of the following (this should be done automatically if the previous Eclipse step was used):
   ```
   <service android:name=".myService"></service>
   ```

3. Override the `onCreate()` and `onDestroy()` methods. (In Eclipse, this can be done by right-clicking on the class file, choosing **Source → Override/Implement Methods...**, and checking the `onCreate()` and `onDestroy()` methods.) These contain the functionality of the service when it is started and stopped.

4. Override the `onBind()` method for cases when a new component binds to this service after it has already been created.

5. Activate the service from an external trigger. The service cannot run by itself but instead needs to be activated by a separate component or trigger in some way. For example, a component can create an intent to start or stop the service using `startService()` or `stopService()` as needed.

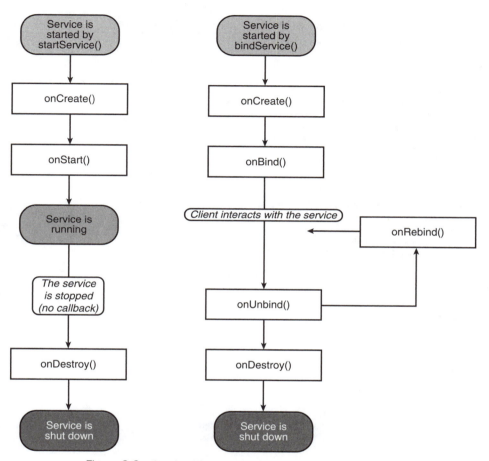

Figure 3.3   Service lifecycle (http://developer.android.com/)

To illustrate the previous process, a simple service is shown in Listing 3.13 to use the play_music() function from the first recipe in this chapter. Note the following:

- A Toast is used to show when the service is started or stopped.
- The onBind() method is overridden but not used. (This can be extended as needed.)
- A thread still needs to be created for playing music so as not to block the UI.
- The service does not stop when the activity is destroyed (for example, by changing the screen orientation) or when the activity is paused (for example, when pressing the Home key). This shows that the service, although launched by the activity, runs as its own entity.

Listing 3.13   src/com/cookbook/simple_service/SimpleService.java

```java
package com.cookbook.simple_service;

import android.app.Service;
import android.content.Intent;
import android.media.MediaPlayer;
import android.os.IBinder;
import android.widget.Toast;

public class SimpleService extends Service {
    @Override
    public IBinder onBind(Intent arg0) {
            return null;
    }

    boolean paused = false;

    @Override
    public void onCreate() {
            super.onCreate();
            Toast.makeText(this,"Service created ...",
                            Toast.LENGTH_LONG).show();
            paused = false;
            Thread initBkgdThread = new Thread(new Runnable() {
                public void run() {
                        play_music();
                }
            });
            initBkgdThread.start();
    }

    @Override
    public void onDestroy() {
            super.onDestroy();
            Toast.makeText(this, "Service destroyed ...",
                            Toast.LENGTH_LONG).show();
            paused = true;
    }

    int[] notes = {R.raw.c5, R.raw.b4, R.raw.a4, R.raw.g4};
    int NOTE_DURATION = 400; //millisec
    MediaPlayer m_mediaPlayer;
    private void play_music() {
        for(int ii=0; ii<12; ii++) {
            //Check to ensure main activity not paused
            if(!paused) {
                if(m_mediaPlayer != null) {m_mediaPlayer.release();}
                m_mediaPlayer = MediaPlayer.create(this, notes[ii%4]);
                m_mediaPlayer.start();
                try {
                    Thread.sleep(NOTE_DURATION);
                } catch (InterruptedException e) {
                    e.printStackTrace();
                }
            }
        }
    }
}
```

The **AndroidManifest.xml** file now has both the activity and service declared, as shown in Listing 3.14.

Listing 3.14   **AndroidManifest.xml**

```xml
<?xml version="1.0" encoding="utf-8"?>
<manifest xmlns:android="http://schemas.android.com/apk/res/android"
          package="com.cookbook.simple_service"
          android:versionCode="1"
          android:versionName="1.0">
    <application android:icon="@drawable/icon"
                 android:label="@string/app_name">
        <activity android:name=".SimpleActivity"
                  android:label="@string/app_name">
            <intent-filter>
              <action android:name="android.intent.action.MAIN" />
              <category android:name="android.intent.category.LAUNCHER" />
            </intent-filter>
        </activity>
        <service android:name=".SimpleService"></service>
    </application>
    <uses-sdk android:minSdkVersion="3" />
</manifest>
```

The example activity that sets up the UI to trigger the start and stop of this service is shown in Listing 3.15, and the associated layout file is shown in Listing 3.16 for the two buttons.

Listing 3.15   **src/com/cookbook/simple_service/SimpleActivity.java**

```java
package com.cookbook.simple_service;

import android.app.Activity;
import android.content.Intent;
import android.os.Bundle;
import android.view.View;
import android.widget.Button;

public class SimpleActivity extends Activity {
    @Override
    protected void onCreate(Bundle savedInstanceState) {
        super.onCreate(savedInstanceState);
        setContentView(R.layout.main);

        Button startButton = (Button) findViewById(R.id.Button01);
        startButton.setOnClickListener(new View.OnClickListener() {
            public void onClick(View view){
                startService(new Intent(SimpleActivity.this,
                                        SimpleService.class));
            }
        });

        Button stopButton = (Button)findViewById(R.id.Button02);
        stopButton.setOnClickListener(new View.OnClickListener() {
```

```
        public void onClick(View v){
            stopService(new Intent(SimpleActivity.this,
                                    SimpleService.class));
        }
    });
    }
}
```

Listing 3.16   res/layout/main.xml

```xml
<?xml version="1.0" encoding="utf-8"?>
<LinearLayout xmlns:android="http://schemas.android.com/apk/res/android"
    android:orientation="vertical"
    android:layout_width="match_parent"
    android:layout_height="match_parent">
  <TextView
    android:layout_width="match_parent"
    android:layout_height="wrap_content"
    android:text="@string/hello"
    />
  <Button android:text="Do it" android:id="@+id/Button01"
    android:layout_width="wrap_content"
    android:layout_height="wrap_content"></Button>
  <Button android:text="Stop it" android:id="@+id/Button02"
    android:layout_width="wrap_content"
    android:layout_height="wrap_content"></Button>
</LinearLayout>
```

Recipe: Adding a WakeLock

When the user presses the power button or the device has not been used for a certain amount of time, the screen goes off and the device goes to standby. While it is on standby, most running processes are shut down or canceled, and the processor goes into sleep mode, saving precious battery life. It is good practice to respect that behavior and not drain the user's battery by preventing standby. That being said, there are cases when it is desirable to keep an app running even if the screen is off, music playback being a prime example. To be able to keep an app running while the screen is off, the app must set a WakeLock. This recipe uses the service from the previous recipe and adds a WakeLock to it, so that music playback continues after the power button on the device has been pressed. Table 3.1 shows which types of WakeLocks are available for use.

There are two main types of WakeLock: partial WakeLock, which lets the screen go off but makes sure the app is still running, and full WakeLock, which also keeps the screen and the keyboard on even if the power button is pressed. Two subtypes building upon partial WakeLock give a bit more fine-grained control over the screen behavior. This recipe uses the partial WakeLock as the screen does not need to be on while audio is playing. For using WakeLocks, a special WakeLock permission is needed. This is added to the **AndroidManifest.xml** file in Listing 3.17.

Table 3.1 **Comparison of Available WakeLocks**

WakeLock Type	CPU	Screen	Hardware Keyboard
PARTIAL_WAKE_LOCK	On	Off	Off
SCREEN_DIM_WAKE_LOCK	On	Dimmed	Off
SCREEN_BRIGHT_WAKE_LOCK	On	Bright	Off
FULL_WAKE_LOCK	On	Bright	Bright

Listing 3.17 **AndroidManifest.xml**

```xml
<?xml version="1.0" encoding="utf-8"?>
<manifest xmlns:android="http://schemas.android.com/apk/res/android"
          package="com.cookbook.simple_service"
          android:versionCode="1"
          android:versionName="1.0">

    <uses-permission android:name="android.permission.WAKE_LOCK"/>

    <application android:icon="@drawable/icon"
                 android:label="@string/app_name">


    <activity android:name=".SimpleActivity"
              android:label="@string/app_name">
        <intent-filter>
            <action android:name="android.intent.action.MAIN" />
            <category android:name="android.intent.category.LAUNCHER" />
        </intent-filter>
    </activity>
    <service android:name=".SimpleService"></service>
    </application>
    <uses-sdk android:minSdkVersion="3" />
</manifest>
```

To acquire a WakeLock, access to the `PowerManager` class is needed. This class is a system service and can be retrieved by calling `Context.getSystemService(Context.PowerService)`. To create a new WakeLock instance, call the following:

```
powerManager.mWakeLock =
    powerManager.newWakeLock(PowerManager.PARTIAL_WAKE_LOCK, LOG_TAG);
```

Here, all the WakeLock properties wanted are specified by concatenating the flags with an OR operation in the first argument, and giving a name tag to the WakeLock in the second, usually the log tag of the service or activity. To activate the WakeLock, simply call `mWakelock.acquire()` whenever needed.

WakeLocks need to be explicitly released if they are not needed anymore. This is done by checking if they are held with `mWakelock.isHeld()` and then calling `mWakelock.release();`. After the WakeLock is released, the device can go back to sleep as it would normally when the screen goes off. One thing to note is that WakeLocks need to be released in the reverse order in which they were acquired, in the rare case that more than one of them is used. This is demonstrated in Listing 3.18.

Listing 3.18 **Simple Service with a WakeLock**

```
public class SimpleService extends Service {
    private static final String LOG_TAG = SimpleService.class.getSimpleName();


        @Override
    public IBinder onBind(Intent arg0) {
        return null;
    }


    boolean paused = false;
        private WakeLock mWakeLock=null;


    @Override
    public void onCreate() {
        super.onCreate();
        Toast.makeText(this,"Service created ...", Toast.LENGTH_LONG).show();
        setWakeLock();
        paused = false;
        Thread initBkgdThread = new Thread(new Runnable() {
            public void run() {
                play_music();
            }
        });
        initBkgdThread.start();
    }


    private void setWakeLock() {
      PowerManager powerManager =
          (PowerManager)getSystemService(Context.POWER_SERVICE);
      mWakeLock=powerManager.newWakeLock(PowerManager.PARTIAL_WAKE_LOCK, LOG_TAG);
        mWakeLock.acquire();
        }


        @Override

    public void onDestroy() {
        super.onDestroy();
        releaseWakeLock();
```

```
                Toast.makeText(this, "Service destroyed ...", Toast.LENGTH_LONG).show();
                paused = true;
        }


        private void releaseWakeLock() {
            if(mWakeLock!=null && mWakeLock.isHeld())
            {
            mWakeLock.release();
            }
            }


            int[] notes = {R.raw.c5, R.raw.b4, R.raw.a4, R.raw.g4};
    int NOTE_DURATION = 400; //millisec
    MediaPlayer m_mediaPlayer;
    private void play_music() {
        for(int ii=0; ii<12; ii++) {
            //Check to ensure main activity not paused
            if(!paused) {
                if(m_mediaPlayer != null) {m_mediaPlayer.release();}
                m_mediaPlayer = MediaPlayer.create(this, notes[ii%4]);
                m_mediaPlayer.start();
                try {
                    Thread.sleep(NOTE_DURATION);
                } catch (InterruptedException e) {
                    e.printStackTrace();
                }
            }
        }
    }
  }
}
```

In Listing 3.18, WakeLock is handled in two separate functions for a cleaner separation; setWakeLock() is called in the onCreate() method of the service so it gets set the moment the service starts. In the onDestroy() method, releaseWakeLock() is called to make sure system resources are released if the service receives a stop request.

Recipe: Using a Foreground Service

Services are meant to run in the background and do short-lived tasks with a lower priority. This means that services are the first thing the system will kill if a foreground process such as an activity needs more memory or computing power. This is the desired behavior in most cases. However, there are some times when it is desirable for a service to stay alive and take priority over other background tasks. Again, playing back music is a prime example. Android allows a service to be marked as a foreground service, but this requires setting a mandatory ongoing notification in the notification bar, so the user is informed about a service taking priority.

Activating the foreground mode is as simple as calling the following:

```
startForeground(NOTIFICATION_ID, getForegroundNotification());
```

The arguments of startForeground are an ID with which to recognize the notification and a new instance of a notification to show.

Foreground mode can easily be stopped by calling stopForeground(true);, the flag telling it to remove the notification now. Again, those two calls are put in separate methods and called from the onCreate() and onDestroy() methods of the service. The biggest hassle here is creating the notification itself, as can be seen in Listing 3.19.

Listing 3.19   **Foreground Service Class**

```java
public class SimpleService extends Service {
    private static final int NOTIFICATION_ID = 1;

        @Override
    public IBinder onBind(Intent arg0) {
            return null;
    }


    boolean paused = false;


    @Override
    public void onCreate() {
        super.onCreate();
        enforceForegroundMode();
        Toast.makeText(this,"Service created ...", Toast.LENGTH_LONG).show();
        paused = false;
        Thread initBkgdThread = new Thread(new Runnable() {
            public void run() {
                play_music();
            }
        });
        initBkgdThread.start();
    }


    @Override
    public void onDestroy() {
        super.onDestroy();
        releaseForegroundMode();
        Toast.makeText(this, "Service destroyed ...", Toast.LENGTH_LONG).show();
        paused = true;
    }


    private final void enforceForegroundMode() {
        startForeground(NOTIFICATION_ID, getForegroundNotification());
    }


    private final void releaseForegroundMode(){
        stopForeground(true);
    }
```

```
protected Notification getForegroundNotification(){
    // Set the icon, scrolling text, and timestamp

    Notification notification = new Notification(R.drawable.icon,
        "playback running",System.currentTimeMillis());


// the PendingIntent to launch the activity if the user selects this notification
    Intent startIntent=new Intent(getApplicationContext(),SimpleActivity.class);
    startIntent.setFlags(Intent.FLA)
 PendingIntent contentIntent = PendingIntent.getActivity(this, 0, startIntent, 0);


    // Set the info for the views that show in the notification panel
    notification.setLatestEventInfo(
            this,
            "Playing Music",
            "Playback running",
            contentIntent
    );


    return notification;
}

    int[] notes = {R.raw.c5, R.raw.b4, R.raw.a4, R.raw.g4};
 int NOTE_DURATION = 400; //millisec
 MediaPlayer m_mediaPlayer;
 private void play_music() {
    for(int ii=0; ii<12; ii++) {
        //Check to ensure main activity not paused
        if(!paused) {
            if(m_mediaPlayer != null) {m_mediaPlayer.release();}
            m_mediaPlayer = MediaPlayer.create(this, notes[ii%4]);
            m_mediaPlayer.start();
            try {
                Thread.sleep(NOTE_DURATION);
            } catch (InterruptedException e) {
                e.printStackTrace();
            }
        }
    }
 }
}
}
```

This listing shows that the code for creating the notification is the biggest change to the service class. First, a new notification instance is created and given an icon and ticker text to show in the collapsed notification bar. An intent is then wrapped into a pending intent that will display the activity if the user clicks on the notification in the fully shown state. That intent is set together with a title and a bit of descriptive text in notification.setLatestEventInfo(..), and then this notification instance is returned to pass it to the startForeground(..) method.

Recipe: Using an IntentService

An `IntentService` is a service that holds a queue of intents it has received and executes them one by one. This is an ideal worker thread for many background tasks like polling servers for new information or downloading large amounts of data. As intents are very flexible and can hold any type of parcelable object in their extras, the amount of configuration given within an intent is almost limitless. This enables sending very complex queries to an `IntentService` and then letting it react. This recipe shows a very simple example of such a service that receives texts to show in a notification. For this, a layout with an edit text field for entering the message and a button to send it are needed, as shown in Listing 3.20.

Listing 3.20   main.xml

```xml
<?xml version="1.0" encoding="utf-8"?>
<LinearLayout xmlns:android="http://schemas.android.com/apk/res/android"
    android:orientation="vertical"
    android:layout_width="match_parent"
    android:layout_height="match_parent"
    >
<TextView
    android:layout_width="match_parent"
    android:layout_height="wrap_content"
    android:text="@string/hello"
    />

<EditText
    android:id="@+id/editText1"
    android:layout_width="match_parent"
    android:layout_height="wrap_content"
    android:ems="10" >

    <requestFocus />
</EditText>

<Button
    android:id="@+id/Button01"
    android:layout_width="wrap_content"
    android:layout_height="wrap_content"
    android:text="send message" />

</LinearLayout>
```

This activity is almost the same as in the other service examples. The edit text box and the button in `onCreate` are registered and an `onClickListener` is set to the button. Within the `onClickListener` the string is read from the edit box and put into the intent as a string extra called `msg`. Then `startService(..)` is called on the intent. This is shown in Listing 3.21.

Listing 3.21 **Main Activity**

```
public class SimpleActivity extends Activity {
    EditText editText;

    @Override
    protected void onCreate(Bundle savedInstanceState) {
        super.onCreate(savedInstanceState);
        setContentView(R.layout.main);

        editText=(EditText) findViewById(R.id.editText1);

        Button sendButton = (Button) findViewById(R.id.Button01);
        sendButton.setOnClickListener(new View.OnClickListener() {
            public void onClick(View view){
                Intent intent =
                    new Intent(SimpleActivity.this, SimpleIntentService.class);
                intent.putExtra("msg",editText.getText().toString());
                startService(intent);
            }
        });

    }
}
```

The `IntentService` class does all the hard work; it will even stop itself after the `IntentQueue` is empty. Only two things need to be implemented: a constructor that gives the queue a name by calling `super("myName")`, and the `handleIntent` method, in which the intent is demarshaled and the query is executed. Not much more is done than creating a notification, as seen in previous recipes, and extracting the message sent with `intent.getStringExtra("msg")`. That string is used to replace the descriptive text of the notification. Listing 3.22 shows the full `IntentService`.

Listing 3.22 **Simple IntentService**

```
public class SimpleIntentService extends IntentService {

    Notification notification=null;
    private NotificationManager mNManager;

    public SimpleIntentService() {
        super("SimpleIntentService");
    }


    @Override
    protected void onHandleIntent(Intent intent) {
        createNotification();
        if(intent.hasExtra("msg")){
            updateNotification(intent.getStringExtra("msg"));
            mNManager.notify(1, notification);
        }

    }
```

```
protected void createNotification(){
    if(mNManager==null){
        mNManager = (NotificationManager)
            getSystemService(Context.NOTIFICATION_SERVICE);
    }
    notification = new Notification(
            R.drawable.icon,
            "New event of importance",
            System.currentTimeMillis());
    // Set the icon, scrolling text, and timestamp



}


protected void updateNotification(final String text){
    // the PendingIntent to launch the activity if the user
    // selects this notification
    Intent startIntent=new Intent(getApplicationContext(),SimpleActivity.class);

    PendingIntent contentIntent =
        PendingIntent.getActivity(this, 0,startIntent, 0);


    // Set the info for the views that show in the notification panel
    notification.setLatestEventInfo(
            this,
            "Message received",
            text,
            contentIntent
    );

}

}
```

Broadcast Receivers

A broadcast receiver listens for relevant broadcast messages to trigger an event. Some examples of broadcasted events already sent from the OS are:

- The camera button was pressed.
- The battery is low.
- A new application was installed.

A user-generated component can also send a broadcast, such as:

- A calculation was finished.
- A particular thread has started.

All broadcast receivers extend the abstract class BroadcastReceiver or one of its subclasses. The lifecycle of a broadcast receiver is simple. A single method, onReceive(), is called when a message arrives for the receiver. After this method is finished, the BroadcastReceiver instance goes inactive.

A broadcast receiver normally initiates a separate component or sends a notification to the user in its onReceive() method, as discussed later in this chapter. If a broadcast receiver needs to do something more time-consuming, it should start a service instead of spawn a thread because an inactive broadcast receiver might be killed by the system.

Recipe: Starting a Service When the Camera Button Is Pressed

This recipe shows how to start a service based on a broadcasted event, such as when the camera button is pressed. The BroadcastReceiver is needed to listen for the specified event(s) and subsequently launch the service. The BroadcastReceiver itself is started in another component. (Here, it is implemented as a stand-alone activity, SimpleActivity.)

The activity shown in Listing 3.23 sets up a BroadcastReceiver and builds an intent with the filter for the camera button. The filter for package-added messages is also added for illustration purposes. Then, the BroadcastReceiver is started and this intent filter is passed to it using the registerReceiver() method.

Listing 3.23   src/com/cookbook/simple_receiver/SimpleActivity.java

```java
package com.cookbook.simple_receiver;

import android.app.Activity;
import android.content.Intent;
import android.content.IntentFilter;
import android.os.Bundle;

public class SimpleActivity extends Activity {
    SimpleBroadcastReceiver intentReceiver =
        new SimpleBroadcastReceiver();

    /** called when the activity is first created */
    @Override
    public void onCreate(Bundle savedInstanceState) {
        super.onCreate(savedInstanceState);
        setContentView(R.layout.main);

        IntentFilter intentFilter =
            new IntentFilter(Intent.ACTION_CAMERA_BUTTON);
        intentFilter.addAction(Intent.ACTION_PACKAGE_ADDED);
        registerReceiver(intentReceiver, intentFilter);
    }

    @Override
    protected void onDestroy() {
        unregisterReceiver(intentReceiver);
        super.onDestroy();
    }
}
```

Note that the receiver is unregistered if the activity is ever destroyed. This is unnecessary, but useful. The BroadcastReceiver component is shown in Listing 3.24. The single lifecycle method onReceive() is overridden to check for any broadcasted event. If it matches the specified event (here, it is the ACTION_CAMERA_BUTTON event), a service is started in the original context.

Listing 3.24   src/com/cookbook/simple_receiver/SimpleBroadcastReceiver.java

```java
package com.cookbook.simple_receiver;

import android.content.BroadcastReceiver;
import android.content.Context;
import android.content.Intent;

public class SimpleBroadcastReceiver extends BroadcastReceiver {
    @Override
    public void onReceive(Context rcvContext, Intent rcvIntent) {
        String action = rcvIntent.getAction();
        if (action.equals(Intent.ACTION_CAMERA_BUTTON)) {
            rcvContext.startService(new Intent(rcvContext,
                    SimpleService2.class));
        }
    }
}
```

The service that is started in the SimpleBroadcastReceiver of Listing 3.24 is shown in Listing 3.25. The service simply shows whether it was started or stopped using Toast.

Listing 3.25   src/com/cookbook/simple_receiver/SimpleService2.java

```java
package com.cookbook.simple_receiver;

import android.app.Service;
import android.content.Intent;
import android.os.IBinder;
import android.widget.Toast;

public class SimpleService2 extends Service {
    @Override
    public IBinder onBind(Intent arg0) {
        return null;
    }

    @Override
    public void onCreate() {
        super.onCreate();
        Toast.makeText(this,"Service created ...",
                Toast.LENGTH_LONG).show();
    }

    @Override
    public void onDestroy() {
```

```
        super.onDestroy();
        Toast.makeText(this, "Service destroyed ...",
                Toast.LENGTH_LONG).show();
    }
}
```

App Widgets

App Widgets are small iconlike views in an application. They implement a subclass of the `BroadcastReceiver` for use in updating this view. Called widgets for short, they can be embedded into other applications, such as the home screen, by long-clicking (in other words, pressing and holding) an empty area of the touchscreen. This displays a menu where a widget can be selected to install at that location. On Android 4 devices they can also be added from the launcher directly. They can be removed by a long click on the widget and dragging to the trash can. In all, they require the following:

- A view describing the appearance of the widget. This is defined in an XML layout resource file and contains text, background, and other layout parameters.

- An App Widget provider that receives broadcast events and interfaces to the widget to update it.

- Detailed information about the App Widget, such as the size and update frequency. Note that the home screen is divided into 4x4 cells for phones and 8x7 cells for tablets, and so a widget is often a multiple of a single cell size.

- Optionally, an App Widget configuration activity can be defined to properly set any parameters of the widget. This activity is launched upon creation of the widget.

Recipe: Creating an App Widget

This recipe creates a simple App Widget that displays some text on the home screen. The text is configured to update every second, but note that by default, the Android system forces the minimum update time to be 30 minutes. This helps prevent poorly written widgets from draining the battery. Listing 3.26 implements `AppWidgetProvider`, which is a subclass of `BroadcastReceiver`. The main method to override is the `onUpdate()` function, which gets called when the system determines it is time to update the widgets.

Listing 3.26   **src/com/cookbook/widget_example/SimpleWidgetProvider.java**

```
package com.cookbook.simple_widget;

import android.appwidget.AppWidgetManager;
import android.appwidget.AppWidgetProvider;
```

```
import android.content.Context;
import android.widget.RemoteViews;

public class SimpleWidgetProvider extends AppWidgetProvider {
    final static int APPWIDGET = 1001;
    @Override
    public void onUpdate(Context context,
            AppWidgetManager appWidgetManager, int[] appWidgetIds) {
        super.onUpdate(context, appWidgetManager, appWidgetIds);
        // Loop through all widgets to display an update
        final int N = appWidgetIds.length;
        for (int i=0; i<N; i++) {
            int appWidgetId = appWidgetIds[i];
            String titlePrefix = "Time since the widget was started:";
            updateAppWidget(context, appWidgetManager, appWidgetId,
                            titlePrefix);
        }
    }

    static void updateAppWidget(Context context, AppWidgetManager
            appWidgetManager, int appWidgetId, String titlePrefix) {
        Long millis = System.currentTimeMillis();
        int seconds = (int) (millis / 1000);
        int minutes = seconds / 60;
        seconds        seconds % 60;

        CharSequence text = titlePrefix;
        text += " " + minutes + ":" + String.format("%02d",seconds));

        // Construct the RemoteViews object
        RemoteViews views = new RemoteViews(context.getPackageName(),
                R.layout.widget_layout);
        views.setTextViewText(R.id.widget_example_text, text);

        // Tell the widget manager
        appWidgetManager.updateAppWidget(appWidgetId, views);
    }
}
```

The XML file describing the detailed information on the widget is shown in Listing 3.27. It shows the size the widget takes on the home screen and how often it should be updated in milliseconds. (The system minimum is 30 minutes.)

Listing 3.27   src/res/xml/widget_info.xml

```
<?xml version="1.0" encoding="utf-8"?>
<appwidget-provider xmlns:android="http://schemas.android.com/apk/res/android"
    android:minWidth="146dp"
    android:minHeight="72dp"
    android:updatePeriodMillis="1000"
    android:initialLayout="@layout/widget_layout">
</appwidget-provider>
```

The view describing the appearance of the widget is laid out in an XML file, as shown in Listing 3.28.

Listing 3.28   **src/res/layout/widget_layout.xml**

```xml
<?xml version="1.0" encoding="utf-8"?>
<TextView xmlns:android="http://schemas.android.com/apk/res/android"
    android:id="@+id/widget_example_text"
    android:layout_width="wrap_content"
    android:layout_height="wrap_content"
    android:textColor="#ff000000"
    android:background="#ffffffff"
```

4

Advanced Threading Techniques

This chapter showcases a collection of threading techniques that are provided by the Android Framework to make the usage of threads easier and more secure. First, the Loaders API that comes with the support package is demonstrated. Next, the AsyncTask API is shown, which is a very flexible and powerful replacement for raw Java threads. Then the ways of using inter-process communication on Android are discussed.

Loaders

Typical usage scenarios for threads are the moments in an application lifecycle when screens are initialized with data from databases or caches. If done on the main thread, these operations can block the loading of the layout itself and leave the user staring at a blank screen for a couple of seconds. To overcome the challenges of dealing with data initialization, Android now provides a Loader API. A loader is a small object that gets started through a manager, executes its query in the background, and then presents the result through a common callback interface. There are two main types of loaders:

- CursorLoaders, used for querying databases and ContentProviders
- AsyncTaskLoaders, used for everything else

Recipe: Using a CursorLoader

This recipe uses a CursorLoader to show all contacts on the phone in a simple ListView. Depending on how many contacts the phone holds, loading this query can take a while. This is a simple activity with a ListView and no fragments. Loaders can be used with both activities and fragments; the methods to override within each class and the steps to do this are the same. To get access to the support API, the activity needs to extend the `FragmentActivity` class. Listing 4.1 shows the activity.

Listing 4.1   **MainActivity.java**

```java
public class MainActivity extends FragmentActivity
    implements LoaderCallbacks<Cursor>{

    private static final int LOADER_ID = 1;
    SimpleCursorAdapter mAdapter;
    ListView mListView;

    static final String[] CONTACTS_PROJECTION = new String[] {
        Contacts._ID,
        Contacts.DISPLAY_NAME
    };


    @Override
    protected void onCreate(Bundle savedInstanceState) {
        super.onCreate(savedInstanceState);
        setContentView(R.layout.activity_main);
        mListView=(ListView)findViewById(R.id.list);


        mAdapter=new SimpleCursorAdapter(
                getApplicationContext(), //context for layout inflation, etc.
                android.R.layout.simple_list_item_1, //the layout file
                null, //We don't have a cursor yet
                new String[]{Contacts.DISPLAY_NAME}, //the name of the data row
                //The ID of the layout for data is displayed
                new int[]{android.R.id.text1}
        );

        mListView.setAdapter(mAdapter);

        getSupportLoaderManager().initLoader(LOADER_ID,null,this);
    }


    @Override
    public Loader<Cursor> onCreateLoader(int loaderId, Bundle args) {
        return new CursorLoader(
                getApplicationContext(),
                Contacts.CONTENT_URI,
                CONTACTS_PROJECTION,
                null,
                null,
                Contacts.DISPLAY_NAME + "COLLATE LOCALIZED ASC"
        );
    }

    @Override
    public void onLoadFinished(Loader<Cursor> loader, Cursor cursor) {
        if(loader.getId()==LOADER_ID){
            mAdapter.swapCursor(cursor);
        }
    }
```

```
    @Override
    public void onLoaderReset(Loader<Cursor> loader) {
        if(loader.getId()==LOADER_ID){
            mAdapter.swapCursor(null);
        }
    }
}
```

To make use of loaders, the activity needs to implement the LoaderCallbacks<T> interface, which has three functions: onCreateLoader, onLoadFinished, and onLoaderReset.

The onCreateLoader(int loaderId, Bundle args) function is called whenever a request is made to initialize a loader. The ID can be used to distinguish the different loaders, or it can be set to 0 if only one loader implementation is used. Here, a new CursorLoader class is returned and given the same arguments that would be used for making a query against a ContentProvider, mainly a content URI, a projection map, a selection string with arguments, and an order function.

The onLoadFinished(Loader<Cursor> loader, Cursor cursor) method is called when the loader is done. The loader's ID can be checked by calling loader.getId(), and if this has the expected value, the resulting cursor is set as a data source for the list by calling mAdapter.swapCursor(). If the adapter had another cursor active before, this would now be closed.

A call to the onLoaderReset(Loader<Cursor> loader) function closes the cursor that is produced by the loader. mAdapter.swapCursor(null) must be called to make sure it is no longer used in the list.

Loaders can also be set to automatically requery the cursor if its underlying data changes, so the presenting views are kept up-to-date. A requery will result in onLoadFinished being called again. This shows that loaders are a simple yet powerful way to do initialization of activities or fragments.

AsyncTasks

AsyncTasks are classes that execute one method in a separate thread, allowing them to take work away from the UI thread easily. The interesting part of AsyncTasks is that only the doInBackground() method runs on a separate thread, allowing the onPreExecute() and onPostExecute() methods to manipulate views or other parts of the activity or fragment that started them. AsyncTasks are typed with a type for Parameters, Progress Reporting, and Result. If any of those types are not used, they can be set to Void. AsyncTasks allow reporting of progress back to the UI thread by calling setProgress(int) in doInBackground(). This will trigger a call to the onProgressChanged() function of the AsyncTask, which is again called on the UI thread and can be used to update a progress dialog.

Recipe: Using an AsyncTask

This recipe uses an AsyncTask that loads an image from a remote location. This image will then be displayed in an ImageView. Loading images from a server is a common scenario for AsyncTasks, as doing this on the main thread could potentially block the UI and should be avoided. Implementing the AsyncTask as an inner class allows the image to be set directly into an ImageView after the download is finished. The complete code is shown in Listing 4.2.

Listing 4.2   **MainActivity**

```java
public class MainActivity extends Activity {
    private static final int LOADER_ID = 1;
    ImageView mImageView;

    private static final String IMAGE_URL =
            "http://developer.android.com/images/brand/Android_Robot_100.png";

    @Override
    protected void onCreate(Bundle savedInstanceState) {
        super.onCreate(savedInstanceState);
        setContentView(R.layout.activity_main);
        mImageView=(ImageView)findViewById(R.id.image);
        new ImageLoaderTask(getApplicationContext()).execute(IMAGE_URL);
    }



    public class ImageLoaderTask extends AsyncTask<String, Void, String>{
        private Context context;

        public ImageLoaderTask(Context context){
            this.context=context;
        }


        @Override
        protected String doInBackground(String. . . params) {
            String path=context.getFilesDir()
                        +File.pathSeparator
                        +"temp_"
                        +System.currentTimeMillis()
                        +".png";


            HttpURLConnection connection=null;


            android.util.Log.v("TASK","opening url="+params[0]);

            try {
                final URL url=new URL(params[0]);
                connection=(HttpURLConnection) url.openConnection();
```

```
                    InputStream in =
                        new BufferedInputStream(connection.getInputStream());

                    OutputStream out= new FileOutputStream(path);
                    int data = in.read();
                    while (data != -1) {
                        out.write(data);
                        data = in.read();
                    }
                } catch (IOException e) {
                    android.util.Log.e("TASK","error loading image",e);
                    e.printStackTrace();
                    return null;
                }finally {
                    if(connection!=null){
                        connection.disconnect();
                    }
                }
                return path;
            }


        @Override
        protected void onPostExecute(String imagePath) {
            super.onPostExecute(imagePath);
            if(imagePath!=null){
                android.util.Log.v("TASK","loading image from temp
➥ file"+imagePath);
                Bitmap bitmap=BitmapFactory.decodeFile(imagePath);
                mImageView.setImageBitmap(bitmap);
            }
        }

    }

}
```

The onCreate() method loads the layout, saves the instance of the ImageView into a field variable, and starts the AsyncTask.

The ImageLoaderTask class takes a string parameter denoting the URL of the image to load and returns a string with the path of the temp file that stores the image. For the path, the application's internal file folder is read from the context and a filename is constructed with a prefix of **temp** followed by the current time in milliseconds and a postfix of **.png**. The doInBackground function uses a simple URLConnection to open an InputStream to the image, read it bytewise, and write it to a FileOutputStream pointing to the path of the temp file.

The onPostExecute method gets the result of doInBackground as a parameter. If this is not null, an image exists at this path. Because onPostExecute is run on the UI thread of the activity, the image can be decoded into a bitmap and the bitmap set into the ImageView of the activity. As the onPreExecute() and onPostExecute() methods are always run on the UI thread, these can be used to communicate with the hosting activity or fragment and manipulate views if needed.

Android Inter-Process Communication

If two applications need to share resources but cannot get permissions, it is possible to define an IPC message. To support IPC, an interface is needed to serve as a bridge between applications. This is provided by the Android Interface Definition Language (AIDL).

Defining AIDL is similar to a Java interface. In fact, it can be easily done in Eclipse by creating a new Java interface and, after the definitions are complete, changing the suffix of the file from **.java** to **.aidl**.

The data types that AIDL currently supports are

- Java primitives that include `int`, `boolean`, and `float`
- `String`
- `CharSequence`
- `List`
- `Map`
- Other AIDL-generated interfaces
- Custom classes that implement the `Parcelable` protocol and are passed by value

Recipe: Implementing a Remote Procedure Call

This recipe implements a remote procedure call (RPC) between two activities. First, an AIDL interface can be defined, as shown in Listing 4.3.

Listing 4.3   **IAdditionalService.aidl under com.cookbook.advance.rpc**

```
package com.cookbook.advance.rpc;

// Declare the interface
interface IAdditionService {
    int factorial(in int value);
}
```

After the AIDL file is created, Eclipse generates an **IAdditionalService.java** file under the **gen/** folder when the project is built. The contents of this file should not be modified. It contains a stub class that is needed to implement the remote service.

Inside the first activity, **rpcService**, an `mBinder` member is declared as the stub from `IAdditionalService`. It can also be interpreted as `IBinder`. In the `onCreate()` method, `mBinder` is initiated and defined to call the `factorial()` function. When the `onBind()` method is called, it returns `mBinder` to the caller. After `onBind()` is ready, the other process activities are able to connect to the service. This is shown in Listing 4.4.

Listing 4.4   **src/com/cookbook/advance/rpc/rpcService.java**

```
package com.cookbook.advance.rpc;

import android.app.Service;
import android.content.Intent;
import android.os.IBinder;
import android.os.RemoteException;

public class RPCService extends Service {

  IAdditionService.Stub mBinder;
  @Override
  public void onCreate() {
    super.onCreate();
    mBinder = new IAdditionService.Stub() {
        public int factorial(int value1) throws RemoteException {
            int result=1;
            for(int i=1; i<=value1; i++){
                result*=i;
            }
            return result;
          }
    };
  }

  @Override
  public IBinder onBind(Intent intent) {
    return mBinder;
  }

  @Override
  public void onDestroy() {
    super.onDestroy();
  }
}
```

   Now the second activity that runs in a different process must be specified. The associated layout file is shown in Listing 4.5. Inside the layout there are three views that actually serve the main roles. EditText takes the input from the user, Button triggers the factorial() function call, and TextView with ID result is used for displaying the result from the factorial.

Listing 4.5   **res/layout/main.xml**

```
<?xml version="1.0" encoding="utf-8"?>
<LinearLayout xmlns:android="http://schemas.android.com/apk/res/android"
  android:orientation="vertical" android:layout_width="fill_parent"
  android:layout_height="match_parent">
  <TextView android:layout_width="match_parent"
    android:layout_height="wrap_content"
    android:text="Android CookBook RPC Demo"
    android:textSize="22dp" />
```

```
<LinearLayout
android:orientation="horizontal"
android:layout_width="match_parent"
android:layout_height="wrap_content">
<EditText android:layout_width="wrap_content"
   android:layout_height="wrap_content" android:id="@+id/value1"
   android:hint="0-30"></EditText>
<Button android:layout_width="wrap_content"
   android:layout_height="wrap_content" android:id="@+id/buttonCalc"
   android:text="GET"></Button>
   </LinearLayout>
<TextView android:layout_width="wrap_content"
   android:layout_height="wrap_content" android:text="result"
   android:textSize="36dp" android:id="@+id/result"></TextView>
</LinearLayout>
```

The **AndroidManifest.xml** file is shown in Listing 4.6. Inside the service tag, there is an extra attribute: android:process=".remoteService". This asks the system to create a new process named remoteService to run the second activity.

Listing 4.6   **AndroidManifest.xml**

```
<?xml version="1.0" encoding="utf-8"?>
<manifest xmlns:android="http://schemas.android.com/apk/res/android"
  package="com.cookbook.advance.rpc"
  android:versionCode="1" android:versionName="1.0">
  <application android:icon="@drawable/icon"
                android:label="@string/app_name" >
    <activity android:name=".rpc" android:label="@string/app_name">
      <intent-filter>
        <action android:name="android.intent.action.MAIN" />
        <category android:name="android.intent.category.LAUNCHER" />
      </intent-filter>
    </activity>

    <service android:name=".rpcService" android:process=".remoteService"/>
  </application>
  <uses-sdk android:minSdkVersion="7" />
</manifest>
```

The second activity is shown in Listing 4.7. It needs to call bindService() to retrieve the factorial() method provided in rpcService. The bindService() method requires a service connection instance as the interface for monitoring the state of an application service. Therefore, this activity has an inner class myServiceConnection that implements the service connection.

The myServiceConnection and IAdditionService classes are instantiated in the rpc activity. The myServiceConnection listens to the onServiceConnected and onServiceDisconnected callback methods. The onServiceConnected callback function passes the IBinder instance to the IAdditionService instance. The

Figure 4.1   Output of the AIDL application

onServiceDisconnected callback method puts the IAdditionService instance to null.

There are also two methods defined inside the rpc activity: initService() and releaseService(). The initService() method tries to initiate a new myServiceConnection. Then, it creates a new intent for a specific package name and class name and passes it to the bindService method along with the myServiceConnection instance and a flag BIND_AUTO_CREATE. After the service is bound, the onServiceConnected callback function is triggered, and it passes the IBinder method to the IAdditionService instance so the rpc activity can start to call the factorial method. The output is shown in Figure 4.1.

Listing 4.7   **src/com/cookbook/advance/rpc/rpc.java**

```java
package com.cookbook.advance.rpc;

import android.app.Activity;
import android.content.ComponentName;
import android.content.Context;
import android.content.Intent;
import android.content.ServiceConnection;
import android.os.Bundle;
import android.os.IBinder;
import android.os.RemoteException;
import android.view.View;
import android.view.View.OnClickListener;
import android.widget.Button;
import android.widget.EditText;
import android.widget.TextView;
import android.widget.Toast;

public class rpc extends Activity {
    IAdditionService service;
    myServiceConnection connection;
```

```java
class myServiceConnection implements ServiceConnection {

  public void onServiceConnected(ComponentName name,
                                  IBinder boundService) {
    service = IAdditionService.Stub.asInterface((IBinder) boundService);
    Toast.makeText(rpc.this, "Service connected", Toast.LENGTH_SHORT)
        .show();
  }

  public void onServiceDisconnected(ComponentName name) {
    service = null;
    Toast.makeText(rpc.this, "Service disconnected", Toast.LENGTH_SHORT)
        .show();
  }
}

private void initService() {
  connection = new myServiceConnection();
  Intent i = new Intent();
  i.setClassName("com.cookbook.advance.rpc",
                com.cookbook.advance.rpc.rpcService.class.getName());
  if(!bindService(i, connection, Context.BIND_AUTO_CREATE)) {
      Toast.makeText(rpc.this, "Bind Service Failed", Toast.LENGTH_LONG)
        .show();
  }
}

private void releaseService() {
  unbindService(connection);
  connection = null;
}

@Override
public void onCreate(Bundle savedInstanceState) {
  super.onCreate(savedInstanceState);
  setContentView(R.layout.main);

  initService();

  Button buttonCalc = (Button) findViewById(R.id.buttonCalc);

  buttonCalc.setOnClickListener(new OnClickListener() {
    TextView result = (TextView) findViewById(R.id.result);
    EditText value1 = (EditText) findViewById(R.id.value1);

    public void onClick(View v) {
      int v1, res = -1;
      try {
          v1 = Integer.parseInt(value1.getText().toString());
          res = service.factorial(v1);
      } catch (RemoteException e) {
        e.printStackTrace();
      }
      result.setText(Integer.toString(res));
    }
  });
}
```

```
   @Override
   protected void onDestroy() {
     releaseService();
   }
}
```

AIDL is good for doing full RPC between processes with different user IDs (which can mean different applications). The downside to this is that AIDL is fully synchronous and slow. If one or more activities need to communicate with a service to pass queries or commands to it and get back the results, there are two simpler and faster ways to do this, as will be shown in the following two recipes.

Recipe: Using Messengers

A `Messenger` class is a reference to a handler in a remote process that can be used to send messages to that handler. Handlers allow messages to be sent into a queue and to be processed one at a time. By providing two handlers, one in the activity and one in the service, those two classes can communicate by sending messages between the handlers. This is done by calling `Messenger.send(msg)`, which will inject the message into the remote handler. The `Message` class has a special field called `Message.replyTo` that can hold a messenger reference. This reference can then be used to send the results of the operation back to the original thread.

The following steps are used to create the service:

1. Create a `Service` class and define integer constants describing messages for registering and unregistering a client, as well as sending results.

2. Create a handler that reacts to those messages.

3. Create a messenger instance that references the handler.

4. In the service onBind function, return the binder object by calling `Messenger.getBinder()`.

This is shown in Listing 4.8.

Listing 4.8 **Messenger Service**

```
package com.cookbook.messenger_service;

/**
 * MessageControlledService is an abstract service implementation that
 * communicates with clients via Messenger objects. Messages are passed
 * directly into the handler of the server/client.
 */
public class MessageControlledService extends Service {

    public static final int MSG_INVALID            = Integer.MIN_VALUE;
    public static final int MSG_REGISTER_CLIENT    = MSG_INVALID+1;
    public static final int MSG_UNREGISTER_CLIENT  = MSG_INVALID+2;
    public static final int MSG_RESULT             = MSG_INVALID+3;
```

```
/** Make sure your message constants are MSG_FIRST_USER+n**/
public static final int MSG_FIRST_USER=1;



private static final String LOG_TAG =
    MessageControlledService.class.getCanonicalName();


/** keeps track of all current registered clients */
ArrayList<Messenger> mClients = new ArrayList<Messenger>();

/**
 * handler of incoming messages from clients
 */
private class CommandHandler extends Handler {

    @Override
    public void handleMessage(Message msg) {
        switch (msg.what) {
        case MSG_REGISTER_CLIENT:
            mClients.add(msg.replyTo);

            break;
        case MSG_UNREGISTER_CLIENT:
            mClients.remove(msg.replyTo);

            break;
        default:
            handleNextMessage(msg);
        }
    }
}


private final Handler mHandler=new CommandHandler();

/**
 * target we publish for clients to send messages to IncomingHandler
 */
private final Messenger mMessenger = new Messenger(mHandler);


/**
 * Call this to send an arbitrary message to the registered clients
 * @param what
 * @param arg1
 * @param arg2
 * @param object
 */
protected final void sendMessageToClients(final int what,final int arg1,
    final int arg2,final Object object) {
    for (int i = mClients.size() - 1; i >= 0; i--) {
        try {
            Message msg = Message.obtain(null, what,arg1,arg2, object);
            mClients.get(i).send(msg);
        } catch (RemoteException e) {
            // The client is dead. Remove it from the list;
```

```
                    // we are going through the list from back to front
                    // so this is safe to do inside the loop.
                    mClients.remove(i);
                }
            }
        }
    }

    //------service stuff

    @Override
    public IBinder onBind(Intent arg0) {
        return mMessenger.getBinder();
    }


    /**
     * This is your main method
     *
     * @param msg the next message in the queue
     */
    public  void handleNextMessage(final Message msg){
        String echo="ECHO: "+(String)msg.obj;
        sendMessageToClients(MSG_RESULT, -1, -1, echo);
    }

}
```

Connected clients are tracked with `ArrayList<Messenger>`. In the handler, clients are added to this list if a `MSG_REGISTER_CLIENT` is received and removed on `MSG_UNREGISTER_CLIENT`. The method `sendMessageToClients(. .)` loops through this list of messengers and calls `send` on all of them. This broadcasts the results to all connected clients and allows communication with more than one activity at a time. All other messages are given as arguments to a call of `handleNextMessage(. .)` where all the real work can be done. In this example, the `message.obj` field is read as a string, the word **Echo** is added to it, and it is sent back to the caller.

In this activity, when a message of type `MSG_RESULT` is received, `message.obj` is cast to a string and displayed as a toast. Whatever is in the edit field is sent to the service if the single button in the activity layout is clicked. This has created an echo service.

The activity has a lot more code for handling the connection than the service itself, as it needs to start the service and bind to it to retrieve its messenger. The steps to create a service connection follow:

1. Create a new `ServiceConnection` instance and implement the `onServiceConnected()` and `onServiceDisconnected()` calls.

2. Implement a handler and create a messenger instance referencing this handler. This messenger instance will be handed over to the service later.

3. In `onCreate()`, start the service by calling `startService(. .)`.

4. In `onResume()`, bind to the service.

5. In `onPause`, disconnect the service by calling `unbindService()`.

The code for the `MessengerActivity` is shown in Listing 4.9.

Listing 4.9   **MessengerActivity**

```
public class MessengerActivity extends Activity {
    private static final String LOG_TAG = null;

    EditText editText;

    /** messenger for communicating with service */
    Messenger mServiceMessenger = null;
    /** flag indicating whether we have called bind on the service */
    boolean mIsBound;


    protected Handler mHandler = new Handler() {
        @Override
        public void handleMessage(Message msg) {
            if(msg.what==MessageControlledService.MSG_RESULT){
                Toast.makeText(
                                            getApplicationContext(),
                                            (String)msg.obj,
                                            Toast.LENGTH_SHORT
                                            ).show();

            }
        }

    };

    Messenger mLocalMessageReceiver=new Messenger(mHandler);

    /**
     * class for interacting with the main interface of the service
     */
    private final ServiceConnection mServiceConnection = new ServiceConnection() {
        @Override
        public void onServiceConnected(ComponentName className, IBinder service){
            // This is called when the connection with the service has been
            // established, giving us the service object we can use to
            // interact with the service. We are communicating with our
            // service through an IDL interface, so get a client-side
            // representation of that from the raw service object.
            mServiceMessenger = new Messenger(service);

            // We want to monitor the service for as long as we are
            // connected to it
            try {
                Message msg = Message.obtain(null,
                  MessageControlledService.MSG_REGISTER_CLIENT);
                msg.replyTo = mLocalMessageReceiver;
                mServiceMessenger.send(msg);

            } catch (RemoteException e) {
                // In this case the service has crashed before we could even
                // do anything with it; we can count on soon being
```

```
                // disconnected (and then reconnected if it can be restarted)
                // so there is no need to do anything here.
            }

            Log.v(LOG_TAG, "service connected");
        }

        @Override
        public void onServiceDisconnected(ComponentName className) {
            // This is called when the connection with the service has been
            // unexpectedly disconnected--that is, its process crashed
            mServiceMessenger = null;
            Log.v(LOG_TAG, "service disconnected");

        }
    };


    @Override
    protected void onResume() {
        super.onResume();
        bindMessengerService();
    }

    @Override
    protected void onPause() {
        super.onPause();
        unbindAccountService();
    }

    void bindMessengerService() {
        Log.v(LOG_TAG,"binding accountservice");
        // Establish a connection with the service. We use an explicit
        // class name because there is no reason to let other
        // applications replace our component.
        bindService(new Intent(getApplicationContext(),
            MessageControlledService.class),
            mServiceConnection, Context.BIND_AUTO_CREATE);
        mIsBound = true;

    }

    protected void unbindAccountService() {
        if (mIsBound) {
            Log.v(LOG_TAG,"unbinding accountservice");
            // If we have received the service, and hence registered with
            // it, now is the time to unregister
            if (mServiceMessenger != null) {

                try
                {
                  Message msg=Message.obtain(
                       null,
                       MessageControlledService.MSG_UNREGISTER_CLIENT
                       );

                  msg.replyTo = mServiceMessenger;
```

```
                    mServiceMessenger.send(msg);

                } catch (RemoteException e) {

                // There is nothing special we need to do if the service

                // has crashed
                }
            }

            // Detach our existing connection
            unbindService(mServiceConnection);
            mIsBound = false;

        }
    }

    protected boolean sendMessageToService(final int what,
        final int arg1,final int arg2,
        final Object object) {
        try {
            Message msg = Message.obtain(null, what, arg1, arg2, object);
            mServiceMessenger.send(msg);
        } catch (RemoteException e) {
            Log.e(LOG_TAG,"unable to send message to account service",e);
            //Retry binding
            bindMessengerService();
            return false;
        }
        return true;

    }
    @Override
    protected void onCreate(Bundle savedInstanceState) {
        super.onCreate(savedInstanceState);
        startService(new Intent(getApplicationContext(),
        MessageControlledService.class));
        setContentView(R.layout.main);

    editText=(EditText) findViewById(R.id.editText1);

        Button sendButton = (Button) findViewById(R.id.Button01);
        sendButton.setOnClickListener(new View.OnClickListener() {
            public void onClick(View view){
                String text=editText.getText().toString();
                sendMessageToService(MessageControlledService.MSG_FIRST_USER,
                    -1,-1,text);
            }
        });


    }

}
```

Once the activity is bound to the service, the `ServiceConnection.onServiceConnected()` method is called. The `Ibinder` that the service returns is its messenger instance (refer back to Listing 4.8), so it gets saved in a field variable. There is a `sendMessageToService()` function that is similar to the `SendMessageToClients()` function of the service but uses the messenger just received. The next step is to register the activity at the service by sending a `MSG_REGISTER_CLIENT` and setting the `Message.replyTo` field to the messenger referencing the activity's local handler.

In the activity's `onPause` method, the service must be unbound to allow it to stop if there are no more connected clients. It is important to send a `MSG_UNREGISTER_CLIENT` to the service before calling unbind on it, or the list of messengers available to the service will go out of sync.

Recipe: Using a ResultReceiver

A `ResultReceiver` is a parcelable class that internally holds an IPC binder to direct calls across different processes. It allows calling `ResultReceiver.send(int ResultCode, Bundle data)` in one process while the instance of the receiver was created in another process. The other process will then be able to read the arguments and react to them. Because `ResultReceiver` is parcelable, it can be given as an argument to an intent. The intent can be used to start another activity or a service, which will be done here. `ResultReceiver` accepts a bundle as an argument, which allows sending even complex objects that implement the parcelable interface.

The `IntentService` from Chapter 3, "Threads, Services, Receivers, and Alerts," is used to implement an echo service similar to the previous recipe. `IntentService` is the perfect class to use with `ResultReceiver`, as it accepts intents as commands and executes them in an ordered queue. The `ResultReceiver` passed within that intent can then be used to send the result back to the calling activity. The service is shown in Listing 4.10.

Listing 4.10   **ResultReceiverIntentService**

```
public class ResultReceiverIntentService extends IntentService {

    public static final String EXTRA_RESULT_RECEIVER = "EXTRA_RESULT_RECEIVER";

    public ResultReceiverIntentService() {
        super("SimpleIntentService");
    }

    @Override
    protected void onHandleIntent(Intent intent) {
        ResultReceiver rr=intent.getParcelableExtra(EXTRA_RESULT_RECEIVER);
        if(intent.hasExtra("msg")){
            String text= "Echo: "+intent.getStringExtra("msg");
            Bundle resultBundle=new Bundle();
```

```
        resultBundle.putString("msg",text);
        rr.send(1, resultBundle);

    }

  }


}
```

This service needs to implement only two functions: the constructor, in which the queue gets a name by calling super("name"); and the onHandleIntent(. .) function. Here, the ResultReceiver is extracted from the intent by calling getParcelableExtra() with a key constant defined as EXTRA_RESULT_RECEIVER. The modified text is then put into a bundle, and the bundle is sent through the receiver's send(. .) method to the originating activity. By using integer constants as result codes, more than one type of message could be sent back to the activity. The activity is shown in Listing 4.11.

Listing 4.11 Main Activity

```
public class SimpleActivity extends Activity {
    EditText editText;

    Handler handler=new Handler();

    ResultReceiver resultReceiver=new ResultReceiver(handler){

        @Override
        protected void onReceiveResult(int resultCode, Bundle resultData) {
            super.onReceiveResult(resultCode, resultData);
            Toast.makeText(
                                SimpleActivity.this,
                                resultData.getString("msg"),
                                Toast.LENGTH_SHORT
                                ).show();

        }

    };

    @Override
    protected void onCreate(Bundle savedInstanceState) {
        super.onCreate(savedInstanceState);
        setContentView(R.layout.main);

        editText=(EditText) findViewById(R.id.editText1);

        Button sendButton = (Button) findViewById(R.id.Button01);
        sendButton.setOnClickListener(new View.OnClickListener() {
```

```
public void onClick(View view){
    Intent intent=new Intent(
                SimpleActivity.this,
                ResultReceiverIntentService.class
                );
    intent.putExtra("msg",editText.getText().toString());

        intent.putExtra(
        ResultReceiverIntentService.EXTRA_RESULT_RECEIVER,
            resultReceiver
            );
    startService(intent);
    }
});


}
}
```

The activity holds an implementation of the `ResultReceiver` that overrides the `onReceiveResult()` method. This is called by the internal binder object, and then another process executes the `send()` function on the `ResultReceiver`. A handler instance must be given to the `ResultReceiver`, which will execute the `onReceiveResult` method on this handler thread. The implementation here will just read the text sent back by the service and display it in a toast.

To send out a command, the string from an edit field is read and put into an intent. The `ResultReceiver` instance is set as an extra into the intent as well. The `IntentService` is called with `startService`, which will start it if it is not already running and deliver the intent with its argument into the queue. The combination of an `IntentService` and a `ResultReceiver` is the easiest way of doing inter-process communication on Android.

5

User Interface Layout

The Android UI consists of screen views, screen touch events, and key presses. The framework for specifying the UI is constructed to support the various Android devices. This chapter focuses on the utilization of this framework for the initial graphical layout and its changes. Chapter 6, "User Interface Events," handles key presses and gestures.

Resource Directories and General Attributes

The UI display uses developer-generated resource files, some of which are discussed in Chapter 2, "Application Basics: Activities and Intents," in the context of the directory structure of an Android project. For completeness, the entire set of resource directories is summarized here:

- **res/anim/**—Frame-by-frame animation or tweened animation objects.
- **res/animator/**—eXtensible Markup Language (XML) files used for property animations.
- **res/color/**—XML files specifying a state list for colors.
- **res/drawable/**—Image resources (bitmap, nine-patch, shapes, animations, state lists, etc.). Note that these images can be modified and optimized during compilation.
- **res/layout/**—XML files specifying screen layouts.
- **res/menu/**—XML files that are used to specify menus.
- **res/values/**—XML files with resource descriptors. As with other resource directories, filenames are arbitrary, but common ones, as used in this book, are **arrays.xml**, **colors.xml**, **dimens.xml**, **strings.xml**, and **styles.xml**.
- **res/xml/**—Other arbitrary XML files not covered previously.
- **res/raw/**—Other arbitrary resources not covered previously, including images that should not be modified or optimized.

Each UI object has three definable attributes that customize the look and feel of the UI: the dimension of the object, text in the object, and the color of the object. The possible values for these three general UI attributes are summarized in Table 5.1. Note that for dimension, it is best to use **dp** or **sp** for device-independent compliance.

To unify the look and feel of the application, a global resource file can be used for each of these attributes. This is also useful in that it is easy to redefine the attributes later, as they are all collected in three files:

- Measurements and dimensions of items are declared in the XML resource file **res/values/dimens.xml**. For example:
  - XML declaration—`<dimen name="large">48sp</dimen>`
  - XML reference—`@dimen/large`
  - Java reference—`getResources().getDimension(R.dimen.large)`
- Labels and text of items are declared in the XML resource file **res/values/strings.xml**. For example:
  - XML declaration—`<string name="start_pt">I\'m here</string>`
  - XML reference—`@string/start_pt`
  - Java reference—`getBaseContext().getString(R.string.start_pt)`

Table 5.1   **Possible Values for the Three General UI Attributes**

Attribute	Possible Values
Dimension	Any number followed by one of the following dimensions: 　`px`—Actual pixels on the screen 　`dp` (or `dip`)—Device-independent pixels relative to a 160dpi screen 　`sp`—Device-independent pixels scaled by user's font size preference 　`in`—Inches based on physical screen size 　`mm`—Millimeters based on physical screen size 　`pt`—1/72 inch based on physical screen size
String	Any string, as long as apostrophes/quotes are escaped: `Don\'t worry` Any properly quoted string: `"Don't worry"` Any formatted string: `Population: %1$d` Can include HTML tags, such as `<b>`, `<i>`, or `<u>` Can include special characters, such as © given by `&#169;`
Color	Possible values are: 　12-bit color `#rgb` 　16-bit color with alpha opacity `#argb` 　24-bit color `#rrggbb` 　32-bit color with alpha opacity `#aarrggbb` Also possible to use the predefined colors in the `Color` class within Java files, such as `Color.CYAN`

- Colors of items are declared in the XML resource file **res/values/colors.xml**. For example:

  - XML declaration—`<color name="red">#f00</color>`

  - XML reference—`@color/red`

  - Java reference—`getResources().getColor(R.color.red)`

Recipe: Specifying Alternate Resources

The resources described in the previous section provide a generic configuration that Android can use by default. The developer has the ability to specify different values for specific configurations distinguished by various qualifiers.

To support multiple languages, the strings can be translated and used in different language **values** directories. For example, American English, British English, French, simplified Chinese (used in mainland China), traditional Chinese (used in Taiwan), and German strings are added using the following:

res/values-en-rUS/strings.xml

res/values-en-rGB/strings.xml

res/values-fr/strings.xml

res/values-zh-rCN/strings.xml

res/values-zh-rTW/strings.xml

res/values-de/strings.xml

Not all strings need to be redefined in these files. Any missing strings from the selected language file fall back to the default **res/values/strings.xml** file, which should contain a complete set of all strings used in the application. If any drawables contain text and require a language-specific form, a similar directory structure should also apply to them (such as **res/drawables-zh-hdpi/**).

To support multiple screen pixel densities, the drawables and raw resources (as needed) can be scaled and used in different dpi value directories. For example, an image file can belong to each of the following directories:

res/drawable-ldpi/

res/drawable-mdpi/

res/drawable-hdpi/

res/drawable-nodpi/

The low-, medium-, and high-density screens are defined as 120dpi, 160dpi, and 240dpi. Not all dpi choices need to be populated. At run-time, Android determines the closest available drawables and scales them appropriately. The `nodpi` choice can be used with bitmap images to prevent them from being scaled. In case both a language and a dpi choice are specified, the directory can contain both qualifiers: **drawable-en-rUS-mdpi/**.

The various types of screens available for Android devices are discussed in Chapter 1, "Overview of Android." It is often useful to define separate XML layouts for the different screen types. The most often used qualifiers are:

- Portrait and landscape screen orientations: **–port** and **–land**
- Regular (QVGA, HVGA, and VGA) and wide aspect ratios (WQVGA, FWVGA, and WVGA): **–notlong** and **–long**
- Small (up to 3.0-inch diagonal), normal (up to 4.5-inch diagonal), and large (above 4.5-inch diagonal) screen sizes: **–small**, **–normal**, and **–large**

If screen orientation or aspect ratio is not defined, the Android system autoscales the UI for the screen (although not always elegantly). However, if layouts for different screens are defined, a special element should be added to the **AndroidManifest.xml** file at the application element level to ensure proper support:

```
<supports-screens
  android:largeScreens="true"
  android:normalScreens="true"
  android:smallScreens="true"
  android:resizable="true"
  android:anyDensity="true" />
```

Note that if `android:minSdkVersion` or `android:targetSdkVersion` is 3 (Android 1.5), by default only `android:normalScreens` (the screen for the G1) is set to `true`. Therefore, it is useful to explicitly declare the `supports-screens` element for the application so more recent phones have a properly scaled UI.

It should also be noted that starting with Android 3.2, some tablets that are 7 inches fit the same category for screen dimensions as 5-inch devices (which would normally use the `large` layout). To compensate for this, several new options have been added: smallest width (`sm<N>dp`), available screen width (`w<N>dp`), and available screen height (`h<N>dp`), where `<N>` is the size of dp values to be supported.

Views and ViewGroups

The basic building block of a graphical layout is a view. Each view is described by a `View` object, which is responsible for drawing a rectangular area and handling events in that area. The `View` is a base class for objects that interact with the user; they are called widgets. Examples of widgets are buttons and check boxes.

A `ViewGroup` object is a type of `View` that acts as a container to hold multiple `Views` (or other `ViewGroups`). For example, a `ViewGroup` object can hold a vertical or horizontal placement of views and widgets, as shown in Figure 5.1. `ViewGroup` is a base class for screen layouts.

The layout defines the user interface elements, their positions, and their actions. It can be specified from either XML or Java. Most often, an initial base layout is declared in XML and any run-time changes are handled in Java. This combines the ease of

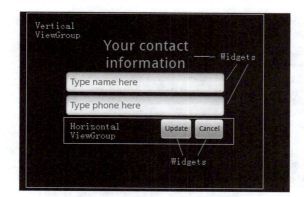

Figure 5.1   View example that contains `ViewGroups` and widgets

developing the overall position of `View` and `ViewGroup` objects using XML and the flexibility to change any component within the application using Java.

Another benefit of separating the XML layout from the Java activity is that the same Android application can produce a different behavior depending on the screen orientation, type of device (such as phone versus tablet), and locale (such as English versus Chinese). These customizations can be abstracted into various XML resource files without cluttering the underlying activity.

Recipe: Building Layouts in the Eclipse Editor

A quick way to get started with layouts is to use the handy graphical layout editor in Eclipse. Take a new activity and open its layout resource XML file. Here, it is the **main.xml** file. Then, click the Layout tab. This shows how the layout would look graphically. Click the black screen and remove everything to start from scratch. Then, follow these steps:

1. Click and drag a layout from the Layouts Selector to the screen area. For example, choose `TableLayout`, which holds multiple `Views` or `ViewGroups` in a column.

2. Click and drag any other layouts to nest them inside the first one. For example, choose `TableRow`, which holds multiple `Views` or `ViewGroups` along a row. Add three of these for this example.

3. Right-click each `TableRow` in the Outline view and add view elements from the Views Selector. For example, add a `Button` and `CheckBox` to the first `TableRow`, two `TextViews` to the second, and a `TimePicker` to the third.

4. Add a `Spinner` and `VideoView` view below the `TableRow` elements.

The result looks like Figure 5.2, and the landscape and portrait view can be toggled to see the difference in the layout. Clicking the **main.xml** tab shows XML code

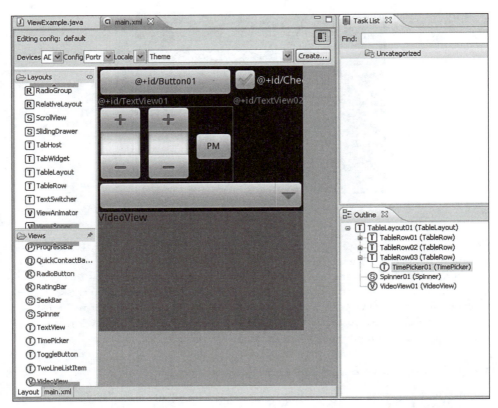

Figure 5.2   Android layout builder example, as seen in Eclipse

like that shown in Listing 5.1. This provides a simple method to build UIs with the
Android look and feel.

Listing 5.1   **main.xml**

```
<?xml version="1.0" encoding="utf-8"?>
<TableLayout android:id="@+id/TableLayout01"
    android:layout_width="match_parent"
    android:layout_height="match_parent"
    xmlns:android="http://schemas.android.com/apk/res/android">
    <TableRow android:id="@+id/TableRow01"
        android:layout_width="wrap_content"
        android:layout_height="wrap_content">
        <Button android:text="@+id/Button01"
            android:id="@+id/Button01"
            android:layout_width="wrap_content"
            android:layout_height="wrap_content" />
        <CheckBox android:text="@+id/CheckBox01"
```

```
                    android:id="@+id/CheckBox01"
                    android:layout_width="wrap_content"
                    android:layout_height="wrap_content" />
          </TableRow>
          <TableRow android:id="@+id/TableRow02"
              android:layout_width="wrap_content"
              android:layout_height="wrap_content">
              <TextView android:text="@+id/TextView01"
                    android:id="@+id/TextView01"
                    android:layout_width="wrap_content"
                    android:layout_height="wrap_content" />
              <TextView android:text="@+id/TextView02"
                    android:id="@+id/TextView02"
                    android:layout_width="wrap_content"
                    android:layout_height="wrap_content" />
          </TableRow>
          <TableRow android:id="@+id/TableRow03"
              android:layout_width="wrap_content"
              android:layout_height="wrap_content">
              <TimePicker android:id="@+id/TimePicker01"
                    android:layout_width="wrap_content"
                    android:layout_height="wrap_content" />
          </TableRow>
          <Spinner android:id="@+id/Spinner01"
              android:layout_width="wrap_content"
              android:layout_height="wrap_content" />
      <VideoView android:id="@+id/VideoView01"
              android:layout_width="wrap_content"
              android:layout_height="wrap_content" />
</TableLayout>
```

Another way to view the layout is by using the Hierarchy Viewer. Running an application in the emulator, the **hierarchyviewer** command can be run from the command line. It resides in the **tools/** directory of the SDK installation. For security reasons, this works only with the emulator as the device because running the Hierarchy Viewer on an actual device might reveal secure settings. Click the window of interest and select **Load View Hierarchy**. This produces a relational view of the different layouts. The result for this recipe is shown in Figure 5.3.

Recipe: Controlling the Width and Height of UI Elements

This recipe shows how specifying the width and height of UI elements changes the overall layout. Each View object must specify a total width (android:layout_width) and total height (android:layout_height) in one of three ways:

- Exact dimension—Provides control, but does not scale to multiple screen types well.
- wrap_content—Just big enough to enclose the contents of the element plus padding.
- match_parent—Size maximized to fill the element's parent, including padding. This replaced fill_parent, which was deprecated in Android 2.2.

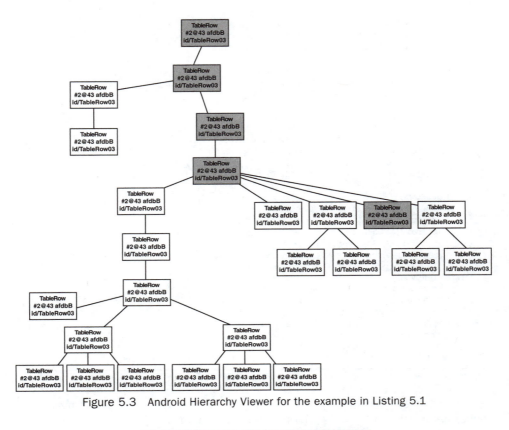

Figure 5.3   Android Hierarchy Viewer for the example in Listing 5.1

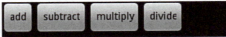

Figure 5.4   `LinearLayout` with four buttons aligned horizontally, as shown in Listing 5.2

Padding is the blank space surrounding an element, and it defaults to zero if it is not specified. It is part of the size of a UI element and must be specified as an exact dimension, but it can be specified using one of two types of attributes:

- `padding`—Sets padding equal on all four sides of an element
- `paddingLeft`, `paddingRight`, `paddingTop`, `paddingBottom`—Sets padding on each side of an element separately

Some developers confuse padding with margins; margins are the spaces around an element but are not included in the size of the UI element.

Another attribute is `android:layout_weight`, which can be assigned an integral number value. It provides the Android system with a way to determine relative importance based on the value for how spacing is handled between different elements of a layout.

Listing 5.2 shows the main layout file as a linear layout with four buttons. This aligns them horizontally on the screen, as shown in Figure 5.4.

Listing 5.2   res/layout/main.xml

```xml
<?xml version="1.0" encoding="utf-8"?>
<LinearLayout xmlns:android="http://schemas.android.com/apk/res/android"
 android:layout_width="match_parent"
 android:layout_height="match_parent">
        <Button android:text="add"
         android:layout_width="wrap_content"
         android:layout_height="wrap_content"
         />
        <Button android:text="subtract"
         android:layout_width="wrap_content"
         android:layout_height="wrap_content"
         />
        <Button android:text="multiply"
         android:layout_width="wrap_content"
         android:layout_height="wrap_content"
         />
        <Button android:text="divide"
         android:layout_width="wrap_content"
         android:layout_height="wrap_content"
         />
</LinearLayout>
```

If the height of the "add" button is changed to match_parent, the button fills the vertical space of its parent while keeping the words aligned. If the width of any button is changed to match_parent, all subsequent buttons in the horizontal layout are washed out. These are shown in Figure 5.5.

Also note in Figure 5.6 that the "multiply" and "divide" buttons have a portion of the last letter cut off in two of the button configurations. This can be fixed by appending a space to the text, such as "multiply " and "divide ". However, a more general method to resolve this uses the layout. Take a look at the various button formats in Figure 5.6.

The four rows of buttons in Figure 5.6 are as follows:

- The first row is the same as what was created in Listing 5.2, but with spaces appended to the end of each word.

- In the second row, the layout width is changed to match_parent for the last button, providing the space needed for the button, but it cannot be used for the earlier buttons on the line as evidenced by the right part of Figure 5.5:

```xml
<Button android:text="divide"
        android:layout_width="match_parent"
        android:layout_height="wrap_content"
/>
```

- In the third row, padding is added to the "multiply" button to make the button bigger, but it does not add this space to the word itself because it was declared as wrap_content:

```
<Button android:text="multiply"
        android:layout_width="wrap_content"
        android:layout_height="wrap_content"
        android:paddingRight="20sp"
/>
```

- In the fourth row, all buttons use match_parent but also add layout_weight and assign it the same value for all buttons. This gives the most satisfying layout:

```
<Button android:text="add"
        android:layout_width="match_parent"
        android:layout_height="wrap_content"
        android:layout_weight="1"
/>
```

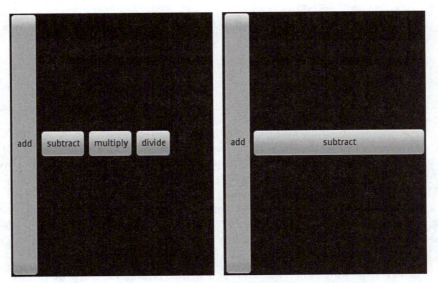

Figure 5.5   The match_parent in height keeps the horizontal alignment, but a match_parent in width washes out the remaining buttons.

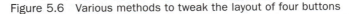

Figure 5.6   Various methods to tweak the layout of four buttons

```
<Button android:text="subtract"
    android:layout_width="match_parent"
    android:layout_height="wrap_content"
    android:layout_weight="1"
/>
<Button android:text="multiply"
    android:layout_width="match_parent"
    android:layout_height="wrap_content"
    android:layout_weight="1"
/>
<Button android:text="divide"
    android:layout_width="match_parent"
    android:layout_height="wrap_content"
    android:layout_weight="1"
/>
```

Recipe: Setting Relative Layout and Layout ID

Sometimes it is more convenient to set the layout relative to a starting object or parent object rather than according to absolute rules. Also, if the UI starts nesting LinearLayouts, it might become inefficient, and it may become simpler to use relative layouts. This can be done using a RelativeLayout view, as shown in Listing 5.3. The layout is shown in Figure 5.7.

Listing 5.3   **RelativeLayout**

```
<?xml version="1.0" encoding="utf-8"?>
<RelativeLayout xmlns:android="http://schemas.android.com/apk/res/android"
    android:layout_width="match_parent"
    android:layout_height="match_parent">
    <TextView android:id="@+id/mid" android:text="middle"
        android:layout_width="wrap_content"
        android:layout_height="wrap_content"
        android:layout_centerInParent="true"/>
    <TextView android:id="@+id/high" android:text="high"
        android:layout_width="wrap_content"
        android:layout_height="wrap_content"
        android:layout_above="@id/mid"/>
    <TextView android:id="@+id/low" android:text="low"
        android:layout_width="wrap_content"
        android:layout_height="wrap_content"
        android:layout_centerHorizontal="true"
        android:layout_below="@id/mid"/>
    <TextView android:id="@+id/left" android:text="left"
        android:layout_width="wrap_content"
        android:layout_height="wrap_content"
        android:layout_alignBottom="@id/high"
        android:layout_toLeftOf="@id/low"/>
</RelativeLayout>
```

Figure 5.7   Four text views from the `RelativeLayout` example

The explanation of these attributes and a list of the different available rules for relative layout are collected in Table 5.2. Because every layout can have portions declared in XML files and other portions in Java code, both methods of referring to layouts are shown. The first three rows of the table show attributes that need to point to a view ID, and the last two rows show attributes that are Boolean.

Recipe: Declaring a Layout Programmatically

The XML layout framework in Android is the preferred method for enabling general device changes and simple development. However, sometimes it is useful to change some layout aspects programmatically—using Java, for example. In fact, the entire layout can be declared using Java. For illustration, a portion of the previous recipe's layout is shown implemented as Java code in Listing 5.4.

Table 5.2   **Possible Rules for Children in a Relative Layout**

XML Attribute (All Start with the `android:` Tag)	Java Constant	Relative Layout Rule
layout_above layout_below layout_toRightOf layout_toLeftOf	ABOVE BELOW RIGHT_OF LEFT_OF	Align this view's edge relative to anchor view's edge.
layout_alignTop layout_alignBottom layout_alignRight layout_alignLeft	ALIGN_TOP ALIGN_BOTTOM ALIGN_RIGHT ALIGN_LEFT	Align this view's edge with anchor view's edge.
layout_alignBaseline	ALIGN_BASELINE	Align this view's text baseline with anchor view's text baseline.
layout_alignParentTop layout_alignParentBottom layout_alignParentRight layout_alignParentLeft	ALIGN_PARENT_TOP ALIGN_PARENT_BOTTOM ALIGN_PARENT_RIGHT ALIGN_PARENT_LEFT	Align this view's edge with parent view's edge.
layout_centerInParent layout_centerHorizontal layout_centerVertical	CENTER_IN_PARENT CENTER_HORIZONTAL CENTER_VERTICAL	Center this view within parent.

It should be stressed that not only is coding layout in Java cumbersome, but it is also discouraged. It does not take advantage of the modular approach to resource directories where a layout can be changed simply without modification of Java code, as discussed in the "Specifying Alternate Resources" recipe.

Listing 5.4   **src/com/cookbook/programmaticlayout/ProgrammaticLayout.java**

```java
package com.cookbook.programmatic_layout;

import android.app.Activity;
import android.os.Bundle;
import android.view.ViewGroup;
import android.view.ViewGroup.LayoutParams;
import android.widget.RelativeLayout;
import android.widget.TextView;

public class ProgrammaticLayout extends Activity {
    private int TEXTVIEW1_ID = 100011;
    @Override
    public void onCreate(Bundle savedInstanceState) {
        super.onCreate(savedInstanceState);

        //Here is an alternative to: setContentView(R.layout.main);
        final RelativeLayout relLayout = new RelativeLayout( this );
        relLayout.setLayoutParams( new RelativeLayout.LayoutParams(
                                    LayoutParams.MATCH_PARENT,
                                    LayoutParams.MATCH_PARENT ) );
        TextView textView1 = new TextView( this );
        textView1.setText("middle");
        textView1.setTag(TEXTVIEW1_ID);

        RelativeLayout.LayoutParams text1layout = new
            RelativeLayout.LayoutParams(   LayoutParams.WRAP_CONTENT,
                                    LayoutParams.WRAP_CONTENT );
        text1layout.addRule( RelativeLayout.CENTER_IN_PARENT );
        relLayout.addView(textView1, text1layout);
        TextView textView2 = new TextView( this );
        textView2.setText("high");

        RelativeLayout.LayoutParams text2Layout = new
            RelativeLayout.LayoutParams(   LayoutParams.WRAP_CONTENT,
                                    LayoutParams.WRAP_CONTENT );
        text2Layout.addRule(RelativeLayout.ABOVE, TEXTVIEW1_ID );
        relLayout.addView( textView2, text2Layout );

        setContentView( relLayout );
    }
}
```

Recipe: Updating a Layout from a Separate Thread

As discussed in Chapter 3, "Threads, Services, Receivers, and Alerts," when a time-consuming activity is being run, care must be taken to ensure that the UI thread stays responsive. This is done by creating a separate thread for the time-consuming task and letting the UI thread continue at high priority. If the separate thread subsequently needs to update the UI, a handler can be used to post updates to the UI thread.

This recipe uses a button to trigger a time–consuming computation in two parts and updates to the screen when each part is done. The layout, represented by the XML in Listing 5.5, consists of status text called computation_status and a trigger button called action. It uses the strings defined in **strings.xml**, as shown in Listing 5.6.

Listing 5.5   **res/layout/main.xml**

```xml
<?xml version="1.0" encoding="utf-8"?>
<LinearLayout
    xmlns:android="http://schemas.android.com/apk/res/android"
    android:orientation="vertical"
    android:layout_width="match_parent"
    android:layout_height="match_parent">
    <TextView android:id="@+id/computation_status"
        android:layout_width="match_parent"
        android:layout_height="wrap_content"
        android:text="@string/hello" android:textSize="36sp"
        android:textColor="#000" />
    <Button android:text="@string/action"
        android:id="@+id/action"
        android:layout_width="wrap_content"
        android:layout_height="wrap_content" />
</LinearLayout>
```

Listing 5.6   **res/layout/strings.xml**

```xml
<?xml version="1.0" encoding="utf-8"?>
<resources>
    <string name="hello">Hello World, HandlerUpdateUi!</string>
    <string name="app_name">HandlerUpdateUi</string>
    <string name="action">Press to Start</string>
    <string name="start">Starting...</string>
    <string name="first">First Done</string>
    <string name="second">Second Done</string>
</resources>
```

The steps to update the UI from a background thread follow:

1. Initialize a handler to the UI object that updates by the background thread. (Here, it is called av.)

2. Define a runnable function (here, it is called mUpdateResults) that updates the UI as needed.

3. Declare a handler to handle the messages between threads. (Here, it is called mHandler.)

4. In the background thread, set flags as appropriate to communicate the change in status. (Here, textString and backgroundColor are to be changed.)

5. In the background thread, have the handler post the UI update function to the main thread.

The activity created by these steps is shown in Listing 5.7.

Listing 5.7   src/com/cookbook/handler_ui/HandlerUpdateUi.java

```java
package com.cookbook.handler_ui;

import android.app.Activity;
import android.graphics.Color;
import android.os.Bundle;
import android.os.Handler;
import android.view.View;
import android.widget.Button;
import android.widget.TextView;

public class HandlerUpdateUi extends Activity {
    TextView av; //UI reference
    int textString = R.string.start;
    int backgroundColor = Color.DKGRAY;

    final Handler mHandler = new Handler();
    // Create runnable for posting results to the UI thread
    final Runnable mUpdateResults = new Runnable() {
        public void run() {
            av.setText(textString);
            av.setBackgroundColor(backgroundColor);
        }
    };

    @Override
    public void onCreate(Bundle savedInstanceState) {
        super.onCreate(savedInstanceState);
        setContentView(R.layout.main);
        av = (TextView) findViewById(R.id.computation_status);

        Button actionButton = (Button) findViewById(R.id.action);
        actionButton.setOnClickListener(new View.OnClickListener() {
            public void onClick(View view) {
                doWork();
            }
        });
    }

    //example of a computationally intensive action with UI updates
    private void doWork() {
        Thread thread = new Thread(new Runnable() {
            public void run() {
                textString=R.string.start;
                backgroundColor = Color.DKGRAY;
                mHandler.post(mUpdateResults);

                computation(1);
                textString=R.string.first;
```

```
            backgroundColor = Color.BLUE;
            mHandler.post(mUpdateResults);

            computation(2);
            textString=R.string.second;
            backgroundColor = Color.GREEN;
            mHandler.post(mUpdateResults);
        }
    });
    thread.start();
}

final static int SIZE=1000; //large enough to take some time
double tmp;
private void computation(int val) {
    for(int ii=0; ii<SIZE; ii++)
        for(int jj=0; jj<SIZE; jj++)
            tmp=val*Math.log(ii+1)/Math.log1p(jj+1);
    }
}
```

Text Manipulation

In views that incorporate text, such as TextView, EditText, and Button, the text
is represented in the XML layout file by the android:text element. As discussed
in the beginning of this chapter, it is good practice to initialize this with a string
defined in the **strings.xml** file, so that all strings are contained in a single place.
Therefore, a way to add text to a UI element, such as TextView, looks like
the following:

```
<TextView android:text="@string/myTextString"
        android:id="@+id/my_text_label"
        android:layout_width="wrap_content"
        android:layout_height="wrap_content" />
```

The default font depends on the Android device and user preferences. To specify
the exact font, use the elements shown in Table 5.3. The default values are shown in
bold in the fourth column.

Recipe: Setting and Changing Text Attributes

This recipe changes the color of displayed text when a button is clicked. It can
easily be extended to change the font size or style instead, as discussed at the end of
the recipe.

The main layout is simply a TextView and Button arranged in a vertical
LinearLayout, as shown in Listing 5.8. The text is identified as mod_text and displays the string changed_text defined in the **strings.xml** file, as shown in Listing 5.9. The button is identified as change and displays the string button_text from
the string's XML file.

Table 5.3 **Useful TextView Attributes**

Attribute	XML Element	Java Method	Values
Display string	android:text	setText(CharSequence)	Any string
Font size	android:textSize	setTextSize(float)	Any dimension
Font color	android:textColor	setTextColor(int)	Any color
Background color	N/A	setBackgroundColor(int)	Any color
Font style	android:textStyle	setTypeface(Typeface)	Bold Italic Bold italic
Font type	android:typeface	setTypeface(Typeface)	**Normal** Sans serif Monospace
Text placement in display area	android:gravity	setGravity(int)	Top Bottom **Left** Right (More . . .)

Listing 5.8   **res/layout/main.xml**

```xml
<?xml version="1.0" encoding="utf-8"?>
<LinearLayout xmlns:android="http://schemas.android.com/apk/res/android"
    android:orientation="vertical"
        android:layout_width="match_parent"
        android:layout_height="match_parent">
        <TextView android:text="@string/changed_text"
                android:textSize="48sp"
                android:id="@+id/mod_text"
                android:layout_width="wrap_content"
                android:layout_height="wrap_content" />
        <Button android:text="@string/button_text"
                android:textSize="48sp"
                android:id="@+id/change"
                android:layout_width="wrap_content"
                android:layout_height="wrap_content" />
</LinearLayout>
```

Listing 5.9   **res/values/strings.xml**

```xml
<?xml version="1.0" encoding="utf-8"?>
<resources>
    <string name="app_name">ChangeFont</string>
    <string name="changed_text">Rainbow Connection</string>
    <string name="button_text">Press to change the font color</string>
</resources>
```

The activity shown in Listing 5.10 uses the **main.xml** layout and identifies the TextView handler to the mod_text ID. Then the button's OnClickListener method is overridden to set the text color as described in Table 5.3.

Listing 5.10   src/com/cookbook/change_font/ChangeFont.java

```java
package com.cookbook.change_font;

import android.app.Activity;
import android.os.Bundle;
import android.view.View;
import android.widget.Button;
import android.widget.TextView;

public class ChangeFont extends Activity {
    TextView tv;
    private int colorVals[]={R.color.start, R.color.mid, R.color.last};
    int idx=0;
    /** called when the activity is first created */
    @Override
    public void onCreate(Bundle savedInstanceState) {
        super.onCreate(savedInstanceState);
        setContentView(R.layout.main);
        tv = (TextView) findViewById(R.id.mod_text);

        Button changeFont = (Button) findViewById(R.id.change);
        changeFont.setOnClickListener(new View.OnClickListener() {
            public void onClick(View view) {
                tv.setTextColor(getResources().getColor(colorVals[idx]));
                idx = (idx+1)%3;
            }
        });
    }
}
```

The possible color resources are defined in a global **colors.xml** file, as shown in Listing 5.11. As defined, the colors are red, green, and blue, but they are named functionally as start, mid, and last. This provides an easy way to change the colors later without needing to change their handler names.

Listing 5.11   res/values/colors.xml

```xml
<?xml version="1.0" encoding="utf-8"?>
<resources>
        <color name="start">#f00</color>
        <color name="mid">#0f0</color>
        <color name="last">#00f</color>
</resources>
```

This recipe can be modified to change the text size (or text style) easily. For example, `colorVals[]` would change to `sizeVals[]` and point to the `R.dimen` resources:

```
private int sizeVals[]={R.dimen.small, R.dimen.medium, R.dimen.large};
tv.setTextSize(getResources().getDimension(sizeVals[idx]));
```

Also, instead of the **colors.xml** file, the **dimens.xml** file would be used, as shown in Listing 5.12.

Listing 5.12   **Similar Usage for the dimens.xml File**

```
<?xml version="1.0" encoding="utf-8"?>
<resources>
        <dimen name="start">12sp</dimen>
        <dimen name="mid">24sp</dimen>
        <dimen name="last">48sp</dimen>
</resources>
```

To change the text string instead, `colorVals[]` would change to `textVals[]` and point to the `R.string` resources as follows:

```
private int textVals[]={R.string.first_text,
                        R.string.second_text, R.string.third_text};
tv.setText(getBaseContext().getString(textVals[idx]));
```

The **strings.xml** file would then be used, as shown in Listing 5.13.

Listing 5.13   **Similar Usage for the strings.xml File**

```
<?xml version="1.0" encoding="utf-8"?>
<resources>
    <string name="app_name">ChangeFont</string>
    <string name="changed_text">Rainbow Connection</string>
    <string name="buttoN_text">Press to Change the Font Color</string>
    <string name="first_text">First</string>
    <string name="second_text">Second</string>
    <string name="third_text">Third</string>
</resources>
```

Recipe: Providing Text Entry

The `EditText` class provides a simple view for user input. It can be declared just like a `TextView` with the most useful attributes shown in Table 5.4. Although each does have a corresponding Java method, it is less illuminating to show those here. Again, the default values are in bold in the last column.

For example, using the following XML code in a layout file shows a text entry window with **Type text here** displayed in grayed-out text as a hint. On devices

Table 5.4   **Useful EditText Attributes**

Attribute	XML Element	Values
Minimum number of lines to display	`android:minLines`	Any integer
Maximum number of lines to display	`android:maxLines`	Any integer
Hint text to show when display is empty	`android:hint`	Any string

Input type	`android:inputType`	**text**
		`textCapSentences`
		`textAutoCorrect`
		`textAutoComplete`
		`textEmailAddress`
		`textNoSuggestions`
		`textPassword`
		`number`
		`phone`
		`date`
		`time`
		(More . . .)

without a keyboard or on those where the keyboard is hidden, selecting the Edit window brings up the soft keyboard for text entry, as shown in Figure 5.8.

```
<EditText  android:id="@+id/text_result"
   android:inputType="text"
   android:textSize="30sp"
   android:hint="Type text here"
   android:layout_width="match_parent"
   android:layout_height="wrap_content" />
```

Figure 5.8   Text entry with soft keyboard

Figure 5.9   Using soft keyboards when `inputText` is set as `"phone"` or `"textEmailAddress"`

By using `android:inputType="phone"` or `="textEmailAddress"`, the soft keyboard for phone number entry or the soft keyboard for email address entry displays when the user selects the Input window. These are shown in Figure 5.9 with appropriately changed `hint` text.

One more note: The text entry method can be specified as shown in Table 5.4 to automatically capitalize each sentence as typed, automatically correct mistyped words, or turn off word suggestions during typing. Control over these choices might be useful depending on the text entry situation.

Recipe: Creating a Form

A form is a graphical layout with areas that can take text input or selection. For text input, an `EditText` object can be used. After it is declared, some Java code needs to capture the text entry at run-time. This is done as shown in Listing 5.14. Note that the content of the text entry `textResult` in this example should not be modified. A copy of the content can be made in case modification is needed.

Listing 5.14   Capturing Text from an EditText Object

```
CharSequence phoneNumber;
EditText textResult = (EditText) findViewById(R.id.text_result);
textResult.setOnKeyListener(new OnKeyListener() {
    public boolean onKey(View v, int keyCode, KeyEvent event) {
        // Register the text when "enter" is pressed
        if ((event.getAction() == KeyEvent.ACTION_UP) &&
            (keyCode == KeyEvent.KEYCODE_ENTER)) {
          // Grab the text for use in the activity
          phoneNumber = textResult.getText();
          return true;
        }
        return false;
    }
});
```

Returning true from the onKey method indicates to the super function that the key press event was consumed (used), and there is no need to process further.

To provide user selection of different options normally used in forms, standard widgets such as check boxes, radio buttons, and drop-down selection menus are implemented using widgets as shown in the next section.

Other Widgets: From Buttons to Seek Bars

The Android system provides some standard graphical widgets that developers can use to create a cohesive user experience across applications. The most common ones are:

- Button—A rectangular graphic that registers when the screen is touched within its bounds. It can contain user-provided text or images.
- CheckBox—A button with a check mark graphic and description text that can be toggled on or off when touched. The ToggleButton is similar and also discussed here.
- RadioButton—A button with a dot graphic that can be selected when touched but cannot then be turned off. Multiple radio buttons can be grouped together into a RadioGroup (as a LinearLayout), which allows only one radio button of the group to be selected at a time.
- Spinner—A button showing the current selection and an arrow graphic to denote a drop-down menu. When the spinner is touched, the list of possible values displays, and when a new selection is made, it is displayed in the spinner.
- ProgressBar—A bar that lights up to visually indicate the percentage of progress (and optionally secondary progress) in an operation. It is not interactive. If a quantitative measure of progress cannot be determined, the ProgressBar can be set in indeterminate mode, which shows a rotating circular motion instead.
- SeekBar—An interactive progress bar that allows progress to be dragged and changed. This is useful to show media playback, for example. It can show how much of the media has been played, and a user can drag to move to an earlier or later place in the file.

The following recipes provide some practical examples of these widgets.

Recipe: Using Image Buttons in a Table Layout

Buttons were introduced in Chapter 2, "Application Basics: Activities and Intents." Like any view, a background image can be added to a button using the android:background attribute. However, using the special ImageButton widget provides some additional layout flexibility. It specifies an image using the android:src attribute as follows:

```
<ImageButton android:id="@+id/imagebutton0"
            android:src="@drawable/android_cupcake"
            android:layout_width="wrap_content"
            android:layout_height="wrap_content" />
```

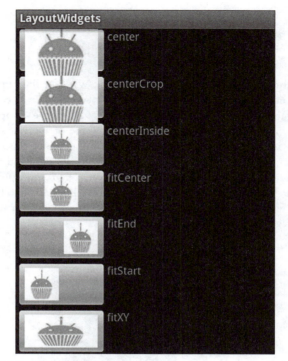

Figure 5.10   Example results of android:scaleType for image views

When used in this way, the image shows on top of a Button widget. The ImageButton widget inherits image placement from the ImageView widget using android:scaleType. Possible values and how they modify a given image are illustrated in Figure 5.10.

Following are some additional possible manipulations used with image buttons:

- Using android:padding to keep buttons from overlapping or to add space between them
- Setting android:background to null (which is @null in the XML layout file) to hide the button and show only the image

When the button is hidden, by default, there is no visual feedback that an image button was pressed. This can be rectified by creating a drawable XML file that contains just a selector element:

```
<?xml version="1.0" encoding="utf-8"?>
<selector xmlns:android="http://schemas.android.com/apk/res/android">
    <item android:drawable="@drawable/myimage_pressed"
          android:state_pressed="true" />
```

```
    <item android:drawable="@drawable/myimage_focused"
        android:state_focused="true" />
    <item android:drawable="@drawable/myimage_normal" />
</selector>
```

This specifies three different images depending on whether the button is pressed, in focus, or just in a normal state. The three different images for these cases should also reside in the drawable resource directory (such as **res/drawable-mdpi/**). Then, the selector file can be specified as the `android:src` attribute of an `ImageButton`.

When multiple image buttons are placed together in a layout, it is often useful to use the table layout, which is also shown in this recipe. The `TableLayout` view group is similar to a `LinearLayout` with vertical orientation. Then, multiple rows can be specified using the `TableRow` view group for each row. The example layout shown in Listing 5.15 specifies an `ImageButton` and `TextView` in each row, producing the screen layout shown in Figure 5.11.

Figure 5.11   `TableLayout` of `ImageButtons` and `TextViews`

Listing 5.15   **res/layout/ibutton.xml**

```
<?xml version="1.0" encoding="utf-8"?>
<TableLayout
    xmlns:android="http://schemas.android.com/apk/res/android"
    android:layout_width="match_parent"
```

```
    android:layout_height="match_parent">
<TableRow>
    <ImageButton android:id="@+id/imagebutton0"
        android:src="@drawable/android_cupcake"
        android:scaleType="fitXY"
        android:background="@null"
        android:padding="5dip"
        android:layout_width="wrap_content"
        android:layout_height="90dip" />
    <TextView android:text="Cupcake"
        android:layout_width="wrap_content"
        android:layout_height="wrap_content" />
</TableRow>
<TableRow>
    <ImageButton android:id="@+id/imagebutton1"
        android:src="@drawable/android_donut"
        android:scaleType="fitXY"
        android:background="@null"
        android:padding="5dip"
        android:layout_width="wrap_content"
        android:layout_height="90dip" />
    <TextView android:text="Donut"
        android:layout_width="wrap_content"
        android:layout_height="wrap_content" />
</TableRow>
<TableRow>
    <ImageButton android:id="@+id/imagebutton2"
        android:src="@drawable/android_eclair"
        android:scaleType="fitXY"
        android:background="@null"
        android:padding="5dip"
        android:layout_width="wrap_content"
        android:layout_height="90dip" />
    <TextView android:text="Eclair"
        android:layout_width="wrap_content"
        android:layout_height="wrap_content" />
</TableRow>
<TableRow>
    <ImageButton android:id="@+id/imagebutton3"
        android:src="@drawable/android_froyo"
        android:scaleType="fitXY"
        android:background="@null"
        android:padding="5dip"
        android:layout_width="wrap_content"
        android:layout_height="90dip" />
    <TextView android:text="FroYo"
        android:layout_width="wrap_content"
        android:layout_height="wrap_content" />
</TableRow>
<TableRow>
    <ImageButton android:id="@+id/imagebutton4"
        android:src="@drawable/android_gingerbread"
        android:scaleType="fitXY"
        android:background="@null"
        android:padding="5dip"
        android:layout_width="wrap_content"
        android:layout_height="90dip" />
```

```
        <TextView android:text="Gingerbread"
            android:layout_width="wrap_content"
            android:layout_height="wrap_content" />
    </TableRow>
</TableLayout>
```

Recipe: Using Check Boxes and Toggle Buttons

Check boxes have a predetermined check mark graphic, colors for selection, and colors for behavior when pressed. This provides a unifying look and feel across Android applications. However, if a custom graphic to denote selection is required, the setButtonDrawable() method can be used.

Sticking with the check box example here, the CheckBox widget needs to be declared in a layout file, as shown in Listing 5.16. The android:text attribute displays as a label after the check box. For illustration, a few text views are also added to the layout.

Listing 5.16   res/layout/ckbox.xml

```
<?xml version="1.0" encoding="utf-8"?>
<LinearLayout
        xmlns:android="http://schemas.android.com/apk/res/android"
        android:orientation="vertical"
        android:layout_width="match_parent"
        android:layout_height="match_parent">
        <CheckBox android:id="@+id/checkbox0"
            android:text="Lettuce"
            android:layout_width="wrap_content"
            android:layout_height="wrap_content" />
        <CheckBox android:id="@+id/checkbox1"
            android:text="Tomato"
            android:layout_width="wrap_content"
            android:layout_height="wrap_content" />
        <CheckBox android:id="@+id/checkbox2"
            android:text="Cheese"
            android:layout_width="wrap_content"
            android:layout_height="wrap_content" />
        <TextView android:text="Lettuce, Tomato, Cheese choices:"
            android:layout_width="wrap_content"
            android:layout_height="wrap_content" />
        <TextView android:id="@+id/status"
            android:layout_width="wrap_content"
            android:layout_height="wrap_content" />
</LinearLayout>
```

The views in the layout file can be associated with view instances in the Java file, as shown in Listing 5.17. Here, a private inner class is used to register the toppings of a sandwich. All three check boxes have an onClickListener method, which keeps track of the changes to the toppings, and this is updated to the text view as an example. The final output with some sample selections is shown in Figure 5.12.

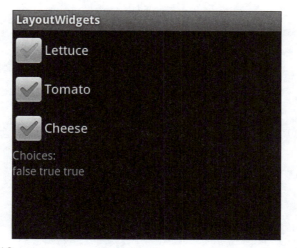

Figure 5.12   CheckBox example showing unselected and selected widgets

Listing 5.17   **src/com/cookbook/layout_widgets/CheckBoxExample.java**

```
package com.cookbook.layout_widgets;

import android.app.Activity;
import android.os.Bundle;
import android.view.View;
import android.view.View.OnClickListener;
import android.widget.CheckBox;
import android.widget.TextView;

public class CheckBoxExample extends Activity {
    private TextView tv;

    @Override
    public void onCreate(Bundle savedInstanceState) {
        super.onCreate(savedInstanceState);
        setContentView(R.layout.ckbox);
        tv = (TextView) findViewById(R.id.status);

        class Toppings {private boolean LETTUCE, TOMATO, CHEESE;}

        final Toppings sandwichToppings = new Toppings();
        final CheckBox checkbox[] = {
                (CheckBox) findViewById(R.id.checkbox0),
                (CheckBox) findViewById(R.id.checkbox1),
                (CheckBox) findViewById(R.id.checkbox2)};

        checkbox[0].setOnClickListener(new OnClickListener() {
            @Override
            public void onClick(View v) {
                if (((CheckBox) v).isChecked()) {
                    sandwichToppings.LETTUCE = true;
```

```
            } else {
                sandwichToppings.LETTUCE = false;
            }
            tv.setText(""+sandwichToppings.LETTUCE + " "
                    +sandwichToppings.TOMATO + " "
                    +sandwichToppings.CHEESE + " ");
        }
    });
    checkbox[1].setOnClickListener(new OnClickListener() {
        @Override
        public void onClick(View v) {
            if (((CheckBox) v).isChecked()) {
                sandwichToppings.TOMATO = true;
            } else {
                sandwichToppings.TOMATO = false;
            }
            tv.setText(""+sandwichToppings.LETTUCE + " "
                    +sandwichToppings.TOMATO + " "
                    +sandwichToppings.CHEESE + " ");
        }
    });
    checkbox[2].setOnClickListener(new OnClickListener() {
        @Override
        public void onClick(View v) {
            if (((CheckBox) v).isChecked()) {
                sandwichToppings.CHEESE = true;
            } else {
                sandwichToppings.CHEESE = false;
            }
            tv.setText(""+sandwichToppings.LETTUCE + " "
                    +sandwichToppings.TOMATO + " "
                    +sandwichToppings.CHEESE + " ");
        }
    });
    }
}
```

Toggle buttons are similar to check boxes but use a different graphic. In addition, the text is incorporated into the button rather than put alongside. Listing 5.16 (and Listing 5.17 for that matter) can be modified to replace each CheckBox with a ToggleButton:

```
<ToggleButton android:id="@+id/ToggleButton0"
            android:textOff="No Lettuce"
            android:textOn="Lettuce"
            android:layout_width="wrap_content"
            android:layout_height="wrap_content" />
```

Note that the android:text element is replaced by an android:textOff (defaults to "OFF" if not specified) and android:textOn (defaults to "ON" if not specified) element for display depending on the selection state of the toggle button. An example output is shown in Figure 5.13.

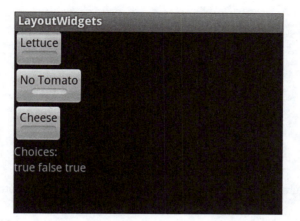

Figure 5.13   `ToggleButton` example with unselected and selected widgets

Recipe: Using Radio Buttons

A radio button is like a check box that cannot be unchecked. Selecting one radio button unselects a previously selected one. Usually a group of radio buttons is put into a `RadioGroup` view group that ensures that only one button of the collection is selected at a time. This is shown in the layout file in Listing 5.18.

Listing 5.18   res/layout/rbutton.xml

```xml
<?xml version="1.0" encoding="utf-8"?>
    <RadioGroup android:id="@+id/RadioGroup01"
            android:layout_width="wrap_content"
            android:layout_height="wrap_content">
        <RadioButton android:text="Republican"
                android:id="@+id/RadioButton02"
                android:layout_width="wrap_content"
                android:layout_height="wrap_content" />
        <RadioButton android:text="Democrat"
                android:id="@+id/RadioButton03"
                android:layout_width="wrap_content"
                android:layout_height="wrap_content" />
        <RadioButton android:text="Independent"
                android:id="@+id/RadioButton01"
                android:layout_width="wrap_content"
                android:layout_height="wrap_content" />
    </RadioGroup>
```

This example activity is similar to the example shown in Listing 5.17, but with `CheckBox` replaced by `RadioButton`. Listing 5.18's layout is shown in Figure 5.14.

Figure 5.14   `RadioGroup` example showing three radio buttons

Recipe: Creating a Spinner

A drop-down menu is called a spinner. It is a widget defined in a normal screen layout such as the one shown in Listing 5.19.

Listing 5.19   **res/layout/spinner.xml**

```xml
<?xml version="1.0" encoding="utf-8"?>
<LinearLayout
        xmlns:android="http://schemas.android.com/apk/res/android"
        android:layout_width="wrap_content"
        android:layout_height="wrap_content">
    <Spinner android:id="@+id/spinner"
                android:prompt="@string/oceaN_prompt"
                android:layout_width="wrap_content"
                android:layout_height="wrap_content" />
</LinearLayout>
```

The title of the drop-down menu can be specified with the `android:prompt` attribute. It needs to be defined in a **strings.xml** file, for example:

```xml
<string name="ocean_prompt">Choose your favorite ocean</string>
```

The spinner also needs a separate layout defined for the drop-down menu appearance, such as Listing 5.20 for the **spinner_entry.xml**.

Listing 5.20   **res/layout/spinner_entry.xml**

```xml
<?xml version="1.0" encoding="utf-8"?>
<TextView
    xmlns:android="http://schemas.android.com/apk/res/android"
    android:gravity="center"
    android:textColor="#000"
    android:textSize="40sp"
```

```
        android:layout_width="match_parent"
        android:layout_height="wrap_content">
</TextView>
```

Note that the spinner entry layout is not limited to text but can include images or any object supported in layouts.

The activity to call the spinner needs to declare an `Adapter` constructor to fill the drop-down menu with the view from the spinner entry layout file. An example of such an activity is shown in Listing 5.21.

Listing 5.21   src/com/cookbook/layout_widgets/SpinnerExample.java

```java
package com.cookbook.layout_widgets;

import android.app.Activity;
import android.os.Bundle;
import android.widget.ArrayAdapter;
import android.widget.Spinner;

public class SpinnerExample extends Activity {
    private static final String[] oceans = {
        "Pacific", "Atlantic", "Indian",
        "Arctic", "Southern" };

    @Override
    protected void onCreate(Bundle savedInstanceState) {
        super.onCreate(savedInstanceState);
        setContentView(R.layout.spinner);

        Spinner favoriteOcean = (Spinner) findViewById(R.id.spinner);

        ArrayAdapter<String> mAdapter = new
            ArrayAdapter<String>(this, R.layout.spinner_entry, oceans);
        mAdapter.setDropDownViewResource(R.layout.spinner_entry);
        favoriteOcean.setAdapter(mAdapter);
    }
}
```

In the previous example, the spinner entries are defined by the string array `oceans[]`, which is passed to the `ArrayAdapter` constructor. This implementation assumes the spinner entries do not change during run-time. To specify a more general case where spinner entries can be added or manipulated, `mAdapter` needs to be built using its `add()` method. The bold part of code in the `onCreate()` method would then become the following:

```java
Spinner favoriteOcean = (Spinner) findViewById(R.id.spinner);
ArrayAdapter<String> mAdapter = new
    ArrayAdapter<String>(this, R.layout.spinner_entry);
mAdapter.setDropDownViewResource(R.layout.spinner_entry);
```

```
for(int idx=0; idx<oceans.length; idx++)
    mAdapter.add(oceans[idx]);
favoriteOcean.setAdapter(mAdapter);
```

This `ArrayAdapter` constructor allows the `add()`, `remove()`, and `clear()` methods to change the selection list during run-time, and `getView()` to improve performance speed by reusing layout views for each spinner entry.

Recipe: Using a Progress Bar

This recipe demonstrates the usage of a progress bar by taking Listing 5.7, which used text to show progress in a computation, and showing the progress graphically instead. This is done by adding a progress bar object to the layout, such as:

```
<ProgressBar  android:id="@+id/ex_progress_bar"
        style="@android:attr/progressBarStyleHorizontal"
        android:layout_width="270dp"
        android:layout_height="50dp"
        android:progress="0"
        android:secondaryProgress="0" />
```

As the progress changes, the `android:progress` attribute can change to show a colored bar going across the screen. The optional `android:secondaryProgress` attribute shows a lighter-colored bar that can be used to indicate a progress milestone, for example.

The activity to update the progress bar is shown in Listing 5.22. It is similar to Listing 5.7, but it uses `ProgressBar` instead of changing background colors. Here, the update results function updates the progress attribute from Java.

Listing 5.22   src/com/cookbook/handler_ui/HandlerUpdateUi.java

```
package com.cookbook.handler_ui;

import android.app.Activity;
import android.os.Bundle;
import android.os.Handler;
import android.view.View;
import android.widget.Button;
import android.widget.ProgressBar;

public class HandlerUpdateUi extends Activity {
    private static ProgressBar m_progressBar; //UI reference
    int percentDone = 0;

    final Handler mHandler = new Handler();
    // Create runnable for posting results to the UI thread
    final Runnable mUpdateResults = new Runnable() {
        public void run() {
            m_progressBar.setProgress(percentDone);
        }
    };
```

```
@Override
public void onCreate(Bundle savedInstanceState) {
    super.onCreate(savedInstanceState);
    setContentView(R.layout.main);
    m_progressBar = (ProgressBar) findViewById(R.id.ex_progress_bar);

    Button actionButton = (Button) findViewById(R.id.action);
    actionButton.setOnClickListener(new View.OnClickListener() {
        public void onClick(View view) {
            doWork();
        }
    });
}

//example of a computationally intensive action with UI updates
private void doWork() {
    Thread thread = new Thread(new Runnable() {
        public void run() {
            percentDone = 0;
            mHandler.post(mUpdateResults);

            computation(1);
            percentDone = 50;
            mHandler.post(mUpdateResults);

            computation(2);
            percentDone = 100;
            mHandler.post(mUpdateResults);
        }
    });
    thread.start();
}

final static int SIZE=1000; //large enough to take some time
double tmp;
private void computation(int val) {
    for(int ii=0; ii<SIZE; ii++)
        for(int jj=0; jj<SIZE; jj++)
            tmp=val*Math.log(ii+1)/Math.log1p(jj+1);
}
}
```

If the updates need to be shown more often, use the postDelayed method of the handler instead of the post method and add postDelayed to the end of the runnable update results function (similar to what was used in "Scheduling a Runnable Task from the Main Thread" recipe in Chapter 3, "Threads, Services, Receivers, and Alerts").

Recipe: Using a Seek Bar

A seek bar is similar to a progress bar, but it can take user input to change the amount of progress. Current progress is indicated by a small sliding box called a thumb. A user

can click and drag the thumb to visually indicate the new place to set the progress.
The main activity is shown in Listing 5.23.

Listing 5.23   **src/com/cookbook/seekbar/SeekBarEx.java**

```java
package com.cookbook.seekbar;

import android.app.Activity;
import android.os.Bundle;
import android.widget.SeekBar;

public class SeekBarEx extends Activity {
    private SeekBar m_seekBar;
    boolean advancing = true;

    @Override
    public void onCreate(Bundle savedInstanceState) {
        super.onCreate(savedInstanceState);
        setContentView(R.layout.main);

        m_seekBar = (SeekBar) findViewById(R.id.SeekBar01);
        m_seekBar.setOnSeekBarChangeListener(new
                        SeekBar.OnSeekBarChangeListener() {
            public void onProgressChanged(SeekBar seekBar,
                    int progress, boolean fromUser) {
                if(fromUser) count = progress;
            }

            public void onStartTrackingTouch(SeekBar seekBar) {}
            public void onStopTrackingTouch(SeekBar seekBar) {}
        });

        Thread initThread = new Thread(new Runnable() {
            public void run() {
                show_time();
            }
        });
        initThread.start();
    }

    int count;
    private void show_time() {
        for(count=0; count<100; count++) {
            m_seekBar.setProgress(count);

            try {
                Thread.sleep(100);
            } catch (InterruptedException e) {
                e.printStackTrace();
            }
        }
    }
}
```

The widget declaration in the layout XML file is shown in Listing 5.24. Note that rather than using the default thumb button, a cupcake image is used, as shown in Figure 5.15.

Listing 5.24   res/layout/main.xml

```xml
<?xml version="1.0" encoding="utf-8"?>
<RelativeLayout
    xmlns:android="http://schemas.android.com/apk/res/android"
    android:layout_width="match_parent"
    android:layout_height="match_parent">
    <TextView android:layout_width="match_parent"
        android:layout_height="wrap_content"
        android:textSize="24sp" android:text="Drag the cupcake"
        android:layout_alignParentTop="true" />
    <SeekBar android:id="@+id/SeekBar01"
        android:layout_centerInParent="true"
        android:layout_width="match_parent"
        android:layout_height="wrap_content"
        android:thumb="@drawable/pink_cupcake_no_bg" />
</RelativeLayout>
```

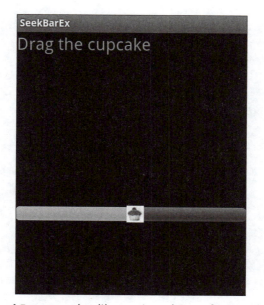

Figure 5.15   SeekBar example with a custom picture of a cupcake as the thumb

6

User Interface Events

The two aspects of a UI are screen layout and event handling. Chapter 5, "User Interface Layout," discussed how layouts are made up of `View` objects, such as text and buttons. This chapter shows how to handle events from a user, such as physical key presses, touch events, and menu navigation. It also shows how to use a few advanced user interface libraries, namely, gestures and 3D graphics.

Event Handlers and Event Listeners

Most user interaction with an Android device is captured by the system and sent to a corresponding callback method. For example, if the physical BACK key is pressed, the `onBackPressed()` method is called. Such events can be handled by extending the class and overriding the methods, called event handlers.

User interaction with `View` or `ViewGroup` objects can also support event listeners. These are methods that wait for the registered event and then trigger the system to send the event information to the corresponding callback method. For example, the `OnClickListener` event listener can be registered for a button and when it is pressed by using `setOnClickListener()`.

Event listeners are the preferred method when available because they avoid the class extension overhead. Furthermore, an activity implementing an event listener gets a callback for *all* the layout objects it contains, allowing for more concise code. Both event listeners and event handlers are demonstrated in this chapter within the context of handling physical key press events and screen touch events.

Recipe: Intercepting a Physical Key Press

A standard Android device has multiple physical keys that can trigger events, as listed in Table 6.1.

The system first sends any `KeyEvent` to the appropriate callback method in the in-focus activity or view. These callback methods are:

Table 6.1   **Possible Physical Keys on an Android Device**

Physical Key	KeyEvent	Description
Power key	KEYCODE_POWER	Turns on the device or wakes it from sleep; brings the UI to the lock screen
BACK key	KEYCODE_BACK	Navigates to the previous screen
MENU key	KEYCODE_MENU	Shows the menu for the active application
HOME key	KEYCODE_HOME	Navigates to the home screen
SEARCH key	KEYCODE_SEARCH	Launches a search in the active application
Camera key	KEYCODE_CAMERA	Launches the camera
Volume key	KEYCODE_VOLUME_UP KEYCODE_VOLUME_DOWN	Controls the volume of the media by context (voice when in a phone call, music when in media playback, or ringer volume)
DPAD	KEYCODE_DPAD_CENTER KEYCODE_DPAD_UP KEYCODE_DPAD_DOWN KEYCODE_DPAD_LEFT KEYCODE_DPAD_RIGHT	Directional pad on some devices
Trackball	KEYCODE_DPAD_CENTER KEYCODE_DPAD_UP KEYCODE_DPAD_DOWN KEYCODE_DPAD_LEFT KEYCODE_DPAD_RIGHT	Directional joystick on some devices
Keyboard	KEYCODE_0, ..., KEYCODE_9, KEYCODE_A, ..., KEYCODE_Z	Pull-out keyboard on some devices
Media button	KEYCODE_HEADSETHOOK	Headset Play/Pause button

- onKeyUp(), onKeyDown(), onKeyLongPress()—Physical key press callbacks
- onTrackballEvent(), onTouchEvent()—Trackball and touchscreen press callbacks
- onFocusChanged()—Called when the view gains or loses focus

These can be overridden by the application to customize with different actions. For example, to turn off the camera button (to avoid accidental presses), just consume the event in the onKeyDown() callback method for the activity. This is done by intercepting the method for the event KeyEvent.KEYCODE_CAMERA and returning true:

```
public boolean onKeyDown(int keyCode, KeyEvent event) {
    if (keyCode == KeyEvent.KEYCODE_CAMERA) {
        return true; // Consume event, hence do nothing on camera button
    }
    return super.onKeyDown(keyCode, event);
}
```

Because the event is consumed, it does not get passed on to other Android components. There are a few exceptions to this:

- The power button and HOME key are intercepted by the system and do not reach the application for customization.
- The BACK, MENU, HOME, and SEARCH keys should not intercept the KeyDown but instead the KeyUp. This coincides with Android 2.0 suggestions because these buttons might not be physical keys in other platforms.

Listing 6.1 shows a variety of examples of intercepting physical key presses, including the following:

- The Camera and DPAD left keys are intercepted in onKeyDown() to show a message to the screen, and then the method is consumed (by returning true).
- The Volume Up key is intercepted to show a message to the screen, but it is not consumed (returning false) and hence also actually increases the volume.
- The SEARCH key is intercepted in onKeyDown(), and the startTracking() method is used to track it through to the KeyUp where a message is sent to the screen.
- The BACK key is intercepted in onBackPressed().

A note on the latter: An Android guideline for usability is that the BACK key should generally not be customized. However, if needed for some reason in an activity or dialog, there is a separate callback method available with API Level 5 (Eclair) and higher to intercept the BACK key: onBackPressed().

For backward compatibility with earlier SDKs, the KeyEvent.KEYCODE_BACK can be intercepted, and the onBackPressed() method can be explicitly called for earlier SDKs, as shown in Listing 6.1. (Note: This code can be compiled only with Android 2.0 or higher due to the explicit mention of Eclair, but it is backward compatible at run-time on all devices.) To intercept the BACK key in a view (not shown here) requires using the startTracking() method, which is similar to the SEARCH key example in Listing 6.1.

Listing 6.1   src/com/cookbook/PhysicalKeyPress.java

```
package com.cookbook.physkey;
import android.app.Activity;
import android.os.Bundle;
import android.view.KeyEvent;
import android.widget.Toast;
```

```java
public class PhysicalKeyPress extends Activity {
    @Override
    public void onCreate(Bundle savedInstanceState) {
        super.onCreate(savedInstanceState);
        setContentView(R.layout.main);
    }
    @Override
    public boolean onKeyDown(int keyCode, KeyEvent event) {
        switch (keyCode) {
            case KeyEvent.KEYCODE_CAMERA:
            Toast.makeText(this, "Pressed Camera Button",
                    Toast.LENGTH_LONG).show();
            return true;
        case KeyEvent.KEYCODE_DPAD_LEFT:
            Toast.makeText(this, "Pressed DPAD Left Button",
                    Toast.LENGTH_LONG).show();
            return true;
        case KeyEvent.KEYCODE_VOLUME_UP:
            Toast.makeText(this, "Pressed Volume Up Button",
                    Toast.LENGTH_LONG).show();
            return false;
        case KeyEvent.KEYCODE_SEARCH:
            //example of tracking through to the KeyUp
            if(event.getRepeatCount() == 0)
                event.startTracking();
            return true;
        case KeyEvent.KEYCODE_BACK:
            // Make new onBackPressed compatible with earlier SDKs
            if (android.os.Build.VERSION.SDK_INT
                    < android.os.Build.VERSION_CODES.ECLAIR
                    && event.getRepeatCount() == 0) {
                onBackPressed();
            }
        }
        return super.onKeyDown(keyCode, event);
    }
    @Override
    public void onBackPressed() {
        Toast.makeText(this, "Pressed BACK Key",
                    Toast.LENGTH_LONG).show();
    }
    @Override
    public boolean onKeyUp(int keyCode, KeyEvent event) {
        if (keyCode == KeyEvent.KEYCODE_SEARCH && event.isTracking()
                && !event.isCanceled()) {
            Toast.makeText(this, "Pressed SEARCH Key",
                    Toast.LENGTH_LONG).show();
            return true;
        }
        return super.onKeyUp(keyCode, event);
    }
}
```

Recipe: Building Menus

A developer can implement three types of menus in Android, and this recipe creates an example of each:

- Options menu—The main menu for an activity that displays when the MENU key is pressed. For Android API Levels 10 and below, it contains an icon menu and possibly an expanded menu when the **More** menu item is selected. For newer levels of Android, only the original options menu is available.

- Context menu—A floating list of menu items that displays when a view is long pressed.

- Submenu—A floating list of menu items that displays when a menu item is pressed.

The options menu is created the first time the MENU key is pressed in an activity. This launches the onCreateOptionsMenu() method that usually contains menu methods, such as:

```
menu.add(GROUP_DEFAULT, MENU_ADD, 0, "Add")
    .setIcon(R.drawable.ic_launcher);
```

The first argument of the add() method labels the group of the menu item. Groups of items can be manipulated together. The second argument is an integer ID that represents the menu item. It is passed to the callback function to determine which menu item was selected. The third argument is the order of the item in the menu. If it is not used, the order falls back to the order in which the items were added to the Menu object. The last argument is the text that displays with the menu item. It can be a String or a string resource such as R.string.myLabel. This is the only menu that also supports adding icons to the menu choices using the setIcon() method.

This method is called only once, and the menu does not need to be built again for the rest of the activity. However, the onPrepareOptionsMenu() method can be used if any of the menu options need to change during run-time.

When an item from the options menu is clicked, the onOptionsItemSelected() method is called. This passes the selected item ID, and a switch statement can be used to determine which option was selected.

For this recipe, the options are to add a note, delete a note, or send a note. These are represented as simple mock functions that increment a counter (itemNum), decrement a counter, or show a Toast to the screen of the current counter value. To show an example of changing the menu options at run-time, the delete option is available only if a note has already been added in the past. This is done by grouping the delete option in a separate group and hiding the group when the itemNum is zero. The activity is shown in Listing 6.2.

Listing 6.2   src/com/cookbook/building_menus/BuildingMenus.java

```
package com.cookbook.building_menus;

import android.app.Activity;
import android.os.Bundle;
import android.view.ContextMenu;
import android.view.Menu;
```

```
import android.view.MenuItem;
import android.view.SubMenu;
import android.view.View;
import android.view.ContextMenu.ContextMenuInfo;
import android.widget.TextView;
import android.widget.Toast;

public class BuildingMenus extends Activity {
    private final int MENU_ADD=1, MENU_SEND=2, MENU_DEL=3;
    private final int GROUP_DEFAULT=0, GROUP_DEL=1;
    private final int ID_DEFAULT=0;
    private final int ID_TEXT1=1, ID_TEXT2=2, ID_TEXT3=3;
    private String[] choices = {"Press Me", "Try Again", "Change Me"};

    private static int itemNum=0;
    private static TextView bv;

    @Override
    public void onCreate(Bundle savedInstanceState) {
        super.onCreate(savedInstanceState);
        setContentView(R.layout.main);
        bv = (TextView) findViewById(R.id.focus_text);

        registerForContextMenu((View) findViewById(R.id.focus_text));
    }

    @Override
    public boolean onCreateOptionsMenu(Menu menu) {
        menu.add(GROUP_DEFAULT, MENU_ADD, 0, "Add")
            .setIcon(R.drawable.ic_launcher); //example of adding icon
        menu.add(GROUP_DEFAULT, MENU_SEND, 0, "Send");
        menu.add(GROUP_DEL, MENU_DEL, 0, "Delete");

        return super.onCreateOptionsMenu(menu);
    }

    @Override
    public boolean onPrepareOptionsMenu(Menu menu) {
        if(itemNum>0) {
            menu.setGroupVisible(GROUP_DEL, true);
        } else {
            menu.setGroupVisible(GROUP_DEL, false);
        }
        return super.onPrepareOptionsMenu(menu);
    }

    @Override
    public boolean onOptionsItemSelected(MenuItem item) {
        switch(item.getItemId()) {
        case MENU_ADD:
            create_note();
            return true;
        case MENU_SEND:
            send_note();
            return true;
        case MENU_DEL:
            delete_note();
```

```
            return true;
        }
        return super.onOptionsItemSelected(item);
    }

    @Override
    public void onCreateContextMenu(ContextMenu menu, View v,
            ContextMenuInfo menuInfo) {
        super.onCreateContextMenu(menu, v, menuInfo);
        if(v.getId() == R.id.focus_text) {
            SubMenu textMenu = menu.addSubMenu("Change Text");
            textMenu.add(0, ID_TEXT1, 0, choices[0]);
            textMenu.add(0, ID_TEXT2, 0, choices[1]);
            textMenu.add(0, ID_TEXT3, 0, choices[2]);
            menu.add(0, ID_DEFAULT, 0,  "Original Text");
        }
    }

    @Override
    public boolean onContextItemSelected(MenuItem item) {
        switch(item.getItemId()) {
        case ID_DEFAULT:
            bv.setText(R.string.hello);
            return true;
        case ID_TEXT1:
        case ID_TEXT2:
        case ID_TEXT3:
            bv.setText(choices[item.getItemId()-1]);
            return true;
        }
        return super.onContextItemSelected(item);
    }

    void create_note() { // mock code to create note
        itemNum++;
    }
    void send_note() { // mock code to send note
        Toast.makeText(this, "Item: "+itemNum,
                Toast.LENGTH_SHORT).show();
    }
    void delete_note() { // mock code to delete note
        itemNum--;
    }
}
```

The activity in Listing 6.2 also shows an example of a context menu and submenu. A TextView focus_text is added to the layout, as shown in Listing 6.3, and registered for a context menu using the registerForContextMenu() function in the onCreate() method of the activity.

When the view is pressed and held, the onCreateContextMenu() method is called to build the context menu. Here, the SubMenu is implemented using the addSubMenu() method for the Menu instance. The submenu items are specified along with the main menu items, and the onContextItemSelected() method is called when an item from either menu is clicked. Here, the recipe shows a change of text based on the menu choice.

Listing 6.3   **res/layout/main.xml**

```xml
<?xml version="1.0" encoding="utf-8"?>
<LinearLayout xmlns:android="http://schemas.android.com/apk/res/android"
    android:orientation="vertical"
    android:layout_width="match_parent"
    android:layout_height="match_parent"
    >
<TextView android:id="@+id/focus_text"
    android:layout_width="match_parent"
    android:layout_height="wrap_content"
    android:textSize="40sp"
    android:text="@string/hello"
    />
</LinearLayout>
```

Figures 6.1 and 6.2 show how the menus look for the different cases.

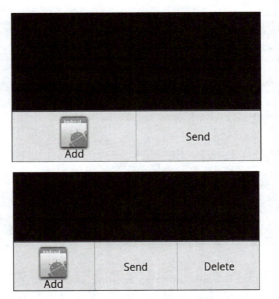

Figure 6.1   Options menu (top) and an added option at run-time (bottom)

Recipe: Defining Menus in XML

Menus can also be built in XML and inflated with the appropriate callback method from the previous recipe. This is a useful context for larger menus. Dynamic choices can still be handled in Java.

Figure 6.2   The context menu that displays with a long click on the text (left) and the sub-menu for the Change Text option that provides three alternate strings for the text view (right)

Menu files are usually kept in the **res/menu/** resources directory. For example, to make the context menu from the previous section, just create the XML file with nested menus, as shown in Listing 6.4.

Listing 6.4   **res/menu/context_menu.xml**

```xml
<?xml version="1.0" encoding="utf-8"?>
<menu xmlns:android="http://schemas.android.com/apk/res/android">
  <item android:id="@+id/submenu" android:title="Change Text">
  <menu xmlns:android="http://schemas.android.com/apk/res/android">
   <item android:id="@+id/text1" android:title="Press Me" />
   <item android:id="@+id/text2" android:title="Try Again" />
   <item android:id="@+id/text3" android:title="Change Me" />
  </menu>
  </item>
  <item android:id="@+id/orig" android:title="Original Text" />
</menu>
```

Then, inflate this XML in the creation of the menu, and reference the IDs from the item selection method. The two methods in Listing 6.2 that would be replaced are shown in Listing 6.5.

Listing 6.5   **Changed Methods in the Main Activity**

```java
@Override
    public void onCreateContextMenu(ContextMenu menu, View v,
            ContextMenuInfo menuInfo) {
        super.onCreateContextMenu(menu, v, menuInfo);
```

```
        MenuInflater inflater = getMenuInflater();
        inflater.inflate(R.menu.context_menu, menu);
    }
@Override
    public boolean onContextItemSelected(MenuItem item) {
        switch(item.getItemId()) {
        case R.id.orig:
            bv.setText(R.string.hello);
            return true;
        case R.id.text1:
            bv.setText(choices[0]);
            return true;
        case R.id.text2:
            bv.setText(choices[1]);
            return true;
        case R.id.text3:
            bv.setText(choices[2]);
            return true;
        }
        return super.onContextItemSelected(item);
    }
```

Recipe: Creating an Action Bar

The action bar is a window feature that was introduced in the release of Android 3.0 (Honeycomb). This was the release of Android that removed the need for a dedicated menu button. To replace it, the `ActionBar` was created. The action bar can be used to display user actions and global menu options. It can be used to reinforce a brand (as it will display an icon or app logo) as well as to switch between fragments, offer drop-down navigation, and display user actions such as search and share.

To get started with an action bar, the Holo theme should be used, and the `android:targetSdkVersion` should be set to 11 or higher. For versions prior to 11, the `ActionBarSherlock`, which is covered later in this chapter, can be used. The following snippet is an example of what can be used in the **AndroidManifest .xml** file:

```
<uses-sdk android:minSdkVersion="11" android:targetSdkVersion="16" />
```

This recipe shows how to create an action bar. The menu is shown in Listing 6.6.

Listing 6.6   res/menu/activity_action_bar.xml

```xml
<menu xmlns:android="http://schemas.android.com/apk/res/android">

<item android:id="@+id/menu_share"
  android:title="Share"
  android:icon="@drawable/ic_launcher"
  android:orderInCategory="0"
  android:showAsAction="ifRoom|withText" />
<item
  android:id="@+id/menu_settings"
```

```
      android:orderInCategory="100"
      android:showAsAction="never"
      android:title="@string/menu_settings"/>

</menu>
```

The action bar works like a menu and is defined in XML. This will be inflated in the ActionBarActivity. This is shown in Listing 6.7.

Listing 6.7   src/com/cookbook/actionbar/ActionBarActivity.java

```java
package com.cookbook.actionbar;

import android.app.Activity;
import android.os.Bundle;
import android.view.Menu;
import android.view.MenuInflater;
import android.view.MenuItem;
import android.widget.Toast;

public class ActionBarActivity extends Activity {

  @Override
  protected void onCreate(Bundle savedInstanceState) {
    super.onCreate(savedInstanceState);
    setContentView(R.layout.activity_action_bar);
  }

  @Override
  public boolean onCreateOptionsMenu(Menu menu) {
    MenuInflater inflater = getMenuInflater();
    inflater.inflate(R.menu.activity_action_bar, menu);
    return true;
  }

  @Override
  public boolean onOptionsItemSelected(MenuItem item) {
    switch (item.getItemId()) {
    case R.id.menu_share:
      Toast.makeText(this, "Implement share options here",
Toast.LENGTH_SHORT).show();
    default:
        return super.onOptionsItemSelected(item);
    }
  }
}
```

The bold section in Listing 6.7 shows the section of code that is added to the default activity in order to handle interaction with the Share menu item. Currently a Toast will be shown when the Share button is tapped, but this could be changed to work with providers to allow integration into other applications and services.

Figures 6.3 and 6.4 show this example on a tablet running Ice Cream Sandwich and a phone running Jelly Bean.

Recipe: Using ActionBarSherlock

The previous section described how to add an action bar to an application when run on Android devices that have Android 3.0 or higher, but what about users with legacy devices? This is where ActionBarSherlock comes into play. ActionBarSherlock bridges the gap between API levels and allows the use of an action bar in Android API levels below 11.

First, go to http://actionbarsherlock.com/ and download ActionBarSherlock. Uncompress the downloaded file, then add the library folder as an "Android Project from Existing Code." After the project has been imported into the workspace, it needs to be added as a library in the Android section of the project properties. Ant or Maven can also be used to build ActionBarSherlock into a project. For details on how, visit http://actionbarsherlock.com/usage.html.

After the project is set up to use the ActionBarSherlock library, it is time to make a few small alterations to the project made in Listing 6.7. The Android Support Library will need to be added, as this is part of what ActionBarSherlock uses to make the action bar work on the versions of Android prior to Honeycomb (API Level 11). If Eclipse is being used as the development IDE, simply right-click on the project folder

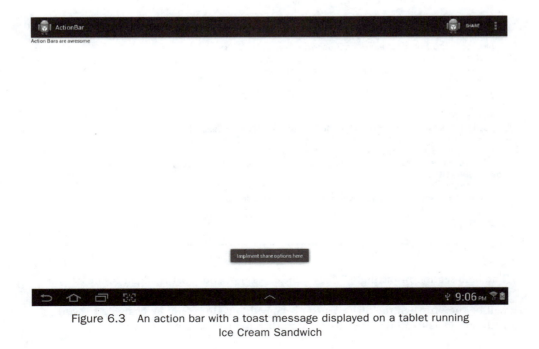

Figure 6.3   An action bar with a toast message displayed on a tablet running
Ice Cream Sandwich

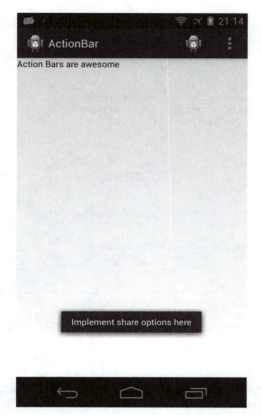

Figure 6.4   An action bar with a toast message displayed on a phone running Jelly Bean

and choose **Android Tools → Add Support Library**. A download will begin and the Support Library will be added to the project when the download has completed.

Now only a few modifications need to be made to add ActionBarSherlock to a project. Listing 6.8 shows the required changes to ActionBarActivity.

Listing 6.8   **src/com/cookbook/actionbar/ActionBarActivity.java**

```
package com.cookbook.actionbar;

import com.actionbarsherlock.app.SherlockActivity;
import android.os.Bundle;
import com.actionbarsherlock.view.Menu;
import com.actionbarsherlock.view.MenuInflater;
import com.actionbarsherlock.view.MenuItem;
import android.widget.Toast;

public class ActionBarActivity extends SherlockActivity {
```

```
    @Override
    protected void onCreate(Bundle savedInstanceState) {
        super.onCreate(savedInstanceState);
        setContentView(R.layout.activity_action_bar);
    }

    @Override
    public boolean onCreateOptionsMenu(Menu menu) {
        MenuInflater inflater = getSupportMenuInflater();
        inflater.inflate(R.menu.activity_action_bar, menu);
        return true;
    }

    @Override
    public boolean onOptionsItemSelected(MenuItem item) {
        switch (item.getItemId()) {
        case R.id.menu_share:
            Toast.makeText(this, "Implement share options here",
Toast.LENGTH_SHORT).show();
        default:
            return super.onOptionsItemSelected(item);
        }
    }
}
```

The boldface code displays the changes from Listing 6.7. These changes are the imports required as well as a change from extends `Activity` to extends `Sherlock-Activity`. A change is also made to the menu inflater, as it will now need to use get-`SupportMenuInflater` instead of getMenuInflater.

In order for the action bar to work on older versions of Android, the **Android Manifest.xml** file must be changed. The following line is an example of what will work:

```
<uses-sdk android:minSdkVersion="7" android:targetSdkVersion="16" />
```

While changes are made to the **AndroidManifest.xml** file, the theme of the application will also need to be changed to allow ActionBarSherlock to display and work properly. The following is an example of what the application settings could look like:

```
<application
    android:allowBackup="true"
    android:icon="@drawable/ic_launcher"
    android:label="@string/app_name"
    android:theme="@style/Theme.Sherlock" >
```

Note that the bolded theme setting has been changed to use the provided Sherlock theme. More information about using themes with ActionBarSherlock can be found at http://actionbarsherlock.com/theming.html.

Figure 6.5 shows a portrait screenshot and Figure 6.6 shows a landscape screenshot taken from an Android device running Gingerbread (Android 2.3, API Level 9). Notice how the word SHARE is removed in portrait mode to conserve space.

Figure 6.5   An action bar working on a device running Gingerbread displayed in portrait

Recipe: Using the SEARCH Key

As of Android 4.1 (Jelly Bean), the SEARCH key on all devices has been hard-coded by Google to be the shortcut key to invoke the Google Now service. This means that developers can no longer redefine this key for their applications. However, those building applications for pre–Jelly Bean devices can map the SEARCH key to trigger

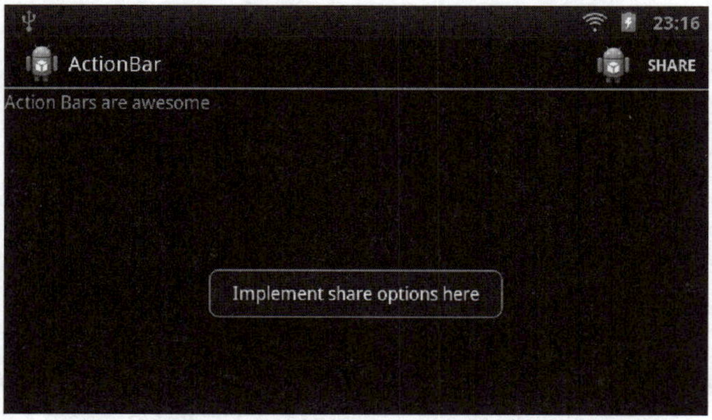

Figure 6.6   An action bar working on a device running Gingerbread displayed in landscape

custom behavior. If an activity in the in-focus application is defined to be searchable, the SEARCH key invokes it. A menu choice or equivalent should always be a redundant way to call the searchable activity to accommodate devices without a SEARCH key. The menu choice simply needs a call to onSearchRequested().

The searchable activity ideally should be declared as singleTop launch mode, as discussed in Chapter 2, "Application Basics: Activities and Intents." This enables multiple searches to take place without clogging the stack with multiple instances of the activity. The manifest file would have the following lines:

```
<activity android:name=".SearchDialogExample"
          android:launchMode="singleTop" >
  <intent-filter>
      <action android:name="android.intent.action.SEARCH" />
  </intent-filter>
  <meta-data android:name="android.app.searchable"
             android:resource="@xml/my_search"/>
</activity>
```

The XML file referencing the details of setting up the search configuration is shown in Listing 6.9. This file must be included when defining search in an application.

Listing 6.9   res/xml/my_search.xml

```
<?xml version="1.0" encoding="utf-8"?>
<searchable xmlns:android="http://schemas.android.com/apk/res/android"
   android:label="@string/app_name" android:hint="Search MyExample Here">
</searchable>
```

This recipe provides a search interface. The simplest main activity is shown in Listing 6.10 with a default **main.xml** file.

Listing 6.10   src/com/cookbook/search_diag/MainActivity.java

```
package com.cookbook.search_diag;

import android.app.Activity;
import android.os.Bundle;

public class MainActivity extends Activity {
    @Override
    protected void onCreate(Bundle savedInstanceState) {
        super.onCreate(savedInstanceState);
        setContentView(R.layout.main);
    }
}
```

Then, if the SEARCH key is selected, the searchable activity is activated. The onCreate() method checks whether the intent is an ACTION_SEARCH, and if it is, it acts on it. Listing 6.11 shows the main activity, which just displays the query to the screen.

Listing 6.11   src/com/cookbook/search_diag/SearchDialogExample.java

```java
package com.cookbook.search_diag;

import android.app.Activity;
import android.app.SearchManager;
import android.content.Intent;
import android.os.Bundle;
import android.widget.Toast;

public class SearchDialogExample extends Activity {
    /** called when the activity is first created */
    @Override
    public void onCreate(Bundle savedInstanceState) {
        super.onCreate(savedInstanceState);
        setContentView(R.layout.main);
        Intent intent = getIntent();

        if (Intent.ACTION_SEARCH.equals(intent.getAction())) {
            String query = intent.getStringExtra(SearchManager.QUERY);
            Toast.makeText(this, "The QUERY: " + query,
                                        Toast.LENGTH_LONG).show();
        }
    }
}
```

Recipe: Reacting to Touch Events

Any interaction with the screen, be it a touch or a navigated selection using the trackball, is an interaction with the corresponding view at that location. Because the screen layout is a hierarchy of views, as described in Chapter 5, "User Interface Layout," the system starts at the top of this hierarchy and passes the event down the tree until it is handled by a view. Some events, if not consumed, can continue to pass down the tree after being handled.

Listing 6.12 shows a button called ex_button that handles both a click and a long click (press and hold) by setting two event listeners. When the event occurs, the corresponding callback method is called and displays a Toast to the screen to show that the method was triggered.

Listing 6.12   src/com/cookbook/touch_examples/TouchExamples.java

```java
package com.cookbook.touch_examples;

import android.app.Activity;
import android.os.Bundle;
import android.view.View;
import android.view.View.OnClickListener;
import android.view.View.OnLongClickListener;
import android.widget.Button;
import android.widget.Toast;
```

```
public class TouchExamples extends Activity {
    @Override
    public void onCreate(Bundle savedInstanceState) {
        super.onCreate(savedInstanceState);
        setContentView(R.layout.main);
        Button ex = (Button) findViewById(R.id.ex_button);

        ex.setOnClickListener(new OnClickListener() {
            public void onClick(View v) {
                Toast.makeText(TouchExamples.this, "Click",
                        Toast.LENGTH_SHORT).show();
            }
        });
        ex.setOnLongClickListener(new OnLongClickListener() {
            public boolean onLongClick(View v) {
                Toast.makeText(TouchExamples.this, "LONG Click",
                        Toast.LENGTH_SHORT).show();
                return true;
            }
        });
    }
}
```

The layout providing the button is given in Listing 6.13.

Listing 6.13   res/layout/main.xml

```xml
<?xml version="1.0" encoding="utf-8"?>
<LinearLayout
    xmlns:android="http://schemas.android.com/apk/res/android"
    android:orientation="vertical"
    android:layout_width="match_parent"
    android:layout_height="match_parent">
    <Button android:id="@+id/ex_button"
        android:text="Press Me"
        android:layout_width="wrap_content"
        android:layout_height="wrap_content" />
</LinearLayout>
```

For compactness, this callback method is defined in place in Listing 6.12, but it can also be defined explicitly for readability and reusability:

```
View.OnClickListener myTouchMethod = new View.OnClickListener() {
    public void onClick(View v) {
        //Insert relevant action here
    }
};
ex.setOnClickListener(myTouchMethod);
```

Another way is to have the activity implement the OnClickListener interface. Then, the method is at the activity level and avoids an extra class load:

```
public class TouchExamples extends Activity implements OnClickListener {
    @Override
    public void onCreate(Bundle savedInstanceState) {
        super.onCreate(savedInstanceState);
        setContentView(R.layout.main);
        Button ex = (Button) findViewById(R.id.ex_button);
        ex.setOnClickListener(this);
    }

    public void onClick(View v) {
        if(v.getId() == R.id.directory_button) {
            // Insert relevant action here
        }
    }
}
```

This implementation of the `onClick()` method at the activity level helps to show how a parent view can handle touch events for multiple children.

Recipe: Listening for Fling Gestures

As discussed in the beginning of the chapter, each view has an `onTouchEvent()` method associated with it. In this recipe, it is overridden with a gesture detector that sets a gesture listener. The possible gestures in the `OnGestureListener` interface are

- `onDown()`—Notifies when a tap-down event occurs
- `onFling()`—Notifies when a tap-down, movement, and matching-up event occurs
- `onLongPress()`—Notifies when a long press occurs
- `onScroll()`—Notifies when a scroll occurs
- `onShowPress()`—Notifies when a tap-down event occurs before any movement or release
- `onSingleTapUp()`—Notifies when a tap-up event occurs

When only a subset of gestures is needed, the `SimpleOnGestureListener` class can be extended instead. It returns `false` for any of the previous methods not explicitly implemented.

A fling consists of two events: a touch down (the first `MotionEvent`) and a release (the second `MotionEvent`). Each motion event has a specified location on the screen given by an (x,y) coordinate pair, where x is the horizontal axis and y is the vertical axis. The (x,y) velocity of the event is also provided.

Listing 6.14 shows an activity that implements the onFling() method. When the movement is large enough (here, defined as 60 pixels), the event is consumed and appends the statement describing the event to the screen.

Listing 6.14   **src/com/cookbook/fling_ex/FlingExample.java**

```
package com.cookbook.fling_ex;

import android.app.Activity;
import android.os.Bundle;
import android.view.GestureDetector;
import android.view.MotionEvent;
import android.view.GestureDetector.SimpleOnGestureListener;
import android.widget.TextView;

public class FlingExample extends Activity {
    private static final int LARGE_MOVE = 60;
    private GestureDetector gestureDetector;
    TextView tv;

    @Override
    public void onCreate(Bundle savedInstanceState) {
        super.onCreate(savedInstanceState);
        setContentView(R.layout.main);
        tv = (TextView) findViewById(R.id.text_result);

        gestureDetector = new GestureDetector(this,
                new SimpleOnGestureListener() {
            @Override
            public boolean onFling(MotionEvent e1, MotionEvent e2,
                    float velocityX, float velocityY) {

                if (e1.getY() - e2.getY() > LARGE_MOVE) {
                    tv.append("\nFling Up with velocity " + velocityY);
                    return true;

                } else if (e2.getY() - e1.getY() > LARGE_MOVE) {
                    tv.append("\nFling Down with velocity " + velocityY);
                    return true;

                } else if (e1.getX() - e2.getX() > LARGE_MOVE) {
                    tv.append("\nFling Left with velocity " + velocityX);
                    return true;

                } else if (e2.getX() - e1.getX() > LARGE_MOVE) {
                    tv.append("\nFling Right with velocity " + velocityX);
                    return true;
                }

                return false;
            } });
    }

    @Override
    public boolean onTouchEvent(MotionEvent event) {
        return gestureDetector.onTouchEvent(event);
    }
}
```

The TextView that contains the descriptive text in the previous activity is defined in the main XML layout shown in Listing 6.15.

Listing 6.15   res/layout/main.xml

```xml
<?xml version="1.0" encoding="utf-8"?>
<LinearLayout
    xmlns:android="http://schemas.android.com/apk/res/android"
    android:orientation="vertical"
    android:layout_width="match_parent"
    android:layout_height="match_parent">
    <TextView android:id="@+id/text_result"
    android:layout_width="match_parent"
    android:layout_height="match_parent"
    android:textSize="16sp"
    android:text="Fling right, left, up, or down\n" />
</LinearLayout>
```

Recipe: Using Multitouch

A multitouch event is when more than one pointer (such as a finger) touches the screen at the same time. This is identified by using a touch listener OnTouchListener, which receives multiple types of motion events:

- ACTION_DOWN—A press gesture has started with a primary pointer (finger).
- ACTION_POINTER_DOWN—A secondary pointer (finger) has gone down.
- ACTION_MOVE—A change in press location has occurred during a press gesture.
- ACTION_POINTER_UP—A secondary pointer was released.
- ACTION_UP—A primary pointer was released, and the press gesture has completed.

This recipe displays an image to the screen and allows the multitouch events to zoom the image in or out. It also checks for single pointer events to drag the picture around the screen. This is shown in the activity in Listing 6.16. First, the activity implements the OnTouchListener that is set in the onCreate() method. When a touch event occurs, the onTouch() method checks the motion event and acts as follows:

- If a first pointer touches the screen, the touch state is declared to be a drag motion, and the touch-down position and Matrix are saved.
- If a second pointer touches the screen when the first pointer is still down, the distance between the two touch-down positions is calculated. As long as it is larger than some threshold (50 pixels here), the touch state is declared to be a zoom motion, and the distance and midpoint of the two events, as well as the Matrix, are saved.
- If a move occurs, the figure is translated for a single touch-down event and scaled for a multitouch event.
- If a pointer goes up, the touch state is declared to be no motion.

Listing 6.16   **src/com/cookbook/multitouch/MultiTouch.java**

```java
package com.cookbook.multitouch;

import android.app.Activity;
import android.graphics.Matrix;
import android.os.Bundle;
import android.util.FloatMath;

import android.view.MotionEvent;
import android.view.View;
import android.view.View.OnTouchListener;
import android.widget.ImageView;

public class MultiTouch extends Activity implements OnTouchListener {
    // Matrix instances to move and zoom image
    Matrix matrix = new Matrix();
    Matrix eventMatrix = new Matrix();

    // possible touch states
    final static int NONE = 0;
    final static int DRAG = 1;
    final static int ZOOM = 2;
    int touchState = NONE;

    @Override
    public void onCreate(Bundle savedInstanceState) {
        super.onCreate(savedInstanceState);
        setContentView(R.layout.main);
        ImageView view = (ImageView) findViewById(R.id.imageView);
        view.setOnTouchListener(this);
    }

    final static float MIN_DIST = 50;
    static float eventDistance = 0;
    static float centerX =0, centerY = 0;
    @Override
    public boolean onTouch(View v, MotionEvent event) {
        ImageView view = (ImageView) v;

        switch (event.getAction() & MotionEvent.ACTION_MASK) {
        case MotionEvent.ACTION_DOWN:
            //Primary touch event starts: remember touch-down location
            touchState = DRAG;
            centerX = event.getX(0);
            centerY = event.getY(0);
            eventMatrix.set(matrix);
            break;

        case MotionEvent.ACTION_POINTER_DOWN:
            //Secondary touch event starts: remember distance and center
            eventDistance = calcDistance(event);
            calcMidpoint(centerX, centerY, event);
            if (eventDistance > MIN_DIST) {
                eventMatrix.set(matrix);

                touchState = ZOOM;
            }
            break;
```

```
    case MotionEvent.ACTION_MOVE:
        if (touchState == DRAG) {
            //single finger drag, translate accordingly
            matrix.set(eventMatrix);
            matrix.setTranslate(event.getX(0) - centerX,
                                event.getY(0) - centerY);

        } else if (touchState == ZOOM) {
            //multifinger zoom, scale accordingly around center
            float dist = calcDistance(event);

            if (dist > MIN_DIST) {
                matrix.set(eventMatrix);
                float scale = dist / eventDistance;

                matrix.postScale(scale, scale, centerX, centerY);
            }
        }

        // Perform the transformation
        view.setImageMatrix(matrix);
        break;

    case MotionEvent.ACTION_UP:
    case MotionEvent.ACTION_POINTER_UP:
        touchState = NONE;
        break;
    }

    return true;
    }

    private float calcDistance(MotionEvent event) {
        float x = event.getX(0) - event.getX(1);
        float y = event.getY(0) - event.getY(1);
        return FloatMath.sqrt(x * x + y * y);
    }

    private void calcMidpoint(float centerX, float centerY,
                             MotionEvent event) {
        centerX = (event.getX(0) + event.getX(1))/2;
        centerY = (event.getY(0) + event.getY(1))/2;
    }
}
```

The layout that specifies a picture to zoom is shown in Listing 6.17. For this recipe, it is taken as the **icon.png**, which is automatically created in Eclipse; however, it can be replaced by any picture.

Listing 6.17   res/layout/main.xml

```xml
<?xml version="1.0" encoding="utf-8"?>
<FrameLayout
    xmlns:android="http://schemas.android.com/apk/res/android"
    android:layout_width="match_parent"
```

```
        android:layout_height="match_parent" >
    <ImageView android:id="@+id/imageView"
          android:layout_width="match_parent"
          android:layout_height="match_parent"
          android:src="@drawable/ic_launcher"
          android:scaleType="matrix" >
    </ImageView>
</FrameLayout>
```

Advanced User Interface Libraries

Some user interface features require complex algorithmic computations. Optimizing this for an embedded system can sometimes be challenging and time-consuming. It is in a developer's best interest to leverage any available UI libraries. The following two recipes provide some illustrative examples to use as a starting point.

Recipe: Using Gestures

A gesture is a hand-drawn shape on a touchscreen. The `android.gesture` package provides libraries to recognize and handle these in a simple way. First, every SDK has a sample program that can be used to build a collection of gestures in **platforms/android-2.0/samples/GestureBuilder/**. The Gesture Builder project can be imported and run on an Android device. It produces a file called **/sdcard/gestures**, which can be copied off of the device and used as a raw resource for this recipe.

As an example, a file of handwritten numbers can be generated as shown in Figure 6.7. Multiple gestures can have the same name, so providing different examples of the same gesture is useful to improve pattern recognition.

After this file is created for all numbers from 0 to 9 in all variants of interest, it can be copied to **res/raw/numbers**, for example. The layout is shown in Listing 6.18, and the main activity is shown in Listing 6.19. In the activity, the `GestureLibrary` is initialized with this raw resource.

This recipe adds a `GestureOverlayView` on top of the screen and implements an `OnGesturePerformedListener`. When a gesture is drawn, the gesture is passed to the `onGesturePerformed()` method, which compares it with all the gestures in the library and returns an ordered list of predictions, starting with the most likely. Each prediction has the name as defined in the library and the score for how correlated the gesture is to the input gesture. As long as the first entry has a score greater than one, it is generally a match.

Listing 6.18   res/layout/main.xml

```xml
<?xml version="1.0" encoding="utf-8"?>
<LinearLayout xmlns:android="http://schemas.android.com/apk/res/android"
    android:orientation="vertical"
    android:layout_width="match_parent"
    android:layout_height="match_parent"
    >
```

```
<TextView
    android:layout_width="match_parent"
    android:layout_height="wrap_content"
    android:gravity="center_horizontal" android:textSize="20sp"
    android:text="Draw a number"
    android:layout_margin="10dip"/>

<android.gesture.GestureOverlayView
    android:id="@+id/gestures"
    android:layout_width="match_parent"
    android:layout_height="0dip"
    android:layout_weight="1.0" />

<TextView android:id="@+id/prediction"
    android:layout_width="match_parent"
    android:layout_height="wrap_content"
    android:gravity="center_horizontal" android:textSize="20sp"
    android:text=""
    android:layout_margin="10dip"/>
</LinearLayout>
```

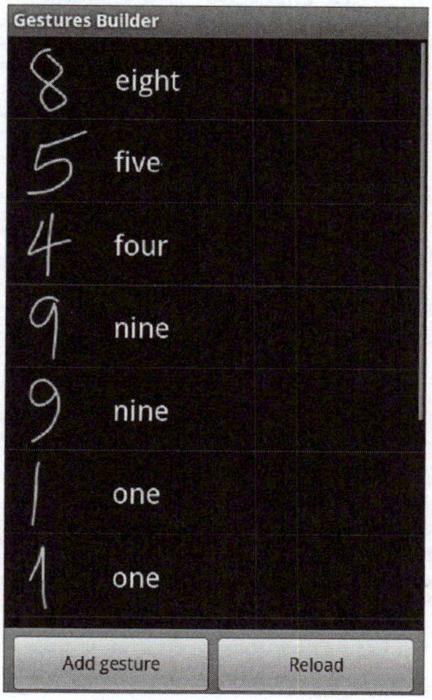

Figure 6.7   The Gesture Builder application, which comes with the Android SDK, can be used to create a gesture library

For illustration, this recipe compiles all the predictions in a String and displays them on the screen. An example output is shown in Figure 6.8. This shows that even though a visual match is not complete, the partial number can match a library number well.

Figure 6.8   The gesture recognition example that shows prediction scores

Listing 6.19   **src/com/cookbook/gestures/Gestures.java**

```java
package com.cookbook.gestures;

import java.text.DecimalFormat;
import java.text.NumberFormat;
import java.util.ArrayList;

import android.app.Activity;
import android.gesture.Gesture;
import android.gesture.GestureLibraries;
import android.gesture.GestureLibrary;
import android.gesture.GestureOverlayView;
import android.gesture.Prediction;
import android.gesture.GestureOverlayView.OnGesturePerformedListener;
import android.os.Bundle;
import android.widget.TextView;

public class Gestures extends Activity
                    implements OnGesturePerformedListener {
    private GestureLibrary mLibrary;
    private TextView tv;

    @Override
    public void onCreate(Bundle savedInstanceState) {
        super.onCreate(savedInstanceState);
        setContentView(R.layout.main);
        tv = (TextView) findViewById(R.id.prediction);
```

```
        mLibrary = GestureLibraries.fromRawResource(this, R.raw.numbers);
        if (!mLibrary.load()) finish();

        GestureOverlayView gestures =
                        (GestureOverlayView) findViewById(R.id.gestures);
        gestures.addOnGesturePerformedListener(this);
    }

    public void onGesturePerformed(GestureOverlayView overlay,
                                   Gesture gesture) {
        ArrayList<Prediction> predictions = mLibrary.recognize(gesture);
        String predList = "";
        NumberFormat formatter = new DecimalFormat("#0.00");
        for(int i=0; i<predictions.size(); i++) {
            Prediction prediction = predictions.get(i);
            predList = predList + prediction.name + " "
                        + formatter.format(prediction.score) + "\n";
        }
        tv.setText(predList);
    }
}
```

Recipe: Drawing 3D Images

Android supports the Open Graphics Library for Embedded Systems (OpenGL ES).
This recipe, based on an Android API demo, shows how to create a three-dimensional
pyramid shape using this library and have it bounce around the screen and spin as it is
deflected off the edges. The main activity requires two separate support classes: one
to define the shape shown in Listing 6.20 and one to render the shape shown in Listing 6.21.

Listing 6.20   src/com/cookbook/open_gl/Pyramid.java

```
package com.cookbook.open_gl;

import java.nio.ByteBuffer;
import java.nio.ByteOrder;
import java.nio.IntBuffer;

import javax.microedition.khronos.opengles.GL10;

class Pyramid {
    public Pyramid() {
        int one = 0x10000;
        /* square base and point top to make a pyramid */
        int vertices[] = {
                -one, -one, -one,
                -one,  one, -one,
                one,   one,  -one,
                one,  -one,  -one,
                0, 0, one
        };
```

```
        /* purple fading to white at the top */
        int colors[] = {
                one,  0,  one,  one,
                one,  0,  one,  one,
                one,  0,  one,  one,
                one,  0,  one,  one,
                one,  one,  one,  one
        };

        /* triangles of the vertices above to build the shape */
        byte indices[] = {
                0, 1, 2,   0, 2, 3, //square base
                0, 3, 4, // side 1
                0, 4, 1, // side 2
                1, 4, 2, // side 3
                2, 4, 3  // side 4
        };

        // buffers to be passed to gl*Pointer() functions
        ByteBuffer vbb = ByteBuffer.allocateDirect(vertices.length*4);
        vbb.order(ByteOrder.nativeOrder());
        mVertexBuffer = vbb.asIntBuffer();
        mVertexBuffer.put(vertices);
        mVertexBuffer.position(0);

        ByteBuffer cbb = ByteBuffer.allocateDirect(colors.length*4);
        cbb.order(ByteOrder.nativeOrder());
        mColorBuffer = cbb.asIntBuffer();
        mColorBuffer.put(colors);
        mColorBuffer.position(0);

        mIndexBuffer = ByteBuffer.allocateDirect(indices.length);
        mIndexBuffer.put(indices);
        mIndexBuffer.position(0);
    }

    public void draw(GL10 gl) {
        gl.glFrontFace(GL10.GL_CW);
        gl.glVertexPointer(3, GL10.GL_FIXED, 0, mVertexBuffer);
        gl.glColorPointer(4, GL10.GL_FIXED, 0, mColorBuffer);
        gl.glDrawElements(GL10.GL_TRIANGLES, 18, GL10.GL_UNSIGNED_BYTE,
                          mIndexBuffer);
    }

    private IntBuffer    mVertexBuffer;
    private IntBuffer    mColorBuffer;
    private ByteBuffer   mIndexBuffer;
}
```

Note that the pyramid has five vertices: four in a square base and one as the raised pointy top. It is important that the vertices be in an order that can be traversed by a line across the figure (not just randomly listed). The center of the shape is at the origin (0, 0, 0).

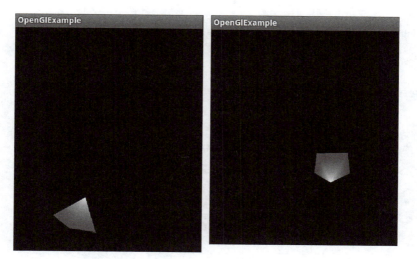

Figure 6.9   The rotating, bouncing pyramid created with OpenGL ES

The five colors in RGBA form correspond to the vertices; the base vertices are defined as purple and the top vertex as white. The library gradates the colors to fill in the shape. Different colors or shading help provide a three-dimensional look.

The main `draw()` method is defined for triangle elements. The square base can be made of two triangles, and each upper side is a triangle, which leads to six total triangles or 18 indices. The pyramid is shown in two different perspectives as it bounces around in Figure 6.9.

Then, a separate class can be created to extend `GLSurfaceView.Renderer` to render this pyramid using the OpenGL ES library, as shown in Listing 6.21. Three methods need to be implemented:

- `onSurfaceCreated()`—One-time initialization of the OpenGL framework
- `onSurfaceChanged()`—Sets the projection at start-up or when the viewport is resized
- `onDrawFrame()`—Draws the graphic image every frame

Listing 6.21   src/com/cookbook/open_gl/PyramidRenderer.java

```
package com.cookbook.open_gl;

import javax.microedition.khronos.egl.EGLConfig;
import javax.microedition.khronos.opengles.GL10;

import android.opengl.GLSurfaceView;

/**
 * Render a tumbling pyramid
 */
```

```
class PyramidRenderer implements GLSurfaceView.Renderer {
    public PyramidRenderer(boolean useTranslucentBackground) {
        mTranslucentBackground = useTranslucentBackground;
        mPyramid = new Pyramid();
    }

    public void onDrawFrame(GL10 gl) {
        /* Clear the screen */
        gl.glClear(GL10.GL_COLOR_BUFFER_BIT | GL10.GL_DEPTH_BUFFER_BIT);

        /* Draw a pyramid rotating */
        gl.glMatrixMode(GL10.GL_MODELVIEW);
        gl.glLoadIdentity();
        gl.glTranslatef(mCenter[0], mCenter[1], mCenter[2]);
        gl.glRotatef(mAngle,        0, 1, 0);
        gl.glRotatef(mAngle*0.25f,  1, 0, 0);

        gl.glEnableClientState(GL10.GL_VERTEX_ARRAY);
        gl.glEnableClientState(GL10.GL_COLOR_ARRAY);
        mPyramid.draw(gl);

        mAngle += mAngleDelta;

        /* Draw it bouncing off the walls */
        mCenter[0] += mVel[0];
        mCenter[1] += mVel[1];

        if(Math.abs(mCenter[0])>4.0f) {
            mVel[0] = -mVel[0];
            mAngleDelta=(float) (5*(0.5-Math.random()));
        }
        if(Math.abs(mCenter[1])>6.0f) {
            mVel[1] = -mVel[1];
            mAngleDelta=(float) (5*(0.5-Math.random()));
        }
    }

    public void onSurfaceChanged(GL10 gl, int width, int height) {
        gl.glViewport(0, 0, width, height);

        /* Set a new projection when the viewport is resized */
        float ratio = (float) width / height;
        gl.glMatrixMode(GL10.GL_PROJECTION);
        gl.glLoadIdentity();
        gl.glFrustumf(-ratio, ratio, -1, 1, 1, 20);
    }

    public void onSurfaceCreated(GL10 gl, EGLConfig config) {
        gl.glDisable(GL10.GL_DITHER);

        /* one-time OpenGL initialization */
        gl.glHint(GL10.GL_PERSPECTIVE_CORRECTION_HINT,
                GL10.GL_FASTEST);

        if (mTranslucentBackground) {
            gl.glClearColor(0,0,0,0);
```

```
        } else {
            gl.glClearColor(1,1,1,1);
        }
        gl.glEnable(GL10.GL_CULL_FACE);
        gl.glShadeModel(GL10.GL_SMOOTH);
        gl.glEnable(GL10.GL_DEPTH_TEST);
    }
    private boolean mTranslucentBackground;
    private Pyramid mPyramid;
    private float mAngle, mAngleDelta=0;
    private float mCenter[]={0,0,-10};
    private float mVel[]={0.025f, 0.03535227f, 0f};
}
```

The dynamics of the bouncing pyramid are captured in the `onDrawFrame()` method. The screen is cleared for the new image, and then the pyramid center is set to `mCenter[]`. The screen is defined as the origin, so the starting point of (0, 0, -10) sets the shape back from right up against the screen. At each update, the shape is rotated by `mAngleDelta` and translated by `mVel[]`. The `mVel`s in the x and y directions are set differently enough to provide a nice diversity of bouncing around the walls. When the shape reaches the edge of the screen, the velocity sign is switched to have it bounce back.

Finally, the main activity must set the content view to the OpenGL ES object, as shown in Listing 6.22. The shape movement can be paused and resumed along with the activity.

Listing 6.22   src/com/cookbook/open_gl/OpenGlExample.java

```java
package com.cookbook.open_gl;

import android.app.Activity;
import android.opengl.GLSurfaceView;
import android.os.Bundle;
/* wrapper activity demonstrating the use of GLSurfaceView, a view
 * that uses OpenGL drawing into a dedicated surface */
public class OpenGlExample extends Activity {
    @Override
    protected void onCreate(Bundle savedInstanceState) {
        super.onCreate(savedInstanceState);

        // Set our Preview view as the activity content
        mGLSurfaceView = new GLSurfaceView(this);
        mGLSurfaceView.setRenderer(new PyramidRenderer(true));
        setContentView(mGLSurfaceView);
    }

    @Override
    protected void onResume() {
        super.onResume();
        mGLSurfaceView.onResume();
    }
```

```
@Override
protected void onPause() {
    super.onPause();
    mGLSurfaceView.onPause();
}

private GLSurfaceView mGLSurfaceView;
}
```

7

Advanced User Interface Techniques

The landscape of Android-powered devices has changed drastically in the last few years. Where phones powered by Android once dominated, the advent of high-resolution small screens, watches, tablets, and even TV screens (through the use of Google TV) have taken applications and their layouts to new heights. This chapter describes creating a custom view, animation, accessing the accessibility features, using gestures, and drawing 3D images. It then discusses tablets and how to display multiple fragments, using an activity wrapper, and using dialog fragments.

Android Custom View

As discussed in Chapter 5, "User Interface Layout," Android has two types of views: `View` objects and `ViewGroup` objects. A custom view can be created by either starting from scratch or inheriting an existing view structure. Some standard widgets are defined by the Android Framework under the `View` and `ViewGroup` classes, and if possible, the customization should start with one of these:

- Views—`Button`, `EditText`, `TextView`, `ImageView`, and so on
- ViewGroups—`LinearLayout`, `ListView`, `RelativeLayout`, `RadioGroup`, and so on

Recipe: Customizing a Button

This recipe customizes a button using a class called `MyButton`. It extends the `Button` widget so that the component inherits most of the `Button` features. To customize a widget, the most important methods are `onMeasure()` and `onDraw()`.

The `onMeasure()` method determines the size requirements for a widget. It takes two parameters: the width and height measure specifications. Customized widgets should calculate the width and height based on the contents inside the widget and then call setMeasuredDimension() with these values. If this is not done, an illegalStateException is thrown by measure().

The onDraw() method allows customized drawing on the widget. Drawing is handled by walking down the tree and rendering view by view. All parents are drawn before the children get drawn. If a background drawable is set for a view, the view draws that before calling back to its onDraw() method.

Inside the MyButton class, eight member methods and two constructors are implemented. The member functions are:

- setText()—Sets the text that is drawn on the button
- setTextSize()—Sets the text size
- setTextColor()—Sets the text color
- measureWidth()—Measures the width of the Button widget
- measureHeight()—Measures the height of the Button widget
- drawArcs()—Draws arcs
- onDraw()—Draws the graphics on the Button widget
- onMeasure()—Measures and sets the boundary of the Button widget

The methods setText(), setTextSize(), and setTextColor() change the text attributes. Every time the text is changed, the invalidate() method needs to be called to force the view to redraw the button widget and reflect the change. The method requestLayout() is called in the setText() and setTextSize() methods but not in the setTextColor() method. This is because the layout is needed only when the boundary of the widget changes, which is not the case with text color changes.

Inside onMeasure(), the setMeasuredDimension() method is called with measureWidth() and measureHeight(). It is an important step for customizing the View.

The methods measureWidth() and measureHeight() are called with the size of the parent view and need to return the proper width and height values of the custom view based on the requested mode of measurement. If the EXACTLY mode of measurement is specified, the method needs to return the value given from the parent View. If the AT_MOST mode is specified, the method can return the smaller of the two values—content size and parent view size—to ensure that the content is sized properly. Otherwise, the method calculates the width and height based on the content inside the widget. In this recipe, the content size is based on the text size.

The method drawArcs() is a straightforward function that draws arcs on the button. This is called by onDraw() as the text is drawn. Animation of the arcs also takes place here. Every time the arc is drawn, its length is incremented a little and the gradient is rotated, making a nice animation.

The class for the custom button is shown in Listing 7.1. A constructor method is required, and here, two MyButton() methods are shown depending on arguments. Each initializes the label view with the custom attributes. The android.graphics.* libraries are similar in format to Java for graphics manipulations, such as Matrix and Paint.

Listing 7.1   **src/com/cookbook/advance/MyButton.java**

```java
package com.cookbook.advance.customcomponent;

import android.content.Context;
import android.graphics.Canvas;
import android.graphics.Color;
import android.graphics.Matrix;
import android.graphics.Paint;
import android.graphics.RectF;
import android.graphics.Shader;
import android.graphics.SweepGradient;
import android.util.AttributeSet;
import android.util.Log;
import android.widget.Button;

public class MyButton extends Button {
    private Paint mTextPaint, mPaint;
    private String mText;
    private int mAscent;
    private Shader mShader;
    private Matrix  mMatrix = new Matrix();
    private float mStart;
    private float mSweep;
    private float mRotate;
    private static final float SWEEP_INC = 2;
    private static final float START_INC = 15;

    public MyButton(Context context) {
        super(context);
        initLabelView();
    }

    public MyButton(Context context, AttributeSet attrs) {
        super(context, attrs);
        initLabelView();
    }

    private final void initLabelView() {
        mTextPaint = new Paint();
        mTextPaint.setAntiAlias(true);
        mTextPaint.setTextSize(16);
        mTextPaint.setColor(0xFF000000);
        setPadding(15, 15, 15, 15);
        mPaint = new Paint();
        mPaint.setAntiAlias(true);
        mPaint.setStrokeWidth(4);
        mPaint.setAntiAlias(true);
        mPaint.setStyle(Paint.Style.STROKE);
        mShader = new SweepGradient(this.getMeasuredWidth()/2,
                                    this.getMeasuredHeight()/2,
                          new int[] { Color.GREEN,
                                      Color.RED,
                                      Color.CYAN,Color.DKGRAY },
                          null);
        mPaint.setShader(mShader);
    }
```

```java
public void setText(String text) {
    mText = text;
    requestLayout();
    invalidate();
}

public void setTextSize(int size) {
    mTextPaint.setTextSize(size);
    requestLayout();
    invalidate();
}

public void setTextColor(int color) {
    mTextPaint.setColor(color);
    invalidate();
}

@Override
protected void onMeasure(int widthMeasureSpec, int heightMeasureSpec){
    setMeasuredDimension(measureWidth(widthMeasureSpec),
            measureHeight(heightMeasureSpec));
}

private int measureWidth(int measureSpec) {
    int result = 0;
    int specMode = MeasureSpec.getMode(measureSpec);
    int specSize = MeasureSpec.getSize(measureSpec);

    if (specMode == MeasureSpec.EXACTLY) {
        // We were told how big to be
        result = specSize;
    } else {
        // Measure the text
        result = (int) mTextPaint.measureText(mText)
                + getPaddingLeft()
                + getPaddingRight();
        if (specMode == MeasureSpec.AT_MOST) {
            result = Math.min(result, specSize);
        }
    }

    return result;
}

private int measureHeight(int measureSpec) {
    int result = 0;
    int specMode = MeasureSpec.getMode(measureSpec);
    int specSize = MeasureSpec.getSize(measureSpec);

    mAscent = (int) mTextPaint.ascent();
    if (specMode == MeasureSpec.EXACTLY) {
        // We were told how big to be
        result = specSize;
    } else {
        // Measure the text (beware: ascent is a negative number)
        result = (int) (-mAscent + mTextPaint.descent())
                        + getPaddingTop() + getPaddingBottom();
        if (specMode == MeasureSpec.AT_MOST) {
            Log.v("Measure Height", "At most Height:"+specSize);
            result = Math.min(result, specSize);
```

```
            }
        }
        return result;
    }

    private void drawArcs(Canvas canvas, RectF oval, boolean useCenter,
            Paint paint) {
        canvas.drawArc(oval, mStart, mSweep, useCenter, paint);
    }

    @Override protected void onDraw(Canvas canvas) {
        mMatrix.setRotate(mRotate, this.getMeasuredWidth()/2,
                            this.getMeasuredHeight()/2);
        mShader.setLocalMatrix(mMatrix);
        mRotate += 3;
        if (mRotate >= 360) {
            mRotate = 0;
        }
        RectF drawRect = new RectF();
        drawRect.set(this.getWidth()-mTextPaint.measureText(mText),
                    (this.getHeight()-mTextPaint.getTextSize())/2,
                    mTextPaint.measureText(mText),
        this.getHeight()-(this.getHeight()-mTextPaint.getTextSize())/2);
        drawArcs(canvas, drawRect, false, mPaint);
        mSweep += SWEEP_INC;
        if (mSweep > 360) {
            mSweep -= 360;
            mStart += START_INC;
            if (mStart >= 360) {
                mStart -= 360;
            }
        }
        if(mSweep >180){
            canvas.drawText(mText, getPaddingLeft(),
                            getPaddingTop() -mAscent, mTextPaint);
        }
        invalidate();
    }
}
```

This custom Button widget can then be used in a layout as shown in Listing 7.2.

Listing 7.2   res/layout/main.xml

```xml
<?xml version="1.0" encoding="utf-8"?>
<LinearLayout xmlns:android="http://schemas.android.com/apk/res/android"
    android:orientation="vertical"
    android:layout_width="match_parent"
    android:layout_height="match_parent"
    android:gravity="center_vertical"
    >
<com.cookbook.advance.customComponent.MyButton
    android:layout_width="wrap_content"
    android:layout_height="wrap_content"
    android:id="@+id/mybutton1"
    />
</LinearLayout>
```

Figure 7.1   An example of a custom button

The layout XML has only one ViewGroup (LinearLayout) and one View, called by its definition location com.cookbook.advance.customComponent.myButton. This can be used in an activity, as shown in Listing 7.3.

Listing 7.3   src/com/cookbook/advance/ShowMyButton.java

```
package com.cookbook.advance.customComponent;

import android.app.Activity;
import android.os.Bundle;

public class ShowMyButton extends Activity{

    @Override
    protected void onCreate(Bundle savedInstanceState) {
        super.onCreate(savedInstanceState);

        setContentView(R.layout.main);
        MyButton myb = (MyButton)findViewById(R.id.mybutton1);
        myb.setText("Hello Students");
        myb.setTextSize(40);

    }
}
```

This shows that the custom button is used the same way as a normal Button widget. The resulting custom button is shown in Figure 7.1.

Android Animation

Android provides two types of animation: frame-by-frame and tween. Frame-by-frame animation shows a sequence of pictures in order. It enables developers to define the pictures to display and then show them like a slide show.

Frame-by-frame animation first needs an `animation-list` element in the layout file containing a list of `item` elements specifying an ordered list of the different pictures to display. The `oneshot` attribute specifies whether the animation is played only once or repeatedly. The animation list XML file is shown in Listing 7.4.

Listing 7.4   res/anim/animated.xml

```
<?xml version="1.0" encoding="utf-8"?>
<animation-list xmlns:android="http://schemas.android.com/apk/res/android"
    android:oneshot="false">
    <item android:drawable="@drawable/anddev1" android:duration="200" />
    <item android:drawable="@drawable/anddev2" android:duration="200" />
    <item android:drawable="@drawable/anddev3" android:duration="200" />
</animation-list>
```

To display the frame-by-frame animation, set the animation to a view's background:

```
ImageView im = (ImageView) this.findViewById(R.id.myanimated);
im.setBackgroundResource(R.anim.animated);
AnimationDrawable ad = (AnimationDrawable)im.getBackground();
ad.start();
```

After the view background is set, a drawable can be retrieved by calling `get Background()` and casting it to `AnimationDrawable`. Then, calling the `start()` method starts the animation.

Tween animation uses a different approach that creates an animation by performing a series of transformations on a single image. In Android, it provides access to the following classes that are the basis for all the animations:

- `AlphaAnimation`—Controls transparency changes
- `RotateAnimation`—Controls rotations
- `ScaleAnimation`—Controls growing or shrinking
- `TranslateAnimation`—Controls position changes

These four animation classes can be used for transitions between activities, layouts, views, and so on. All these can be defined in the layout XML file as `<alpha>`, `<rotate>`, and `<scale>`, and `<translate>`. They all have to be contained within an AnimationSet `<set>`:

- `<alpha>` attributes:
    android:fromAlpha, android:toAlpha

The alpha value translates the opacity from 0.0 (transparent) to 1.0 (opaque).

- `<rotate>` attributes:

  `android:fromDegrees, android:toDegrees,`
  `android:pivotX, android:pivotY`

  The rotate specifies the angle to rotate an animation around a center of rotation defined as the pivot.

- `<scale>` attributes:

  `android:fromXScale, android:toXScale,`
  `android:fromYScale, android:toYScale,`
  `android:pivotX, android:pivotY`

  The scale specifies how to change the size of a view in the x axis or y axis. The pivot location that stays fixed under the scaling can also be specified.

- `<translate>` attributes:

  `android:fromXDelta, android:toXDelta,`
  `android:fromYDelta, android:toYDelta`

  The translate specifies the amount of translation to perform on a view.

Recipe: Creating an Animation

This recipe creates a new mail animation that can be used when mail is received. The main layout file is shown in Listing 7.5, and the new mail animation is shown in Figure 7.2.

Listing 7.5   res/layout/main.xml

```xml
<?xml version="1.0" encoding="utf-8"?>
<LinearLayout xmlns:android="http://schemas.android.com/apk/res/android"
    android:orientation="vertical"
    android:layout_width="match_parent"
    android:layout_height="match_parent"
    android:gravity="center"
    >

    <ImageView
    android:id="@+id/myanimated"
    android:layout_width="wrap_content"
    android:layout_height="wrap_content"
        android:src="@drawable/mail"
    />
    <Button
    android:id="@+id/startanimated"
    android:layout_width="wrap_content"
    android:layout_height="wrap_content"
    android:text="you've got mail"
    />
</LinearLayout>
```

To animate this view, an animation set needs to be defined. In Eclipse, right-click the **res/** folder and select **New → Android XML File**. Then, fill in the filename as **animated.xml** and select the file type as **Animation**. Then, the file can be edited to create the content shown in Listing 7.6.

Figure 7.2   Basic layout for the animation

Listing 7.6   res/anim/animated.xml

```
<?xml version="1.0" encoding="utf-8"?>

<set xmlns:android="http://schemas.android.com/apk/res/and-
roid" android:interpolator="@android:anim/accelerate_interpolator">

    <translate android:fromXDelta="100%p" android:toXDelta="0"
android:duration="5000" />
    <alpha android:fromAlpha="0.0" android:toAlpha="1.0" android:duration="3000" />
            <rotate
            android:fromDegrees="0"
            android:toDegrees="-45"
            android:toYScale="0.0"
            android:pivotX="50%"
            android:pivotY="50%"
            android:startOffset="700"
            android:duration="3000" />
```

```
            <scale
               android:fromXScale="0.0"
               android:toXScale="1.4"
               android:fromYScale="0.0"
               android:toYScale="1.0"
               android:pivotX="50%"
               android:pivotY="50%"
               android:startOffset="700"
               android:duration="3000"
               android:fillBefore="false" />
</set>
```

The main activity is shown in Listing 7.7. It is a simple activity that creates an Animation object by using AnimationUtils to load the animationSet defined in the animation. Then, every time the user clicks on the button, it uses the ImageView object to run the animation by calling the startAnimation() method using the Animation object already loaded.

Listing 7.7   **src/com/cookbook/advance/MyAnimation.java**

```
package com.cookbook.advance;

import android.app.Activity;
import android.os.Bundle;
import android.view.View;
import android.view.View.OnClickListener;
import android.view.animation.Animation;
import android.view.animation.AnimationUtils;
import android.widget.Button;
import android.widget.ImageView;

public class MyAnimation extends Activity {
    /** called when the activity is first created */
    @Override
    public void onCreate(Bundle savedInstanceState) {
        super.onCreate(savedInstanceState);
        setContentView(R.layout.main);

        final ImageView im
                    = (ImageView) this.findViewById(R.id.myanimated);
        final Animation an
                    = AnimationUtils.loadAnimation(this, R.anim.animated);

        im.setVisibility(View.INVISIBLE);
        Button bt = (Button) this.findViewById(R.id.startanimated);
        bt.setOnClickListener(new OnClickListener(){
            public void onClick(View view){
                    im.setVisibility(View.VISIBLE);
                    im.startAnimation(an);
            }

        });
    }
}
```

Recipe: Using Property Animations

Starting with Honeycomb (API Level 11), objects such as buttons can also be animated by changing their properties. In this recipe, there are three buttons that when clicked will perform various animations based on property value changes.

Changes to property values can be done either directly in the activity code or loaded in a separate XML file. When choosing an animation style, it is important to remember that coding the animations in the activity allows for greater control over dynamic data, whereas XML files make complex animations easier to implement.

An important note regarding change with animations is that XML files that use `ValueAnimator`, `ObjectAnimator`, and `AnimatorSet` tags should put resources in the **res/animator** folder to distinguish between legacy animation XML files that are stored in the **res/anim** folder.

Listing 7.8 shows the code for an activity that uses both inline animation code and references to an XML file. `OnClickListener` is used to bind each button to a function that animates the button.

`btnShift` uses `ValueAnimator` along with `ObjectAnimator` to set the values that will be applied to the button when clicked.

`btnRotate` has commented-out code that displays a rotation animation using inline code. It also shows how to use an XML file, located in the **res/animator** directory and shown in Listing 7.9, to perform the same animation.

`btnSling` also uses an XML file, shown in Listing 7.10, for animation but contains two animations instead of one. Multiple animations can be included in the XML file and will run simultaneously. The property of `android:startOffset` is used to delay the start of animations. This will "queue" animations to run in order.

Listing 7.8   src/com/cookbook/propertyanimation/MainActivity.java

```
package com.cookbook.propertyanimation;

import android.animation.ArgbEvaluator;
import android.animation.ObjectAnimator;
import android.animation.ValueAnimator;
import android.app.Activity;
import android.graphics.Color;
import android.os.Bundle;
import android.view.View;
import android.view.animation.AnimationUtils;
import android.widget.Button;

public class MainActivity extends Activity {

  Button btnShift;
  Button btnRotate;
  Button btnSling;

  @Override
  protected void onCreate(Bundle savedInstanceState) {
    super.onCreate(savedInstanceState);
```

```
        setContentView(R.layout.activity_main);

        btnShift = (Button)this.findViewById(R.id.button);
        btnRotate = (Button)this.findViewById(R.id.button1);
        btnSling = (Button)this.findViewById(R.id.button2);

        btnShift.setOnClickListener(new Button.OnClickListener() {
            public void onClick(View v) {
                int start = Color.rgb(0xcc, 0xcc, 0xcc);
                    int end = Color.rgb(0x00, 0xff, 0x00);
                ValueAnimator va =
                        ObjectAnimator.ofInt(btnShift, "backgroundColor", start, end);
                va.setDuration(750);
                va.setRepeatCount(1);
                va.setRepeatMode(ValueAnimator.REVERSE);
                va.setEvaluator(new ArgbEvaluator());
                va.start();
            }
        });

        btnRotate.setOnClickListener(new Button.OnClickListener() {
            public void onClick(View v) {
                // Use ValueAnimator
                /*
                ValueAnimator va = ObjectAnimator.ofFloat(btnRotate, "rotation", 0f, 360f);
                va.setDuration(750);
                    va.start();
                */
                // Or use an XML-defined animation
                btnRotate.startAnimation(AnimationUtils.loadAnimation(MainActivity.this,
                        R.animator.rotation));
            }
        });

        btnSling.setOnClickListener(new Button.OnClickListener() {
            public void onClick(View v) {
                btnSling.startAnimation(AnimationUtils.loadAnimation(MainActivity.this,
                        R.animator.sling));
            }
        });
    }
}
```

Listing 7.9   **res/animator/rotation.xml**

```
<?xml version="1.0" encoding="utf-8"?>
<rotate
    xmlns:android="http://schemas.android.com/apk/res/android"
    android:fromDegrees="0"
    android:toDegrees="360"
    android:pivotX="50%"
    android:pivotY="50%"
    android:duration="500" android:fillAfter="true">
</rotate>
```

Listing 7.10   res/animator/sling.xml

```xml
<?xml version="1.0" encoding="utf-8"?>
<set xmlns:android="http://schemas.android.com/apk/res/android">
  <scale
    android:interpolator="@android:anim/accelerate_decelerate_interpolator"
    android:fromXScale="0.0"
    android:toXScale="1.8"
    android:fromYScale="0.0"
    android:toYScale="1.4"
    android:pivotX="50%"
    android:pivotY="50%"
    android:fillAfter="false"
    android:duration="1000" />
  <scale
    android:fromXScale="1.8"
    android:toXScale="0.0"
    android:fromYScale="1.4"
    android:toYScale="0.0"
    android:pivotX="50%"
    android:pivotY="50%"
    android:startOffset="1000"
    android:duration="300"
    android:fillBefore="false" />
</set>
```

Accessibility

Android comes with several accessibility features baked into the platform. TalkBack is a service that is installed on most Android devices. It works by using voice synthesis to read what is displayed on the screen. If a device does not have TalkBack installed, it can be downloaded from Google Play.

TalkBack can be enabled by navigating to the settings section of the device and to the item named "Accessibility." When TalkBack is installed, a toggle for TalkBack can be enabled. When it is turned on, the way a user interacts with the Android device is changed. The entire screen becomes an input surface that allows gestures and swipes to navigate between various applications and screens. An application must first be selected, and then the screen must be double-tapped to open it.

Soft keys such as the Back or Home key must be selected and then double-tapped.

Recipe: Using Accessibility Features

Google recommends the following checklist for creating accessible applications:

- Make sure that the component is described. This can be done with `android:contentDescription` in the layout XML file.
- Make sure that the components used are focusable.
- Take advantage of the accessibility interfaces if using any custom controls.

- Do not use audio only for interaction. Always add a visual cue or even haptic feedback to applications.
- Test applications without looking at the screen using TalkBack.

When adding descriptions to interface components, the editText field uses android:hint instead of android:contentDescription. When the field is empty, the value of android:hint will be read out loud. If the field contains text that has been entered by the user, that will be read out loud in place of the hint. Listing 7.11 shows a layout file with the fields populated.

Listing 7.11   res/layout/activity_main.xml

```xml
<RelativeLayout xmlns:android="http://schemas.android.com/apk/res/android"
    xmlns:tools="http://schemas.android.com/tools"
    android:layout_width="match_parent"
    android:layout_height="match_parent"
    tools:context=".MainActivity" >

    <EditText
        android:id="@+id/edittext1"
        android:layout_width="wrap_content"
        android:layout_height="wrap_content"
        android:layout_alignParentTop="true"
        android:layout_centerHorizontal="true"
        android:ems="10"
        android:hint="Enter some text here"
        android:nextFocusDown="@+id/button1" >

        <requestFocus />
    </EditText>

    <TextView
        android:id="@+id/textview1"
        android:layout_width="wrap_content"
        android:layout_height="wrap_content"
        android:layout_below="@+id/editText1"
        android:layout_centerHorizontal="true"
        android:layout_marginTop="35dp"
        android:contentDescription="Text messages will appear here"
        android:text="This is a TextView" />

    <RadioGroup
        android:id="@+id/radiogroup1"
        android:layout_width="wrap_content"
        android:layout_height="wrap_content"
        android:layout_below="@+id/textView1"
        android:layout_centerHorizontal="true"
        android:layout_marginTop="21dp" >

        <RadioButton
            android:id="@+id/radio0"
            android:layout_width="wrap_content"
            android:layout_height="wrap_content"
            android:checked="true"
```

```
        android:contentDescription="Select for a banana"
        android:text="Banana" />

    <RadioButton
        android:id="@+id/radio1"
        android:layout_width="wrap_content"
        android:layout_height="wrap_content"
        android:contentDescription="Select for a coconut"
        android:text="Coconut" />

    <RadioButton
        android:id="@+id/radio2"
        android:layout_width="wrap_content"
        android:layout_height="wrap_content"
        android:contentDescription="Select for a grape"
        android:text="Grape" />
    </RadioGroup>

</RelativeLayout>
```

Fragments

On large-screen devices, how the application will display information in a pleasing and easy-to-use manner must be considered. Knowing that tablets have a larger physical viewing area than most phones, developers can plan on having their applications display data differently from the way they do on a small-screen device.

Some great examples of this are applications that are already built into both phones and tablet devices such as the Contacts or People application. When one of those applications is opened on a phone, users are treated to a list view that allows them to scroll through their contacts and then tap contacts to open information about them. On a tablet, the list view is smaller and displayed on the left side of the screen; the right side of the screen shows the extended information about the contact.

The Calendar application has a similar function, showing a small and precise amount of data on a phone while showing extended information on the bottom portion of the screen on a tablet.

The ability to display extended data is done through the use of fragments. Fragments are modular portions of an activity that can be used to change the presentation of an application. A fragment acts similarly to an activity, but it has a different lifecycle and way of processing logic. The recipes in this section focus on using fragments to optimize the display of content across devices with various screen sizes.

Recipe: Displaying Multiple Fragments at Once

This recipe includes two fragments to display a list using a `ListFragment` and to display a `TextView` using a fragment. On small-screen devices, the list is best displayed in one window and the text in a separate window. On large-screen devices, both the list and the text can be displayed in the same window.

To start, the XML layout files are defined using two XML files in the **res/layout** folder for small-screen devices, and a layout file in the **res/layout-large** folder for large-screen devices.

Listing 7.12 shows the **activity_main.xml** file. The layout file is rather minimal, as the ListFragment that will be loaded into the FrameLayout will provide most of the layout needed.

Listing 7.12   res/layout/activity_main.xml

```
<?xml version="1.0" encoding="utf-8"?>

<FrameLayout xmlns:android="http://schemas.android.com/apk/res/android"
    android:id="@+id/fragment_container"
    android:layout_width="match_parent"
    android:layout_height="match_parent" />
```

To continue the layout for small-screen devices, another layout that can be used to display text values is needed. Listing 7.13 shows the contents of **text_view.xml**.

Listing 7.13   res/layout/text_view.xml

```
<?xml version="1.0" encoding="utf-8"?>

<TextView xmlns:android="http://schemas.android.com/apk/res/android"
    android:id="@+id/text"
    android:layout_width="match_parent"
    android:layout_height="match_parent"
    android:padding="16dp"
    android:textSize="18sp" />
```

For large-screen devices, a folder named **layout-large** will need to be created inside the **res** directory. Once that folder has been created, another layout XML file is needed. In this instance, another **activity_main.xml** file is added. Listing 7.14 shows the contents of the file that will be used for the large-screen layout.

Listing 7.14   res/layout-large/activity_main.xml

```
<LinearLayout xmlns:android="http://schemas.android.com/apk/res/android"
    android:orientation="horizontal"
    android:layout_width="match_parent"
    android:layout_height="match_parent">

    <fragment android:name="com.cookbook.fragments.ItemFragment"
            android:id="@+id/item_fragment"
            android:layout_weight="1"
            android:layout_width="0dp"
            android:layout_height="match_parent" />
```

```
<fragment android:name="com.cookbook.fragments.TextFragment"
            android:id="@+id/text_fragment"
            android:layout_weight="2"
            android:layout_width="0dp"
            android:layout_height="match_parent" />

</LinearLayout>
```

The fragment elements inside Listing 7.15 reference a class file that holds the logic used for each fragment. The listing shows the contents of a fragment element that references **src/com/cookbook/fragments/ItemFragment.java**. The **ItemFragment.java** file uses getFragmentManager to determine if the device should use the large layout or not. Also note that ItemFragment references Strings.Items, which is an array created in Strings.java that is imported in **TextFragment.java**.

Listing 7.15   **src/com/cookbook/fragments/ItemFragment.java**

```java
package com.cookbook.fragments;

import android.app.Activity;
import android.os.Build;
import android.os.Bundle;
import android.support.v4.app.ListFragment;
import android.view.View;
import android.widget.ArrayAdapter;
import android.widget.ListView;

public class ItemFragment extends ListFragment {
  OnItemSelectedListener mCallback;

    public interface OnItemSelectedListener {
        public void onItemSelected(int position);
    }

    @Override
    public void onCreate(Bundle savedInstanceState) {
        super.onCreate(savedInstanceState);

        // Older than Honeycomb requires a different layout
        int layout = Build.VERSION.SDK_INT >= Build.VERSION_CODES.HONEYCOMB ?
                android.R.layout.simple_list_item_activated_1 :
                android.R.layout.simple_list_item_1;

        setListAdapter(new ArrayAdapter<String>(getActivity(), layout,
            Strings.Items));
    }

    @Override
    public void onStart() {
        super.onStart();
        if (getFragmentManager().findFragmentById(R.id.item_fragment) != null) {
            getListView().setChoiceMode(ListView.CHOICE_MODE_SINGLE);
        }
    }
```

```
    @Override
    public void onAttach(Activity activity) {
        super.onAttach(activity);

        try {
            mCallback = (OnItemSelectedListener) activity;
        } catch (ClassCastException e) {
            throw new ClassCastException(activity.toString()
                + " must implement OnItemSelectedListener");
        }
    }

    @Override
    public void onListItemClick(ListView l, View v, int position, long id) {
        mCallback.onItemSelected(position);
        getListView().setItemChecked(position, true);
    }
}
```

Listing 7.16 shows the contents of the fragment element that references **src/com/
cookbook/fragments/TextFragment.java**.

Listing 7.16   **src/com/cookbook/fragments/TextFragment.java**

```
package com.cookbook.fragments;

import com.cookbook.fragments.Strings;
import com.cookbook.fragments.R;

import android.os.Bundle;
import android.support.v4.app.Fragment;
import android.view.LayoutInflater;
import android.view.View;
import android.view.ViewGroup;
import android.widget.TextView;

public class TextFragment extends Fragment {
    final static String ARG_POSITION = "position";
    int mCurrentPosition = -1;

    @Override
    public View onCreateView(LayoutInflater inflater,
        ViewGroup container, Bundle savedInstanceState) {
        return inflater.inflate(R.layout.text_view, container, false);
    }

    @Override
    public void onStart() {
        super.onStart();

        Bundle args = getArguments();
        if (args != null) {
            updateTextView(args.getInt(ARG_POSITION));
```

```
        } else if (mCurrentPosition != -1) {
            updateTextView(mCurrentPosition);
        } else {
            TextView tv = (TextView) getActivity().findViewById(R.id.text);
            tv.setText("Select an item from the list.");
        }

    }

    public void updateTextView(int position){
        TextView tv = (TextView) getActivity().findViewById(R.id.text);
        tv.setText(Strings.Text[position]);
        mCurrentPosition = position;
    }

    @Override
    public void onSaveInstanceState(Bundle outState) {
        super.onSaveInstanceState(outState);
        outState.putInt(ARG_POSITION, mCurrentPosition);
    }
}
```

Now that the layout has been set up and the fragments have been created, List-ing 7.17 shows the contents of **MainActivity.java**. The fragments are handled by the FragmentManager by means of a FragmentTransaction. The FragmentTransaction keeps track of what fragments are available in the view. Whenever FragmentTransaction is used to add, remove, or replace fragments, the commit() method must be called.

Listing 7.17   src/com/cookbook/fragments/MainActivity.java

```
package com.cookbook.fragments;

import android.os.Bundle;
import android.support.v4.app.FragmentActivity;
import android.support.v4.app.FragmentTransaction;

// When using the support lib, use FragmentActivity
public class MainActivity extends FragmentActivity implements
    ItemFragment.OnItemSelectedListener {

    @Override
    protected void onCreate(Bundle savedInstanceState) {
        super.onCreate(savedInstanceState);
        setContentView(R.layout.activity_main);

        //If using large layout, use the Support Fragment Manager
        if (findViewById(R.id.fragment_container) != null) {
            if(savedInstanceState != null){
                return;
            }
```

```
            ItemFragment firstFragment = new ItemFragment();
            firstFragment.setArguments(getIntent().getExtras());

    getSupportFragmentManager().beginTransaction().add(R.id.fragment_container,
    firstFragment).commit();
        }

    }

    public void onItemSelected(int position) {
        TextFragment textFrag =
            (TextFragment) getSupportFragmentManager()
                .findFragmentById(R.id.text_fragment);

        if (textFrag != null) {
            textFrag.updateTextView(position);
        } else {
            TextFragment newFragment = new TextFragment();
            Bundle args = new Bundle();
            args.putInt(TextFragment.ARG_POSITION, position);
            newFragment.setArguments(args);

            FragmentTransaction transaction =
                getSupportFragmentManager().beginTransaction();
            transaction.replace(R.id.fragment_container, newFragment);
            transaction.addToBackStack(null);
            transaction.commit();
        }
    }
}
```

Recipe: Using Dialog Fragments

In addition to changing the layout of a page, a DialogFragment can be used
to display a dialog window that contains a fragment. A DialogFragment is exactly
what it sounds like: a dialog that is contained inside a fragment. It is recommended to
always build dialogs with DialogFragments; the support library can help with porting
code to previous versions of Android. Listing 7.18 shows how the activity is set up to
use DialogFragment. Note that because it is using a fragment, it must extend
FragmentActivity.

Listing 7.18   src/com/cookbook/dialogfragment/MainActivity.java

```
package com.cookbook.dialogfragment;

import android.os.Bundle;
import android.support.v4.app.FragmentActivity;
import android.view.View;
import android.widget.Button;
import android.widget.Toast;
```

```
public class MainActivity extends FragmentActivity {

    @Override
    public void onCreate(Bundle savedInstanceState) {
        super.onCreate(savedInstanceState);
        setContentView(R.layout.activity_main);

        Button buttonOpenDialog = (Button) findViewById(R.id.opendialog);
        buttonOpenDialog.setOnClickListener(new Button.OnClickListener() {

            @Override
            public void onClick(View arg0) {
                openDialog();
            }
        });

    }

    void openDialog() {
        MyDialogFragment myDialogFragment = MyDialogFragment.newInstance();
        myDialogFragment.show(getSupportFragmentManager(), "myDialogFragment");
    }

    public void protestClicked() {
        Toast.makeText(MainActivity.this, "Your protest has been recorded", Toast.
➡LENGTH_LONG).show();
    }

    public void forgetClicked() {
        Toast.makeText(MainActivity.this,
            "You have chosen to forget", Toast.LENGTH_LONG).show();
    }

}
```

Listing 7.19 shows the logic for DialogFragment. Here, the class MyDialogFragment extends DialogFragment. The onCreateDialog method is overridden, and a new Dialog is built along with some onClick logic.

Listing 7.19   src/com/cookbook/dialogfragment/MyDialogFragment.java

```
package com.cookbook.dialogfragment;

import android.app.AlertDialog;
import android.app.Dialog;
import android.content.DialogInterface;
import android.os.Bundle;
import android.support.v4.app.DialogFragment;

public class MyDialogFragment extends DialogFragment {
    static MyDialogFragment newInstance() {
        MyDialogFragment mdf = new MyDialogFragment();
        Bundle args = new Bundle();
```

```java
        args.putString("title", "Dialog Fragment");
        mdf.setArguments(args);
        return mdf;
    }

    @Override
    public Dialog onCreateDialog(Bundle savedInstanceState) {
        String title = getArguments().getString("title");
        Dialog myDialog = new AlertDialog.Builder(getActivity())
            .setIcon(R.drawable.ic_launcher)
            .setTitle(title)
            .setPositiveButton("Protest", new DialogInterface.OnClickListener() {

                @Override
                public void onClick(DialogInterface dialog, int which) {
                    ((MainActivity) getActivity()).protestClicked();
                }
            })
            .setNegativeButton("Forget", new DialogInterface.OnClickListener() {

                @Override
                public void onClick(DialogInterface dialog, int which) {
                    ((MainActivity) getActivity()).forgetClicked();
                }
            }).create();

        return myDialog;
    }
}
```

8

Multimedia Techniques

The Android platform provides comprehensive multimedia functionality. This chapter introduces techniques to manipulate images, record and play back audio, and record and play back video. Most decoders are supported by Android for reading multimedia, but only a subset of encoders is available for creating multimedia. Basic media framework support in Android 4.1 is summarized in Table 8.1. Vendor-specific versions of Android are known to support more formats than this. This is specifically true for Google TV devices.

An application that records any type of media requires setting the appropriate permission in the **AndroidManifest.xml** file (one or both of the following):

```
<uses-permission android:name="android.permission.RECORD_AUDIO"/>
<uses-permission android:name="android.permission.RECORD_VIDEO"/>
```

Images

Images local to an application are usually put in the **res/drawable/** directory, as discussed in Chapter 5, "User Interface Layout," and are packaged with the application. They can be accessed with the appropriate resource identifier, such as R.drawable .my_picture. Images on the Android device filesystem can be accessed using the normal Java classes, such as an InputStream. However, the preferred method in Android to read an image into memory for manipulation is to use the built-in class BitmapFactory.

BitmapFactory creates bitmap objects from files, streams, or byte arrays. A resource or a file can be loaded like this:

```
Bitmap myBitmap1 = BitmapFactory.decodeResource(getResources(),
                                          R.drawable.my_picture);
Bitmap myBitmap2 = BitmapFactory.decodeFile(filePath);
```

Table 8.1   **Supported Media Types in Android 4.1 for Reading and Writing**

Format/Code	Encoder	Decoder	Details	Supported File Type(s)/ Container Formats
Image				
JPEG	X	X	Base + progressive	JPEG (.jpg)
GIF		X		GIF (.gif)
PNG	X	X		PNG (.png)
BMP		X		BMP (.bmp)
WEBP	X (Android 4.0+)	X (Android 4.0+)		WebP (.webp)
Audio				
AAC LC	X	X	Support for mono/ stereo/5.0/5.1 content with standard sampling rates from 8 to 48kHz	• 3GPP (.3gp) • MPEG-4 (.mp4, .m4a) • ADTS raw AAC (.aac, decode in Android 3.1+, encode in Android 4.0+, ADIF not supported) • MPEG-TS (.ts, not seekable, Android 3.0+)
HE-AACv1 (AAC+)	X (Android 4.1+)	X		
HE-AACv2 (enhanced AAC+)		X	Support for stereo/5.0/5.1 content with standard sampling rates from 8 to 48kHz	
AAC ELD (enhanced low-delay AAC)	X (Android 4.1+)	X (Android 4.1+)	Support for mono/stereo content with standard sampling rates from 16 to 48kHz	
AMR-NB	X	X	4.75–12.2kbps sampled @ 8kHz	3GPP (.3gp)
AMR-WB	X	X	9 rates from 6.60kbit/s to 23.85kbit/s sampled @ 16kHz	3GPP (.3gp)

(continues)

Table 8.1   (*Continued*)

Format/Code	Encoder	Decoder	Details	Supported File Type(s)/ Container Formats
FLAC		X (Android 3.1+)	• Mono/stereo (no multichannel) • Sample rates up to 48kHz (but up to 44.1kHz is recommended on devices with 44.1kHz output, as the 48–44.1kHz downsampler does not include a low-pass filter) • 16-bit recommended • No dither applied for 24-bit	FLAC (.flac) only
MP3		X	Mono/stereo 8–320Kbps constant (CBR) or variable bit-rate (VBR)	MP3 (.mp3)
MIDI		X	• MIDI Type 0 and 1 • DLS Version 1 and 2 • XMF and Mobile XMF • Support for ringtone formats RTTTL/RTX, OTA, and iMelody	• Type 0 and 1 (.mid, .xmf, .mxmf) • RTTTL/RTX (.rtttl, .rtx) • OTA (.ota) • iMelody (.imy)
Vorbis		X		• Ogg (.ogg) • Matroska (.mkv, Android 4.0+)
PCM/WAVE	X (Android 4.1+)	X	• 8- and 16-bit linear PCM (rates up to limit of hardware) • Sampling rates for raw PCM recordings at 8000, 16,000, and 44,100Hz	WAVE (.wav)
Video				
H.263	X	X		• 3GPP (.3gp) • MPEG-4 (.mp4)
H.264 AVC	X (Android 3.0+)	X	Baseline Profile (BP)	• 3GPP (.3gp) • MPEG-4 (.mp4) • MPEG-TS (.ts, AAC audio only, not seekable, Android 3.0+)
MPEG-4 SP		X		3GPP (.3gp)
VP8		X (Android 2.3.3+)	Streamable only in Android 4.0 and above	• WebM (.webm) • Matroska (.mkv, Android 4.0+)

After the image is in memory, it can be manipulated using the bitmap methods, such as `getPixel()` and `setPixel()`. However, most images are too large to manipulate full scale on an embedded device. Instead, consider subsampling the image:

```
Bitmap bm = Bitmap.createScaledBitmap(myBitmap2, 480, 320, false);
```

This helps to avoid `OutOfMemory` run-time errors. The following recipe shows an optimized method for loading large images.

Recipe: Loading and Displaying an Image for Manipulation

This recipe shows an example of an image cut into four pieces and scrambled before being displayed to the screen. It also shows how to create a selectable list of images.

When a picture is taken on a device, it is put in the **DCIM/Camera/** directory, which is used as an example image directory in this recipe. The image directory is passed to the `ListFiles` activity, which lists all files and returns the one chosen by the user. The `ListFiles` activity is shown in Listing 8.1.

Listing 8.1   ListFiles.java

```java
public class ListFiles extends ListActivity {
    private List<String> directoryEntries = new ArrayList<String>();

    @Override
    public void onCreate(Bundle savedInstanceState) {
        super.onCreate(savedInstanceState);
        Intent i = getIntent();
        File directory = new File(i.getStringExtra("directory"));

        if (directory.isDirectory()){
            File[] files = directory.listFiles();

            //Sort in descending date order
            Arrays.sort(files, new Comparator<File>(){
                public int compare(File f1, File f2) {
                    returnLong.valueOf(
                        f1.lastModified()).compareTo(f2.lastModified()
                    );
                }
            });

            //Fill list with files
            this.directoryEntries.clear();
            for (File file : files){
                this.directoryEntries.add(file.getPath());
            }

            ArrayAdapter<String> directoryList = new ArrayAdapter<String>(
                    this,
                    R.layout.file_row, this.directoryEntries);

            //Alphabetize entries
```

```
            //directoryList.sort(null);
            this.setListAdapter(directoryList);
        }
    }

    @Override
    protected void onListItemClick(ListView l, View v,
                                    int position, long id) {
        File clickedFile = new File(this.directoryEntries.get(position));
        Intent i = getIntent();
        i.putExtra("clickedFile", clickedFile.toString());
        setResult(RESULT_OK, i);
        finish();
    }
}
```

A `File` object is created based on the directory string passed to the activity. If it is a directory, the files are sorted in reverse chronological order by specifying a new `compare()` method based on the `lastModified()` flag of the files.

If instead an alphabetical list is desired, the `sort()` method can be used. (This is in the `ListFiles` activity, too, but commented out.) The list is then built and displayed on the screen using a separate layout file `R.layout.file_row`, which is shown in Listing 8.2.

Listing 8.2   res/layout/file_row.xml

```
<?xml version="1.0" encoding="utf-8"?>
<TextView
    xmlns:android="http://schemas.android.com/apk/res/android"
    android:layout_width="match_parent"
    android:layout_height="wrap_content"
    android:textSize="20sp"
    android:padding="3pt"
/>
```

`ListFiles` returns the path of the selected file to the calling activity, which can read this from the bundle in its `onActivityResult(. .)` method.

The chosen picture is then loaded into memory for manipulation. If the file is too large, it can be subsampled as it is loaded to save memory; just replace the single bolded statement in `onActivityResult` of Listing 8.3 with the following:

```
BitmapFactory.Options options = new BitmapFactory.Options();
options.inSampleSize = 4;
Bitmap imageToChange = BitmapFactory.decodeFile(tmp, options);
```

An `inSampleSize` of four creates an image 1/16 the size of the original (four times smaller in each of the pixel dimensions). The limit can be adaptive based on the original image size.

Another method to save memory is to resize the bitmap in memory before manipulations. This is done using the `createScaledBitmap()` method, as shown in this recipe. Listing 8.3 shows the main activity.

Listing 8.3   ImageManipulation.java

```java
package cc.dividebyzero.android.cookbook.chapter8.image;

import cc.dividebyzero.android.cookbook.chapter8.ListFiles;
import cc.dividebyzero.android.cookbook.chapter8.R;
import cc.dividebyzero.android.cookbook.chapter8.R.id;
import cc.dividebyzero.android.cookbook.chapter8.R.layout;
import android.app.Activity;
import android.content.Intent;
import android.graphics.Bitmap;
import android.graphics.BitmapFactory;
import android.os.Bundle;
import android.os.Environment;
import android.widget.ImageView;

public class ImageManipulation extends Activity {
    static final String CAMERA_PIC_DIR = "/DCIM/Camera/";
    ImageView iv;

    @Override
    public void onCreate(Bundle savedInstanceState) {
        super.onCreate(savedInstanceState);
        setContentView(R.layout.image_manipulation);
        iv = (ImageView) findViewById(R.id.my_image);

        String imageDir =
            Environment.getExternalStorageDirectory().getAbsolutePath()
            + CAMERA_PIC_DIR;

        Intent i = new Intent(this, ListFiles.class);
        i.putExtra("directory", imageDir);
        startActivityForResult(i,0);
    }

    @Override
    protected void onActivityResult(int requestCode,
            int resultCode, Intent data) {
        super.onActivityResult(requestCode, resultCode, data);
        if(requestCode == 0 && resultCode==RESULT_OK) {
            String tmp = data.getExtras().getString("clickedFile");
            Bitmap imageToChange= BitmapFactory.decodeFile(tmp);
            process_image(imageToChange);
        }

    }

    void process_image(Bitmap image) {
        Bitmap bm = Bitmap.createScaledBitmap(image, 480, 320, false);
        int width = bm.getWidth();
        int height = bm.getHeight();
```

```
        int x = width>>1;
        int y = height>>1;
        int[] pixels1 = new int[(width*height)];
        int[] pixels2 = new int[(width*height)];
        int[] pixels3 = new int[(width*height)];
        int[] pixels4 = new int[(width*height)];
        bm.getPixels(pixels1, 0, width, 0, 0, width>>1, height>>1);
        bm.getPixels(pixels2, 0, width, x, 0, width>>1, height>>1);
        bm.getPixels(pixels3, 0, width, 0, y, width>>1, height>>1);
        bm.getPixels(pixels4, 0, width, x, y, width>>1, height>>1);
        if(bm.isMutable()) {
            bm.setPixels(pixels2, 0, width, 0, 0, width>>1, height>>1);
            bm.setPixels(pixels4, 0, width, x, 0, width>>1, height>>1);
            bm.setPixels(pixels1, 0, width, 0, y, width>>1, height>>1);
            bm.setPixels(pixels3, 0, width, x, y, width>>1, height>>1);
        }
        iv.setImageBitmap(bm);
    }
}
```

The associated main layout is shown in Listing 8.4.

Listing 8.4   image_manipulation.xml

```xml
<?xml version="1.0" encoding="utf-8"?>
<LinearLayout
    xmlns:android="http://schemas.android.com/apk/res/android"
    android:orientation="vertical"
    android:layout_width="match_parent"
    android:layout_height="match_parent">
    <TextView android:layout_width="match_parent"
        android:layout_height="wrap_content"
        android:textSize="30sp"
        android:text="Scrambled Picture" />
    <ImageView android:id="@+id/my_image"
        android:layout_width="wrap_content"
        android:layout_height="wrap_content" />
</LinearLayout>
```

The **AndroidManifest.xml** file must declare both the activities, as shown in Listing 8.5. An example of the output is shown in Figure 8.1.

Listing 8.5   AndroidManifest.xml

```xml
<manifest xmlns:android="http://schemas.android.com/apk/res/android"
    package="cc.dividebyzero.android.cookbook.chapter8"
    android:versionCode="1"
    android:versionName="1.0">
    <uses-sdk android:minSdkVersion="8" android:targetSdkVersion="15" />
    <application android:label="@string/app_name"
        android:icon="@drawable/ic_launcher"
        android:theme="@style/AppTheme">
```

```
        <activity android:name=".Chapter8">
            <intent-filter >
              <action android:name="android.intent.action.MAIN" />
              <category android:name="android.intent.category.LAUNCHER" />
            </intent-filter>
        </activity>
        <activity android:name=".ListFiles">
            <intent-filter >
              <action android:name="android.intent.action.PICK" />
              <category android:name="android.intent.category.DEFAULT" />
            </intent-filter>
        </activity>
        <activity android:name=".audio.AudioPlayback"/>
        <activity android:name=".audio.AudioRecording"/>
        <activity android:name=".audio.AudioSoundPool"/>

        <activity android:name=".video.VideoViewActivity"/>
        <activity android:name=".video.VideoPlayback"/>
        <activity android:name=".image.ImageManipulation"/>
    </application>
</manifest>
```

Audio

There are two distinct frameworks for recording and playing audio. The choice of which to use depends on the application:

- `MediaPlayer/MediaRecorder`—This is the standard method to manipulate audio but the data must be file- or stream-based. It creates its own thread for processing. `SoundPool` uses this framework.

- `AudioTrack/AudioRecorder`—This method provides direct access to raw audio and is useful for manipulating audio in memory, writing to the buffer while

Figure 8.1   Scrambled image

already playing, or any other usage that does not require a file or stream. It does not create its own thread for processing.

These methods are used in the following recipes.

Recipe: Choosing and Playing Back Audio Files

The `MediaRecorder` and `MediaPlayer` classes are used to record and play back either audio or video. This recipe focuses on audio, and the usage is straightforward. For playback, the steps are as follows:

1. Create an instance of the `MediaPlayer`:

```
MediaPlayer m_mediaPlayer = new MediaPlayer();
```

2. Specify the source of media. It can be created from a raw resource:

```
m_mediaPlayer = MediaPlayer.create(this, R.raw.my_music);
```

Another option is to select a file from the filesystem (which then also needs a prepare statement):

```
m_mediaPlayer.setDataSource(path);
m_mediaPlayer.prepare();
```

In any case, these statements need to be surrounded by a try-catch block because the specified resource might not exist.

3. Start playback of the audio:

```
m_mediaPlayer.start();
```

4. When the playback is done, stop the `MediaPlayer` and release the instance to free up resources:

```
m_mediaPlayer.stop();
m_mediaPlayer.release();
```

This recipe uses the same `ListFiles` activity shown in Listings 8.1 and 8.2 to create a selectable list of audio files for playback. It is assumed that audio files are in the **/sdcard/music/** directory of the Android device, but this is configurable.

When the `ListFiles` activity returns a file, it is initialized as the `MediaPlayer` media source, and the method `startMP()` is called. This starts the `MediaPlayer` and sets the button text to show "Pause." Similarly, the `pauseMP()` method pauses the `MediaPlayer` and sets the button text to show "Play." At any time, the user can click the button to pause or continue the playback of the music.

In general, the `MediaPlayer` creates its own background thread and does not pause when the main activity pauses. This is reasonable behavior for a music player, but in general, the developer might want control over this. Therefore, for illustration purposes, in this recipe the music playback is paused and resumed along with the main activity by overriding the `onPause()` and `onResume()` methods. This is shown in Listing 8.6.

Listing 8.6   **AudioPlayback.java**

```java
package cc.dividebyzero.android.cookbook.chapter8.audio;

import cc.dividebyzero.android.cookbook.chapter8.ListFiles;
import cc.dividebyzero.android.cookbook.chapter8.R;
import cc.dividebyzero.android.cookbook.chapter8.R.id;
import cc.dividebyzero.android.cookbook.chapter8.R.layout;
import android.app.Activity;
import android.content.Intent;
import android.media.MediaPlayer;
import android.os.Bundle;
import android.os.Environment;
import android.view.View;
import android.widget.Button;

public class AudioPlayback extends Activity {
    static final String MUSIC_DIR = "/music/";
    Button playPauseButton;

    private MediaPlayer m_mediaPlayer;

    @Override
    protected void onCreate(Bundle savedInstanceState) {
        super.onCreate(savedInstanceState);

        setContentView(R.layout.audio_playback);
        playPauseButton = (Button) findViewById(R.id.play_pause);

        m_mediaPlayer= new MediaPlayer();

        String musicDir = Environment.getExternalStorageDirectory()
        .getAbsolutePath() + MUSIC_DIR;

        //Show a list of music files to choose
        Intent i = new Intent(this, ListFiles.class);
        i.putExtra("directory", musicDir);
        startActivityForResult(i,0);

        playPauseButton.setOnClickListener(new View.OnClickListener() {
            public void onClick(View view) {
                if(m_mediaPlayer.isPlaying()) {
                    //Stop and give option to start again
                    pauseMP();
                } else {
                    startMP();
                }
            }
        });
    }

    @Override
    protected void onActivityResult(int requestCode, int resultCode,
                                    Intent data) {
        super.onActivityResult(requestCode, resultCode, data);
        if(requestCode == 0 && resultCode==RESULT_OK) {
            String tmp = data.getExtras().getString("clickedFile");
```

```
            try {
                m_mediaPlayer.setDataSource(tmp);
                m_mediaPlayer.prepare();
            } catch (Exception e) {
                e.printStackTrace();
            }
            startMP();
        }
    }

    void pauseMP() {
        playPauseButton.setText("Play");
        m_mediaPlayer.pause();
    }

    void startMP() {
        m_mediaPlayer.start();
        playPauseButton.setText("Pause");
    }

    boolean needToResume = false;
    @Override
    protected void onPause() {
        if(m_mediaPlayer != null && m_mediaPlayer.isPlaying()) {
            needToResume = true;
            pauseMP();
        }
        super.onPause();
    }

    @Override
    protected void onResume() {
        super.onResume();
        if(needToResume && m_mediaPlayer != null) {
            startMP();
        }
    }
}
```

The associated main XML layout with the Play/Pause button is shown in Listing 8.7.

Listing 8.7   res/layout/audio_playback.xml

```xml
<?xml version="1.0" encoding="utf-8"?>
<LinearLayout
    xmlns:android="http://schemas.android.com/apk/res/android"
    android:orientation="vertical"
    android:layout_width="match_parent"
    android:layout_height="match_parent">
    <Button android:id="@+id/play_pause"
        android:text="Play"
        android:textSize="20sp"
        android:layout_width="wrap_content"
        android:layout_height="wrap_content" />
</LinearLayout>
```

Recipe: Recording Audio Files

Recording audio using `MediaRecorder` is similar to playback from the previous recipe, except a few more things need to be specified (`DEFAULT` can also be used and is the same as the first choice in these lists):

- `MediaRecorder.AudioSource`:
  - `MIC`—Built-in microphone
  - `VOICE_UPLINK`—Transmitted audio during voice call
  - `VOICE_DOWNLINK`—Received audio during voice call
  - `VOICE_CALL`—Both uplink and downlink audio during voice call
  - `CAMCORDER`—Microphone associated with camera if available
  - `VOICE_RECOGNITION`—Microphone tuned for voice recognition if available
- `MediaRecorder.OutputFormat`:
  - `THREE_GPP`—3GPP media file format
  - `MPEG_4`—MPEG4 media file format
  - `AMR_NB`—Adaptive multirate narrowband file format
- `MediaRecorder.AudioEncoder`:
  - `AMR_NB`—Adaptive multirate narrowband vocoder

The steps to record audio are as follows:

1. Create an instance of the `MediaRecorder`:

   ```
   MediaRecorder m_Recorder = new MediaRecorder();
   ```

2. Specify the source of media, for example, the microphone:

   ```
   m_Recorder.setAudioSource(MediaRecorder.AudioSource.MIC);
   ```

3. Set the output file format and encoding, such as:

   ```
   m_Recorder.setOutputFormat(MediaRecorder.OutputFormat.THREE_GPP);
   m_Recorder.setAudioEncoder(MediaRecorder.AudioEncoder.AMR_NB);
   ```

4. Set the path for the file to be saved:

   ```
   m_Recorder.setOutputFile(path);
   ```

5. Prepare and start the recording:

   ```
   m_Recorder.prepare();
   m_Recorder.start();
   ```

These steps for audio recording can be used just as they were in the previous recipe for playback.

Recipe: Manipulating Raw Audio

The `MediaRecorder`/`MediaPlayer` framework is useful for most audio uses, but to manipulate raw audio straight from the microphone, process it without saving to a file, and/or play back raw audio, use `AudioRecord`/`AudioTrack` instead. First, set the permission in the **AndroidManifest.xml** file:

```
<uses-permission android:name="android.permission.RECORD_AUDIO" />
```

Then, the steps to record are the following:

1. Create an `AudioRecord` instance, specifying the following to the constructor:

   - Audio source—Use one of the `MediaRecorder.AudioSource` choices described in the previous recipe; for example, use `MediaRecorder.AudioSource.MIC`.

   - Sampling frequency in hertz—Use `44100` for CD-quality audio or half-rates such as `22050` or `11025` (which are sufficient for voice and are the only sampling frequencies guaranteed to be supported).

   - Channel configuration—Use `AudioFormat.CHANNEL_IN_STEREO` to record stereo sound and `CHANNEL_IN_MONO` to record mono sound.

   - Audio encoding—Use either `AudioFormat.ENCODING_PCM_8BIT` for 8-bit quantization or `AudioFormat.ENCODING_PCM_16BIT` for 16-bit.

   - Buffer size in bytes—This is the total size of allotted memory in static mode or the size of chunks used in streaming mode. This must be at least `getMinBufferSize()` bytes.

2. Start recording from the `AudioRecord` instance.

3. Read audio data to memory `audioData[]` using one of the following methods:

   ```
   read(short[] audioData, int offsetInShorts, int sizeInShorts)
   read(byte[] audioData, int offsetInBytes, int sizeInBytes)
   read(ByteBuffer audioData, int sizeInBytes)
   ```

4. Stop recording.

For example, the following is suitable to record voice from the built-in microphone to a memory buffer `myRecordedAudio`, which can be declared a `short[]` (for instance, 16 bits each sample). Using a `short[]` has the advantage of not having to worry about byte ordering when reassembling the byte values into a short. Note that 11,025 samples per second and a buffer size of 10,000 samples means this recording is a little less than a second long:

```
short[] myRecordedAudio = new short[10000];
AudioRecord audioRecord = new AudioRecord(
         MediaRecorder.AudioSource.MIC, 11025,
         AudioFormat.CHANNEL_IN_MONO,
         AudioFormat.ENCODING_PCM_16BIT, 10000);
```

```
audioRecord.startRecording();
audioRecord.read(myRecordedAudio, 0, 10000);
audioRecord.stop();
audioRecord.release();
```

Then, the steps to play back the audio are as follows:

1. Create an `AudioTrack` instance specifying the following to the constructor:

   - Stream type—Use `AudioManager.STREAM_MUSIC` for capturing from the microphone or playback to the speaker. Other choices are `STREAM_VOICE_CALL`, `STREAM_SYSTEM`, `STREAM_RING`, and `STREAM_ALARM`.

   - Sampling frequency in hertz—This has the same meaning as during recording.

   - Channel configuration—Use `AudioFormat.CHANNEL_OUT_STEREO` to play back stereo sound. There are many other choices such as `CHANNEL_OUT_MONO` and `CHANNEL_OUT_5POINT1` (for surround sound).

   - Audio encoding—This has the same meaning as for recording.

   - Buffer size in bytes—This is the size of chunks of data to play at a time.

   - Buffer mode—Use `AudioTrack.MODE_STATIC` for short sounds that can fully fit in memory, avoiding transfer overheads. Otherwise, use `AudioTrack.MODE_STREAM` to write data to hardware in buffer chunks.

2. Start playback from the `AudioTrack` instance.

3. Write memory `audioData[]` to hardware using one of the following methods:
   ```
   write(short[] audioData, int offsetInShorts, int sizeInShorts)
   write(byte[] audioData, int offsetInBytes, int sizeInBytes)
   ```

4. Stop playback (optional).

For example, the following is suitable to play back the voice data in the previous record example:

```
AudioTrack audioTrack = new AudioTrack(
          AudioManager.STREAM_MUSIC, 11025,
          AudioFormat.CHANNEL_OUT_MONO,
          AudioFormat.ENCODING_PCM_16BIT, 4096,
          AudioTrack.MODE_STREAM);
audioTrack.play();
audioTrack.write(myRecordedAudio, 0, 10000);
audioTrack.stop();
audioTrack.release();
```

This recipe uses these two options to record audio to memory and play it back. The layout specifies two buttons on the screen: one to record audio and another to play back that recorded audio, as declared in the main layout file shown in Listing 8.8.

Listing 8.8   **audio_recording.xml**

```xml
<?xml version="1.0" encoding="utf-8"?>
<LinearLayout xmlns:android="http://schemas.android.com/apk/res/android"
    android:orientation="vertical"
    android:layout_width="match_parent"
    android:layout_height="match_parent">
    <TextView android:id="@+id/status"
        android:text="Ready" android:textSize="20sp"
        android:layout_width="wrap_content"
        android:layout_height="wrap_content" />
    <Button android:id="@+id/record"
        android:text="Record for 5 seconds"
        android:textSize="20sp" android:layout_width="wrap_content"
        android:layout_height="wrap_content" />
    <Button android:id="@+id/play"
        android:text="Play" android:textSize="20sp"
        android:layout_width="wrap_content"
        android:layout_height="wrap_content" />
</LinearLayout>
```

The main activity shown in Listing 8.9 first creates an `OnClickListener` for these buttons to record or play back the in-memory audio buffer. The `onClick()` callback method creates the appropriate background thread because neither `AudioTrack` nor `AudioRecord` should be run in the UI thread. For illustration, two different methods of creating the thread are shown: The `record_thread()` has a local thread with the UI updated through a `Handler`, and the play thread uses the main activity's `run()` method.

The buffer is kept in memory. For illustration, the recording is kept to 5 seconds.

Listing 8.9   **AudioRecording.java**

```java
package cc.dividebyzero.android.cookbook.chapter8.audio;

import cc.dividebyzero.android.cookbook.chapter8.R;
import cc.dividebyzero.android.cookbook.chapter8.R.id;
import cc.dividebyzero.android.cookbook.chapter8.R.layout;
import android.app.Activity;
import android.media.AudioFormat;
import android.media.AudioManager;
import android.media.AudioRecord;
import android.media.AudioTrack;
import android.media.MediaRecorder;
import android.os.Bundle;
import android.os.Handler;
import android.util.Log;
import android.view.View;
import android.widget.Button;
import android.widget.TextView;

public class AudioRecording extends Activity implements Runnable {
    private TextView statusText;
```

```java
public void onCreate(Bundle savedInstanceState) {
    super.onCreate(savedInstanceState);
    setContentView(R.layout.audio_recording);

    statusText = (TextView) findViewById(R.id.status);

    Button actionButton = (Button) findViewById(R.id.record);
    actionButton.setOnClickListener(new View.OnClickListener() {
        public void onClick(View view) {
            record_thread();
        }
    });

    Button replayButton = (Button) findViewById(R.id.play);
    replayButton.setOnClickListener(new View.OnClickListener() {
        public void onClick(View view) {
            Thread thread = new Thread(AudioRecording.this);
            thread.start();
        }
    });
}

String text_string;
final Handler mHandler = new Handler();
// Create runnable for posting
final Runnable mUpdateResults = new Runnable() {
    public void run() {
        updateResultsInUi(text_string);
    }
};

private void updateResultsInUi(String update_txt) {
    statusText.setText(update_txt);
}

private void record_thread() {
    Thread thread = new Thread(new Runnable() {
        public void run() {
            text_string = "Starting";
            mHandler.post(mUpdateResults);

            record();

            text_string = "Done";
            mHandler.post(mUpdateResults);
        }
    });
    thread.start();
}

private int audioEncoding = AudioFormat.ENCODING_PCM_16BIT;
int frequency = 11025; //hertz
int bufferSize = 50*AudioTrack.getMinBufferSize(
        frequency,
        AudioFormat.CHANNEL_OUT_MONO,
        audioEncoding
        );
// Create new AudioRecord object to record the audio
```

```
public AudioRecord audioRecord = new AudioRecord(
        MediaRecorder.AudioSource.MIC,
        frequency,
        AudioFormat.CHANNEL_IN_MONO,
        audioEncoding,
        bufferSize
        );
// Create new AudioTrack object w/same parameters as AudioRecord obj
public AudioTrack audioTrack = new AudioTrack(
        AudioManager.STREAM_MUSIC,
        frequency,
        AudioFormat.CHANNEL_OUT_MONO,
        audioEncoding,
        4096,
        AudioTrack.MODE_STREAM
        );
short[] buffer = new short[bufferSize];

public void record() {
    try {
        audioRecord.startRecording();
        audioRecord.read(buffer, 0, bufferSize);
        audioRecord.stop();
        audioRecord.release();
    } catch (Throwable t) {
        Log.e("AudioExamplesRaw","Recording Failed");
    }
}

public void run() { //Play audio using runnable activity
    audioTrack.play();
    int i=0;
    while(i<bufferSize) {
        audioTrack.write(buffer, i++, 1);
    }
    return;
}

@Override
protected void onPause() {
    if(audioTrack!=null) {
        if(audioTrack.getPlayState()==AudioTrack.PLAYSTATE_PLAYING) {
            audioTrack.pause();
        }
    }
    super.onPause();
}
}
```

Recipe: Using Sound Resources Efficiently

To keep the smaller memory requirements of compressed audio files but also the benefit of lower-latency playback of raw audio files, the SoundPool class can be used. This uses the MediaPlayer service to decode audio and provides methods to repeat sound buffers and also speed them up or slow them down.

Usage is similar to the other sound methods described in previous recipes: initialize, load a resource, play, and release. However, note that the `SoundPool` launches a background thread, so a `play()` right after a `load()` might not produce sound if the resource does not have time to load. Similarly, a `release()` called right after a `play()` releases the resource before it can be played. Therefore, it is best to tie `Sound-Pool` resources to activity lifecycle events (such as `onCreate` and `onPause`) and tie the playback of `SoundPool` resources to a user-generated event (such as a button press or advancement in a game).

Using the same layout file as in Listing 8.7, the main activity of this recipe is shown in Listing 8.10. A button press triggers the `SoundPool` to repeat a drumbeat eight times (the initial time plus seven repeats). Also, the rate alternates from half-speed to double speed between button presses. Up to ten streams can play at once, which means that ten quick button presses can launch ten drumbeats playing simultaneously.

Listing 8.10   AudioSoundPool.java

```java
package cc.dividebyzero.android.cookbook.chapter8.audio;

import cc.dividebyzero.android.cookbook.chapter8.R;
import cc.dividebyzero.android.cookbook.chapter8.R.id;
import cc.dividebyzero.android.cookbook.chapter8.R.layout;
import cc.dividebyzero.android.cookbook.chapter8.R.raw;
import android.app.Activity;
import android.media.AudioManager;
import android.media.SoundPool;
import android.os.Bundle;
import android.view.View;
import android.widget.Button;

public class AudioSoundPool extends Activity {
    static float rate = 0.5f;
    @Override
    protected void onCreate(Bundle savedInstanceState) {
        super.onCreate(savedInstanceState);

        setContentView(R.layout.audio_soundpool);
        Button playDrumButton = (Button) findViewById(R.id.play_pause);

        final SoundPool mySP = new SoundPool(
                            10,
                            AudioManager.STREAM_MUSIC,
                            0);
        final int soundId = mySP.load(this, R.raw.drum_beat, 1);

        playDrumButton.setOnClickListener(new View.OnClickListener() {
            public void onClick(View view) {
                rate = 1/rate;
                mySP.play(soundId, 1f, 1f, 1, 7, rate);
            }
        });
    }
}
```

Recipe: Adding Media and Updating Paths

After an application creates a newly recorded audio file, that file can be registered with the system as available for use. This is done using the `MediaStore` class. For example, Listing 8.11 shows how to register a saved audio file `myFile` as a possible ringtone, notification, and alarm, but not to be seen by an MP3 player (because `IS_MUSIC` is false).

Listing 8.11   Example of Registering an Audio File to the System

```
//Reload MediaScanner to search for media and update paths
sendBroadcast(new Intent(Intent.ACTION_MEDIA_MOUNTED,
                Uri.parse("file://"
                    + Environment.getExternalStorageDirectory())));
ContentValues values = new ContentValues();
values.put(MediaStore.MediaColumns.DATA, myFile.getAbsolutePath());
values.put(MediaStore.MediaColumns.TITLE, myFile.getName());
values.put(MediaStore.MediaColumns.TIMESTAMP,
                                    System.currentTimeMillis());
values.put(MediaStore.MediaColumns.MIME_TYPE,
                                    recorder.getMimeContentType());
values.put(MediaStore.Audio.Media.ARTIST, SOME_ARTIST_HERE);
values.put(MediaStore.Audio.Media.IS_RINGTONE, true);
values.put(MediaStore.Audio.Media.IS_NOTIFICATION, true);
values.put(MediaStore.Audio.Media.IS_ALARM, true);
values.put(MediaStore.Audio.Media.IS_MUSIC, false);
ContentResolver contentResolver = new ContentResolver();
Uri base = MediaStore.Audio.INTERNAL_CONTENT_URI;
Uri newUri = contentResolver.insert(base, values);
String path = contentResolver.getDataFilePath(newUri);
```

Here, `ContentValues` is used to declare some standard properties of the file, such as `TITLE`, `TIMESTAMP`, and `MIME_TYPE`, and `ContentResolver` is used to create an entry in the `MediaStore` content database with the file's path automatically added.

Video

There are two different ways of displaying video. One uses the `MediaPlayer` framework similar to the audio examples discussed previously. The other uses a `VideoView` class that takes care of most of the work and is recommended for simpler use cases.

Recipe: Using the VideoView

Using a `VideoView` is very easy. Once it is declared in the XML layout and the layout has been loaded, all that needs to be done is to give a URL of the video to the `VideoView` and it will start playing immediately. It will even show an error dialog, if the video format is not supported by the framework or some other error occurred.

To make things easier for the user, there is another helper class called the `MediaController`. This adds Play/Pause, Forward, and Rewind buttons and a Seeking

Bar control. All that needs to be done is to hook up the MediaController to the VideoView to act as its anchor with .setAnchorView. This way, a full video player can be obtained with just a few lines of code, as can be seen in Listing 8.12.

Listing 8.12   **VideoViewActivity.java**

```java
public class VideoViewActivity extends Activity {

    private static final String VIDEO_DIR =
    File.separator+"DCIM"+File.separator+"Camera";
    private VideoView videoView;

    @Override
    public void onCreate(Bundle savedInstanceState){
        super.onCreate(savedInstanceState);

        setContentView(R.layout.video_view);
        videoView=(VideoView)findViewById(R.id.videoView1);
        MediaController controller=new MediaController(this);
        controller.setMediaPlayer(videoView);
        controller.setAnchorView(videoView);

        videoView.setMediaController(controller);


    String videoDir = Environment.getExternalStorageDirectory()
    .getAbsolutePath() + VIDEO_DIR;

    //Show a list of video files to choose
    Intent i = new Intent(this, ListFiles.class);
    i.putExtra("directory", videoDir);
    startActivityForResult(i,0);

    }

    @Override
    protected void onActivityResult(int requestCode,
                                    int resultCode, Intent data) {
        super.onActivityResult(requestCode, resultCode, data);
        if(requestCode == 0 && resultCode==RESULT_OK) {
            String path = data.getExtras().getString("clickedFile");

            videoView.setVideoPath(path);
            videoView.start();

        }
    }
}
```

The accompanying layout is seen in Listing 8.13.

Listing 8.13   **video_view.xml**

```xml
<?xml version="1.0" encoding="utf-8"?>
<LinearLayout xmlns:android="http://schemas.android.com/apk/res/android"
    android:layout_width="match_parent"
    android:layout_height="match_parent"
    android:orientation="vertical" >

    <VideoView
        android:id="@+id/videoView1"
        android:layout_width="match_parent"
        android:layout_height="wrap_content"
    />

</LinearLayout>
```

Recipe: Video Playback Using the MediaPlayer

The `MediaPlayer` framework can also be used to play videos. The main difference from playing audio is that a surface for rendering the video frames must be provided. This is done using the `SurfaceView` class, which is added to the layout just beneath the Play/Pause button in Listing 8.14.

Listing 8.14   **video_playback.xml**

```xml
<?xml version="1.0" encoding="utf-8"?>
<LinearLayout
    xmlns:android="http://schemas.android.com/apk/res/android"
    android:orientation="vertical"
    android:layout_width="match_parent"
    android:layout_height="match_parent">
    <Button android:id="@+id/play_pause"
        android:text="Play"
        android:textSize="20sp"
        android:layout_width="wrap_content"
        android:layout_height="wrap_content" />
    <SurfaceView
            android:id="@+id/surface"
            android:layout_width="match_parent"
            android:layout_height="0dip"
            android:layout_weight="1"
            android:visibility="visible"
        />
</LinearLayout>
```

Creating the surface can take some time. Because of this, the `SurfaceHolder.Callback` method is used to set the display of the `MediaPlayer` after the surface is created. Once this is done, videos can be played. If a video is started without attaching a display or if `setDisplay` is called with a null argument, only the audio track of the video is played.

9

Hardware Interface

Android devices have multiple types of hardware that are built in and accessible to developers. Sensors, such as a camera, accelerometer, magnetometer, pressure sensor, temperature sensor, and proximity sensor, are available on most devices. Telephony, Bluetooth, near field communication (NFC), and other wireless connections are also accessible to the developer in some form. This chapter shows how to leverage these hardware APIs to enrich the experience of an application. Note that these recipes are best run on actual Android devices because the emulator might not provide accurate or realistic behavior of hardware interfaces.

Camera

The camera is the most visible and most used sensor in an Android device. It is a selling point for most consumers, and the capabilities are getting better with each generation. Image-processing applications normally work on an image after it is taken, but other applications, such as augmented reality, use the camera in real time with overlays.

There are two ways to access the camera from an application. The first is by declaring an implicit intent as described in Chapter 2, "Application Basics: Activities and Intents." The implicit intent launches the default camera interface:

```
Intent intent = new Intent("android.media.action.IMAGE_CAPTURE");
startActivity(intent);
```

The second way leverages the `Camera` class, which provides more flexibility in the settings. This creates a custom camera interface, which is the focus of the recipes that follow. Camera hardware access requires explicit permission in the **Android Manifest.xml** file:

```
<uses-permission android:name="android.permission.CAMERA" />
```

This is implied in the following recipe.

Recipe: Customizing the Camera

Control of the camera is abstracted into various components in the Android system:

- `Camera` class—Accesses the camera hardware
- `Camera.Parameters` class—Specifies the camera parameters such as picture size, picture quality, flash modes, and method to assign GPS location
- `Camera Preview` methods—Sets the camera output display and toggles streaming video preview to the display
- `SurfaceView` class—Dedicates a drawing surface at the lowest level of the view hierarchy as a placeholder to display the camera preview

Before describing how these are tied together, the layout structure is introduced. The main layout is shown in Listing 9.1 and includes a `SurfaceView` class to hold the camera output.

Listing 9.1   res/layout/main.xml

```
<LinearLayout
    xmlns:android="http://schemas.android.com/apk/res/android"
    android:layout_width="match_parent"
    android:layout_height="match_parent"
    android:orientation="vertical">

  <SurfaceView android:id="@+id/surface"
      android:layout_width="match_parent"
      android:layout_height="match_parent">
  </SurfaceView>

</LinearLayout>
```

A control interface can be added on top of this view by using a separate layout, as shown in Listing 9.2. This layout contains a button at the bottom center of the screen to take a picture.

Listing 9.2   res/layout/cameraoverlay.xml

```
<LinearLayout xmlns:android="http://schemas.android.com/apk/res/android"
    android:layout_width="match_parent"
    android:layout_height="match_parent"
    android:orientation="vertical"
    android:gravity="bottom"
    android:layout_gravity="bottom">

    <LinearLayout
    xmlns:android="http://schemas.android.com/apk/res/android"
        android:layout_width="match_parent"
        android:layout_height="wrap_content"
        android:orientation="horizontal"
        android:gravity="center_horizontal">
```

```
        <Button
        android:id="@+id/button"
        android:layout_width="wrap_content"
        android:layout_height="wrap_content"
        android:text="take picture"
        />
    </LinearLayout>
</LinearLayout>
```

The main activity involves multiple functionalities. First, the layout is set up as follows:

1. The window settings are changed to be translucent and full screen. (In this instance, they hide the title and notification bar.)

2. The SurfaceView class defined in the previous layout (R.id.surface) is then filled by the camera preview. Each SurfaceView contains a SurfaceHolder class for access and control over the surface. The activity is added as the SurfaceHolder's callback, and the type is set to SURFACE_TYPE_PUSH_ BUFFERS, which means it creates a "push" surface and the object does not own the buffer. This makes video streaming more efficient.

3. A LayoutInflater class is declared to inflate another layout (**cameraoverlay .xml**) over the original (**main.xml**) layout.

Next, the activity sets a trigger for taking a picture:

1. An OnClickListener class is added on the button from the cameraoverlay layout, so when clicked, it takes a picture (mCamera.takePicture()).

2. The takePicture() method needs to have the following interfaces implemented:

   - ShutterCallback() to define any effects needed after the picture is taken, such as a sound to let the user know that the picture has been captured.

   - PictureCallback() for raw picture data if the hardware has enough memory to support this feature. (Otherwise, the data might return as null.)

   - A second PictureCallback() method for the compressed picture data. This calls the local method done() to save the picture.

Then, the activity saves any pictures that were taken:

1. The compressed picture byte array is saved to a local variable tempData for manipulation. BitmapFactory is used to decode the byte array into a Bitmap object.

2. The media content provider is used to save the bitmap and return a URL. If this main activity were called by another activity, this URL would be the return information to the caller activity to retrieve the image.

3. After this process, finish() is called to kill the activity.

Finally, the activity sets up a response to a change in the surface view:

1. A `SurfaceHolder.CallBack` interface is implemented. This requires three methods to be overridden:

   - `surfaceCreated()`—Called when the surface is first created. Initialize objects here.

   - `surfaceChanged()`—Called after surface creation and when the surface changes (for example, format or size).

   - `surfaceDestroyed()`—Called between removing the surface from the view of the user and destroying the surface. This is used for memory cleanup.

2. The parameters for the camera are changed when the surface is changed (such as `PreviewSize` based on the surface size).

These functionalities are in the complete activity shown in Listing 9.3.

Listing 9.3   src/com/cookbook/hardware/CameraApplication.java

```java
package com.cookbook.hardware;

import android.app.Activity;
import android.content.Intent;
import android.graphics.Bitmap;
import android.graphics.BitmapFactory;
import android.graphics.PixelFormat;
import android.hardware.Camera;
import android.hardware.Camera.PictureCallback;
import android.hardware.Camera.ShutterCallback;
import android.os.Bundle;
import android.provider.MediaStore.Images;
import android.util.Log;
import android.view.LayoutInflater;
import android.view.SurfaceHolder;
import android.view.SurfaceView;
import android.view.View;
import android.view.Window;
import android.view.WindowManager;
import android.view.View.OnClickListener;
import android.view.ViewGroup.LayoutParams;
import android.widget.Button;
import android.widget.Toast;

public class CameraApplication extends Activity
                            implements SurfaceHolder.Callback {
    private static final String TAG = "cookbook.hardware";
    private LayoutInflater mInflater = null;
    Camera mCamera;
    byte[] tempData;
    boolean mPreviewRunning = false;
    private SurfaceHolder mSurfaceHolder;
    private SurfaceView mSurfaceView;
    Button takepicture;
```

```java
    @Override
    public void onCreate(Bundle savedInstanceState) {
        super.onCreate(savedInstanceState);

        getWindow().setFormat(PixelFormat.TRANSLUCENT);
        requestWindowFeature(Window.FEATURE_NO_TITLE);
        getWindow().setFlags(WindowManager.LayoutParams.FLAG_FULLSCREEN,
                WindowManager.LayoutParams.FLAG_FULLSCREEN);

        setContentView(R.layout.main);

        mSurfaceView = (SurfaceView)findViewById(R.id.surface);
        mSurfaceHolder = mSurfaceView.getHolder();
        mSurfaceHolder.addCallback(this);
// Uncomment the following line if using less than Android 3.0 (API 11)
        // mSurfaceHolder.setType(SurfaceHolder.SURFACE_TYPE_PUSH_BUFFERS);

        mInflater = LayoutInflater.from(this);
        View overView = mInflater.inflate(R.layout.cameraoverlay, null);
        this.addContentView(overView,
                new LayoutParams(LayoutParams.MATCH_PARENT,
                        LayoutParams.MATCH_PARENT));
        takepicture = (Button) findViewById(R.id.button);
        takepicture.setOnClickListener(new OnClickListener(){
            public void onClick(View view){
                mCamera.takePicture(mShutterCallback,
                        mPictureCallback, mjpeg);
            }
        });
    }

    ShutterCallback mShutterCallback = new ShutterCallback(){
        @Override
        public void onShutter() {}
    };
    PictureCallback mPictureCallback = new PictureCallback() {
        public void onPictureTaken(byte[] data, Camera c) {}
    };
    PictureCallback mjpeg = new PictureCallback() {
        public void onPictureTaken(byte[] data, Camera c) {
            if(data !=null) {
                tempdata=data;
                done();
            }
        }
    };

    void done() {
        Bitmap bm = BitmapFactory.decodeByteArray(tempdata,
                                                0, tempdata.length);
        String url = Images.Media.insertImage(getContentResolver(),
                bm, null, null);
        bm.recycle();
        Bundle bundle = new Bundle();
        if(url!=null) {
            bundle.putString("url", url);
```

```
                Intent mIntent = new Intent();
                mIntent.putExtras(bundle);
                setResult(RESULT_OK, mIntent);
        } else {
                Toast.makeText(this, "Picture cannot be saved",
                                Toast.LENGTH_SHORT).show();
        }
        finish();
}
@Override
public void surfaceChanged(SurfaceHolder holder, int format,
                                int w, int h) {
        Log.e(TAG, "surfaceChanged");
        try {
                if (mPreviewRunning) {
                        mCamera.stopPreview();
                        mPreviewRunning = false;
                }

                Camera.Parameters p = mCamera.getParameters();
                p.setPreviewSize(w, h);

                mCamera.setParameters(p);
                mCamera.setPreviewDisplay(holder);
                mCamera.startPreview();
                mPreviewRunning = true;
        } catch(Exception e) {
                Log.d("",e.toString());
        }
}

@Override
public void surfaceCreated(SurfaceHolder holder) {
        Log.e(TAG, "surfaceCreated");
        mCamera = Camera.open();
}

@Override
public void surfaceDestroyed(SurfaceHolder holder) {
        Log.e(TAG, "surfaceDestroyed");
        mCamera.stopPreview();
        mPreviewRunning = false;
        mCamera.release();
        mCamera=null;
}
}
```

Note that the camera preview from the camera hardware is not standardized, and some Android devices might show the preview sideways. In this case, simply add the following to the onCreate() method of the CameraPreview activity:

```
this.setRequestedOrientation(ActivityInfo.SCREEN_ORIENTATION_LANDSCAPE);
```

Other Sensors

The proliferation of small and low-power micro-electro-mechanical systems (MEMS) is becoming more evident. Smartphones are becoming aggregators of sensors, and the push for sensor accuracy by smartphone manufacturers is driving the need for better-performing devices.

As discussed in Chapter 1, "Overview of Android," each Android phone has a selection of different sensors. The standard two are a three-axis accelerometer to determine device tilt and a three-axis magnetometer to determine compass direction. Other devices that might be integrated are temperature sensor, proximity sensor, light sensor, and gyroscope. Following are the currently supported sensors in the Android SDK:

- TYPE_ACCELEROMETER—Measures acceleration in meters per second squared
- TYPE_AMBIENT_TEMPERATURE—Measures temperature in degrees Celsius (replaced TYPE_TEMPERATURE in API Level 14)
- TYPE_GRAVITY—Measures movement on a three-dimensional axis including the magnitude of gravity
- TYPE_GYROSCOPE—Measures orientation based on angular momentum
- TYPE_LIGHT—Measures ambient light in lux
- TYPE_LINEAR_ACCELERATION—Measures movement on a three-dimensional axis without the effects of gravity
- TYPE_MAGNETIC_FIELD—Measures magnetic field in microteslas
- TYPE_PRESSURE—Measures air pressure
- TYPE_PROXIMITY—Measures the distance of a blocking object in centimeters
- TYPE_RELATIVE_HUMIDITY—Measures humidity as a percentage
- TYPE_TEMPERATURE—Measures temperature in degrees Celsius

The getSensorList() method lists all the available sensors in a particular device. SensorManager manages all sensors. It provides various sensor event listeners with two callback functions—onSensorChanged() and onAccuracyChanged()—that are used to listen for sensor value and accuracy changes.

Recipe: Getting a Device's Rotational Attitude

Ideally, the accelerometer measures the Earth's gravitational field as $G = 9.8m/sec^2$, and the magnetometer measures the Earth's magnetic field that ranges from $H = 30\mu T$ to $60\mu T$ depending on the device's location in the world. These two vectors are enough to implement a simple textbook estimation of rotation, as used in the getRotationMatrix() method. This recipe shows how to use this information.

The coordinate system of the device (also known as the body) frame is defined in this way:

- The x axis is defined along the direction of the short side of the screen (along the menu keys).
- The y axis is defined along the direction of the long side of the screen.
- The z axis is defined as pointing out of the screen.

The coordinate system of the world (also known as inertial) frame is defined in this way:

- The x axis is the cross-product of the y axis with the z axis.
- The y axis is tangential to the ground and points toward the North Pole.
- The z axis points perpendicular to the ground toward the sky.

These two systems are aligned when the device is flat on a table with the screen facing up and pointing north. In this case, the accelerometer measures (0, 0, G) in the x, y, and z directions. At most locations, the magnetic field of the Earth points slightly toward the ground at an angle (and even when the device points north is given by (0, H cos((), -H sin(()).

As the device tilts and rotates, `SensorManager.getRotationMatrix()` provides the 3×3 rotation matrix `R[]` to get from the device coordinate system to the world coordinate system and 3×3 inclination matrix `I[]` (rotation around the x axis) to get from the true magnetic field direction to the ideal case (0, H, 0).

Note that if the device is accelerating or is near a strong magnetic field, the values measured do not necessarily reflect the proper reference frame of the Earth.

Another way to express the rotation is by using `SensorManager.getOrientation()`. This provides the rotation matrix `R[]` and the attitude vector `attitude[]`:

- `attitude[0]`—Azimuth (in radians) is the rotation angle around the world-frame z axis required to have the device facing north. It takes values between –PI and PI, with 0 representing north and PI/2 representing east.
- `attitude[1]`—Pitch (in radians) is the rotation angle around the world-frame x axis required to have the device face straight up along the long dimension of the screen. It takes values between –PI and PI with 0 representing device face up, and PI/2 means it points toward the ground.
- `attitude[2]`—Roll (in radians) is the rotation angle around the world-frame y axis required to have the device face straight up along the short dimension of the screen. It takes values between –PI and PI with 0 representing device face up, and PI/2 means it points toward the right.

This recipe displays the attitude information to the screen. The layout provides a text with ID `attitude`, as shown in Listing 9.4.

Listing 9.4   res/layout/main.xml

```
<?xml version="1.0" encoding="utf-8"?>
<LinearLayout xmlns:android="http://schemas.android.com/apk/res/android"
    android:orientation="vertical"
```

```
        android:layout_width="match_parent"
        android:layout_height="match_parent"
        >
<TextView android:id="@+id/attitude"
        android:layout_width="match_parent"
        android:layout_height="wrap_content"
        android:text="Azimuth, Pitch, Roll"
        />
</LinearLayout>
```

The main activity is shown in Listing 9.5. The accelerometer and magnetometer are registered to return data to the sensor listener. SensorEventListener then assigns values based on which sensor triggered the callback. The attitude information is determined based on the rotation matrix, converted from radians to degrees, and is displayed on the screen. Note that the refresh rate of the sensors can take on different values as follows:

- SENSOR_DELAY_FASTEST—Fastest update rate possible

- SENSOR_DELAY_GAME—Update rate suitable for games

- SENSOR_DELAY_NORMAL—The default update rate suitable for screen orientation changes

- SENSOR_DELAY_UI—Update rate suitable for the user interface

Listing 9.5   src/com/cookbook/orientation/OrientationMeasurements.java

```java
package com.cookbook.orientation;

import android.app.Activity;
import android.hardware.Sensor;
import android.hardware.SensorEvent;
import android.hardware.SensorEventListener;
import android.hardware.SensorManager;
import android.os.Bundle;
import android.widget.TextView;

public class OrientationMeasurements extends Activity {
    private SensorManager myManager = null;
    TextView tv;

    @Override
    public void onCreate(Bundle savedInstanceState) {
        super.onCreate(savedInstanceState);
        setContentView(R.layout.main);
        tv = (TextView) findViewById(R.id.attitude);
        // Set Sensor Manager
        myManager = (SensorManager)getSystemService(SENSOR_SERVICE);
        myManager.registerListener(mySensorListener,
                myManager.getDefaultSensor(Sensor.TYPE_ACCELEROMETER),
                SensorManager.SENSOR_DELAY_GAME);
        myManager.registerListener(mySensorListener,
```

```
                          myManager.getDefaultSensor(Sensor.TYPE_MAGNETIC_FIELD),
                          SensorManager.SENSOR_DELAY_GAME);
      }

      float[] mags = new float[3];
      float[] accels = new float[3];
      float[] rotationMat = new float[9];
      float[] inclinationMat = new float[9];
      float[] attitude = new float[3];
      final static double RAD2DEG = 180/Math.PI;
      private final SensorEventListener mySensorListener
                                     = new SensorEventListener() {
          @Override
          public void onSensorChanged(SensorEvent event)
          {
              int type = event.sensor.getType();

              if(type == Sensor.TYPE_MAGNETIC_FIELD) {
                  mags = event.values;
              }
              if(type == Sensor.TYPE_ACCELEROMETER) {
                  accels = event.values;
              }

              SensorManager.getRotationMatrix(rotationMat,
                      inclinationMat, accels, mags);
              SensorManager.getOrientation(rotationMat, attitude);
              tv.setText("Azimuth, Pitch, Roll:\n"
                      + attitude[0]*RAD2DEG + "\n"
                      + attitude[1]*RAD2DEG + "\n"
                      + attitude[2]*RAD2DEG);
          }

          public void onAccuracyChanged(Sensor sensor, int accuracy) {}
      };
  }
```

For consistent data, it is good practice to avoid putting computationally intensive code into the onSensorChanged() method. Also note that SensorEvent is reused for subsequent sensor data. Therefore, for precise data, it is good practice to use the clone() method on event values, for example:

```
accels = event.values.clone();
```

This ensures that if the accels data is used elsewhere in the class, it does not keep changing as the sensors continue sampling.

Recipe: Using the Temperature and Light Sensors

The temperature sensor is used to determine the temperature of the phone for internal hardware calibration. The light sensor measures ambient light and is used to automatically adjust the brightness of the screen.

These sensors are not available on all phones, but if they exist, the developer can use them for alternative reasons. The code to read the values from these sensors is shown in Listing 9.6. It can be added to the activity in the previous recipe to see the result.

Listing 9.6   **Accessing the Temperature and Light Sensors**

```
private final SensorEventListener mTListener
                                  = new SensorEventListener(){
    @Override
    public void onAccuracyChanged(Sensor sensor, int accuracy) {}

    @Override
    public void onSensorChanged(SensorEvent event) {
        Log.v("test Temperature",
            "onSensorChanged:"+event.sensor.getName());
        if(event.sensor.getType()==Sensor.TYPE_AMBIENT_TEMPERATURE){
            tv2.setText("Temperature:"+event.values[0]);
        }
    }
};

private final SensorEventListener mLListener
                                  = new SensorEventListener(){
    @Override
    public void onAccuracyChanged(Sensor sensor, int accuracy) {}

    @Override
    public void onSensorChanged(SensorEvent event) {
        Log.v("test Light",
            "onSensorChanged:"+event.sensor.getName());
        if(event.sensor.getType()==Sensor.TYPE_LIGHT){
            tv3.setText("Light:"+event.values[0]);
        }
    }
};

myManager.registerListener(mTListener, sensorManager
                .getDefaultSensor(Sensor.TYPE_TEMPERATURE),
                SensorManager.SENSOR_DELAY_FASTEST);
myManager.registerListener(mLListener, sensorManager
                .getDefaultSensor(Sensor.TYPE_LIGHT),
                SensorManager.SENSOR_DELAY_FASTEST);
```

Telephony

The Android telephony API provides a way to monitor basic phone information, such as the network type, connection state, and utilities for manipulating phone number strings.

Recipe: Using the Telephony Manager

The telephony API has a `TelephonyManager` class, which is an Android system service, to access information about the telephony services on the device. Some of the telephony information is permission protected, so access must be declared in the **AndroidManifest.xml** file:

```
<uses-permission android:name="android.permission.READ_PHONE_STATE" />
```

The main activity is shown in Listing 9.7.

Listing 9.7   **src/com/cookbook/hardware.telephony/TelephonyApp.java**

```java
package com.cookbook.hardware.telephony;

import android.app.Activity;
import android.os.Bundle;
import android.telephony.TelephonyManager;
import android.widget.TextView;

public class TelephonyApp extends Activity {
    TextView tv1;
    TelephonyManager telManager;
    @Override
    public void onCreate(Bundle savedInstanceState) {
        super.onCreate(savedInstanceState);
        setContentView(R.layout.main);
        tv1 =(TextView) findViewById(R.id.tv1);
        telManager = (TelephonyManager)
                        getSystemService(TELEPHONY_SERVICE);

        StringBuilder sb = new StringBuilder();
        sb.append("deviceid:")
          .append(telManager.getDeviceId()).append("\n");
        sb.append("device Software Ver:")
          .append(telManager.getDeviceSoftwareVersion()).append("\n");
        sb.append("Line number:")
          .append(telManager.getLine1Number()).append("\n");
        sb.append("Network Country ISO:")
          .append(telManager.getNetworkCountryIso()).append("\n");
        sb.append("Network Operator:")
          .append(telManager.getNetworkOperator()).append("\n");
        sb.append("Network Operator Name:")
          .append(telManager.getNetworkOperatorName()).append("\n");
        sb.append("Sim Country ISO:")
          .append(telManager.getSimCountryIso()).append("\n");
        sb.append("Sim Operator:")
          .append(telManager.getSimOperator()).append("\n");
        sb.append("Sim Operator Name:")
          .append(telManager.getSimOperatorName()).append("\n");
        sb.append("Sim Serial Number:")
          .append(telManager.getSimSerialNumber()).append("\n");
        sb.append("Subscriber Id:")
          .append(telManager.getSubscriberId()).append("\n");
```

```
        sb.append("Voice Mail Alpha Tag:")
          .append(telManager.getVoiceMailAlphaTag()).append("\n");
        sb.append("Voice Mail Number:")
          .append(telManager.getVoiceMailNumber()).append("\n");
        tv1.setText(sb.toString());
    }
}
```

The main layout XML file, shown in Listing 9.8, outputs the screen shown in Figure 9.1.

Listing 9.8   res/layout/main.xml

```
<?xml version="1.0" encoding="utf-8"?>
<LinearLayout xmlns:android="http://schemas.android.com/apk/res/android"
    android:orientation="vertical"
    android:layout_width="match_parent"
    android:layout_height="match_parent"
    >
<TextView
    android:id="@+id/tv1"
    android:layout_width="match_parent"
    android:layout_height="wrap_content"
    android:text="@string/hello"
    />
</LinearLayout>
```

Figure 9.1   Output using the TelephonyManager class

Recipe: Listening for Phone States

The `PhoneStateListener` class provides information about the different telephony states on the device, including network service state, signal strength, and message-waiting indicator (voicemail). Some require explicit permission, as shown in Table 9.1.

For example, to listen for an incoming call, `TelephonyManager` needs to register a listener for the `PhoneStateListener.LISTEN_CALL_STATE` event. The three possible call states are:

- `CALL_STATE_IDLE`—Device not being used for a phone call
- `CALL_STATE_RINGING`—Device receiving a call
- `CALL_STATE_OFFHOOK`—Call in progress

This recipe lists the phone call state changes as they occur. By using the LogCat tool (discussed in Chapter 16, "Debugging"), these different states can be seen when an incoming call or outgoing call occurs.

The main activity is shown in Listing 9.9. It creates a new inner class extending `PhoneStateListener`, which overrides the `onCallStateChanged` method to catch the phone call state changes. Other methods that can be overridden are `onCallForwardingIndicator()`, `onCellLocationChanged()`, and `onDataActivity()`.

Table 9.1   Possible Phone State Listener Events and Required Permissions

Phone State Listener	Description	Permission
LISTEN_CALL_ FORWARDING_INDICATOR	Listen for call forward indicator changes	READ_PHONE_STATE
LISTEN_CALL_STATE	Listen for call state changes	READ_PHONE_STATE
LISTEN_CELL_INFO	Listen for changes to observed cell information	None
LISTEN_CELL_LOCATION	Listen for cell location changes	ACCESS_COARSE_LOCATION
LISTEN_DATA_ACTIVITY	Listen for direction of data traffic on cellular changes	READ_PHONE_STATE
LISTEN_DATA_ CONNECTION_STATE	Listen for data connection state changes	None
LISTEN_MESSAGE_ WAITING_INDICATOR	Listen for message-waiting indicator changes	READ_PHONE_STATE
LISTEN_NONE	Remove listeners	None
LISTEN_SERVICE_STATE	Listen for network service state changes	None
LISTEN_SIGNAL_ STRENGTHS	Listen for network signal strength changes	None

Listing 9.9   **src/com/cookbook/hardware.telephony/HardwareTelephony.java**

```
package com.cookbook.hardware.telephony;

import android.app.Activity;
import android.os.Bundle;
import android.telephony.PhoneStateListener;
import android.telephony.TelephonyManager;
import android.util.Log;
import android.widget.TextView;

public class HardwareTelephony extends Activity {
    TextView tv1;
    TelephonyManager telManager;
    @Override
    public void onCreate(Bundle savedInstanceState) {
        super.onCreate(savedInstanceState);
        setContentView(R.layout.main);
        tv1 =(TextView) findViewById(R.id.tv1);
        telManager = (TelephonyManager)
                        getSystemService(TELEPHONY_SERVICE);

        telManager.listen(new TelListener(),
                        PhoneStateListener.LISTEN_CALL_STATE);
    }
{
    private class TelListener extends PhoneStateListener {
        public void onCallStateChanged(int state, String incomingNumber)
            super.onCallStateChanged(state, incomingNumber);

            Log.v("Phone State", "state:"+state);
            switch (state) {
                case TelephonyManager.CALL_STATE_IDLE:
                    Log.v("Phone State",
                        "incomingNumber:"+incomingNumber+" ended");
                    break;
                case TelephonyManager.CALL_STATE_OFFHOOK:
                    Log.v("Phone State",
                        "incomingNumber:"+incomingNumber+"
picked up");
                    break;
                case TelephonyManager.CALL_STATE_RINGING:
                    Log.v("Phone State",
                        "incomingNumber:"+incomingNumber+" received");
                    break;
                default:
                    break;
            }
        }
    }
}
```

Recipe: Dialing a Phone Number

To make a phone call from an application, the following permission needs to be added to the **AndroidManifest.xml** file:

```
<uses-permission android:name="android.permission.CALL_PHONE" />
```

The act of making a call can use either the ACTION_CALL or ACTION_DIALER implicit intent. When using the ACTION_DIALER intent, the phone dialer user interface is displayed with the specified phone number ready to call. This is created using:

```
startActivity(new Intent(Intent.ACTION_CALL,
  Uri.parse("tel:15102345678")));
```

When using the ACTION_CALL intent, the phone dialer is not shown and the specified phone number is just dialed. This is created using:

```
startActivity(new Intent(Intent.ACTION_DIAL,
  Uri.parse("tel:15102345678")));
```

Bluetooth

Bluetooth from the IEEE standard 802.15.1 is an open, wireless protocol for exchanging data between devices over short distances. A common example is from a phone to a headset, but other applications can include proximity tracking. To communicate between devices using Bluetooth, four steps need to be performed:

1. Turn on Bluetooth for the device.

2. Find paired or available devices in a valid range.

3. Connect to devices.

4. Transfer data between devices.

To use the Bluetooth service, the application needs to have BLUETOOTH permission to receive and transmit and BLUETOOTH_ADMIN permission to manipulate Bluetooth settings or initiate device discovery. These require the following lines in the **AndroidManifest.xml** file:

```
<uses-permission android:name="android.permission.BLUETOOTH" />
<uses-permission android:name="android.permission.BLUETOOTH_ADMIN" />
```

All the Bluetooth API functionality resides in the android.bluetooth package. There are five main classes that provide the features:

- BluetoothAdapter—Represents the Bluetooth radio interface that is used to discover devices and instantiate Bluetooth connections

- BluetoothClass—Describes the general characteristics of the Bluetooth device

- BluetoothDevice—Represents a remote Bluetooth device

- BluetoothSocket—Represents the socket or connection point for data exchange with another Bluetooth device

- BluetoothServerSocket—Represents an open socket listening for incoming requests

These are discussed in detail in the following recipes.

Recipe: Turning on Bluetooth

Bluetooth is initialized using the `BluetoothAdapter` class. The `getDefaultAdapter()` method retrieves information about the Bluetooth radio interface. If `null` is returned, it means the device does not support Bluetooth:

```
BluetoothAdapter myBluetooth = BluetoothAdapter.getDefaultAdapter();
```

Activate Bluetooth using this `BluetoothAdapter` instance to query the status. If not enabled, the Android built-in activity `ACTION_REQUEST_ENABLE` can be used to ask the user to start Bluetooth:

```
if(!myBluetooth.isEnabled()) {
    Intent enableIntent = new Intent(BluetoothAdapter
                                 .ACTION_REQUEST_ENABLE);
    startActivity(enableIntent);
}
```

Recipe: Discovering Bluetooth Devices

After Bluetooth is activated, to discover paired or available Bluetooth devices, use the `BluetoothAdapter` instance's `startDiscovery()` method as an asynchronous call. This requires registering a `BroadcastReceiver` to listen for `ACTION_FOUND` events that tell the application whenever a new remote Bluetooth device is discovered. This is shown in the example code in Listing 9.10.

Listing 9.10   **Discovering Bluetooth Devices**

```
private final BroadcastReceiver mReceiver = new BroadcastReceiver() {
    public void onReceive(Context context, Intent intent) {
        String action = intent.getAction();
        // When discovery finds a device
        if (BluetoothDevice.ACTION_FOUND.equals(action)) {
            // Get the BluetoothDevice object from the intent
            BluetoothDevice device = intent.getParcelableExtra(
                                    BluetoothDevice.EXTRA_DEVICE);
            Log.v("BlueTooth Testing",device.getName() + "\n"
                    + device.getAddress());
        }
    }
};

IntentFilter filter = new IntentFilter(BluetoothDevice.ACTION_FOUND);
registerReceiver(mReceiver, filter);
myBluetooth.startDiscovery();
```

The `BroadcastReceiver` can also listen for `ACTION_DISCOVERY_STARTED` events and `ACTION_DISCOVERY_FINISHED` events that tell the application when the discovery starts and ends.

For other Bluetooth devices to discover the current device, the application can enable discoverability using the ACTION_REQUEST_DISCOVERABLE intent. This activity displays another dialog on top of the application to ask users whether or not they want to make the current device discoverable:

```
Intent discoverableIntent
        = new Intent(BluetoothAdapter.ACTION_REQUEST_DISCOVERABLE);
startActivity(discoverableIntent);
```

Recipe: Pairing with Bonded Bluetooth Devices

Bonded Bluetooth devices are those that have already paired with the current device sometime in the past. When pairing two Bluetooth devices, one connects as a server and the other as the client using the BluetoothSocket and BluetoothServerSocket classes. To get the bonded Bluetooth devices, the BluetoothAdapter instance's method getBondedDevices() can be used:

```
Set<BluetoothDevice> pairedDevices = mBluetoothAdapter.getBondedDevices();
```

Recipe: Opening a Bluetooth Socket

To establish a Bluetooth connection with another device, the application needs to implement either the client-side or server-side socket. After the server and client are bonded, there is a connected Bluetooth socket for each device on the same RFCOMM (Bluetooth transport protocol). However, the client device and server device obtain the Bluetooth socket in different ways. The server receives the Bluetooth socket instance when an incoming connection is accepted. The client receives the instance when it opens an RFCOMM channel to the server.

Server-side initialization uses the generic client-server programming model with applications requiring an open socket for accepting incoming requests (similar to TCP). The interface BluetoothServerSocket should be used to create a server listening port. After the connection is accepted, a BluetoothSocket class is returned and can be used to manage the connection.

BluetoothServerSocket can be obtained from the BluetoothAdapter instance's method listenUsingRfcommWithServiceRecord(). After the socket is obtained, the accept() method starts listening for a request and returns only when either a connection has been accepted or an exception has occurred. The BluetoothSocket class then returns when accept() returns a valid connection. Finally, the close() method should be called to release the server socket and its resources because RFCOMM allows only one connected client per channel at a time. This does not close the connected BluetoothSocket. The following excerpt shows how these steps are done:

```
BluetoothServerSocket myServerSocket
    = myBluetoothAdapter.listenUsingRfcommWithServiceRecord(name, uuid);
myServerSocket.accept();
myServerSocket.close();
```

Note that the `accept()` method is a blocking call and so it should not be implemented inside the main thread. It is a better idea to implement this inside a working thread, as shown in Listing 9.11.

Listing 9.11   **Establishing a Bluetooth Socket**

```
private class AcceptThread extends Thread {
    private final BluetoothServerSocket mmServerSocket;

    public AcceptThread() {
        // Use a temporary object that is later assigned
        // to mmServerSocket, because mmServerSocket is final
        BluetoothServerSocket tmp = null;
        try {
            // MY_UUID is the app's UUID string, also used by the client
            tmp = mAdapter.listenUsingRfcommWithServiceRecord(NAME,MY_UUID);
        } catch (IOException e) { }
        mmServerSocket = tmp;
    }

    public void run() {
        BluetoothSocket socket = null;
        // Keep listening until an exception occurs or a socket is returned
        while (true) {
            try {
                socket = mmServerSocket.accept();
            } catch (IOException e) {
                break;
            }
            // If a connection was accepted
            if (socket != null) {
                // Do work to manage the connection (in a separate thread)
                manageConnectedSocket(socket);
                mmServerSocket.close();
                break;
            }
        }
    }

    /** will cancel the listening socket and cause thread to finish */
    public void cancel() {
        try {
            mmServerSocket.close();
        } catch (IOException e) { }
    }
}
```

To implement the client device mechanism, the `BluetoothDevice` needs to be obtained from the remote device. Then the socket needs to be retrieved to make the connection. To retrieve the `BluetoothSocket` class, use the `BluetoothDevice` method `createRfcommSocketToServiceRecord(UUID)` with the UUID used in `listenUsingRfcommWithServiceRecord`. After the socket is retrieved, the connect() method can be used to initiate a connection. This method is also blocking and should also be implemented in a separate thread, as shown in Listing 9.12. The UUID is inside the BluetoothDevice object that is found during discovery.

Listing 9.12   **Connecting to a Bluetooth Socket**

```
private class ConnectThread extends Thread {
    private final BluetoothSocket mmSocket;
    private final BluetoothDevice mmDevice;

    public ConnectThread(BluetoothDevice device) {
        // Use a temporary object that is later assigned to mmSocket,
        // because mmSocket is final
        BluetoothSocket tmp = null;
        mmDevice = device;

        // Get a BluetoothSocket to connect with the given BluetoothDevice
        try {
        // MY_UUID is the app's UUID string, also used by the server code
        tmp = device.createRfcommSocketToServiceRecord(MY_UUID);
        } catch (IOException e) { }
        mmSocket = tmp;
    }

    public void run() {
        // Cancel discovery because it will slow down the connection
        mAdapter.cancelDiscovery();

        try {
            // Connect the device through the socket. This will block
            // until it succeeds or throws an exception.
            mmSocket.connect();
        } catch (IOException connectException) {
            // Unable to connect; close the socket and get out
            try {
                mmSocket.close();
            } catch (IOException closeException) { }
            return;
        }

        // Do work to manage the connection (in a separate thread)
        manageConnectedSocket(mmSocket);
    }

    /** will cancel an in-progress connection and close the socket */
    public void cancel() {
        try {
            mmSocket.close();
        } catch (IOException e) { }
    }
}
```

After the connection is established, the normal `InputStream` and `OutputStream` can be used to read and send data between the Bluetooth devices.

Recipe: Using Device Vibration

Device vibration is a common feature in all cellular phones. To control vibration on an Android device, a permission must be defined in the **AndroidManifest.xml** file:

```
<uses-permission android:name="android.permission.VIBRATE" />
```

Then, using the device vibrator is just another Android system service provided by the framework. It can be accessed using the `Vibrator` class:

```
Vibrator myVib = (Vibrator) getSystemService(Context.VIBRATOR_SERVICE);
```

With a `Vibrator` instance, just call the `vibrate()` method to start device vibration:

```
myVib.vibrate(3000); //Vibrate for 3 seconds
```

If needed, the `cancel()` method can be used to stop a vibration before it finishes:

```
myVib.cancel(); //Cancel the vibration
```

It is also possible to vibrate in a rhythmic pattern. This is specified as a vibration-pause sequence. For example:

```
long[] pattern = {2000,1000,5000};
 myVib.vibrate(pattern,1);
```

This causes the device to wait for 2 seconds and then start a pattern of vibrating for 1 second, then pausing for 5 seconds, indefinitely. The second argument to the `vibrate()` method is the index of the pattern at which to start repeating. This can be set to -1 to cause no repeat of the pattern at all.

Recipe: Accessing the Wireless Network

Many applications use the network connectivity of the Android device. To better understand how to handle application behavior due to network changes, Android provides access to the underlying network state. This is done by broadcasting intents to notify application components of changes in network connectivity and offer control over network settings and connections.

Android provides a system service through the `ConnectivityManager` class to let developers monitor the connectivity state, set the preferred network connection, and manage connectivity failover. This is initialized as follows:

```
ConnectivityManager myNetworkManager
 = (ConnectivityManager) getSystemService(Context.CONNECTIVITY_SERVICE);
```

To use the connectivity manager, the appropriate permission is needed in the **AndroidManifest.xml** file for the application:

```
<uses-permission android:name="android.permission.ACCESS_NETWORK_STATE" />
```

The connectivity manager does provide the two methods, getNetworkInfo() and getActiveNetworkInfo(), to obtain the details of the current network in a NetworkInfo class. However, a better way to monitor the network changes is to create a broadcast receiver, as shown in the following example:

```
private BroadcastReceiver mNetworkReceiver = new BroadcastReceiver(){
    public void onReceive(Context c, Intent i){
        Bundle b = i.getExtras();
        NetworkInfo ni = (NetworkInfo)
                        b.get(ConnectivityManager.EXTRA_NETWORK_INFO);
        if(ni.isConnected()){
            //Do the operation
        }else{
            //Announce to the user the network problem
        }
    }
};
```

After a broadcast receiver is defined, it can be registered to listen for Connectivity Manager.CONNECTIVITY_ACTION intents:

```
this.registerReceiver(mNetworkReceiver,
        new IntentFilter(ConnectivityManager.CONNECTIVITY_ACTION));
```

The mNetworkReceiver class defined previously extracts only the NetworkInfo from ConnectivityManager.EXTRA_NETWORK_INFO. However, the connectivity manager has more information that can be exposed. Following are the different types of information available:

- EXTRA_EXTRA_INFO—Contains additional information about the network state
- EXTRA_IS_FAILOVER—Returns a boolean value if the current connection is the result of a failover network
- EXTRA_NETWORK_INFO—Returns a NetworkInfo object
- EXTRA_NETWORK_TYPE—Triggers a CONNECTIVITY_ACTION broadcast
- EXTRA_NO_CONNECTIVITY—Returns a boolean value if there is no network connectivity
- EXTRA_OTHER_NETWORK_INFO—Returns a NetworkInfo object about the available network for failover when the network is disconnected
- EXTRA_REASON—Returns a String value that describes the reason for connection failure

ConnectivityManager also provides the capability to control network hardware and failover preferences. The setNetworkPreference() method can be used to select a network type. To change the network, the application needs to set another permission in the **AndroidManifest.xml** file:

```
<uses-permission android:name="android.permission.CHANGE_NETWORK_STATE" />
```

Near Field Communication (NFC)

NFC is a wireless technology that is built into many Android devices. When there are two devices with NFC capability, and small amounts of data such as playlists, web addresses, and contact information are to be moved, NFC is a fantastic medium for communication. It is ideal because it does not require complicated passwords, discovery, or device pairing. When using Android Beam, a simple tap on one device with an accept dialog tap on the other will transfer data using NFC between devices.

NFC reads and transfers small bits of data between devices through the use of encoded NFC Data Exchange Format (NDEF) messages. Each NDEF message contains at least one NDEF record. This record will contain the following fields:

- 3-bit type name format (TNF)
- Variable-length type
- Variable-length ID (optional)
- Variable-length payload

The 3-bit TNF field can contain many different values that are used by Android as part of the tag dispatch system to decide how to map a MIME type or URI to the NDEF message being read. If the tag is recognized, the ACTION_NDEF_DISCOVERED intent is used and an activity that handles this intent will be started. If no activities are registered when a tag is scanned or if the data is unrecognized, the ACTION_TECH_DISCOVERED intent is started and the user will be prompted to choose a program to open. When developing an application, developers may want to take advantage of the foreground dispatch system to keep the Android system from exiting the app and opening another to process the NFC data.

Using NFC in applications requires permission to access the NFC hardware. The following can be added to the **AndroidManifest.xml** file:

```
<uses-permission android:name="android.permission.NFC" />
```

By using a minimum SDK level of 10, read and write support for NFC, as well as enhanced NDEF options, is available for use in applications. For those wanting to use Android Beam, a minimum level of 14 must be used.

Recipe: Reading NFC Tags

Working with NFC is generally tied to reading and writing. The code in Listing 9.13 can be used to build a reader that will return some of the data stored in NFC tags. This data is then shown inside a TextView.

Listing 9.13   src/com/cookbook/nfcreader/MainActivity.java

```
package com.cookbook.nfcreader;

import com.cookbook.nfcreader.R;
```

```java
import android.app.Activity;
import android.app.PendingIntent;
import android.content.Intent;
import android.content.IntentFilter;
import android.nfc.NdefMessage;
import android.nfc.NdefRecord;
import android.nfc.NfcAdapter;
import android.os.Bundle;
import android.os.Parcelable;
import android.util.Log;
import android.widget.TextView;

public class MainActivity extends Activity {

    protected NfcAdapter nfcAdapter;
    protected PendingIntent nfcPendingIntent;

    private static final String TAG = MainActivity.class.getSimpleName();

        @Override
        protected void onCreate(Bundle savedInstanceState) {
            super.onCreate(savedInstanceState);
            setContentView(R.layout.activity_main);

            nfcAdapter = NfcAdapter.getDefaultAdapter(this);
        nfcPendingIntent = PendingIntent.getActivity(this, 0,
            new Intent(this, this.getClass()).addFlags(Intent.FLAG_ACTIVITY_SINGLE_TOP),
            0);
        }

        public void enableForegroundMode() {
        Log.d(TAG, "enableForegroundMode");

        IntentFilter tagDetected = new IntentFilter(NfcAdapter.ACTION_TAG_DISCOVERED);
        IntentFilter[] writeTagFilters = new IntentFilter[] {tagDetected};
        nfcAdapter.enableForegroundDispatch(this, nfcPendingIntent,
            writeTagFilters, null);
    }

        public void disableForegroundMode() {
        Log.d(TAG, "disableForegroundMode");

        nfcAdapter.disableForegroundDispatch(this);
    }

        @Override
        public void onNewIntent(Intent intent) {
        Log.d(TAG, "onNewIntent");
        String stringOut = "";

        if (NfcAdapter.ACTION_TAG_DISCOVERED.equals(intent.getAction())) {
            TextView textView = (TextView) findViewById(R.id.main_tv);

            Parcelable[] messages =
    intent.getParcelableArrayExtra(NfcAdapter.EXTRA_NDEF_MESSAGES);
```

```
        if (messages != null) {
          for (int i = 0; i < messages.length; i++) {
            NdefMessage message = (NdefMessage)messages[i];
            NdefRecord[] records = message.getRecords();

            for (int j = 0; j < records.length; j++) {
              NdefRecord record = records[j];
              stringOut += "TNF: " + record.getTnf() + "\n";
              stringOut += "MIME Type: " + new String(record.getType()) + "\n";
              stringOut += "Payload: " + new String(record.getPayload()) + "\n\n";
              textView.setText(stringOut);
            }
          }
        }
      }
    }
  }

  @Override
  protected void onResume() {
    Log.d(TAG, "onResume");

    super.onResume();

    enableForegroundMode();
  }

  @Override
  protected void onPause() {
    Log.d(TAG, "onPause");

    super.onPause();

    disableForegroundMode();
  }
}
```

The application built in Listing 9.13 uses the foreground dispatch system to ensure that the application is used to process any scanned NFC tags. Note that in the onPause() method, disableForegroundMode() is called to stop the application from being the default handler for NFC tags. The onResume() method restores this capability.

Recipe: Writing NFC Tags

Android devices that support NFC are also able to write to unprotected NFC tags. Listing 9.14 shows a sample application that will write information to an NFC tag. Note that when writing to NFC tags, the information on the card will be erased and replaced with the information written to it.

Listing 9.14   src/com/cookbook/nfcwriter/MainActivity.java

```java
package com.cookbook.nfcwriter;

import java.io.IOException;
import java.nio.charset.Charset;

import android.app.Activity;
import android.app.PendingIntent;
import android.content.Intent;
import android.content.IntentFilter;
import android.nfc.NdefMessage;
import android.nfc.NdefRecord;
import android.nfc.NfcAdapter;
import android.nfc.Tag;
import android.nfc.tech.Ndef;
import android.nfc.tech.NdefFormatable;
import android.os.Bundle;
import android.view.View;
import android.view.View.OnClickListener;
import android.widget.Button;
import android.widget.Toast;

public class MainActivity extends Activity implements OnClickListener {

    protected NfcAdapter nfcAdapter;
    private Button mainButton;
    private boolean mInWriteMode;

    @Override
    protected void onCreate(Bundle savedInstanceState) {
        super.onCreate(savedInstanceState);
        setContentView(R.layout.activity_main);

        nfcAdapter = NfcAdapter.getDefaultAdapter(this);

        mainButton = (Button)findViewById(R.id.main_button);
            mainButton.setOnClickListener(this);

    }

    public void onClick(View v) {
        displayMessage("Touch and hold tag against phone to write.");
        beginWrite();
    }

    @Override
    protected void onPause() {
        super.onPause();
        stopWrite();
    }

    @Override
    public void onNewIntent(Intent intent) {
        if(mInWriteMode) {
            mInWriteMode = false;
            Tag tag = intent.getParcelableExtra(NfcAdapter.EXTRA_TAG);
            writeTag(tag);
```

```
      }
      }

   private void beginWrite() {
     mInWriteMode = true;

         PendingIntent pendingIntent = PendingIntent.getActivity(this, 0,
new Intent(this, getClass()).addFlags(Intent.FLAG_ACTIVITY_SINGLE_TOP), 0);
         IntentFilter tagDetected =
new IntentFilter(NfcAdapter.ACTION_TAG_DISCOVERED);
         IntentFilter[] filters = new IntentFilter[] { tagDetected };

     nfcAdapter.enableForegroundDispatch(this, pendingIntent, filters, null);
   }

   private void stopWrite() {
     nfcAdapter.disableForegroundDispatch(this);
   }

   private boolean writeTag(Tag tag) {
     byte[] payload = "Text stored in an NFC tag".getBytes();
     byte[] mimeBytes = "text/plain".getBytes(Charset.forName("US-ASCII"));
         NdefRecord cardRecord = new NdefRecord(NdefRecord.TNF_MIME_MEDIA,
         mimeBytes, new byte[0], payload);
         NdefMessage message = new NdefMessage(new NdefRecord[] { cardRecord });

     try {
       Ndef ndef = Ndef.get(tag);
       if (ndef != null) {
         ndef.connect();

         if (!ndef.isWritable()) {
           displayMessage("This is a read-only tag.");
           return false;
         }

         int size = message.toByteArray().length;
         if (ndef.getMaxSize() < size) {
           displayMessage("There is not enough space to write.");
           return false;
         }

         ndef.writeNdefMessage(message);
         displayMessage("Write successful.");
         return true;
       } else {
         NdefFormatable format = NdefFormatable.get(tag);
         if (format != null) {
           try {
             format.connect();
             format.format(message);
             displayMessage("Write successful\nLaunch a scanning app or scan and
choose to read.");
             return true;
           } catch (IOException e) {
             displayMessage("Unable to format tag to NDEF.");
             return false;
           }
```

```
        } else {
          displayMessage("Tag doesn't appear to support NDEF format.");
          return false;
        }
      }
    } catch (Exception e) {
      displayMessage("Write failed.");
    }

        return false;
    }

  private void displayMessage(String message) {
    Toast.makeText(MainActivity.this, message, Toast.LENGTH_LONG).show();
  }
}
```

The application built in Listing 9.14 will write "Text stored in an NFC tag" as the payload for the message with a MIME type of "text/plain." You can see these values being placed in the `writeTag()` method. By changing these values, you can change how the NFC tag will be handled by the Android system.

Universal Serial Bus (USB)

Starting with Android 3.1, USB devices can be used in Android in either host or accessory mode. Older Android devices running Gingerbread 2.3.4 can use accessory mode provided that the Google support APIs are included. The following two classes are used when developing for accessory mode:

- `UsbManager`—Allows communication with connected USB accessories
- `UsbAccessory`—Represents a USB device with methods for retrieving information about it

Host mode allows the Android-powered device to control whatever is connected. This also means that the Android device will be powering the USB device. Examples of devices that would be used in host mode include keyboards, mice, and other input devices. Host mode is available in Android 3.1 and above. The following classes are used when developing in host mode:

- `UsbManager`—Accesses the state of USB connections and communicates with USB devices
- `UsbDevice`—Represents the USB device that is plugged in
- `UsbInterface`—An interface on a `UsbDevice`
- `UsbEndpoint`—An endpoint of a `UsbInterface`
- `UsbDeviceConnection`—Sends and receives messages to a USB device

- `UsbRequest`—Represents a USB request packet
- `UsbConstants`—Constants that are used for the USB protocol

Accessory mode allows the USB device to power the Android device. USB devices that use accessory mode must follow the rules of the Android Accessory Development Kit (ADK). Examples of USB devices that would be used in accessory mode include external diagnostic devices, music controllers, docking stations, and other similar devices.

When developing with a USB device plugged in, developers will probably not be able to use USB debugging. When this is the case, LogCat can still be used, but over a wireless connection. This is done by using ADB (Android Debug Bridge) over TCP. To do this, start with the Android device in debug mode and connected to a computer. Enable Wi-Fi on the device and find the current IP address. Open the terminal or command prompt and navigate to the **SDK installation** directory and into the **platform-tools** directory. Type the following into the command prompt or terminal:

adb tcpip 5555

This will change the connection mode from USB to TCP/IP. If this is not changed, attempts to connect to the device over the network will fail. To connect to the device, type the following, where **DEVICEIPADDRESS** is the IP address of the device to be connected:

adb connect DEVICEIPADDRESS:5555

Note that for some operating systems, the port (**:5555**) does not need to be added to the command. The port number is not limited to 5555; any open port can be used. If the connect command is run with the port and it fails, try running the command again without specifying any port number.

Once connected, all of the commands can be run that would normally run under ADB. Of these, `adb logcat` is probably the most important.

After using the network to debug an application and to revert to USB, type **adb usb** into the console and ADB will restart, looking for USB connections.

For more information on ADB and how to use it, visit http://developer.android.com/tools/help/adb.html.

10

Networking

Network-based applications provide increased value for a user, in that content can be dynamic and interactive. Networking enables multiple features, from social networking to cloud computing.

This chapter focuses on the network state, short message service (SMS), Internet resource-based applications, and social networking applications. Knowing the network state is important to applications that fetch or update information that is available through a network connection. SMS is a communication service component that enables the exchange of short text messages between mobile phone devices. Internet resource-based applications rely on web content such as HTML (HyperText Markup Language), XML (eXtensible Markup Language), and JSON (JavaScript Object Notation). Social networking applications, such as Twitter, are important methods for people to connect with each other.

Reacting to the Network State

Knowing how and if a device is connected to a network is a very important facet of Android development. Applications that stream information from a network server may need to warn users about the large amount of data that may be charged to their accounts. Application latency issues may also be a concern. Making some simple queries enables users to find out if they are currently connected through a network device and how to react when the connection state changes.

Recipe: Checking for Connectivity

The `ConnectivityManager` is used for determining the connectivity of a device. This recipe can be used to determine what network interfaces are connected to a network. Listing 10.1 uses the `ConnectivityManager` to display if the device is connected via Wi-Fi or Bluetooth.

Listing 10.1   src/com/cookbook/connectivitycheck/MainActivity.java

```java
package com.cookbook.connectivitycheck;

import android.app.Activity;
import android.content.Context;
import android.net.ConnectivityManager;
import android.net.NetworkInfo;
import android.os.Bundle;
import android.widget.TextView;

public class MainActivity extends Activity {
  TextView tv;

  @Override
  protected void onCreate(Bundle savedInstanceState) {
    super.onCreate(savedInstanceState);
    setContentView(R.layout.activity_main);
    tv = (TextView) findViewById(R.id.tv_main);
    try {
      String service = Context.CONNECTIVITY_SERVICE;
      ConnectivityManager cm = (ConnectivityManager)getSystemService(service);
      NetworkInfo activeNetwork = cm.getActiveNetworkInfo();

      boolean isWiFi = activeNetwork.getType() == ConnectivityManager.TYPE_WIFI;
      boolean isBT = activeNetwork.getType() == ConnectivityManager.TYPE_BLUETOOTH;

      tv.setText("WiFi connected: "+isWiFi+"\nBluetooth connected: "+isBT);
    } catch(Exception nullPointerException)   {
      tv.setText("No connected networks found");
    }
  }
}
```

Listing 10.1 uses the constants TYPE_WIFI and TYPE_BLUETOOTH to check for connectivity on these networks. In addition to TYPE_WIFI and TYPE_BLUETOOTH, the following constants can also be used to determine connectivity:

- TYPE_DUMMY—For dummy data connections
- TYPE_ETHERNET—For the default Ethernet connection
- TYPE_MOBILE—For the default mobile data connection
- TYPE_MOBILE_DUN—For DUN-specific mobile data connections
- TYPE_MOBILE_HIPRI—For high-priority mobile data connections
- TYPE_MOBILE_MMS—For an MMS-specific mobile data connection
- TYPE_MOBILE_SUPL—For an SUPL-specific mobile data connection
- TYPE_WIMAX—For the default WiMAX data connection

Figure 10.1   Checking for device connectivity

Figure 10.1 shows an application running with the code from Listing 10.1. Even though Bluetooth has been enabled, it reports false for being connected because it does not currently have an active connection.

Recipe: Receiving Connectivity Changes

A broadcast receiver can be used to check the status of network connectivity when it is necessary to react to changes in connectivity status.

A broadcast receiver can be declared in the application manifest, or it can be a subclass inside the main activity. While both are accessible, this recipe uses a subclass in conjunction with the onCreate() and onDestroy() methods to register and unregister the receiver.

As this recipe checks for connectivity, the following permissions need to be added to the application manifest:

```
<uses-permission android:name="android.permission.INTERNET" />
<uses-permission android:name="android.permission.ACCESS_NETWORK_STATE" />
```

Listing 10.2 shows the code needed to check for connectivity changes. When a change is detected, the application will display a toast message informing the user of the change.

Listing 10.2 src/com/cookbook/connectivitychange/MainActivity.java

```
package com.cookbook.connectivitychange;

import android.app.Activity;
import android.content.BroadcastReceiver;
import android.content.Context;
import android.content.Intent;
import android.content.IntentFilter;
import android.net.ConnectivityManager;
import android.net.NetworkInfo;
import android.os.Bundle;
import android.widget.Toast;

public class MainActivity extends Activity {

  private ConnectivityReceiver receiver = new ConnectivityReceiver();

  @Override
  protected void onCreate(Bundle savedInstanceState) {
    super.onCreate(savedInstanceState);
    setContentView(R.layout.activity_main);

    IntentFilter filter = new IntentFilter(ConnectivityManager.CONNECTIVITY_ACTION);
        receiver = new ConnectivityReceiver();
        this.registerReceiver(receiver, filter);
  }

  @Override
    public void onDestroy() {
        super.onDestroy();
        if (receiver != null) {
            this.unregisterReceiver(receiver);
        }
    }

  public class ConnectivityReceiver extends BroadcastReceiver {

    @Override
    public void onReceive(Context context, Intent intent) {
      ConnectivityManager conn =
(ConnectivityManager)context.getSystemService(Context.CONNECTIVITY_SERVICE);
      NetworkInfo networkInfo = conn.getActiveNetworkInfo();

      if (networkInfo != null && networkInfo.getType() == ConnectivityManager.
TYPE_WIFI) {
        Toast.makeText(context, "WiFi is connected", Toast.LENGTH_SHORT).show();
        } else if (networkInfo != null) {
          Toast.makeText(context, "WiFi is disconnected", Toast.LENGTH_SHORT).show();
```

```
        } else {
          Toast.makeText(context, "No active connection", Toast.LENGTH_SHORT).show();
        }
      }
    }
}
```

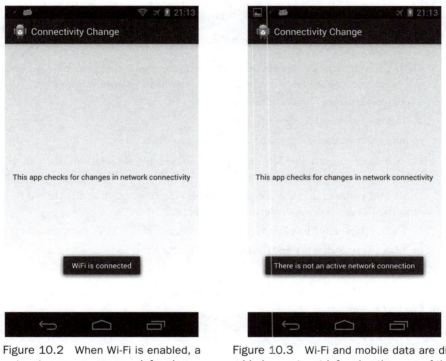

Figure 10.2   When Wi-Fi is enabled, a toast message appears informing the user of the connection

Figure 10.3   Wi-Fi and mobile data are disabled, so a toast informing the user of the lack of network connectivity is displayed

Figure 10.2 shows the message that appears when Wi-Fi is connected. Figure 10.3 shows the message that appears when both Wi-Fi and mobile data have been disconnected.

Using SMS

The Android Framework provides full access to SMS functionality using the SmsManager class. Early versions of Android placed SmsManager in the android.telephony.gsm package. Since Android 1.5, where SmsManager supports both GSM and CDMA mobile telephony standards, the SmsManager class is now placed in the android.telephony package.

Sending an SMS through the SmsManager class is fairly straightforward:

1. Set the permission in the **AndroidManifest.xml** file to send SMS:

```
<uses-permission android:name="android.permission.SEND_SMS" />
```

2. Use the SmsManager.getDefault() static method to get an SMS manager instance:

```
SmsManager mySMS = SmsManager.getDefault();
```

3. Define the destination phone number and the message that is to be sent. Use the sendTextMesssage() method to send the SMS to another device:

```
String destination = "16501234567";

String msg = "Sending my first message";

mySMS.sendTextMessage(destination, null, msg, null, null);
```

This is sufficient to send an SMS message. However, the three additional parameters in the previous call set to null can be used as follows:

- The second parameter is the specific SMS service center to use. Set this to null to use the default service center from the carrier.
- The fourth parameter is a PendingIntent to track if the SMS message was sent.
- The fifth parameter is a PendingIntent to track if the SMS message was received.

To use the fourth and fifth parameters, a sent message and a delivered message intent need to be declared:

```
String SENT_SMS_FLAG = "SENT_SMS";
String DELIVER_SMS_FLAG = "DELIVER_SMS";

Intent sentIn = new Intent(SENT_SMS_FLAG);
PendingIntent sentPIn = PendingIntent.getBroadcast(this,0,sentIn,0);

Intent deliverIn = new Intent(SENT_SMS_FLAG);
PendingIntent deliverPIn
                = PendingIntent.getBroadcast(this,0,deliverIn,0);
```

Then, a BroadcastReceiver class needs to be registered for each PendingIntent to receive the result:

```
BroadcastReceiver sentReceiver = new BroadcastReceiver(){
    @Override public void onReceive(Context c, Intent in) {
        switch(getResultCode()){
            case Activity.RESULT_OK:
                //sent SMS message successfully;
```

```
                break;
            default:
                //sent SMS message failed
                break;
        }
    }
};
BroadcastReceiver deliverReceiver = new BroadcastReceiver(){
    @Override public void onReceive(Context c, Intent in) {
        //SMS delivered actions
    }
};

 registerReceiver(sentReceiver, new IntentFilter(SENT_SMS_FLAG));
 registerReceiver(deliverReceiver, new IntentFilter(DELIVER_SMS_FLAG));
```

Most SMSs are restricted to 140 characters per text message. To make sure the message is within this limitation, use the divideMessage() method that divides the text into fragments in the maximum SMS message size. Then, the method sendMultipartTextMessage() should be used instead of the sendTextMessage() method. The only difference is the use of an ArrayList of messages and pending intents:

```
ArrayList<String> multiSMS = mySMS.divideMessage(msg);
ArrayList<PendingIntent> sentIns = new ArrayList<PendingIntent>();
ArrayList<PendingIntent> deliverIns = new ArrayList<PendingIntent>();

for(int i=0; i< multiSMS.size(); i++){
    sentIns.add(sentIn);
    deliverIns.add(deliverIn);
}

mySMS.sendMultipartTextMessage(destination, null,
                        multiSMS, sentIns, deliverIns);
```

Recipe: Autosending an SMS Based on a Received SMS

Because most SMS messages are not read by the recipient until hours later, this recipe sends an autoresponse SMS when an SMS is received. This is done by creating an Android service in the background that can receive incoming SMSs. An alternative method is to register a broadcast receiver in the **AndroidManifest.xml** file.

The application must declare permission to send and receive SMSs in the **AndroidManifest.xml** file, as shown in Listing 10.3. It also declares a main activity SMSResponder that creates the autoresponse and a service ResponderService to send the response when an SMS is received.

Listing 10.3   **AndroidManifest.xml**

```xml
<?xml version="1.0" encoding="utf-8"?>
<manifest xmlns:android="http://schemas.android.com/apk/res/android"
      package="com.cookbook.SMSResponder"
      android:versionCode="1"
      android:versionName="1.0">
    <application android:icon="@drawable/icon"
                   android:label="@string/app_name">
        <activity android:name=".SMSResponder"
                     android:label="@string/app_name">
            <intent-filter>
              <action android:name="android.intent.action.MAIN" />
              <category android:name="android.intent.category.LAUNCHER" />
            </intent-filter>
        </activity>
        <service android:enabled="true" android:name=".ResponderService">
        </service>
    </application>

    <uses-permission android:name="android.permission.RECEIVE_SMS"/>
    <uses-permission android:name="android.permission.SEND_SMS"/>
</manifest>
```

The main layout file shown in Listing 10.4 contains a LinearLayout with three views: a TextView to display the message used for the autoresponse, Button used to commit changes on the reply message inside the application, and EditText where the user can enter a reply message.

Listing 10.4   **res/layout/main.xml**

```xml
<?xml version="1.0" encoding="utf-8"?>
<LinearLayout xmlns:android="http://schemas.android.com/apk/res/android"
    android:orientation="vertical"
    android:layout_width="match_parent"
    android:layout_height="match_parent">
      <TextView android:id="@+id/display"
      android:layout_width="match_parent"
      android:layout_height="wrap_content"
      android:text="@string/hello"
      android:textSize="18dp"
      />
      <Button android:id="@+id/submit"
      android:layout_width="wrap_content"
      android:layout_height="wrap_content"
      android:text="Change my response"
      />
      <EditText android:id="@+id/editText"
      android:layout_width="match_parent"
      android:layout_height="match_parent"
      />
</LinearLayout>
```

The main activity is shown in Listing 10.5. It starts the service that listens and auto-responds to SMS messages. It also allows the user to change the reply message and save it in SharedPreferences for future use.

Listing 10.5   src/com/cookbook/SMSresponder/SMSResponder.java

```java
package com.cookbook.SMSresponder;

import android.app.Activity;
import android.content.Intent;
import android.content.SharedPreferences;
import android.content.SharedPreferences.Editor;
import android.os.Bundle;
import android.preference.PreferenceManager;
import android.util.Log;
import android.view.View;
import android.view.View.OnClickListener;
import android.widget.Button;
import android.widget.EditText;
import android.widget.TextView;

public class SMSResponder extends Activity {
    TextView tv1;
    EditText ed1;
    Button bt1;
    SharedPreferences myprefs;
    Editor updater;
    String reply=null;

    @Override
    public void onCreate(Bundle savedInstanceState) {
        super.onCreate(savedInstanceState);
        setContentView(R.layout.main);

        myprefs = PreferenceManager.getDefaultSharedPreferences(this);
        tv1 = (TextView) this.findViewById(R.id.display);
        ed1 = (EditText) this.findViewById(R.id.editText);
        bt1 = (Button) this.findViewById(R.id.submit);

        reply = myprefs.getString("reply",
                "Thank you for your message. I am busy now."
              + "I will call you later");
        tv1.setText(reply);

        updater = myprefs.edit();
        ed1.setHint(reply);
        bt1.setOnClickListener(new OnClickListener() {
            public void onClick(View view) {
                updater.putString("reply", ed1.getText().toString());
                updater.commit();
                SMSResponder.this.finish();
            }
        });

        try {
```

```
            // Start service
            Intent svc = new Intent(this, ResponderService.class);
            startService(svc);
        }
        catch (Exception e) {
            Log.e("onCreate", "service creation problem", e);
        }
    }
}
```

The majority of code is contained in the service, as shown in Listing 10.6. It retrieves `SharedPreferences` for this application first. Then, it registers a broadcast receiver for listening to incoming and outgoing SMS messages. The broadcast receiver for outgoing SMS messages is not used here but is shown for completeness.

The incoming SMS broadcast receiver uses a bundle to retrieve the protocol description unit (PDU), which contains the SMS text and any additional SMS metadata, and parses it into an `Object` array. The method `createFromPdu()` converts the `Object` array into an `SmsMessage`. Then the method `getOriginatingAddress()` can be used to get the sender's phone number, and `getMessageBody()` can be used to get the text message.

In this recipe, after the sender address is retrieved, the `respond()` method is called. This method tries to get the data stored inside `SharedPreferences` for the auto-respond message. If no data is stored, it uses a default value. Then, it creates two `PendingIntents` for sent status and delivered status. The method `divideMessage()` is used to make sure the message is not oversized. After all the data is managed, it is sent using `sendMultiTextMessage()`.

Listing 10.6   src/com/cookbook/SMSresponder/ResponderService.java

```
package com.cookbook.SMSresponder;

import java.util.ArrayList;

import android.app.Activity;
import android.app.PendingIntent;
import android.app.Service;
import android.content.BroadcastReceiver;
import android.content.Context;
import android.content.Intent;
import android.content.IntentFilter;
import android.content.SharedPreferences;
import android.os.Bundle;
import android.os.IBinder;
import android.preference.PreferenceManager;
import android.telephony.SmsManager;
import android.telephony.SmsMessage;
import android.util.Log;
import android.widget.Toast;

public class ResponderService extends Service {
```

```java
//the action fired by the Android system when an SMS was received
private static final String RECEIVED_ACTION =
                        "android.provider.Telephony.SMS_RECEIVED";
private static final String SENT_ACTION="SENT_SMS";
private static final String DELIVERED_ACTION="DELIVERED_SMS";

String requester;
String reply="";
SharedPreferences myprefs;

@Override
public void onCreate() {
    super.onCreate();
    myprefs = PreferenceManager.getDefaultSharedPreferences(this);

    registerReceiver(sentReceiver, new IntentFilter(SENT_ACTION));
    registerReceiver(deliverReceiver,
                        new IntentFilter(DELIVERED_ACTION));

    IntentFilter filter = new IntentFilter(RECEIVED_ACTION);
    registerReceiver(receiver, filter);

    IntentFilter attemptedfilter = new IntentFilter(SENT_ACTION);
    registerReceiver(sender,attemptedfilter);
}

private BroadcastReceiver sender = new BroadcastReceiver(){
    @Override
    public void onReceive(Context c, Intent i) {
        if(i.getAction().equals(SENT_ACTION)) {
            if(getResultCode() != Activity.RESULT_OK) {
                String recipient = i.getStringExtra("recipient");
                requestReceived(recipient);
            }
        }
    }
};
BroadcastReceiver sentReceiver = new BroadcastReceiver() {
    @Override public void onReceive(Context c, Intent in) {
        switch(getResultCode()) {
            case Activity.RESULT_OK:
                //sent SMS message successfully;
                smsSent();
                break;
            default:
                //sent SMS message failed
                smsFailed();
                break;
        }
    }
};

public void smsSent() {
    Toast.makeText(this, "SMS sent", Toast.LENGTH_SHORT);
}
public void smsFailed() {
    Toast.makeText(this, "SMS sent failed", Toast.LENGTH_SHORT);
```

```
    }
public void smsDelivered() {
    Toast.makeText(this, "SMS delivered", Toast.LENGTH_SHORT);
}

BroadcastReceiver deliverReceiver = new BroadcastReceiver() {
    @Override public void onReceive(Context c, Intent in) {
        //SMS delivered actions
        smsDelivered();
    }
};

public void requestReceived(String f) {
    Log.v("ResponderService","In requestReceived");
    requester=f;
}

BroadcastReceiver receiver = new BroadcastReceiver() {
    @Override
    public void onReceive(Context c, Intent in) {
        Log.v("ResponderService","On Receive");
        reply="";
        if(in.getAction().equals(RECEIVED_ACTION)) {
            Log.v("ResponderService","On SMS RECEIVE");

            Bundle bundle = in.getExtras();
            if(bundle!=null) {
                Object[] pdus = (Object[])bundle.get("pdus");
                SmsMessage[] messages = new SmsMessage[pdus.length];
                for(int i = 0; i<pdus.length; i++) {
                    Log.v("ResponderService","FOUND MESSAGE");
                    messages[i] =
                            SmsMessage.createFromPdu((byte[])pdus[i]);
                }
                for(SmsMessage message: messages) {
                    requestReceived(message.getOriginatingAddress());
                }
                respond();
            }
        }
    }
};

@Override
public void onStart(Intent intent, int startId) {
    super.onStart(intent, startId);
}

public void respond() {
    Log.v("ResponderService","Responding to " + requester);
    reply = myprefs.getString("reply",
                        "Thank you for your message. I am busy now."
                        + "I will call you later.");
    SmsManager sms = SmsManager.getDefault();
    Intent sentIn = new Intent(SENT_ACTION);
    PendingIntent sentPIn = PendingIntent.getBroadcast(this,
                                                0,sentIn,0);
```

```
        Intent deliverIn = new Intent(DELIVERED_ACTION);
        PendingIntent deliverPIn = PendingIntent.getBroadcast(this,
                                              0,deliverIn,0);
        ArrayList<String> Msgs = sms.divideMessage(reply);
        ArrayList<PendingIntent> sentIns = new ArrayList<PendingIntent>();
        ArrayList<PendingIntent> deliverIns =
                                new ArrayList<PendingIntent>();

        for(int i=0; i< Msgs.size(); i++) {
            sentIns.add(sentPIn);
            deliverIns.add(deliverPIn);
        }

        sms.sendMultipartTextMessage(requester, null,
                                  Msgs, sentIns, deliverIns);
    }

    @Override
    public void onDestroy() {
        super.onDestroy();
        unregisterReceiver(receiver);
        unregisterReceiver(sender);
    }

    @Override
    public IBinder onBind(Intent arg0) {
        return null;
    }
}
```

Using Web Content

To launch an Internet browser to display web content, the implicit intent
ACTION_VIEW can be used as discussed in Chapter 2, "Application Basics: Activities
and Intents," for example:

```
Intent i = new Intent(Intent.ACTION_VIEW);
i.setData(Uri.parse("http://www.google.com"));
startActivity(i);
```

It is also possible for developers to create their own web browser by using WebView,
which is a View that displays web content. As with any view, it can occupy the full
screen or only a portion of the layout in an activity. WebView uses WebKit, the open
source browser engine used in Apple's Safari, to render web pages.

Recipe: Customizing a Web Browser

There are two ways to obtain a WebView object. It can be instantiated from the
constructor:

```
WebView webview = new WebView(this);
```

Alternatively, a `WebView` can be used in a layout and declared in the activity:

```
WebView webView = (WebView) findViewById(R.id.webview);
```

After the object is retrieved, a web page can be displayed using the `loadURL()` method:

```
webview.loadUrl("http://www.google.com/");
```

The `WebSettings` class can be used to define the features of the browser. For example, network images can be blocked in the browser to reduce the data loading using the `setBlockNetworkImage()` method. The font size of the displayed web content can be set using the `setDefaultFontSize()` method. Some other commonly used settings are shown in the following example:

```
WebSettings webSettings = webView.getSettings();
webSettings.setSaveFormData(false);
webSettings.setJavaScriptEnabled(true);
webSettings.setSavePassword(false);
webSettings.setSupportZoom(true);
```

Recipe: Using an HTTP GET

Besides launching a browser or using the `WebView` widget to include a WebKit-based browser control in an activity, developers might also want to create native Internet-based applications. This means the application relies on only the raw data from the Internet, such as images, media files, and XML data. Just the data of relevance can be loaded. This is important for creating social networking applications. Two packages are useful in Android to handle network communication: `java.net` and `android.net`.

In this recipe, an HTTP GET is used to retrieve XML or JSON data (see www.json .org/ for an overview). In particular, the Google search Representational State Transfer (REST) API is demonstrated, and the following query is used:

```
http://ajax.googleapis.com/ajax/services/search/web?v=1.0&q=
```

To search for any topic, the topic just needs to be appended to the query. For example, to search for information on the National Basketball Association (NBA), the following query returns JSON data:

```
http://ajax.googleapis.com/ajax/services/search/web?v=1.0&q=NBA
```

The activity needs Internet permission to run. So, the following should be added to the **AndroidManifest.xml** file:

```
<uses-permission android:name="android.permission.INTERNET"/>
```

The main layout is shown in Listing 10.7. It has three views: `EditText` for user input of the search topic, `Button` to trigger the search, and `TextView` to display the search result.

Listing 10.7   res/layout/main.xml

```xml
<?xml version="1.0" encoding="utf-8"?>
<LinearLayout xmlns:android="http://schemas.android.com/apk/res/android"
    android:orientation="vertical"
    android:layout_width="match_parent"
    android:layout_height="match_parent"
    >
            <EditText
            android:id="@+id/editText"
            android:layout_width="match_parent"
            android:layout_height="wrap_content"
            android:singleLine="true"
             />
            <Button
                android:id="@+id/submit"
            android:layout_width="wrap_content"
            android:layout_height="wrap_content"
            android:text="Search"
            />
            <TextView
            android:id="@+id/display"
            android:layout_width="match_parent"
            android:layout_height="match_parent"
            android:text="@string/hello"
            android:textSize="18dp"
            />
</LinearLayout>
```

The main activity is shown in Listing 10.8. It initiates the three layout elements in onCreate(). Inside the OnClickListener class for the button, it calls searchRequest(). This composes the search item using the Google REST API URL and then initiates a URL class instance. The URL class instance is then used to get an HttpURLConnection instance.

The HttpURLConnection instance can retrieve the status of the connection. When HttpURLConnection returns a result code of HTTP_OK, it means the whole HTTP transaction went through. Then, the JSON data returned from the HTTP transaction can be dumped into a string. This is done using an InputStreamReader passed to a BufferReader to read the data and create a String instance. After the result from HTTP is obtained, it uses another function processResponse() to parse the JSON data.

Listing 10.8   src/com/cookbook/internet/search/GoogleSearch.java

```java
package com.cookbook.internet.search;

import java.io.BufferedReader;
import java.io.IOException;
import java.io.InputStreamReader;
import java.net.HttpURLConnection;
import java.net.MalformedURLException;
```

```java
import java.net.URL;
import java.security.NoSuchAlgorithmException;

import org.json.JSONArray;
import org.json.JSONException;
import org.json.JSONObject;

import android.app.Activity;
import android.os.Bundle;
import android.util.Log;
import android.view.View;
import android.view.View.OnClickListener;
import android.widget.Button;
import android.widget.EditText;
import android.widget.TextView;

public class GoogleSearch extends Activity {
    /** called when the activity is first created */
    TextView tv1;
    EditText ed1;
    Button bt1;
    static String url =
"http://ajax.googleapis.com/ajax/services/search/web?v=1.0&q=";

    @Override
    public void onCreate(Bundle savedInstanceState) {
        super.onCreate(savedInstanceState);
        setContentView(R.layout.main);
        tv1 = (TextView) this.findViewById(R.id.display);
        ed1 = (EditText) this.findViewById(R.id.editText);
        bt1 = (Button) this.findViewById(R.id.submit);

        bt1.setOnClickListener(new OnClickListener() {
            public void onClick(View view) {
                    if(ed1.getText().toString()!=null) {
                        try{
                            processResponse(
                              searchRequest(ed1.getText().toString()));
                        } catch(Exception e) {
                            Log.v("Exception Google search",
                                "Exception:"+e.getMessage());
                        }
                    }
                    ed1.setText("");
            }
        });
    }

    public String searchRequest(String searchString)
                        throws MalformedURLException, IOException {
        String newFeed=url+searchString;
        StringBuilder response = new StringBuilder();
        Log.v("gsearch","gsearch url:"+newFeed);
        URL url = new URL(newFeed);

        HttpURLConnection httpconn
                            = (HttpURLConnection) url.openConnection();
```

```
        if(httpconn.getResponseCode()==HttpURLConnection.HTTP_OK) {
            BufferedReader input = new BufferedReader(
                    new InputStreamReader(httpconn.getInputStream()),
                    8192);
            String strLine = null;
            while ((strLine = input.readLine()) != null) {
                response.append(strLine);
            }
            input.close();
        }
        return response.toString();
    }

    public void processResponse(String resp) throws IllegalStateException,
                    IOException, JSONException, NoSuchAlgorithmException {
        StringBuilder sb = new StringBuilder();
        Log.v("gsearch","gsearch result:"+resp);
        JSONObject mResponseObject = new JSONObject(resp);
        JSONObject responObject
                        = mResponseObject.getJSONObject("responseData");
        JSONArray array = responObject.getJSONArray("results");
        Log.v("gsearch","number of results:"+array.length());
        for(int i = 0; i<array.length(); i++) {
            Log.v("result",i+"] "+array.get(i).toString());
            String title = array.getJSONObject(i).getString("title");
            String urllink = array.getJSONObject(i)
                                    .getString("visibleUrl");
            sb.append(title);
            sb.append("\n");
            sb.append(urllink);
            sb.append("\n");
        }
        tv1.setText(sb.toString());
    }
}
```

The detailed mechanism used requires an understanding of the incoming JSON data structure. In this case, the Google REST API provides all the result data under the results JSONArray. Figure 10.4 shows the search result for NBA.

Note that this recipe will run on Android projects only prior to API Level 11. This is due to running network requests on the main thread. The next recipe, "Using HTTP POST," uses an AsyncTask to fix the NetworkOnMainThreadException that is thrown.

Recipe: Using HTTP POST

Sometimes, raw binary data needs to be retrieved from the Internet such as an image, video, or audio file. This can be achieved with the HTTP POST protocol by using setRequestMethod(), such as:

```
httpconn.setRequestMethod(POST);
```

Figure 10.4   The search result from the Google REST API query

Accessing data through the Internet can be time-consuming and unpredictable. Therefore, a separate thread should be spawned anytime network data is required.

In addition to the methods shown in Chapter 3, "Threads, Services, Receivers, and Alerts," there is a built-in Android class called AsyncTask that allows background operations to be performed and publishes results on the UI thread without needing to manipulate threads or handlers. So, the POST method can be implemented asynchronously with the following code:

```
private class MyGoogleSearch extends AsyncTask<String, Integer, String> {

    protected String doInBackground(String... searchKey) {

        String key = searchKey[0];

        try {
            return searchRequest(key);
        } catch(Exception e) {
            Log.v("Exception Google search",
                    "Exception:"+e.getMessage());
            return "";
        }
    }
```

```
        protected void onPostExecute(String result) {
            try {
                processResponse(result);
            } catch(Exception e) {
                Log.v("Exception Google search",
                        "Exception:"+e.getMessage());
            }
        }
    }
}
```

This excerpt can be added to the end of the **GoogleSearch.java** activity in List-ing 10.8. It provides the same result with one additional change to the code inside the button `OnClickListener` to

```
new MyGoogleSearch().execute(ed1.getText().toString());
```

Recipe: Using WebViews

WebViews are useful for displaying content that may change on a semiregular basis, or for data that may need to be changed without having to force an update to the applica-tion. WebViews can also be used to allow web applications access to some client-side features of the Android system such as using the toast messaging system.

To add a WebView to an application, the following should be added to the layout XML:

```
<WebView   xmlns:android="http://schemas.android.com/apk/res/android"
    android:id="@+id/webview"
    android:layout_width="match_parent"
    android:layout_height="match_parent" />
```

The following permission must also be added to the application manifest:

```
<uses-permission android:name="android.permission.INTERNET" />
```

To create a simple page without any user interaction, add the following to the `onCreate()` method of the main activity:

```
WebView myWebView = (WebView) findViewById(R.id.webview);
myWebView.loadUrl("http://www.example.com/");
```

In order to enable JavaScript on the page inside of the WebView, the WebSettings must be changed. This can be done using the following:

```
WebSettings webSettings = myWebView.getSettings();
webSettings.setJavaScriptEnabled(true);
```

To trigger native methods from JavaScript, a class that can be used as an inter-face needs to be created. Listing 10.9 shows an activity with all of the pieces put together.

Listing 10.9   **src/com/cookbook/viewtoaweb/MainActivity.java**

```java
package com.cookbook.viewtoaweb;

import android.app.Activity;
import android.content.Context;
import android.os.Bundle;
import android.webkit.JavascriptInterface;
import android.webkit.WebSettings;
import android.webkit.WebView;
import android.widget.Toast;

public class MainActivity extends Activity {

  @Override
  protected void onCreate(Bundle savedInstanceState) {
    super.onCreate(savedInstanceState);
    setContentView(R.layout.activity_main);

    WebView myWebView = (WebView) findViewById(R.id.webview);
    WebSettings webSettings = myWebView.getSettings();
    webSettings.setJavaScriptEnabled(true);
    myWebView.addJavascriptInterface(new WebAppInterface(this), "Android");
    myWebView.loadUrl("http://www.devcannon.com/androidcookbook/chapter10/webview/");
  }

  public class WebAppInterface {
      Context context;

      WebAppInterface(Context c) {
          context = c;
      }

      @JavascriptInterface
      public void triggerToast(String toast) {
          Toast.makeText(context, toast, Toast.LENGTH_SHORT).show();
      }
  }
}
```

The following HTML is used to trigger the code from Listing 10.9:

```html
<input type="text" name="toastText" id="toastText" />
<button id="btn" onClick="androidToast()">Toast it</button>
```

The following JavaScript is used to trigger the code:

```javascript
function androidToast() {
  var input = document.getElementById('toastText');
  Android.triggerToast(input.value);
}
```

Figure 10.5 displays the WebView with a toast that was launched from the page being viewed.

Figure 10.5   Triggering a toast message from a page inside a WebView

Recipe: Parsing JSON

JSON is a very popular format for data transfer, especially when used with web services. Android has included a set of classes in the `org.json` package that can be imported into code to allow manipulation of JSON data.

To get started parsing, first a JSON object needs to be created; this can be done like so:

```
private JSONObject jsonObject;
```

Some data in JSON format is also needed. The following creates a string containing some JSON data:

```
private String jsonString =
"{\"item\":{\"name\":\"myName\",\"numbers\":[{\"id\":\"1\"},{\"id\":\"2\"}]}}";
```

Because a string is not a JSON object, one will need to be created that contains the value of the string. This can be done like so:

```
jsonObject = new JSONObject(jsonString);
```

Now that there is an object to manipulate, data can be gotten from it. If the `getString()` method were used to pull data from an "object" that is inside the

jsonObject, a JSONException would be thrown. This is because it is not a string.
To pull a specific value, another object must be set up that contains the desired string,
like so:

```
JSONObject itemObject = jsonObject.getJSONObject("item");
```

The value of "name" can be gotten by using the following:

```
String jsonName = itemObject.getString("name");
```

A loop may be used to get the information stored in the "numbers" section of
jsonObject. This can be done by creating a JSONArray object and looping through it,
as follows:

```
JSONArray numbersArray = itemObject.getJSONArray("numbers");


for(int i = 0;i < numbersArray.length();i++){
  numbersArray.getJSONObject(i).getString("id");
}
```

Listing 10.10 shows how parsing may be put together inside an activity and displayed in a TextView. Note that when pulling JSON data from a remote location, such
as through a web service, a separate class or AsyncTask must be used so that the main
UI thread is not blocked.

Listing 10.10   src/com/cookbook/parsejson/MainActivity.java

```
package com.cookbook.parsejson;

import org.json.JSONArray;
import org.json.JSONException;
import org.json.JSONObject;

import android.app.Activity;
import android.os.Bundle;
import android.widget.TextView;

public class MainActivity extends Activity {

  TextView tv;
  private JSONObject jsonObject;
  private String jsonString =
"{\"item\":{\"name\":\"myName\",\"numbers\":[{\"id\":\"1\"},{\"id\":\"2\"}]}}";

  @Override
  protected void onCreate(Bundle savedInstanceState) {
    super.onCreate(savedInstanceState);
    setContentView(R.layout.activity_main);
    tv = (TextView) findViewById(R.id.tv_main);

    try {
      jsonObject = new JSONObject(jsonString);
      JSONObject itemObject = jsonObject.getJSONObject("item");
      String jsonName = "name: " +itemObject.getString("name");
```

```
            JSONArray numbersArray = itemObject.getJSONArray("numbers");
            String jsonIds = "";

            for(int i = 0;i < numbersArray.length();i++){
              jsonIds += "id: " +
                  numbersArray.getJSONObject(i).getString("id").toString() + "\n";
            }

            tv.setText(jsonName+"\n"+jsonIds);

        } catch (JSONException e) {
          e.printStackTrace();
        }
      }
    }

}
```

Recipe: Parsing XML

The official Android documentation recommends the use of XmlPullParser for parsing XML data. You may use any method you prefer to get XML data; however, for this recipe, a simple one-node XML string will be used. Listing 10.11 shows an activity that will display the process of reading the XML document, including the node and text value, into a TextView.

The XML data is processed one line at a time, with the next() method moving to the next line. In order to parse for specific nodes inside the XML data, an if else statement must be added for them in the while loop.

Listing 10.11   src/com/cookbook/parsexml/MainActivity.java

```
package com.cookbook.parsexml;

import java.io.IOException;
import java.io.StringReader;

import org.xmlpull.v1.XmlPullParser;
import org.xmlpull.v1.XmlPullParserException;
import org.xmlpull.v1.XmlPullParserFactory;

import android.app.Activity;
import android.os.Bundle;
import android.widget.TextView;

public class MainActivity extends Activity {

  TextView tv;

  @Override
  protected void onCreate(Bundle savedInstanceState) {
    super.onCreate(savedInstanceState);
    setContentView(R.layout.activity_main);
    tv = (TextView) findViewById(R.id.tv_main);
```

```
String xmlOut = "";
XmlPullParserFactory factory = null;
try {
  factory = XmlPullParserFactory.newInstance();
} catch (XmlPullParserException e) {
  e.printStackTrace();
}
factory.setNamespaceAware(true);
XmlPullParser xpp = null;
try {
  xpp = factory.newPullParser();
} catch (XmlPullParserException e) {
  e.printStackTrace();
}

try {
  xpp.setInput(new StringReader("<node>This is some text</node>"));
} catch (XmlPullParserException e) {
  e.printStackTrace();
}

int eventType = 0;
try {
  eventType = xpp.getEventType();
} catch (XmlPullParserException e) {
  e.printStackTrace();
}

while (eventType != XmlPullParser.END_DOCUMENT) {
  if(eventType == XmlPullParser.START_DOCUMENT) {
    xmlOut += "Start of XML Document";
  } else if (eventType == XmlPullParser.START_TAG) {
    xmlOut += "\nStart of tag: "+xpp.getName();
  } else if (eventType == XmlPullParser.END_TAG) {
    xmlOut += "\nEnd of tag: "+xpp.getName();
  } else if (eventType == XmlPullParser.TEXT) {
    xmlOut += "\nText: "+xpp.getText();
  }
  try {
    eventType = xpp.next();
  } catch (XmlPullParserException e) {
    e.printStackTrace();
  } catch (IOException e) {
    e.printStackTrace();
  }
}
xmlOut += "\nEnd of XML Document";

tv.setText(xmlOut);
}
}
```

Social Networking

Twitter is a social networking and microblogging service that enables its users to send and read messages known as tweets. Twitter is described as the "SMS of the Internet," and indeed, each tweet cannot exceed 140 characters (although links are converted to shorter links and not counted against the 140-character limit). Twitter users can follow other people's tweets or be followed by others.

Recipe: Reading the Owner Profile

Starting with API Level 14 (Ice Cream Sandwich), developers are able to access the owner profile. This is a special contact that stores `RawContact` data. To read the owner profile of a device, the following permission must be added to the **AndroidManifest. xml** file:

```
<uses-permission android:name="android.permission.READ_PROFILE" />
```

The following enables access to profile data:

```
// sets the columns to retrieve for the owner profile - RawContact data
String[] mProjection = new String[]
    {
        Profile._ID,
        Profile.DISPLAY_NAME_PRIMARY,
        Profile.LOOKUP_KEY,
        Profile.PHOTO_THUMBNAIL_URI
    };
```

```
// retrieves the profile from the Contacts Provider
Cursor mProfileCursor =
    getContentResolver().query(Profile.CONTENT_URI,mProjection,null,null,null);
// Set the cursor to the first entry (instead of -1)
boolean b = mProfileCursor.moveToFirst();
for(int i = 0, length = mProjection.length;i < length;i++) {
  System.out.println("*** " +
      mProfileCursor.getString(mProfileCursor.getColumnIndex(mProjection[i])));
}
```

Note that where `System.out.println()` is used is the place where logic can be inserted to process the profile information. It is also worth mentioning that the output will be shown in LogCat, even though it is not a method from `Log.*`.

Recipe: Integrating with Twitter

Some third-party libraries exist to assist in integrating Twitter into Android applications (from http://dev.twitter.com/pages/libraries#java):

- Twitter4J by Yusuke Yamamoto—An open source, Mavenized, and Google App Engine-safe Java library for the Twitter API, released under the BSD license
- Scribe by Pablo Fernandez—OAuth module for Java, Mavenized, and works with Facebook, LinkedIn, Twitter, Evernote, Vimeo, and more

For this recipe, the Twitter4J library by Yusuke Yamamoto is used, which has documentation at http://twitter4j.org/en/javadoc/overview-summary.html. The recipe enables users to log in to Twitter by using OAuth and make a tweet.

Twitter has made changes to its authentication system that now require applications to register in order to access the public feed. To get started, an application has to be registered at https://dev.twitter.com/apps/new. During the registration process, OAuth public and private keys will be generated. They will be used in this recipe, so take note of them.

As this application will be accessing the Internet, it will need the INTERNET permission. There will also be a check to make sure that the device is connected to a network, so the ACCESS_NETWORK_STATE permission is also required. This is done by editing the **AndroidManifest.xml** file, as shown in Listing 10.12.

Listing 10.12   AndroidManifest.xml

```xml
<?xml version="1.0" encoding="utf-8"?>
<manifest xmlns:android="http://schemas.android.com/apk/res/android"
    package="com.cookbook.tcookbook"
    android:versionCode="1"
    android:versionName="1.0" >

    <uses-sdk
        android:minSdkVersion="9"
        android:targetSdkVersion="17" />

    <uses-permission android:name="android.permission.INTERNET" />
    <uses-permission android:name="android.permission.ACCESS_NETWORK_STATE" />

    <application
        android:allowBackup="true"
        android:icon="@drawable/ic_launcher"
        android:label="@string/app_name"
        android:theme="@style/AppTheme" >
        <activity
            android:name="com.cookbook.tcookbook.MainActivity"
            android:label="@string/app_name" >
            <intent-filter>
                <action android:name="android.intent.action.MAIN" />

                <category android:name="android.intent.category.LAUNCHER" />
            </intent-filter>
            <intent-filter>
                <action android:name="android.intent.action.VIEW" />
                <category android:name="android.intent.category.DEFAULT" />
                <category android:name="android.intent.category.BROWSABLE" />
                <data android:scheme="oauth" android:host="tcookbook"/>
```

```
            </intent-filter>
        </activity>
    </application>
</manifest>
```

For the layout of the application, everything will be put into the **activity_main.xml** file. This file will contain a button that is visible on page load and then several buttons, TextViews, and an `EditText` widget. Note that some of these will be hidden with `android:visibility="gone"`. Listing 10.13 shows the contents of the **activity_main.xml** file.

Listing 10.13   res/layout/activity_main.xml

```xml
<LinearLayout xmlns:android="http://schemas.android.com/apk/res/android"
    xmlns:tools="http://schemas.android.com/tools"
    android:layout_width="match_parent"
    android:layout_height="match_parent"
    android:orientation="vertical" >
    tools:context=".MainActivity" >

    <Button android:id="@+id/btnLoginTwitter"
        android:layout_width="match_parent"
        android:layout_height="wrap_content"
        android:text="Login with OAuth"
        android:layout_marginLeft="10dip"
        android:layout_marginRight="10dip"
        android:layout_marginTop="30dip"/>

    <TextView android:id="@+id/lblUserName"
        android:layout_width="match_parent"
        android:layout_height="wrap_content"
        android:padding="10dip"
        android:layout_marginTop="30dip"/>

    <TextView android:id="@+id/lblUpdate"
        android:text="Enter Your Tweet:"
        android:layout_width="match_parent"
        android:layout_height="wrap_content"
        android:layout_marginLeft="10dip"
        android:layout_marginRight="10dip"
        android:visibility="gone"/>

    <EditText android:id="@+id/txtUpdateStatus"
        android:layout_width="match_parent"
        android:layout_height="wrap_content"
        android:layout_margin="10dip"
        android:visibility="gone"/>

    <Button android:id="@+id/btnUpdateStatus"
        android:layout_width="match_parent"
        android:layout_height="wrap_content"
        android:text="Tweet it!"
        android:layout_marginLeft="10dip"
```

```
            android:layout_marginRight="10dip"
            android:visibility="gone"/>

    <Button android:id="@+id/btnLogoutTwitter"
            android:layout_width="match_parent"
            android:layout_height="wrap_content"
            android:text="Logout/invalidate OAuth"
            android:layout_marginLeft="10dip"
            android:layout_marginRight="10dip"
            android:layout_marginTop="50dip"
            android:visibility="gone"/>
</LinearLayout>
```

One activity is used in the application, and two classes are used: one to help with connection detection and one to display an alert message when the wrong application OAuth keys are used.

In the main activity, several constants are set up for use. These include the OAuth Consumer key and Consumer secret. A connectivity check is run to make sure that the user can reach Twitter. Several OnClickListener classes are also registered to trigger logic such as login, logout, and update when clicked.

As Twitter handles authentication for the user, the information passed back is saved in application preferences and is checked again when the user attempts to log in to the application. An AsyncTask is also used to move any tweets made to a background thread.

Listing 10.14 shows the contents of the activity in full.

Listing 10.14   **src/com/cookbook/tcookbook/MainActivity.java**

```
package com.cookbook.tcookbook;

import twitter4j.Twitter;
import twitter4j.TwitterException;
import twitter4j.TwitterFactory;
import twitter4j.User;
import twitter4j.auth.AccessToken;
import twitter4j.auth.RequestToken;
import twitter4j.conf.Configuration;
import twitter4j.conf.ConfigurationBuilder;
import android.app.Activity;
import android.app.ProgressDialog;
import android.content.Intent;
import android.content.SharedPreferences;
import android.content.SharedPreferences.Editor;
import android.content.pm.ActivityInfo;
import android.net.Uri;
import android.os.AsyncTask;
import android.os.Build;
import android.os.Bundle;
import android.os.StrictMode;
import android.text.Html;
import android.util.Log;
```

```java
import android.view.View;
import android.widget.Button;
import android.widget.EditText;
import android.widget.TextView;
import android.widget.Toast;

public class MainActivity extends Activity {

    // Replace the following value with the Consumer key
    static String TWITTER_CONSUMER_KEY = "01189998819991197253";
    // Replace the following value with the Consumer secret
    static String TWITTER_CONSUMER_SECRET =
        "616C6C20796F75722062617365206172652062656C6F6E6720746F207573";

    static String PREFERENCE_NAME = "twitter _ oauth";
    static final String PREF_KEY_OAUTH_TOKEN = "oauth_token";
    static final String PREF_KEY_OAUTH_SECRET = "oauth_token_secret";
    static final String PREF_KEY_TWITTER_LOGIN = "isTwitterLoggedIn";

    static final String TWITTER_CALLBACK_URL = "oauth://tcookbook";

    static final String URL_TWITTER_AUTH = "auth_url";
    static final String URL_TWITTER_OAUTH_VERIFIER = "oauth_verifier";
    static final String URL_TWITTER_OAUTH_TOKEN = "oauth_token";

    Button btnLoginTwitter;
    Button btnUpdateStatus;
    Button btnLogoutTwitter;
    EditText txtUpdate;
    TextView lblUpdate;
    TextView lblUserName;

    ProgressDialog pDialog;

    private static Twitter twitter;
    private static RequestToken requestToken;

    private static SharedPreferences mSharedPreferences;

    private ConnectionDetector cd;

    AlertDialogManager adm = new AlertDialogManager();

    @Override
    public void onCreate(Bundle savedInstanceState) {
      super.onCreate(savedInstanceState);
      setContentView(R.layout.activity_main);
      // used for Android 2.3+
      if (Build.VERSION.SDK_INT > Build.VERSION_CODES_GINGERBREAD) {
        StrictMode.ThreadPolicy policy =
            new StrictMode.ThreadPolicy.Builder().permitAll().build();
        StrictMode.setThreadPolicy(policy);
      }

      setRequestedOrientation(ActivityInfo.SCREEN_ORIENTATION_PORTRAIT);

      cd = new ConnectionDetector(getApplicationContext());
```

```
if (!cd.isConnectingToInternet()) {
  adm.showAlertDialog(MainActivity.this, "Internet Connection Error",
      "Please connect to working Internet connection", false);
  return;
}

if(TWITTER_CONSUMER_KEY.trim().length() == 0 ||
    TWITTER_CONSUMER_SECRET.trim().length() == 0){
  adm.showAlertDialog(MainActivity.this,
      "Twitter OAuth tokens",
      "Please set your Twitter OAuth tokens first!", false);
  return;
}

btnLoginTwitter = (Button) findViewById(R.id.btnLoginTwitter);
btnUpdateStatus = (Button) findViewById(R.id.btnUpdateStatus);
btnLogoutTwitter = (Button) findViewById(R.id.btnLogoutTwitter);
txtUpdate = (EditText) findViewById(R.id.txtUpdateStatus);
lblUpdate = (TextView) findViewById(R.id.lblUpdate);
lblUserName = (TextView) findViewById(R.id.lblUserName);

mSharedPreferences = getApplicationContext().getSharedPreferences("MyPref", 0);

btnLoginTwitter.setOnClickListener(new View.OnClickListener() {
  @Override
  public void onClick(View arg0) {
    // Call login Twitter function
    loginToTwitter();
  }
});

btnUpdateStatus.setOnClickListener(new View.OnClickListener() {
  @Override
  public void onClick(View v) {
    String status = txtUpdate.getText().toString();

    if (status.trim().length() > 0) {
      new updateTwitterStatus().execute(status);
    } else {
      Toast.makeText(getApplicationContext(),
          "Please enter status message", Toast.LENGTH_SHORT).show();
    }
  }
});

btnLogoutTwitter.setOnClickListener(new View.OnClickListener() {
  @Override
  public void onClick(View arg0) {
    // Call logout Twitter function
    logoutFromTwitter();
  }
});

if (!isTwitterLoggedInAlready()) {
  Uri uri = getIntent().getData();
```

```
            if (uri != null && uri.toString().startsWith(TWITTER_CALLBACK_URL)) {
               String verifier = uri.getQueryParameter(URL_TWITTER_OAUTH_VERIFIER);

               try {
                  AccessToken accessToken = twitter.getOAuthAccessToken(requestToken,
➡verifier);

                  Editor e = mSharedPreferences.edit();

                  e.putString(PREF_KEY_OAUTH_TOKEN, accessToken.getToken());
                  e.putString(PREF_KEY_OAUTH_SECRET,accessToken.getTokenSecret());
                  e.putBoolean(PREF_KEY_TWITTER_LOGIN, true);
                  e.commit();

//                Log.e("Twitter OAuth Token", "> " + accessToken.getToken());

                  btnLoginTwitter.setVisibility(View.GONE);

                  lblUpdate.setVisibility(View.VISIBLE);
                  txtUpdate.setVisibility(View.VISIBLE);
                  btnUpdateStatus.setVisibility(View.VISIBLE);
                  btnLogoutTwitter.setVisibility(View.VISIBLE);

                  long userID = accessToken.getUserId();
                  User user = twitter.showUser(userID);
                  String username = user.getName();

                  lblUserName.setText(Html.fromHtml("<b>Welcome " + username + "</b>"));
               } catch (Exception e) {
                  Log.e("***Twitter Login Error: ",e.getMessage());
               }
            }
         }

      }

      private void loginToTwitter() {
         if (!isTwitterLoggedInAlready()) {
            ConfigurationBuilder builder = new ConfigurationBuilder();
            builder.setOAuthConsumerKey(TWITTER_CONSUMER_KEY);
            builder.setOAuthConsumerSecret(TWITTER_CONSUMER_SECRET);
            Configuration configuration = builder.build();

            TwitterFactory factory = new TwitterFactory(configuration);
            twitter = factory.getInstance();

            if(!(Build.VERSION.SDK_INT >= Build.VERSION_CODES.HONEYCOMB)) {
              try {
                 requestToken = twitter.getOAuthRequestToken(TWITTER_CALLBACK_URL);
                 this.startActivity(new Intent(Intent.ACTION_VIEW,
                     Uri.parse(requestToken.getAuthenticationURL())));
              } catch (TwitterException e) {
                 e.printStackTrace();
              }
            } else {
              new Thread(new Runnable() {
```

```
            public void run() {
              try {
                requestToken = twitter.getOAuthRequestToken(TWITTER_CALLBACK_URL);
                MainActivity.this.startActivity(new Intent(Intent.ACTION_VIEW,
                    Uri.parse(requestToken.getAuthenticationURL())));
              } catch (TwitterException e) {
                e.printStackTrace();
              }
            }
          }).start();
        }
      } else {
        Toast.makeText(getApplicationContext(),"Already logged into Twitter",
            Toast.LENGTH_LONG).show();
      }
    }

    class updateTwitterStatus extends AsyncTask<String, String, String> {
      @Override
      protected void onPreExecute() {
        super.onPreExecute();
        pDialog = new ProgressDialog(MainActivity.this);
        pDialog.setMessage("Updating to Twitter...");
        pDialog.setIndeterminate(false);
        pDialog.setCancelable(false);
        pDialog.show();
      }

      protected String doInBackground(String... args) {
//        Log.d("*** Text Value of Tweet: ",args[0]);
        String status = args[0];
        try {
          ConfigurationBuilder builder = new ConfigurationBuilder();
          builder.setOAuthConsumerKey(TWITTER_CONSUMER_KEY);
          builder.setOAuthConsumerSecret(TWITTER_CONSUMER_SECRET);

          String access_token =
              mSharedPreferences.getString(PREF_KEY_OAUTH_TOKEN, "");
          String access_token_secret =
              mSharedPreferences.getString(PREF_KEY_OAUTH_SECRET, "");

          AccessToken accessToken =
              new AccessToken(access_token, access_token_secret);
          Twitter twitter =
              new TwitterFactory(builder.build()).getInstance(accessToken);

          twitter4j.Status response = twitter.updateStatus(status);

//          Log.d("*** Update Status: ",response.getText());
        } catch (TwitterException e) {
          Log.d("*** Twitter Update Error: ", e.getMessage());
        }
        return null;
      }
```

```
    protected void onPostExecute(String file_url) {
      pDialog.dismiss();
      runOnUiThread(new Runnable() {
        @Override
        public void run() {
          Toast.makeText(getApplicationContext(),
             "Status tweeted successfully", Toast.LENGTH_SHORT).show();
          txtUpdate.setText("");
        }
      });
    }

  }

  private void logoutFromTwitter() {
    Editor e = mSharedPreferences.edit();
    e.remove(PREF_KEY_OAUTH_TOKEN);
    e.remove(PREF_KEY_OAUTH_SECRET);
    e.remove(PREF_KEY_TWITTER_LOGIN);
    e.commit();

    btnLogoutTwitter.setVisibility(View.GONE);
    btnUpdateStatus.setVisibility(View.GONE);
    txtUpdate.setVisibility(View.GONE);
    lblUpdate.setVisibility(View.GONE);
    lblUserName.setText("");
    lblUserName.setVisibility(View.GONE);

    btnLoginTwitter.setVisibility(View.VISIBLE);
  }

  private boolean isTwitterLoggedInAlready() {
    return mSharedPreferences.getBoolean(PREF_KEY_TWITTER_LOGIN, false);
  }

  protected void onResume() {
    super.onResume();
  }

}
```

More information on using Twitter4j can be found in the following resources:

- www.androidhive.info/2012/09/android-twitter-oauth-connect-tutorial/ by Ravi Tamada

- http://blog.doityourselfandroid.com/2011/08/08/improved-twitter-oauth -android/ by Do-it-yourself Android

- http://davidcrowley.me/?p=410 by David Crowley

- https://tutsplus.com/tutorials/?q=true&filter_topic=90 by Sue Smith

- http://blog.blundell-apps.com/sending-a-tweet/ by Blundell

Recipe: Integrating with Facebook

Facebook has changed rapidly in the last couple of years, and it remains one of the top social networking sites. One thing the Facebook team has done recently is to clean up their documentation to help developers. The official documentation can be found at https://developers.facebook.com/docs/getting-started/facebook-sdk-for-android/3.0/.

To get started with Facebook development, first download the Facebook SDK and the Facebook android package (APK) from https://developers.facebook.com /resources/facebook-android-sdk-3.0.zip. The APK is provided as a means of authentication without having to use a WebView. If the Facebook application is already installed on the phone, the APK file need not be installed.

Next, add the Facebook SDK as a library project to the Eclipse installation. This is done by choosing **File → Import** and then **General → Existing Projects into Workspace**. Note that Facebook warns against using the "Copy projects into workspace" options, as this may build incorrect filesystem paths and cause the SDK to function incorrectly.

After the Facebook SDK has been imported, the sample projects are available for experimentation. Note that most of the projects require the generation of a key hash that will be used to sign applications and that developers can add to their Facebook developer profile for quick SDK project access.

The key is generated by using the `keytool` utility that comes with Java. Open a terminal or command prompt and type the following to generate the key:

OS X:

```
keytool -exportcert -alias androiddebugkey -keystore ~/.android/debug.keystore |
[ccc]openssl sha1 -binary | openssl base64
```

Windows:

```
keytool -exportcert -alias androiddebugkey -keystore %HOMEPATH%\.android\debug.
keystore [ccc]| openssl sha1 -binary | openssl base64
```

The command should be typed in a single line, although terminals or command prompt windows may show it breaking into multiple lines. When the command is executed, a password prompt should appear. The password to enter is **android**. After the key has been generated successfully, it will be displayed. Note that if a "`'keytool' is not recognized as an internal or external command . . .`" error is generated, move to the **bin** directory of the JRE installation directory and try again. If there is a similar error for "openssl," download OpenSSL from http://code.google .com/p/openssl-for-windows/. If there are still errors, make sure that the **bin** directories have been added to the system path or that the exact directories are being used instead of **%HOMEPATH%**.

If more than one computer will be used for development, a hash must be generated for each one and added to the developer profile at https://developers.facebook.com/.

Once that is done, dig into the sample applications and log in with them. The showcase example project, called **HelloFacebookSample**, demonstrates how to access a profile, update a status, and even upload photos.

The last step in creating an application that integrates with Facebook is to create a Facebook app that will then be tied to the Android application by using a generated key hash. This will take care of integration and allow users to authenticate themselves while using the application.

The developer site gives a terrific breakdown of all the pieces needed to get started. Be sure to read the official Scrumptious tutorial, which can be found at http://developers.facebook.com/docs/tutorials/androidsdk/3.0/scrumptious/.

11

Data Storage Methods

Complicated and robust Android applications often need to use some type of data storage. Depending on the situation, different data storage methods are available to the developer:

- `SharedPreferences` for lightweight usage, such as saving application settings and the UI state
- A built-in SQLite database for more complicated usage, such as saving application records
- The standard Java flat file storage methods: `InputFileStream` and `OutputFileStream`

These are discussed in this chapter. Also discussed is the `ContentProvider` Android component that is used to share data between applications. It should be noted that another basic data storage method managed by the Android system, the `onSaveInstanceState()` and `onRestoreInstanceState()` pair, was already discussed in Chapter 2, "Application Basics: Activities and Intents." The optimal method to use depends on the situation, as discussed in each recipe.

Shared Preferences

`SharedPreferences` is an interface that an application can use to quickly and efficiently save data in name-value pairs, similar to a bundle. The information is stored in an XML file on the Android device. For example, if the application `com.cookbook.datastorage` creates a shared preference, the Android system creates a new XML file under the **/data/data/com.cookbook.datastorage/shared_prefs** directory.

Shared preferences are usually used for saving application settings such as user settings, theme, and other general application properties. They can also save login information such as username, password, auto-login flag, and remember-user flag. The shared preferences data is accessible by every component of the application that created it.

Recipe: Creating and Retrieving Shared Preferences

The shared preferences for an activity can be accessed using the getPreferences()
method, which specifies the operating mode for the default preferences file. If instead
multiple preference files are needed, each can be specified using the getShared
Preferences() method. If the shared preferences XML file exists in the data directory, it is opened; otherwise, it is created. The operating mode provides control over
the different kinds of access permission to the preferences:

- MODE_PRIVATE—Only the calling application has access to the XML file.
- MODE_WORLD_READABLE—All applications can read the XML file. This setting has
  been deprecated in API Level 17; use ContentProvider, BroadcastReceiver, or
  a service instead.
- MODE_WORLD_WRITEABLE—All applications can write to the XML file.
  This setting has been deprecated in API Level 17; use ContentProvider,
  BroadcastReceiver, or a service instead.

After a SharedPreferences object is retrieved, an Editor object is needed to
write the name-value pairs to the XML file using the put() method. Currently, five
primitive types are supported: int, long, float, String, and boolean. The following
code shows how to create and store shared preferences data:

```
SharedPreferences prefs = getSharedPreferences("myDataStorage",
                                               MODE_PRIVATE);

Editor mEditor = prefs.edit();
mEditor.putString("username","datastorageuser1");
mEditor.putString("password","password1234");
mEditor.apply();
```

Note that when developing with Android 2.3 (Level 9) or above, the apply()
method should be used to commit changes, as this will trigger an async request to
update the file. Previous versions of Android require using the commit() method.

The following shows how to retrieve shared preferences data:

```
SharedPreferences prefs = getSharedPreferences("myDataStorage",
                                               MODE_PRIVATE);
String username = prefs.getString("username", "");
String password = prefs.getString("password", "");
```

Recipe: Using the Preferences Framework

Android provides a standardized framework for setting preferences across all applica-
tions. The framework uses category preferences and screens to group related settings.
PreferenceCategory is used to declare a set of preferences into one category.
PreferenceScreen presents a group of preferences in a new screen.

This recipe uses the preferences defined in the XML file in Listing 11.1. A `PreferenceScreen` is the root element with two `EditTextPreference` elements for username and password. Other possible elements are `CheckBoxPreference`, `RingtonePreference`, and `DialogPreference`. The Android system then generates a UI to manipulate the preferences, as shown in Figure 11.1. These preferences are stored in shared preferences, which means they can be retrieved by calling `get Preferences()`.

Listing 11.1   res/xml/preferences.xml

```xml
<?xml version="1.0" encoding="utf-8"?>
<PreferenceScreen xmlns:android="http://schemas.android.com/apk/res/android">
  <EditTextPreference
    android:title="User Name"
    android:key="username"
     android:summary="Please provide user name">
  </EditTextPreference>
  <EditTextPreference
    android:title="Password"
    android:password="true"
    android:key="password"
    android:summary="Please enter your password">
  </EditTextPreference>
</PreferenceScreen>
```

Then, an activity extending `PreferenceActivity` calls the `addPreferences FromResource()` method to include these preferences in the activity, as shown in Listing 11.2. Note that when developing with an API level of 11 or higher, a `PreferenceFragment` must be used to call the `addPreferencesFromResource()` method.

Listing 11.2   src/com/cookbook/datastorage/MyPreferences.java

```java
package com.cookbook.datastorage;

import android.os.Bundle;
import android.preference.PreferenceActivity;

public class MyPreferences extends PreferenceActivity {

  @Override
  public void onCreate(Bundle savedInstanceState) {
    super.onCreate(savedInstanceState);

    addPreferencesFromResource(R.xml.preferences);
  }
}
```

The main activity merely needs to launch `PreferenceActivity` when needed (for example, when the Menu key is pressed). Listing 11.3 shows a simple example of showing the preferences upon start-up of the activity.

Listing 11.3   **src/com/cookbook/datastorage/DataStorage.java**

```java
package com.cookbook.datastorage;

import android.app.Activity;
import android.content.Intent;
import android.os.Bundle;

public class DataStorage extends Activity {
    /** called when the activity is first created */
    @Override
    public void onCreate(Bundle savedInstanceState) {
        super.onCreate(savedInstanceState);
        setContentView(R.layout.main);
        Intent i = new Intent(this, MyPreferences.class);
        startActivity(i);
    }
}
```

The **AndroidManifest.xml** file needs to include all activities, including the new `PreferenceActivity`, as shown in Listing 11.4. This creates the preferences screen shown in Figure 11.1.

Listing 11.4   **AndroidManifest.xml**

```xml
<?xml version="1.0" encoding="utf-8"?>
<manifest xmlns:android="http://schemas.android.com/apk/res/android"
      package="com.cookbook.datastorage"
      android:versionCode="1"
      android:versionName="1.0">
    <application android:icon="@drawable/icon" android:label="@string/app_name">
        <activity android:name=".DataStorage"
                    android:label="@string/app_name">
            <intent-filter>
                <action android:name="android.intent.action.MAIN" />
                <category android:name="android.intent.category.LAUNCHER"
            />
            </intent-filter>
        </activity>
        <activity android:name=".MyPreferences" />
    </application>
    <uses-sdk android:minSdkVersion="7" />
</manifest>
```

Recipe: Changing the UI Based on Stored Data

The `DataStorage` activity of the previous recipe can be extended to check the shared preferences when loading, altering the behavior accordingly. In this recipe, if a user-

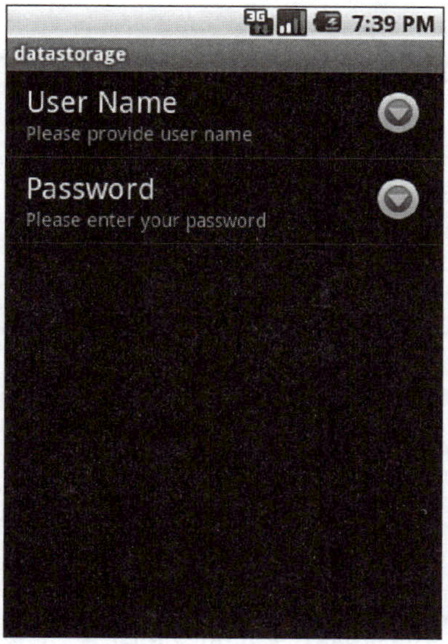

Figure 11.1   The preferences UI generated by the Android system from an XML preferences file

name and password are already saved in the `SharedPreferences` file, a login page is displayed. After a successful login, the activity can successfully continue. If no login information is on file, the activity continues directly.

The **main.xml** layout file can be modified to be a login page, as shown in Listing 11.5. This uses two `EditText` objects for username and password, as covered in Chapter 5, "User Interface Layout."

Listing 11.5   **res/layout/main.xml**

```xml
<?xml version="1.0" encoding="utf-8"?>
<LinearLayout xmlns:android="http://schemas.android.com/apk/res/android"
    android:orientation="vertical"
    android:layout_width="match_parent"
    android:layout_height="match_parent">
    <TextView
        android:layout_width="match_parent"
        android:layout_height="wrap_content"
        android:text="username"
    />
    <EditText
        android:id="@+id/usertext"
        android:layout_width="match_parent"
        android:layout_height="wrap_content"
    />
    <TextView
        android:layout_width="match_parent"
        android:layout_height="wrap_content"
        android:text="password"
    />
```

```
        <EditText
            android:id="@+id/passwordtext"
            android:layout_width="match_parent"
            android:layout_height="wrap_content"
            android:password="true"
    />
    <Button
            android:id="@+id/loginbutton"
            android:layout_width="wrap_content"
            android:layout_height="wrap_content"
            android:text="login"
            android:textSize="20dp"
    />
</LinearLayout>
```

The main activity DataStorage, as shown in Listing 11.6, is modified to first read the username and password data from the SharedPreferences instance. If this data is not set, the application launches the MyPreferences activity (Listing 11.2) directly to set the preferences. If the data is set, the application displays the login layout **main .xml** shown in Figure 11.2.

The button has an onClickListener that verifies whether the login information matches the username and password from the SharedPreferences file. A successful login enables the application to continue, which in this case just launches the MyPreferences activity. Any login attempt shows a toast message of success or failure for illustration purposes.

Listing 11.6   **src/com/cookbook/datastorage/DataStorage.java**

```java
package com.cookbook.datastorage;

import android.app.Activity;
import android.content.Intent;
import android.content.SharedPreferences;
import android.os.Bundle;
import android.preference.PreferenceManager;
import android.view.View;
import android.view.View.OnClickListener;
import android.widget.Button;
import android.widget.EditText;
import android.widget.Toast;

public class DataStorage extends Activity {
    SharedPreferences myprefs;
    EditText userET, passwordET;
    Button loginBT;
    @Override
    public void onCreate(Bundle savedInstanceState) {
        super.onCreate(savedInstanceState);
        myprefs = PreferenceManager.getDefaultSharedPreferences(this);
        final String username = myprefs.getString("username", null);
        final String password = myprefs.getString("password", null);
        if (username != null && password != null){
            setContentView(R.layout.main);
```

```
userET = (EditText)findViewById(R.id.usertext);
passwordET = (EditText)findViewById(R.id.passwordtext);
loginBT = (Button)findViewById(R.id.loginbutton);
loginBT.setOnClickListener(new OnClickListener() {
    public void onClick(View v) {
        try {
            if(username.equals(userET.getText().toString())
                && password.equals(
                            passwordET.getText().toString())) {
                Toast.makeText(DataStorage.this,
                            "login passed!!",
                            Toast.LENGTH_SHORT).show();
                Intent i = new Intent(DataStorage.this,
                                    MyPreferences.class);
                startActivity(i);
            } else {
                Toast.makeText(DataStorage.this,
                            "login failed!!",
                            Toast.LENGTH_SHORT).show();
            }
        } catch (Exception e) {
            e.printStackTrace();
        }
    }
});
} else {
    Intent i = new Intent(this, MyPreferences.class);
    startActivity(i);
}
}
}
```

Figure 11.2   The login screen described
by Listing 11.5

Recipe: Adding an End User License Agreement

As discussed in Chapter 1, "Overview of Android," it is often useful to display an end user license agreement (EULA) when a user first installs and runs an app. If the user does not accept it, the downloaded application does not run. After a user does accept it, the EULA is never shown again.

This EULA functionality is already implemented and available publicly under the Apache License as the `Eula` class shown in Listing 11.7. It uses `SharedPreferences` with the Boolean `PREFERENCE_EULA_ACCEPTED` to determine whether the EULA was previously accepted or not accepted.

Listing 11.7   **src/com/cookbook/eula_example/Eula.java**

```
/*
 * Copyright (C) 2008 The Android Open Source Project
 *
 * Licensed under the Apache License, Version 2.0 (the "License");
 * you may not use this file except in compliance with the License.
 * You may obtain a copy of the License at
 *
 *      http://www.apache.org/licenses/LICENSE-2.0
 *
 * Unless required by applicable law or agreed to in writing, software
 * distributed under the License is distributed on an "AS IS" BASIS,
 * WITHOUT WARRANTIES OR CONDITIONS OF ANY KIND, either expressed or implied.
 * See the License for the specific language governing permissions and
 * limitations under the License.
 */

package com.cookbook.eula_example;

import android.app.Activity;
import android.app.AlertDialog;
import android.content.DialogInterface;
import android.content.SharedPreferences;

import java.io.IOException;
import java.io.BufferedReader;
import java.io.InputStreamReader;
import java.io.Closeable;

/**
 * displays a EULA ("End User License Agreement") that the user has to accept before
 * using the application
 */
class Eula {
    private static final String ASSET_EULA = "EULA";
    private static final String PREFERENCE_EULA_ACCEPTED = "eula.accepted";
    private static final String PREFERENCES_EULA = "eula";

    /**
     * callback to let the activity know when the user accepts the EULA
     */
```

```java
static interface OnEulaAgreedTo {
    void onEulaAgreedTo();
}

/**
 * displays the EULA if necessary
 */
static boolean show(final Activity activity) {

    final SharedPreferences preferences =
                    activity.getSharedPreferences(
                            PREFERENCES_EULA, Activity.MODE_PRIVATE);
    //to test:
    //  preferences.edit()
    //      .putBoolean(PREFERENCE_EULA_ACCEPTED, false).commit();

    if (!preferences.getBoolean(PREFERENCE_EULA_ACCEPTED, false)) {
        final AlertDialog.Builder builder =
                    new AlertDialog.Builder(activity);
        builder.setTitle(R.string.eula_title);
        builder.setCancelable(true);
        builder.setPositiveButton(R.string.eula_accept,
                            new DialogInterface.OnClickListener() {
            public void onClick(DialogInterface dialog, int which) {
                accept(preferences);
                if (activity instanceof OnEulaAgreedTo) {
                    ((OnEulaAgreedTo) activity).onEulaAgreedTo();
                }
            }
        });
        builder.setNegativeButton(R.string.eula_refuse,
                            new DialogInterface.OnClickListener() {
            public void onClick(DialogInterface dialog, int which) {
                refuse(activity);
            }
        });
        builder.setOnCancelListener(
                            new DialogInterface.OnCancelListener() {
            public void onCancel(DialogInterface dialog) {
                refuse(activity);
            }
        });
        builder.setMessage(readEula(activity));
        builder.create().show();
        return false;
    }
    return true;
}

private static void accept(SharedPreferences preferences) {
    preferences.edit().putBoolean(PREFERENCE_EULA_ACCEPTED,
                            true).commit();
}

private static void refuse(Activity activity) {
    activity.finish();
```

```
    }

    private static CharSequence readEula(Activity activity) {
        BufferedReader in = null;
        try {
            in = new BufferedReader(new InputStreamReader(activity.getAssets().
➡open(ASSET_EULA)));
            String line;
            StringBuilder buffer = new StringBuilder();
            while ((line = in.readLine()) != null)
                buffer.append(line).append('\n');
            return buffer;
        } catch (IOException e) {
            return "";
        } finally {
            closeStream(in);
        }
    }

    /**
     * closes the specified stream
     */
    private static void closeStream(Closeable stream) {
        if (stream != null) {
            try {
                stream.close();
            } catch (IOException e) {
                // Ignore
            }
        }
    }
}
```

The Eula class needs to be customized as follows:

1. The actual text of the EULA needs to be put in a text file called **EULA** (as specified by the ASSET_EULA variable in Listing 11.7) and placed in the **assets/** directory of the Android project. This is loaded by the readEula() method of the Eula class.

2. A few strings need to be specified for the Acceptance dialog box. These can be collected in the string's resource file. Example wording is shown in Listing 11.8.

Listing 11.8   **res/values/strings.xml**

```xml
<?xml version="1.0" encoding="utf-8"?>
<resources>
    <string name="hello">Welcome to MyApp</string>
    <string name="app_name">MyApp</string>
    <string name="eula_title">License Agreement</string>
    <string name="eula_accept">Accept</string>
    <string name="eula_refuse">Don\'t Accept</string>
</resources>
```

Then, any application can automatically have the EULA functionality if the following line in the onCreate() method of the main activity of the application is included:

```
Eula.show(this);
```

SQLite Database

For more complex data structures, a database provides a quicker and more flexible access method than flat files or shared preferences. Android provides a built-in database called SQLite that provides full relational database capability using SQL commands. Each application that uses SQLite has its own instance of the database, which is by default accessible only from the application itself. The database is stored in the **/data/data/<package_name>/databases** folder of an Android device. A content provider can be used to share the database information between applications. The steps for using SQLite follow:

1. Create a database.

2. Open the database.

3. Create a table.

4. Create an insert interface for datasets.

5. Create a query interface for datasets.

6. Close the database.

The next recipe provides a general method to accomplish these steps.

Recipe: Creating a Separate Database Package

A good modular structure of classes is essential for more complicated Android projects. Here, the database class is put in its own package, com.cookbook.data, so it is easy to reuse. This package contains three classes: MyDB, MyDBhelper, and Constants.

The MyDB class is shown in Listing 11.9. It contains a SQLiteDatabase instance and a MyDBhelper class (described in the following) with the methods that follow:

- MyDB()—Initializes a MyDBhelper instance (the constructor).

- open()—Initializes a SQLiteDatabase instance using MyDBhelper. This opens a writeable database connection. If SQLite throws any exception, it tries to get a readable database instead.

- close()—Closes the database connection.

- insertDiary()—Saves a diary entry to the database as name-value pairs in a ContentValues instance and then passes the data to the SQLiteDatabase instance to do an insert.

- getDiaries()—Reads the diary entries from the database, saves them in a Cursor class, and returns them from the method.

Listing 11.9   src/com/cookbook/data/MyDB.java

```java
package com.cookbook.data;

import android.content.ContentValues;
import android.content.Context;
import android.database.Cursor;
import android.database.sqlite.SQLiteDatabase;
import android.database.sqlite.SQLiteException;
import android.util.Log;

public class MyDB {
    private SQLiteDatabase db;
    private final Context context;
    private final MyDBhelper dbhelper;
    public MyDB(Context c){
        context = c;
        dbhelper = new MyDBhelper(context, Constants.DATABASE_NAME, null,
                                        Constants.DATABASE_VERSION);
    }
    public void close()
    {
        db.close();
    }
    public void open() throws SQLiteException
    {
        try {
            db = dbhelper.getWriteableDatabase();
        } catch(SQLiteException ex) {
            Log.v("Open database exception caught", ex.getMessage());
            db = dbhelper.getReadableDatabase();
        }
    }
    public long insertDiary(String title, String content)
    {
        try{
            ContentValues newTaskValue = new ContentValues();
            newTaskValue.put(Constants.TITLE_NAME, title);
            newTaskValue.put(Constants.CONTENT_NAME, content);
            newTaskValue.put(Constants.DATE_NAME,
                            java.lang.System.currentTimeMillis());
            return db.insert(Constants.TABLE_NAME, null, newTaskValue);
        } catch(SQLiteException ex) {
            Log.v("Insert into database exception caught",
                    ex.getMessage());
            return -1;
        }
    }
    public Cursor getDiaries()
    {
        Cursor c =  db.query(Constants.TABLE_NAME, null, null,
                            null, null, null, null);
        return c;
    }
}
```

The MyDBhelper class, shown in Listing 11.10, extends SQLiteOpenHelper. The SQLiteOpenHelper framework provides methods to manage database creation and upgrades. The database is initialized in the class constructor MyDBhelper(). This requires the context and database name to be specified for creation of the database file under **/data/data/com.cookbook.datastorage/databases** and the database schema version to determine whether the onCreate() or onUpgrade() method is called.

Tables can be added in the onCreate() method using a custom SQL command such as:

```
create table MyTable (key_id integer primary key autoincrement,
                      title text not null, content text not null,
                      recordDate long);
```

Whenever a database needs to be upgraded (when a user downloads a new version of an application, for example), the change in database version number calls the onUpgrade() method. This can be used to alter or drop tables as needed to update the tables to the new schema.

Listing 11.10   **src/com/cookbook/data/MyDBhelper.java**

```java
package com.cookbook.data;

import android.content.Context;
import android.database.sqlite.SQLiteDatabase;
import android.database.sqlite.SQLiteException;
import android.database.sqlite.SQLiteOpenHelper;
import android.database.sqlite.SQLiteDatabase.CursorFactory;
import android.util.Log;

public class MyDBhelper extends SQLiteOpenHelper{
    private static final String CREATE_TABLE="create table "+
    Constants.TABLE_NAME+" ("+
    Constants.KEY_ID+" integer primary key autoincrement, "+
    Constants.TITLE_NAME+" text not null, "+
    Constants.CONTENT_NAME+" text not null, "+
    Constants.DATE_NAME+" long);";

    public MyDBhelper(Context context, String name, CursorFactory factory,
                      int version) {
        super(context, name, factory, version);
    }

    @Override
    public void onCreate(SQLiteDatabase db) {
        Log.v("MyDBhelper onCreate","Creating all the tables");
        try {
            db.execSQL(CREATE_TABLE);
        } catch(SQLiteException ex) {
            Log.v("Create table exception", ex.getMessage());
        }
    }

    @Override
    public void onUpgrade(SQLiteDatabase db, int oldVersion,
                          int newVersion) {
```

```
        Log.w("TaskDBAdapter", "Upgrading from version "+oldVersion
                            +" to "+newVersion
                            +", which will destroy all old data");
        db.execSQL("drop table if exists "+Constants.TABLE_NAME);
        onCreate(db);
    }
}
```

The third file of the com.cookbook.data package is the Constants class, shown in
Listing 11.11. This class is used to hold all the String constants because they are used
in both MyDB and MyDBhelper.

Listing 11.11   src/com/cookbook/data/Constants.java

```
package com.cookbook.data;

public class Constants {
    public static final String DATABASE_NAME="datastorage";
    public static final int DATABASE_VERSION=1;
    public static final String TABLE_NAME="diaries";
    public static final String TITLE_NAME="title";
    public static final String CONTENT_NAME="content";
    public static final String DATE_NAME="recordDate";
    public static final String KEY_ID="_id";
}
```

Recipe: Using a Separate Database Package

This recipe demonstrates SQLite data storage using the previous recipe's database
package. It also ties together the login screen from the "Changing the UI Based on
Stored Data" recipe and enables the creation and listing of personal diary entries. First,
a layout XML file for creating diary entries—**diary.xml**—is shown in Listing 11.12
and its output screen in Figure 11.3.

Listing 11.12   res/layout/diary.xml

```
<?xml version="1.0" encoding="utf-8"?>
<LinearLayout xmlns:android="http://schemas.android.com/apk/res/android"
    android:orientation="vertical"
    android:layout_width="match_parent"
    android:layout_height="match_parent"
    >
    <TextView
        android:layout_width="match_parent"
        android:layout_height="wrap_content"
        android:text="Diary Title"
    />
    <EditText
        android:id="@+id/diarydescriptiontext"
        android:layout_width="match_parent"
        android:layout_height="wrap_content"
    />
```

```
    <TextView
        android:layout_width="match_parent"
        android:layout_height="wrap_content"
        android:text="Content"
    />
    <EditText
        android:id="@+id/diarycontenttext"
        android:layout_width="match_parent"
        android:layout_height="200dp"
    />
    <Button
        android:id="@+id/submitbutton"
        android:layout_width="wrap_content"
        android:layout_height="wrap_content"
        android:text="submit"
        android:textSize="20dp"
    />
</LinearLayout>
```

Figure 11.3   The diary entry creation screen

The main activity is **Diary.java**, shown in Listing 11.13. The com.cookbook.data package needs to be imported, and the MyDB object is declared, initialized, and opened for use. It also displays the **diary.xml** layout and handles the "submit" button press to save data to the database.

Listing 11.13   **src/com/cookbook/datastorage/Diary.java**

```
package com.cookbook.datastorage;

import android.app.Activity;
import android.content.Intent;
import android.os.Bundle;
import android.view.View;
import android.view.View.OnClickListener;
import android.widget.Button;
import android.widget.EditText;

import com.cookbook.data.MyDB;
public class Diary extends Activity {
    EditText titleET, contentET;
    Button submitBT;
    MyDB dba;

    @Override
    public void onCreate(Bundle savedInstanceState) {
        super.onCreate(savedInstanceState);
        setContentView(R.layout.diary);
        dba = new MyDB(this);
        dba.open();
        titleET = (EditText)findViewById(R.id.diarydescriptiontext);
        contentET = (EditText)findViewById(R.id.diarycontenttext);
        submitBT = (Button)findViewById(R.id.submitbutton);
        submitBT.setOnClickListener(new OnClickListener() {
            public void onClick(View v) {
                try {
                    saveItToDB();
                } catch (Exception e) {
                    e.printStackTrace();
                }
            }
        });
    }
    public void saveItToDB() {
        dba.insertDiary(titleET.getText().toString(),
                        contentET.getText().toString());
        dba.close();
        titleET.setText("");
        contentET.setText("");
        Intent i = new Intent(Diary.this, DisplayDiaries.class);
        startActivity(i);
    }
}
```

The DataStorage.java class is the same as in Listing 11.6 with MyPreferences. class changed to launch Diary.class when the login is successful:

```
Toast.makeText(DataStorage.this, "login passed!!",
            Toast.LENGTH_SHORT).show();
Intent i = new Intent(DataStorage.this, Diary.class);
startActivity(i);
```

Finally, the **AndroidManifest.xml** file must be updated to include the new activities, as shown in Listing 11.14.

Listing 11.14   **AndroidManifest.xml**

```
<?xml version="1.0" encoding="utf-8"?>
<manifest xmlns:android="http://schemas.android.com/apk/res/android"
      package="com.cookbook.datastorage"
      android:versionCode="1" android:versionName="1.0">
    <application android:icon="@drawable/icon"
                  android:label="@string/app_name">
        <activity android:name=".DataStorage"
                  android:label="@string/app_name">
            <intent-filter>
               <action android:name="android.intent.action.MAIN" />
               <category android:name="android.intent.category.LAUNCHER" />
            </intent-filter>
        </activity>
        <activity android:name=".MyPreferences" />
        <activity android:name=".Diary"/>
    </application>
    <uses-sdk android:minSdkVersion="7" />
</manifest>
```

Now that a separate database has been integrated, the layout for the list of entries is discussed in the next recipe to complete the diary application.

Recipe: Creating a Personal Diary

This recipe leverages the `ListView` object to display multiple entries from a SQLite database table. It shows these items in a vertically scrolling list. The `ListView` needs a data adapter to tell the view whenever the underlying data changes. Two XML files need to be created: **diaries.xml**, which populates the `ListView` shown in Listing 11.15, and **diaryrow.xml**, which populates the row inside the `ListView` shown in Listing 11.16.

Listing 11.15   **res/layout/diaries.xml**

```
<?xml version="1.0" encoding="utf-8"?>
<LinearLayout xmlns:android="http://schemas.android.com/apk/res/android"
    android:orientation="vertical"
    android:layout_width="match_parent"
    android:layout_height="match_parent">
        <ListView
            android:layout_width="match_parent" android:dividerHeight="1px"
            android:layout_height="match_parent"
            android:id="list">
        </ListView>
</LinearLayout>
```

Listing 11.16   **res/layout/diaryrow.xml**

```
<?xml version="1.0" encoding="utf-8"?>
<RelativeLayout android:layout_width="wrap_content"
    android:layout_height="wrap_content"
    android:layout_alignLeft="@+id/name" android:layout_below="@+id/name"
    xmlns:android="http://schemas.android.com/apk/res/android"
    android:padding="12dip">
    <TextView android:layout_width="wrap_content"
        android:layout_height="wrap_content" android:id="@+id/name"
        android:layout_marginRight="4dp" android:text="Diary Title"
        android:textStyle="bold" android:textSize="16dip"  />
    <TextView android:id="@+id/datetext"
        android:layout_width="wrap_content"
        android:layout_height="wrap_content" android:text="Date Recorded"
        android:textSize="14dip"  />
</RelativeLayout>
```

The activity `DisplayDiaries.java` extends `ListActivity` to display a `ListView`.
Inside this class, two inner classes are defined: `MyDiary` is a data class to hold the content of the diary entry (title, content, and date), and `DiaryAdapter` is a `BaseAdapter`
class to handle data retrieval from the database (using `getData()`). The following
methods are derived from `BaseAdapter` and called by `ListView`:

- `getCount()`—Returns how many items are on the adapter
- `getItem()`—Returns the item specified
- `getItemID()`—Returns the ID of the item (for this example, there is no item ID)
- `getView()`—Returns a view for each item

Note that `ListView` calls `getView()` to draw the view for each item. To improve
the UI rendering performance, the view returned by `getView()` should be recycled as
much as possible. This is done by creating a `ViewHolder` class to hold the views.

When `getView()` is called, the view currently displayed to the user is also passed in,
which is when it is saved in the `ViewHolder` and tagged. On subsequent calls to
`getView()` with the same view, the tag identifies the view as already in the `ViewHolder`.
In this case, the content can be changed on the existing view rather than a newly created one.

The main activity is shown in Listing 11.17, and the resulting view of diary entries
in a `ListView` is shown in Figure 11.4 on page 307.

Listing 11.17   **src/com/cookbook/datastorage/DisplayDiaries.java**

```
package com.cookbook.datastorage;

import java.text.DateFormat;
import java.util.ArrayList;
import java.util.Date;

import android.app.ListActivity;
import android.content.Context;
```

```
import android.database.Cursor;
import android.os.Bundle;
import android.view.LayoutInflater;
import android.view.View;
import android.view.ViewGroup;
import android.widget.BaseAdapter;
import android.widget.TextView;

import com.cookbook.data.Constants;
import com.cookbook.data.MyDB;

public class DisplayDiaries extends ListActivity {
    MyDB dba;
    DiaryAdapter myAdapter;
    private class MyDiary{
        public MyDiary(String t, String c, String r){
            title=t;
            content=c;
            recordDate=r;
        }
        public String title;
        public String content;
        public String recordDate;
    }
    @Override
    protected void onCreate(Bundle savedInstanceState) {
        dba = new MyDB(this);
        dba.open();
        setContentView(R.layout.diaries);

        super.onCreate(savedInstanceState);
        myAdapter = new DiaryAdapter(this);
        this.setListAdapter(myAdapter);
    }

    private class DiaryAdapter extends BaseAdapter {
        private LayoutInflater mInflater;
        private ArrayList<MyDiary> diaries;
        public DiaryAdapter(Context context) {
            mInflater = LayoutInflater.from(context);
            diaries = new ArrayList<MyDiary>();
            getData();
        }
        public void getData(){
            Cursor c = dba.getDiaries();
            startManagingCursor(c);
            if(c.moveToFirst()){
                do{
                    String title =
                        c.getString(c.getColumnIndex(Constants.TITLE_NAME));
                    String content =
                     c.getString(c.getColumnIndex(Constants.CONTENT_NAME));
                    DateFormat dateFormat =
                     DateFormat.getDateTimeInstance();
                    String dateData = dateFormat.format(new
                     Date(c.getLong(c.getColumnIndex(
                                        Constants.DATE_NAME))).getTime());
                    MyDiary temp = new MyDiary(title,content,dateData);
```

```
                    diaries.add(temp);
                } while(c.moveToNext());
            }
        }

        @Override
        public int getCount() {return diaries.size();}
        public MyDiary getItem(int i) {return diaries.get(i);}
        public long getItemId(int i) {return i;}
        public View getView(int arg0, View arg1, ViewGroup arg2) {
            final ViewHolder holder;
            View v = arg1;
            if ((v == null) || (v.getTag() == null)) {
                v = mInflater.inflate(R.layout.diaryrow, null);
                holder = new ViewHolder();
                holder.mTitle = (TextView)v.findViewById(R.id.name);
                holder.mDate = (TextView)v.findViewById(R.id.datetext);
                v.setTag(holder);
            } else {
                holder = (ViewHolder) v.getTag();
            }

            holder.mdiary = getItem(arg0);
            holder.mTitle.setText(holder.mdiary.title);
            holder.mDate.setText(holder.mdiary.recordDate);

            v.setTag(holder);

            return v;
        }

        public class ViewHolder {
            MyDiary mdiary;
            TextView mTitle;
            TextView mDate;
        }
    }
}
```

Content Provider

Every application has its own sandbox and cannot access data from other applications. If access to functions not provided by its own sandbox is required, the application must explicitly declare permission up front before installation. Android provides an interface called ContentProvider to act as a bridge between applications, enabling them to share and change each other's data. A content provider allows a clean separation between the application layer and the data layer. It requires a permission setting in the **AndroidManifest.xml** file and can be accessed using a simple URI model.

Following are some of the native databases Android makes available as content providers:

- Browser—Read or modify bookmarks, browser history, or web searches.

Figure 11.4   The `ListView` of diary entries

- CallLog—View or update the call history.
- Contacts—Retrieve, modify, or store personal contacts. Contact information is stored in a three-tier data model of tables under a `ContactsContract` object:
  - `ContactsContract.Data`—Contains all kinds of personal data. There is a predefined set of common data, such as phone numbers and email addresses, but the format of this table can be application-specific.
  - `ContactsContract.RawContacts`—Contains a set of data objects associated with a single account or person.
  - `ContactsContract.Contacts`—Contains an aggregate of one or more RawContacts, presumably describing the same person.
- LiveFolder—A special folder whose content is provided by a content provider.
- MediaStore—Access audio, video, and images.
- Setting—View and retrieve Bluetooth settings, ringtones, and other device preferences.
- SearchRecentSuggestions—Configure to operate with a search-suggestions provider.
- SyncStateContract—View the content provider contract for associating data with a data array account. Providers that want to store this data in a standard way can use this.
- UserDictionary—Store user-defined words used by input methods during

predictive text input. Applications and input methods can add words to the dictionary. Words can have associated frequency information and locale information.

To access a content provider, the application needs to get a `ContentResolver` instance to query, insert, delete, and update the data from the content provider, as shown in the following example:

```
ContentResolver crInstance = getContentResolver(); //Get a ContentResolver instance
crInstance.query(People.CONTENT_URI, null, null, null, null); //Query contacts
ContentValues new_Values= new ContentValues();
crInstance.insert(People.CONTENT_URI, new_Values); //Insert new values
crInstance.delete(People_URI, null, null); //Delete all contacts

ContentValues update_Values= new ContentValues();
crInstance.update(People_URI, update_Value, null,null); //Update values
```

Each content provider needs to have a URI, which is used for registration and permission access. The URI must be unique from provider to provider and have the generic suggested format:

```
content://<package name>.provider.<custom ContentProvider name>/<DataPath>
```

For simplicity, it can also be just `content://com.cookbook.datastorage/diaries`, which is used in the next recipe. The `UriMatcher` class is used in the `ContentProvider` interface to ensure that a proper URI is passed.

Recipe: Creating a Custom Content Provider

Having seen how to use a content provider, it is time to integrate one into the diary project used in previous recipes. This recipe shows how to expose diary entries to other selected applications. A custom content provider just extends the Android `ContentProvider` class, which contains six methods to optionally override:

- `query()`—Allows third-party applications to retrieve content
- `insert()`—Allows third-party applications to insert content
- `update()`—Allows third-party applications to update content
- `delete()`—Allows third-party applications to delete content
- `getType()`—Allows third-party applications to read each of the URI structures supported
- `onCreate()`—Creates a database instance to help retrieve the content

For example, if other applications are allowed to read only content from the provider, just `onCreate()` and `query()` need to be overridden.

A custom `ContentProvider` class is shown in Listing 11.18; it has one URI added to `UriMatcher` based on the package `com.cookbook.datastorage` and the database table name `diaries`. The `onCreate()` method forms a `MyDB` object with code from Listing 11.9. It is responsible for the database access. The `query()` method retrieves all records from the diaries database, which is passed as the `uri` argument. In case of a more specific selection of records, the other arguments of this method would be used.

Listing 11.18   **src/com/cookbook/datastorage/DiaryContentProvider.java**

```
package com.cookbook.datastorage;

import android.content.ContentProvider;
import android.content.ContentValues;
import android.content.UriMatcher;
import android.database.Cursor;
import android.database.sqlite.SQLiteQueryBuilder;
import android.net.Uri;

import com.cookbook.data.Constants;
import com.cookbook.data.MyDB;

public class DiaryContentProvider extends ContentProvider {

    private MyDB dba;
    private static final  UriMatcher sUriMatcher;
    //the code returned for URI match to components
    private static final int DIARIES=1;
    public static final String AUTHORITY = "com.cookbook.datastorage";
    static {
            sUriMatcher = new UriMatcher(UriMatcher.NO_MATCH);
            sUriMatcher.addURI(AUTHORITY, Constants.TABLE_NAME,
                               DIARIES);
    }
    @Override
    public int delete(Uri uri, String selection, String[] selectionArgs) {
        return 0;
    }
    public String getType(Uri uri) {return null;}
    public Uri insert(Uri uri, ContentValues values) {return null;}
    public int update(Uri uri, ContentValues values, String selection,
        String[] selectionArgs) {return 0;}

    @Override
    public boolean onCreate() {
        dba = new MyDB(this.getContext());
        dba.open();
        return false;
    }

    @Override
    public Cursor query(Uri uri, String[] projection, String selection,
            String[] selectionArgs, String sortOrder) {
        Cursor c=null;
        switch (sUriMatcher.match(uri)) {
                case DIARIES:
```

```
                    c = dba.getDiaries();
                    break;
                default:
                    throw new IllegalArgumentException(
                                            "Unknown URI" + uri);

        }
        c.setNotificationUri(getContext().getContentResolver(), uri);
        return c;
    }
}
```

The provider needs to be specified in the **AndroidManifest.xml** file to be accessible, as shown in Listing 11.19.

Listing 11.19   AndroidManifest.xml

```
<?xml version="1.0" encoding="utf-8"?>
<manifest xmlns:android="http://schemas.android.com/apk/res/android"
      package="com.cookbook.datastorage"
      android:versionCode="1"
      android:versionName="1.0">
    <application android:icon="@drawable/icon"
                    android:label="@string/app_name">
        <activity android:name=".DataStorage"
                    android:label="@string/app_name">
            <intent-filter>
              <action android:name="android.intent.action.MAIN" />
              <category android:name="android.intent.category.LAUNCHER" />
            </intent-filter>
        </activity>
        <activity android:name=".MyPreferences" />
        <activity android:name=".Diary"/>
        <activity android:name=".DisplayDiaries"/>
        <provider android:name="DiaryContentProvider"
            android:authorities="com.cookbook.datastorage" />
    </application>
    <uses-sdk android:minSdkVersion="7" />
</manifest>
```

Now the content provider is ready for other applications to use. To test this content provider, a new Android project can be created called **DataStorageTester** with main activity DataStorageTester. This is shown in Listing 11.20. An instance of Content Resolver is created to query the data from the DataStorage content provider. After a Cursor is returned, the testing function parses the second column of each data entry and concatenates it into a String to display on the screen using a StringBuilder object.

Listing 11.20   src/com/cookbook/datastorage_tester/DataStorageTester.java

```
package com.cookbook.datastorage_tester;

import android.app.Activity;
import android.content.ContentResolver;
```

```java
import android.database.Cursor;
import android.net.Uri;
import android.os.Bundle;
import android.widget.TextView;

public class DataStorageTester extends Activity {
    TextView tv;

    @Override
    public void onCreate(Bundle savedInstanceState) {
        super.onCreate(savedInstanceState);
        setContentView(R.layout.main);
        tv = (TextView) findViewById(R.id.output);
        String myUri = "content://com.cookbook.datastorage/diaries";
        Uri CONTENT_URI = Uri.parse(myUri);
        //Get ContentResolver instance
        ContentResolver crInstance = getContentResolver();
        Cursor c = crInstance.query(CONTENT_URI, null, null, null, null);
        startManagingCursor(c);
        StringBuilder sb = new StringBuilder();
        if(c.moveToFirst()){
            do{
                sb.append(c.getString(1)).append("\n");

            }while(c.moveToNext());
        }
        tv.setText(sb.toString());

    }
}
```

Inside the **main.xml** layout file, an ID needs to be added for the TextView output, as shown in Listing 11.21.

Listing 11.21   res/layout/main.xml

```xml
<?xml version="1.0" encoding="utf-8"?>
<LinearLayout xmlns:android="http://schemas.android.com/apk/res/android"
    android:orientation="vertical"
    android:layout_width="match_parent"
    android:layout_height="match_parent"
    >
<TextView
    android:id="@+id/output"
    android:layout_width="match_parent"
    android:layout_height="wrap_content"
    android:text="@string/hello"
    />
</LinearLayout>
```

Running the testing function displays the diary entry titles, as shown in Figure 11.5.

Figure 11.5   The result of a query in a content provider to the separate diary application

File Saving and Loading

In addition to the Android-specific data storage methods mentioned previously, the standard java.io.File Java package is available. This provides for flat file manipulation, such as FileInputStream, FileOutputStream, InputStream, and OutputStream. An example is reading from and writing to a file:

```
FileInputStream fis = openFileInput("myfile.txt");
FileOutputStream fos = openFileOutput("myfile.txt",
                                Context.MODE_WORLD_WRITEABLE);
```

Another example is saving the bitmap camera picture to a PNG file, as follows:

```
Bitmap takenPicture;
FileOutputStream out = openFileOutput("mypic.png",
                                Context.MODE_WORLD_WRITEABLE);
takenPicture.compress(CompressFormat.PNG, 100, out);
out.flush();
out.close();
```

The files in the resources directories can also be opened. For example, to open **myrawfile.txt** located in the **res/raw** folder, use the following:

```
InputStream is = this.getResource()
                .openRawResource(R.raw.myrawfile.txt);
```

Recipe: Using AsyncTask for Asynchronous Processing

To maximize application performance, it is best to ensure that the main thread is not blocked. Tasks can be offloaded to separate threads that will run in the background. This recipe uses the `AsyncTask` class to perform some logic off the main thread.

The `AsyncTask` class takes three arguments: `Params`, `Progress`, and `Result`. Using all of them is not required, and in such a case passing `Void` is acceptable. The four main methods that are used as logical steps when executed using `AsyncTask` are as follows:

- `onPreExecute()`—This method runs on the main thread and is generally used for setup of the asynchronous task.
- `doInBackground()`—This method is where the logic of a task is run. A separate thread is used so that thread blocking does not exist. It uses the `publishProgress()` method to pass updates back to the main thread.
- `onProgressUpdate()`—This method is used during the `publishProgress()` method to update the main thread with visual updates.
- `onPostExecute()`—This method is called immediately after the `doInBackground()` method completes, and it includes a parameter passed from that method.

Note that when using the `AsyncTask` class, any threads that are used will be destroyed when the current view is removed or destroyed.

The code in Listing 11.22 will take a sentence and look for the word *meow*. As it processes, the progress bar will be updated.

Listing 11.22 src/com/cookbook/async/MainActivity.java

```java
package com.cookbook.async;

import java.util.regex.Matcher;
import java.util.regex.Pattern;

import android.app.Activity;
import android.os.AsyncTask;
import android.os.Bundle;
import android.view.View;
import android.widget.ProgressBar;
import android.widget.TextView;

public class MainActivity extends Activity {

  TextView mainTextView;
  ProgressBar mainProgress;

  @Override
  protected void onCreate(Bundle savedInstanceState) {
    super.onCreate(savedInstanceState);
    setContentView(R.layout.activity_main);
    mainTextView = (TextView) findViewById(R.id.maintextview);
    mainProgress = (ProgressBar) findViewById(R.id.mainprogress);
  }
```

```java
private class MyAsyncTask extends AsyncTask<String, Integer, String> {
  @Override
  protected String doInBackground(String... parameter) {
    String result = "";

    Pattern pattern = Pattern.compile("meow");
    Matcher matcher = pattern.matcher(parameter[0]);

    int count = 0;
    while (matcher.find()){
      count++;
      try {
        Thread.sleep(100);
      } catch (InterruptedException e) {
        // Remember to error handle
      }
      publishProgress(count + 20);
    }

    result = "meow was found "+count+" times";

    return result;
  }

  @Override
  protected void onProgressUpdate(Integer... progress) {
    mainProgress.setProgress(progress[0]);
  }

  @Override
  protected void onPostExecute(String result) {
    mainTextView.setText(result);
  }
}

public void executeAsync(View view) {
  MyAsyncTask task = new MyAsyncTask();
  task.execute("Meow, meow, meow many times do you have meow?");
}

}
```

12

Location-Based Services

Location-based services (LBSs) enable some of the most popular mobile applications. Location can be integrated with many functions, such as Internet searching, picture taking, gaming, and social networking. Developers can leverage the available location technology to make their applications more relevant and local.

This chapter introduces methods to obtain the device's location and then track, geocode, and map it. In addition, there are recipes for overlaying the map with markers and views.

Location Basics

An application requires the following to access the location services from the Android system:

- LocationManager—Class providing access to Android system location services
- LocationListener—Interface for receiving notifications from the LocationManager when the location has changed
- Location—Class representing a geographic location determined at a particular time

The LocationManager class needs to be initialized with the Android system service called LOCATION_SERVICE. This provides the application with the device's current location and movement and can also alert when the device enters or leaves a defined area. An example of initialization follows:

```
LocationManager mLocationManager;
mLocationManager = (LocationManager)
            getSystemService(Context.LOCATION_SERVICE);
```

After the LocationManager instance is initiated, a location provider needs to be selected. Different location technologies might be available on the device (such as Assisted Global Positioning System (AGPS), Wi-Fi, and so on), and a general way to find a proper location provider is to define the accuracy and power requirements. This can be done using the `Criteria` class defined in `android.location.Criteria`. This enables the Android system to find the best available location technology for the specified requirements. Following is an example of selecting a location provider based on criteria:

```
Criteria criteria = new Criteria();
criteria.setAccuracy(Criteria.ACCURACY_FINE);
criteria.setPowerRequirement(Criteria.POWER_LOW);
String locationprovider =
            mLocationManager.getBestProvider(criteria, true);
```

It is also possible to specify the location estimation technology using the location manager's `getProvider()` method. The two most common providers are the satellite-based GPS (specified by `LocationManager.GPS_PROVIDER`) and cell-tower/Wi-Fi identification (specified by `LocationManager.NETWORK_PROVIDER`). The former is more accurate, but the latter is useful when a direct view of the sky is not available, such as indoors.

Unless otherwise noted, all recipes in this chapter will use the following two support files. First, the main layout needs a `TextView`, as shown in Listing 12.1, for displaying the location data.

Listing 12.1   **res/layout/main.xml**

```
<?xml version="1.0" encoding="utf-8"?>
<LinearLayout xmlns:android="http://schemas.android.com/apk/res/android"
    android:orientation="vertical"
    android:layout_width="match_parent"
    android:layout_height="match_parent"
    >
<TextView
    android:id="@+id/tv1"
    android:layout_width="match_parent"
    android:layout_height="wrap_content"
    android:text="@string/hello"
    />
</LinearLayout>
```

Second, permission to use location information needs to be granted in the **AndroidManifest.xml** file, as shown in Listing 12.2 (only the package name needs to be changed for each recipe). For a more accurate location, such as GPS, add the `ACCESS_FINE_LOCATION` permission. Otherwise, add the `ACCESS_COARSE_LOCATION` permission. It should be noted that `ACCESS_FINE_LOCATION` also enables the same sensors that are used for `ACCESS_COARSE_LOCATION`.

Listing 12.2   **AndroidManifest.xml**

```
<?xml version="1.0" encoding="utf-8"?>
<manifest xmlns:android="http://schemas.android.com/apk/res/android"
```

```
        package="com.cookbook.mylocationpackage"
        android:versionCode="1"
        android:versionName="1.0">
<uses-permission android:name="android.permission.ACCESS_FINE_LOCATION"/>

    <application android:icon="@drawable/icon"
                android:label="@string/app_name">
        <activity android:name=".MyLocation"
                android:label="@string/app_name">
            <intent-filter>
                <action android:name="android.intent.action.MAIN" />
                <category android:name="android.intent.category.LAUNCHER" />
            </intent-filter>
        </activity>
    </application>
    <uses-sdk android:minSdkVersion="4" />

</manifest>
```

Recipe: Retrieving Last Location

Because it might take time to produce a location estimation, getLastKnownLocation()
can be called to retrieve the location last saved for a given provider. The location
contains a latitude, longitude, and Coordinated Universal Time (CUT) timestamp.
Depending on the provider, information on altitude, speed, and bearing might also
be included (use getAltitude(), getSpeed(), and getBearing() on the location
object to retrieve these and getExtras() to retrieve satellite information). Latitude
and longitude are displayed to the screen in this recipe. Another option that may be
used is PASSIVE_PROVIDER, which is a constant that is a special location provider that
stores the last request for location. The main activity is shown in Listing 12.3.

Listing 12.3 src/com/cookbook/lastlocation/MyLocation.java

```java
package com.cookbook.lastlocation;

import android.app.Activity;
import android.content.Context;
import android.location.Criteria;
import android.location.Location;
import android.location.LocationManager;
import android.os.Bundle;
import android.widget.TextView;

public class MyLocation extends Activity {
    LocationManager mLocationManager;
    TextView tv;

    @Override
    public void onCreate(Bundle savedInstanceState) {
```

```
        super.onCreate(savedInstanceState);
        setContentView(R.layout.main);
        tv = (TextView) findViewById(R.id.tv1);

        mLocationManager = (LocationManager)
                getSystemService(Context.LOCATION_SERVICE);

        Criteria criteria = new Criteria();
        criteria.setAccuracy(Criteria.ACCURACY_FINE);
        criteria.setPowerRequirement(Criteria.POWER_LOW);
        String locationprovider =
                mLocationManager.getBestProvider(criteria,true);
        Location mLocation =
                mLocationManager.getLastKnownLocation(locationprovider);

        tv.setText("Last location lat:" + mLocation.getLatitude()
                + "long:" + mLocation.getLongitude());
    }
}
```

Recipe: Updating Location Upon Change

The LocationListener interface is used to receive notifications when the location has changed. The location manager's requestLocationUpdates() method needs to be called after a location provider is initialized to specify when the current activity is to be notified of changes. It depends on the following parameters:

- provider—The location provider the application uses
- minTime—The minimum time between updates in milliseconds (although the system might increase this time to conserve power)
- minDistance—The minimum distance change before updates in meters
- listener—The location listener that should receive the updates

The location listener's onLocationChanged() method can be overridden to specify an action to be done with the new location. Listing 12.4 shows how this is put together for 5 seconds of time and changes of more than 2 meters between updates. An actual implementation should use larger values between updates to save battery life. Also note that no heavy processing should be done in the onLocationChanged() method. Rather, copy the data and pass it off to a thread.

Listing 12.4   **src/com/cookbook/update_location/MyLocation.java**

```
package com.cookbook.update_location;

import android.app.Activity;
import android.content.Context;
import android.location.Criteria;
import android.location.Location;
import android.location.LocationListener;
```

```
import android.location.LocationManager;
import android.os.Bundle;
import android.widget.TextView;

public class MyLocation extends Activity implements LocationListener {
    LocationManager mLocationManager;
    TextView tv;
    Location mLocation;

    @Override
    public void onCreate(Bundle savedInstanceState) {
        super.onCreate(savedInstanceState);
        setContentView(R.layout.main);
        tv = (TextView) findViewById(R.id.tv1);

        mLocationManager = (LocationManager)
                    getSystemService(Context.LOCATION_SERVICE);

        Criteria criteria = new Criteria();
        criteria.setAccuracy(Criteria.ACCURACY_FINE);
        criteria.setPowerRequirement(Criteria.POWER_LOW);
        String locationprovider =
                    mLocationManager.getBestProvider(criteria,true);

        mLocation =
                    mLocationManager.getLastKnownLocation(locationprovider);
        mLocationManager.requestLocationUpdates(
                        locationprovider, 5000, 2.0, this);
    }

    @Override
    public void onLocationChanged(Location location) {
        mLocation = location;
        showupdate();
    }
    // These methods are required
    public void onProviderDisabled(String arg0) {}
    public void onProviderEnabled(String provider) {}
    public void onStatusChanged(String a, int b, Bundle c) {}

    public void showupdate(){
        tv.setText("Last location lat:"+mLocation.getLatitude()
                    + "long:" + mLocation.getLongitude());
    }
}
```

Note that rather than implementing the LocationListener at the activity level, it can also be declared as a separate inner class as follows. This can easily be added to any of the following recipes to provide an update mechanism to the location:

```
mLocationManager.requestLocationUpdates(
                    locationprovider, 5000, 2.0, myLocL);
}
```

```
private final LocationListener myLocL = new LocationListener(){
    @Override
    public void onLocationChanged(Location location){
        mLocation = location;
        showupdate();
    }

    // These methods are required
    public void onProviderDisabled(String arg0) {}
    public void onProviderEnabled(String provider) {}
    public void onStatusChanged(String a, int b, Bundle c) {}
};
```

Recipe: Listing All Enabled Providers

This recipe lists the different location providers available on a given Android device.
One example output is shown in Figure 12.1, but output may be different depending on
the device. The main activity is shown in Listing 12.5. To see a list of possible providers,
the getProviders(true) method is used. To contrast with the previous recipe,
LocationListener is declared as an anonymous inner class without loss of functionality.

Figure 12.1   Example output of all enabled location
providers at their last known location using an actual
Android device

Listing 12.5   **src/com/cookbook/show_providers/MyLocation.java**

```java
package com.cookbook.show_providers;

import java.util.List;

import android.app.Activity;
import android.content.Context;
import android.location.Criteria;
import android.location.Location;
import android.location.LocationListener;
import android.location.LocationManager;
import android.os.Bundle;
import android.widget.TextView;

public class MyLocation extends Activity {
    LocationManager mLocationManager;
    TextView tv;
    Location mLocation;

    @Override
    public void onCreate(Bundle savedInstanceState) {
        super.onCreate(savedInstanceState);
        setContentView(R.layout.main);
        tv = (TextView) findViewById(R.id.tv1);
        mLocationManager = (LocationManager)
                            getSystemService(Context.LOCATION_SERVICE);
        Criteria criteria = new Criteria();
        criteria.setAccuracy(Criteria.ACCURACY_FINE);
        criteria.setPowerRequirement(Criteria.POWER_LOW);
        String locationprovider =
                        mLocationManager.getBestProvider(criteria,true);

        List<String> providers = mLocationManager.getProviders(true);
        StringBuilder mSB = new StringBuilder("Providers:\n");
        for(int i = 0; i<providers.size(); i++) {
          mLocationManager.requestLocationUpdates(
             providers.get(i), 5000, 2.0f, new LocationListener(){

             // These methods are required
             public void onLocationChanged(Location location) {}
             public void onProviderDisabled(String arg0) {}
             public void onProviderEnabled(String provider) {}
             public void onStatusChanged(String a, int b, Bundle c) {}
          });
          mSB.append(providers.get(i)).append(": \n");
          mLocation =
             mLocationManager.getLastKnownLocation(providers.get(i));
          if(mLocation != null) {
             mSB.append(mLocation.getLatitude()).append(" , ");
             mSB.append(mLocation.getLongitude()).append("\n");
          } else {
             mSB.append("Location cannot be found");
          }
        }
        tv.setText(mSB.toString());
    }
}
```

Recipe: Translating a Location to an Address (Reverse Geocoding)

The `Geocoder` class provides a method to translate from an address into latitude-longitude coordinates (geocoding) and from latitude-longitude coordinates into an address (reverse geocoding). Reverse geocoding might produce only a partial address, such as city and postal code, depending on the level of detail available to the location provider.

This recipe uses reverse geocoding to get an address from the device's location and display to the screen, as shown in Figure 12.2. The `Geocoder` instance needs to be initiated with a context and optionally with a locale if different from the system locale. Here, it is explicitly set to `Locale.ENGLISH`. Then the `getFromLocation()` method provides a list of addresses associated with the area around the provided location. Here, the maximum number of returned results is set to one (for instance, the most likely address).

Figure 12.2 Reverse geocoding example, which converts latitude-longitude coordinates into an address

The geocoder returns a list of `android.location.Address` objects. This translation to an address depends on a backend service that is not included in the core Android Framework. The Google Maps API provides a client geocoder service, for example. However, the translation returns an empty list if no such service exists on the target device. The address as a list of strings is dumped line by line into a `String` for display on the screen. The main activity is shown in Listing 12.6.

Listing 12.6   **src/com/cookbook/rev_geocoding/MyLocation.java**
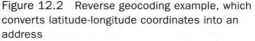

```java
package com.cookbook.rev_geocoding;

import java.io.IOException;
import java.util.List;
import java.util.Locale;
```

```
import android.app.Activity;
import android.content.Context;
import android.location.Address;
import android.location.Criteria;
import android.location.Geocoder;
import android.location.Location;
import android.location.LocationListener;
import android.location.LocationManager;
import android.os.Bundle;
import android.util.Log;
import android.widget.TextView;

public class MyLocation extends Activity {
    LocationManager mLocationManager;
    Location mLocation;
    TextView tv;

    @Override
    public void onCreate(Bundle savedInstanceState) {
        super.onCreate(savedInstanceState);

        setContentView(R.layout.main);
        tv = (TextView) findViewById(R.id.tv1);

        mLocationManager = (LocationManager)
                getSystemService(Context.LOCATION_SERVICE);

        Criteria criteria = new Criteria();
        criteria.setAccuracy(Criteria.ACCURACY_FINE);
        criteria.setPowerRequirement(Criteria.POWER_LOW);
        String locationprovider =
                mLocationManager.getBestProvider(criteria,true);

        mLocation =
                mLocationManager.getLastKnownLocation(locationprovider);

        List<Address> addresses;
        try {
          Geocoder mGC = new Geocoder(this, Locale.ENGLISH);
          addresses = mGC.getFromLocation(mLocation.getLatitude(),
                                        mLocation.getLongitude(), 1);
          if(addresses != null) {
            Address currentAddr = addresses.get(0);
            StringBuilder mSB = new StringBuilder("Address:\n");
            for(int i=0; i<currentAddr.getMaxAddressLineIndex(); i++) {
              mSB.append(currentAddr.getAddressLine(i)).append("\n");
            }

            tv.setText(mSB.toString());
          }
        } catch(IOException e) {
            tv.setText(e.getMessage());
        }
    }
}
```

Recipe: Translating an Address to a Location (Geocoding)

This recipe shows how to translate an address to longitude–latitude coordinates, which is the geocoding process. It is almost the same as the reverse geocoding process used in the previous recipe, except the getFromLocationName() method is used instead of getFromLocation(). Listing 12.7 takes a specific address in the String myAddress, converts it to a location, and then displays it to the screen, as shown in Figure 12.3.

Listing 12.7   src/com/cookbook/geocoding/MyLocation.java

```java
package com.cookbook.geocoding;

import java.io.IOException;
import java.util.List;
import java.util.Locale;

import android.app.Activity;
import android.content.Context;
import android.location.Address;
import android.location.Criteria;
import android.location.Geocoder;
import android.location.Location;
import android.location.LocationListener;
import android.location.LocationManager;
import android.os.Bundle;
import android.widget.TextView;

public class MyLocation extends Activity {
    LocationManager mLocationManager;
    Location mLocation;
    TextView tv;

    @Override
    public void onCreate(Bundle savedInstanceState) {
        super.onCreate(savedInstanceState);

        setContentView(R.layout.main);
        tv = (TextView) findViewById(R.id.tv1);

        mLocationManager = (LocationManager)
                getSystemService(Context.LOCATION_SERVICE);

        Criteria criteria = new Criteria();
        criteria.setAccuracy(Criteria.ACCURACY_FINE);
        criteria.setPowerRequirement(Criteria.POWER_LOW);
        String locationprovider =
                mLocationManager.getBestProvider(criteria,true);

        mLocation =
                mLocationManager.getLastKnownLocation(locationprovider);

        List<Address> addresses;

        String myAddress="Seattle,WA";
        Geocoder gc = new Geocoder(this);
```

```
        try {
            addresses = gc.getFromLocationName(myAddress, 1);
            if(addresses != null) {
                Address x = addresses.get(0);
                StringBuilder mSB = new StringBuilder("Address:\n");

                mSB.append("latitude: ").append(x.getLatitude());
                mSB.append("\nlongitude: ").append(x.getLongitude());
                tv.setText(mSB.toString());
            }
        } catch(IOException e) {
            tv.setText(e.getMessage());
        }
    }
}
```

Figure 12.3   Geocoding example, which converts an address string into latitude-longitude coordinates

Using Google Maps

Google Maps can be used on the Android system in two ways: user access through a browser, and application access through the Google Maps API. The MapView class is a wrapper around the Google Maps API. To use MapView and version 1 of Google Maps, the following setup is needed:

1. Download and install the Google API's SDK as follows:

   - Use the Android SDK and AVD manager in Eclipse to download the Google API.

   - Right-click the project that uses the API, and then select **Properties**.

- Select **Android,** and then select **Google API** to enable it for this project.

2. Obtain a valid Maps API key to use the Google Maps service as follows (see http://code.google.com/android/add-ons/google-apis/mapkey.html):

   - Use the `keytool` command to generate an MD5 certificate fingerprint for the key `alias _ name`:

     ```
     > keytool -list -alias alias_name -keystore my.keystore

     > result:(Certificate fingerprint (MD5):

              94:1E:43:49:87:73:BB:E6:A6:88:D7:20:F1:8E:B5)
     ```

   - Use the MD5 keystore to sign up for the Google Maps service at http://code.google.com/android/maps-api-signup.html.

   - A Maps API key is provided upon signup. Use this key with `MapView`.

3. Include `<uses-library android:name="com.google.android.maps" />` in the **AndroidManifest.xml** file to inform the Android system that the application uses the `com.google.android.maps` library from the Google API's SDK.

4. Add the `android.permission.INTERNET` permission to the **AndroidManifest.xml** file so the application is allowed to use the Internet to receive data from the Google Maps service.

5. Include a `MapView` in the layout XML file.

More specifically, the two supporting files needed for a Google Maps activity follow. First, the **AndroidManifest.xml** file needs the proper maps library and permissions, as shown in Listing 12.8.

Listing 12.8   AndroidManifest.xml

```xml
<?xml version="1.0" encoding="utf-8"?>
<manifest xmlns:android="http://schemas.android.com/apk/res/android"
      package="com.cookbook.using_gmaps"
      android:versionCode="1"
      android:versionName="1.0">
   <application android:icon="@drawable/icon"
               android:label="@string/app_name">
      <activity android:name=".MyLocation"
               android:label="@string/app_name">
         <intent-filter>
            <action android:name="android.intent.action.MAIN" />
            <category android:name="android.intent.category.LAUNCHER" />
         </intent-filter>
      </activity>
      <uses-library android:name="com.google.android.maps" />
   </application>
   <uses-sdk android:minSdkVersion="4" />
<uses-permission android:name="android.permission.INTERNET" />
```

```
<uses-permission android:name="android.permission.ACCESS_FINE_LOCATION"/>
</manifest>
```

Second, the layout XML file needs the proper `MapView` declared in order to display the Google map, as shown in Listing 12.9. It can also declare whether the user can interact with the map by declaring the `clickable` element, which is `false` by default. This is used in the following recipes.

Listing 12.9   **res/layout/main.xml**

```
<?xml version="1.0" encoding="utf-8"?>
<LinearLayout xmlns:android="http://schemas.android.com/apk/res/android"
    android:orientation="vertical"
    android:layout_width="match_parent"
    android:layout_height="match_parent"
    >
<TextView
    android:id="@+id/tv1"
    android:layout_width="match_parent"
    android:layout_height="wrap_content"
    android:text="@string/hello"
    />
<com.google.android.maps.MapView
    android:id="@+id/map1"
    android:layout_width="match_parent"
    android:layout_height="match_parent"
    android:clickable="true"
    android:apiKey="0ZDUMMY13442HjX491CODE44MSsJzfDVlIQ"
    />
</LinearLayout>
```

Note that there are several changes in Google Maps API version 2:

- Acquiring an API key is now done through the Google API console (https://code.google.com/apis/console/).

- The following permissions are now required:

      android.permission.INTERNET

      android.permission.ACCESS_NETWORK_STATE

      android.permission.WRITE_EXTERNAL_STORAGE

      com.google.android.providers.gsf.permission.READ_GSERVICES

- OpenGL ES version 2 is now required and is obtained by including the following `<uses-feature>` element:

      <uses-feature

        android:glEsVersion="0x00020000"

        android:required="true"/>

- In the main layout XML file, add the following fragment:

```
<fragment xmlns:android="http://schemas.android.com/apk/res/android"

    android:id="@+id/map"

    android:layout_width="match_parent"

    android:layout_height="match_parent"

    android:name="com.google.android.gms.maps.MapFragment"/>
```

- In onCreate(), make sure to use setContentView to the XML file that contains the fragment. For example:

```
setContentView(R.layout.main);
```

For more information about using Google Maps Android API version 2, visit https://developers.google.com/maps/documentation/android/start.

Recipe: Adding Google Maps to an Application

To display a Google map, the main activity should extend MapActivity, as shown in Listing 12.10. It also must point to the layout ID for the map in the main layout XML file, called map1 here. Note that the isRouteDisplayed() method needs to be implemented, too. The resulting display is shown in Figure 12.4.

Listing 12.10 src/com/cookbook/using_gmaps/MyLocation.java

```java
package com.cookbook.using_gmaps;

import android.content.Context;
import android.location.Criteria;
import android.location.Location;
import android.location.LocationManager;
import android.os.Bundle;
import android.widget.TextView;

import com.google.android.maps.MapActivity;
import com.google.android.maps.MapView;

public class MyLocation extends MapActivity {
    LocationManager mLocationManager;
    Location mLocation;
    TextView tv;

    @Override
    public void onCreate(Bundle savedInstanceState) {
        super.onCreate(savedInstanceState);

        setContentView(R.layout.main);
        MapView mapView = (MapView) findViewById(R.id.map1);
        tv = (TextView) findViewById(R.id.tv1);

        mLocationManager = (LocationManager)
                getSystemService(Context.LOCATION_SERVICE);
```

```
        Criteria criteria = new Criteria();
        criteria.setAccuracy(Criteria.ACCURACY_FINE);
        criteria.setPowerRequirement(Criteria.POWER_LOW);
        String locationprovider =
                mLocationManager.getBestProvider(criteria,true);

        mLocation =
                mLocationManager.getLastKnownLocation(locationprovider);

        tv.setText("Last location lat:" + mLocation.getLatitude()
                + "long:" + mLocation.getLongitude());
    }

    @Override
    protected boolean isRouteDisplayed() {
        // This method is required
        return false;
    }
}
```

Recipe: Adding Markers to a Map

The ItemizedOverlay class provides a way to draw markers and overlays on top of
a MapView. It manages a set of OverlayItem elements, such as an image, in a list and

Figure 12.4   Example of Google Maps used from
inside an application

handles the drawing, placement, click handling, focus control, and layout optimization for each element. Create a class that extends ItemizedOverlay and override the following:

- addOverlay()—Adds an OverlayItem to the ArrayList. This calls populate(), which reads the item and prepares it to be drawn.
- createItem()—Called by populate() to retrieve the given OverlayItem.
- size()—Returns the number of OverlayItem elements in the ArrayList.
- onTap()—Callback method when a marker is clicked.

The newly created class is given in Listing 12.11, and Figure 12.5 shows the result.

Listing 12.11   src/com/cookbook/adding_markers/MyMarkerLayer.java

```java
package com.cookbook.adding_markers;

import java.util.ArrayList;

import android.app.AlertDialog;
import android.content.DialogInterface;
import android.graphics.drawable.Drawable;

import com.google.android.maps.ItemizedOverlay;
import com.google.android.maps.OverlayItem;

public class MyMarkerLayer extends ItemizedOverlay {

    private ArrayList<OverlayItem> mOverlays =
            new ArrayList<OverlayItem>();

    public MyMarkerLayer(Drawable defaultMarker) {
        super(boundCenterBottom(defaultMarker));
        populate();
    }
    public void addOverlayItem(OverlayItem overlay) {
        mOverlays.add(overlay);
        populate();
    }
    @Override
    protected OverlayItem createItem(int i) {
        return mOverlays.get(i);
    }
    @Override
    public int size() {
        return mOverlays.size();
    }
    @Override
    protected boolean onTap(int index) {
        AlertDialog.Builder dialog =
                new AlertDialog.Builder(MyLocation.mContext);
        dialog.setTitle(mOverlays.get(index).getTitle());
        dialog.setMessage(mOverlays.get(index).getSnippet());
        dialog.setPositiveButton("OK",
```

```
                 new DialogInterface.OnClickListener() {
                   public void onClick(DialogInterface dialog, int whichButton) {
                       dialog.cancel();
                   }
              });
              dialog.setNegativeButton("Cancel",
                 new DialogInterface.OnClickListener() {
                   public void onClick(DialogInterface dialog, int whichButton) {
                       dialog.cancel();
                   }
              });
              dialog.show();
              return super.onTap(index);
          }
}
```

Figure 12.5   Adding a clickable marker to a map

A few comments on the `MyMarkerLayer` class that are highlighted in Listing 12.11:

- An `OverlayItem` container `mOverlays` is declared to save all the items passed to the overlay.

- A binding point for where all overlaid items are attached to the map needs to be defined before any overlay item is drawn. To specify the bottom center of the map as that point, `boundCenterBottom` is added to the class constructor.

- The required methods are overridden: `addOverlay()`, `createItem()`, `size()`, and `onTap()`. Here, the `onTap()` method provides a dialog box when the item is clicked.

- The populate() method is added to the end of the constructor and addOverlay(). This tells the MyMarkerLayer class to prepare all OverlayItem elements and draw each one on the map.

Now this ItemizedOverlay can be added to the MapActivity created in the previous recipe. As highlighted in Listing 12.12, the activity:

- Retrieves the existing map overlay items using the getOverlays() method from MapView. The marker layer is added to this container at the end of the function.
- Defines an instance of the MyMarkerLayer to handle the overlay items.
- Retrieves the latitude and longitude (in degrees) of the address. This defines the point of interest using a GeoPoint class. GeoPoint takes input in microdegrees, so the latitude and longitude need to be multiplied by one million (1E6).
- Uses a map controller to animate to the GeoPoint and zoom the view. Also, it enables user-controlled zoom using setBuiltInZoomControls().
- Defines an OverlayItem as a message at the GeoPoint of interest.
- Adds the item to the MyMarkerLayer using the addOverlayItem() method. It then puts the now-defined MyMarkerLayer into the existing overlay list retrieved in step 1.

Listing 12.12   src/com/cookbook/adding_markers/MyLocation.java

```
package com.cookbook.adding_markers;

import java.io.IOException;
import java.util.List;

import android.content.Context;
import android.graphics.drawable.Drawable;
import android.location.Address;
import android.location.Geocoder;
import android.os.Bundle;
import android.widget.TextView;

import com.google.android.maps.GeoPoint;
import com.google.android.maps.MapActivity;
import com.google.android.maps.MapController;
import com.google.android.maps.MapView;
import com.google.android.maps.Overlay;

public class MyLocation extends MapActivity {
    TextView tv;
    List<Overlay> mapOverlays;
    MyMarkerLayer markerlayer;
    private MapController mc;
    public static Context mContext;

    @Override
    public void onCreate(Bundle savedInstanceState) {
        super.onCreate(savedInstanceState);
```

```
    mContext = this;
    setContentView(R.layout.main);
    MapView mapView = (MapView) findViewById(R.id.map1);
    tv = (TextView) findViewById(R.id.tv1);

    mapOverlays = mapView.getOverlays();
    Drawable drawable =
            this.getResources().getDrawable(R.drawable.icon);
    markerlayer = new MyMarkerLayer(drawable);

    List<Address> addresses;
    String myAddress="1600 Amphitheatre Parkway, Mountain View, CA";

    int geolat = 0;
    int geolon = 0;

    Geocoder gc = new Geocoder(this);
    try {
        addresses = gc.getFromLocationName(myAddress, 1);
        if(addresses != null) {
          Address x = addresses.get(0);

          geolat = (int)(x.getLatitude()*1E6);
          geolon = (int)(x.getLongitude()*1E6);
        }
    } catch(IOException e) {
        tv.setText(e.getMessage());
    }

    mapView.setBuiltInZoomControls(true);
    GeoPoint point = new GeoPoint(geolat,geolon);
    mc = mapView.getController();
    mc.animateTo(point);
    mc.setZoom(3);

    OverlayItem overlayitem =
            new OverlayItem(point, "Google Campus", "I am at Google");
    markerlayer.addOverlayItem(overlayitem);
    mapOverlays.add(markerlayer);
    }

    @Override
    protected boolean isRouteDisplayed() { return false; }
}
```

Recipe: Adding Views to a Map

Developers can add any View or ViewGroup to the MapView. This recipe shows the addition of two simple elements to a map: TextView and Button. When the button is clicked, the text in the TextView changes.

These two views are added to MapView by calling the addView() method with LayoutParams. Here, the location of the elements is specified in (x,y) screen coordinates, but developers can also provide a GeoPoint class to LayoutParams instead.

Listing 12.13 shows the main activity, which also requires the `MyMarkerLayer` class defined in the previous recipe (Listing 12.11 with the first line changed to reflect the proper package). This results in the `MapView` shown in Figure 12.6.

Listing 12.13   **src/com/cookbook/mylocation/MyLocation.java**

```
package com.cookbook.mylocation;

import java.io.IOException;
import java.util.List;

import android.content.Context;
import android.content.Intent;
import android.graphics.Color;
import android.graphics.drawable.Drawable;
import android.location.Address;
import android.location.Geocoder;
import android.os.Bundle;
import android.view.View;
import android.view.View.OnClickListener;
import android.widget.Button;
import android.widget.TextView;
import com.google.android.maps.GeoPoint;
import com.google.android.maps.MapActivity;
import com.google.android.maps.MapController;
import com.google.android.maps.MapView;
import com.google.android.maps.Overlay;

public class MyLocation extends MapActivity {
    TextView tv;
    List<Overlay> mapOverlays;
    MyMarkerLayer markerlayer;
    private MapController mc;
    MapView.LayoutParams mScreenLayoutParams;
    public static Context mContext;

    @Override
    public void onCreate(Bundle savedInstanceState) {
        super.onCreate(savedInstanceState);
        mContext = this;
        setContentView(R.layout.main);

        MapView mapView = (MapView) findViewById(R.id.map1);
        mc = mapView.getController();
        tv = (TextView) findViewById(R.id.tv1);
        mapOverlays = mapView.getOverlays();
        Drawable drawable =
                    this.getResources().getDrawable(R.drawable.icon);
        markerlayer = new MyMarkerLayer(drawable);

        List<Address> addresses;
        String myAddress="1600 Amphitheatre Parkway, Mountain View, CA";

        int geolat = 0;
        int geolon = 0;
```

```
Geocoder gc = new Geocoder(this);
try {
    addresses = gc.getFromLocationName(myAddress, 1);
    if(addresses != null) {
        Address x = addresses.get(0);

        StringBuilder mSB = new StringBuilder("Address:\n");
        geolat =(int)(x.getLatitude()*1E6);
        geolon = (int)(x.getLongitude()*1E6);
        mSB.append("latitude: ").append(geolat).append("\n");
        mSB.append("longitude: ").append(geolon);
        tv.setText(mSB.toString());
    }
} catch(IOException e) {
    tv.setText(e.getMessage());
}

int x = 50;
int y = 50;
mScreenLayoutParams =
        new MapView.LayoutParams(MapView.LayoutParams.WRAP_CONTENT,
                                 MapView.LayoutParams.WRAP_CONTENT,
                                 x,y,MapView.LayoutParams.LEFT);

final TextView tv = new TextView(this);
tv.setText("Adding View to Google Map");
tv.setTextColor(Color.BLUE);
tv.setTextSize(20);
mapView.addView(tv, mScreenLayoutParams);

x = 250;
y = 250;
mScreenLayoutParams =
        new MapView.LayoutParams(MapView.LayoutParams.WRAP_CONTENT,
                                 MapView.LayoutParams.WRAP_CONTENT,
                                 x,y,
                                 MapView.LayoutParams.BOTTOM_CENTER);

Button clickMe = new Button(this);
clickMe.setText("Click Me");
clickMe.setOnClickListener(new OnClickListener() {
    public void onClick(View v) {
        tv.setTextColor(Color.RED);
        tv.setText("Let's play");
    }
});

mapView.addView(clickMe, mScreenLayoutParams);
}

@Override
protected boolean isRouteDisplayed() { return false; }
}
```

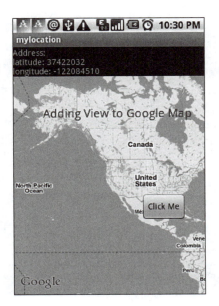

Figure 12.6   Adding a `TextView` and a button to a map

Recipe: Setting Up a Proximity Alert

`LocationManager` provides a method to set a proximity alert. This triggers an alert when a user enters or leaves a defined area. The area is specified by creating variables for latitude-longitude coordinates as well as a variable containing the radius in meters. The alert is specified with a `PendingIntent` that will be launched whenever a user enters or leaves the specified area. An expiration time, set in milliseconds, for the alert can also be defined. An example of how to implement this is shown in Listing 12.14.

Listing 12.14   Creating a Proximity Alert without an Expiration

```
double mlatitude=35.41;
double mlongitude=139.46;

float mRadius=500f; // in meters

long expiration=-1; //-1 never expires or use milliseconds

Intent mIntent = new Intent("You entered the defined area");
PendingIntent mFireIntent
            = PendingIntent.getBroadCast(this, -1, mIntent, 0);

mLocationManager.addProximityAlert(mlatitude, mlongitude,
                              mRadius, expiration, mFireIntent);
```

Using the Little Fluffy Location Library

Dealing with location accuracy as well as maintaining sensible battery usage can at times be tricky. If a user must leave the GPS on in order to get a location fix, the application will use a considerable amount of battery power. If an application needs only a rough estimate of where the user is, some battery power can be saved by using coarse location. However, many applications benefit from using both coarse and fine location, and this leaves developers trying to plan how to handle getting a location, balancing which location method to use (fine or coarse), and how to deal with acquiring the location when the application has been moved into the background without using more battery power than is necessary.

Kenton Price of Little Fluffy Toys Ltd. has written a library for Android 2.1+ called Little Fluffy Location Library that has taken these issues into account. Projects that include his library can tap into a broadcast action that contains a `LocationInfo` object with the following fields:

- `lastLocationUpdateTimestamp`—Time of the last location update in milliseconds
- `lastLocationBroadcastTimestamp`—Time of the last location update broadcast in milliseconds
- `lastLat`—Latitude of the last update in degrees
- `lastLong`—Longitude of the last update in degrees
- `lastAccuracy`—Accuracy of the last update in meters

In addition, the object also contains the following utility methods:

- `refresh`—Refreshes all fields with the latest information
- `anyLocationDataReceived`—Determines if any location data has been received since the last reboot
- `anyLocationDataBroadcast`—Determines if any location information has been broadcast since the last reboot
- `hasLatestDataBeenBroadcast`—Determines if the data contained in the `LocationInfo` object has already been broadcast
- `getTimestampAgeInSeconds`—Returns how old the last location update is in seconds

To start using the Little Fluffy Location Library, download the **littleflufffylocationlibrary.jar** file from http://code.google.com/p/little-fluffy -location-library/ and include it in the project by copying it into the **/libs** folder. After it has been copied, right-click on the file and choose **Build Path → Add to Build Path**.

Recipe: Adding a Notification with the Little Fluffy Location Library

To use the Little Fluffy Location Library in a project, add the following permissions to the manifest:

- `ACCESS_FINE_LOCATION`
- `INTERNET`
- `RECEIVE_BOOT_COMPLETED`
- `ACCESS_COARSE_LOCATION`
- `ACCESS_FINE_LOCATION`

The following features should also be added to the manifest:

- `Android.hardware.location`
- `Android.hardware.location.gps`

The following elements will also be needed inside the `application` element:

```
<service android:name="com.littlefluffytoys.littlefluffylocationlibrary.
➥ LocationBroadcastService" />
<receiver android:name="
➥com.littlefluffytoys.littlefluffylocationlibrary.StartupBroadcastReceiver
➥" android:exported="true">
  <intent-filter>
    <action android:name="android.intent.action.BOOT_COMPLETED" />
  </intent-filter>
</receiver>
<receiver
➥android:name="com.littlefluffytoys.littlefluffylocationlibrary.PassiveLocation
➥ChangedReceiver" android:exported="true" />
<receiver android:name=".FluffyBroadcastReceiver">
    <intent-filter>
        <action
➥android:name="com.cookbook.fluffylocation.littlefluffylocationlibrary.
➥LOCATION_CHANGED" android:exported="true"/>
    </intent-filter>
</receiver>
```

The added elements will set up a service as well as a receiver that is used to get data from the Little Fluffy Location Library. The last block will set up a broadcast receiver that will be used to trigger notifications. Listing 12.15 shows the class that is referenced in the manifest file as the receiver.

Listing 12.15   **/src/com/cookbook/fluffylocation/FluffyBroadcastReceiver.java**

```java
package com.cookbook.fluffylocation;

import android.app.Notification;
import android.app.NotificationManager;
import android.app.PendingIntent;
import android.content.BroadcastReceiver;
import android.content.Context;
import android.content.Intent;
import android.util.Log;

import com.littlefluffytoys.littlefluffylocationlibrary.LocationInfo;
import com.littlefluffytoys.littlefluffylocationlibrary.LocationLibraryConstants;

public class FluffyBroadcastReceiver extends BroadcastReceiver{
  @Override
    public void onReceive(Context context, Intent intent) {
        Log.d("LocationBroadcastReceiver", "onReceive: received location update");

        final LocationInfo locationInfo = (LocationInfo) intent
            .getSerializableExtra(LocationLibraryConstants
                .LOCATION_BROADCAST_EXTRA_LOCATIONINFO);

        // For API 16+ use Notification.Builder instead of Notification
        Notification notification = new Notification(R.drawable.ic_launcher,
            "Locaton updated " +
            locationInfo.getTimestampAgeInSeconds() +
            " seconds ago", System.currentTimeMillis());

        Intent contentIntent = new Intent(context, MainActivity.class);
        PendingIntent contentPendingIntent = PendingIntent.getActivity(context,
            0, contentIntent, PendingIntent.FLAG_UPDATE_CURRENT);

        notification.setLatestEventInfo(context, "Location update broadcast received",
            "Timestamped " +
            LocationInfo
                .formatTimeAndDay(locationInfo.lastLocationUpdateTimestamp, true),
                contentPendingIntent);

        ((NotificationManager) context
            .getSystemService(Context.NOTIFICATION_SERVICE))
                .notify(1234, notification);
  }
}
```

Listing 12.15 shows the basic setup for a broadcast receiver. Using the Log.d() method shows that logging has been put in place to help debug the application.

Something else to take into account is how the notification is built. The notify() method currently uses a value of 1234; this is an ID that is tied to the notification. If there already is a global notification port, such as NOTIFICATION_PORT, it can be substituted here. The current notification will work from Gingerbread to Honeycomb;

however, the `Notification` constructor has been deprecated starting with API Level 16 (Jelly Bean). For future development, the `Notification` constructor must be converted to `Notification.Builder`.

Now that a receiver is in place, an application class needs to be set up. To do this, make sure that the application has been named. In the manifest file, the application element should contain the following property:

```
android:name="com.cookbook.fluffylocation.FluffyApplication"
```

The full path to the application class must be referenced. In this example snippet, `com.cookbook.fluffylocation.FluffyApplication` was used. Listing 12.16 shows the class file found in this location.

Listing 12.16   /src/com/cookbook/fluffylocation/FluffyApplication.java

```java
package com.cookbook.fluffylocation;

import com.littlefluffytoys.littlefluffylocationlibrary.LocationLibrary;

import android.app.Application;
import android.util.Log;

public class FluffyApplication extends Application {
    @Override
    public void onCreate() {
        super.onCreate();
        // Show debugging information
        Log.d("FluffyApplication", "onCreate()");

        LocationLibrary.showDebugOutput(true);

        // Default call would be the following:
        // LocationLibrary.initialiseLibrary(getBaseContext(),
        //      "com.cookbook.fluffylocation");

        // For testing, make request every 1 minute, and force a location update
        // if one hasn't happened in the last 2 minutes
        LocationLibrary.initializeLibrary(getBaseContext(),
            60 * 1000, 2 * 60 * 1000, "com.cookbook.fluffylocation");
    }
}
```

Listing 12.16 shows an `onCreate()` method setting up logging by use of the `Log.d()` method as well as enabling extra debug information by using `showDebugOutput(true)`. This debug information will be useful because it indicates when the library has been loaded and when information is passed to and from the application. The call to initialize the Little Fluffy Location Library can be seen in both the comments and near the end of the `onCreate()` method. The call being used is overkill for getting location data but for development purposes will inform the user every minute if new location data has been retrieved. Figure 12.7 shows the Little Fluffy Location Library in use.

Figure 12.7   A notification displaying information
gathered from the Little Fluffy Location Library

13

In-App Billing

Creating applications that have the ability to up-sell, allow the purchase of items, or add functionality can fill an important role in the application's marketing strategy. Most users are familiar with "pay-to-win" strategies as well as "gifting" systems. Pay-to-win systems often allow users to download the application for free but penalize them with lesser power-ups or limited playing time unless they purchase upgrades. Gifting systems work on a similar principle, allowing users to purchase items for others instead of powering up themselves.

Until recently, Google did not have an official support system in place for these models for the Android Platform, and developers had to create their own system or integrate with third parties for selling additional services or products. Google has since changed that and now provides a very robust system for billing integration. This chapter explains how to implement the official in-app billing solution from Google.

Google Play In-App Billing

Google has provided an API that developers can use to add in-app billing to applications. Only digital goods can be sold; no physical items or tangible goods may be sold with any version of the API. Items that are sold as an in-app purchase are either owned by the user (such as premium upgrades) or consumed by the user (such as power-ups or currency). Purchases made with in-app billing are nonrefundable.

There are currently two versions of the API, although version 2 has been suspended and Google is urging users to upgrade to version 3. While there is not a final date for when support for version 2 of the API will be dropped, new developers getting started with the API should use version 3. In early 2013, it was announced that version 3 of the API would be upgraded to allow for subscriptions and add support for all features that were introduced in version 2 of the API. API version 2 requires at least Android 1.6 (API Level 4) and requires Google Play version 3.5. API version 3 requires a minimum installation of Android 2.2 (API Level 8) with Google Play 3.9.16.

A stipulation for using any version of the Google-provided in-app billing API is that an application must be offered in the Google Play store and abide by the terms of

service for app distribution. The application must also be able to communicate with
the Google Play servers over a network connection.

Developers who wish to use in-app billing through Google Play must have a merchant account. If a developer account has already been created in the Play market, log
in to the developer console (https://play.google.com/apps/publish/) and find the link
to set up a merchant account at Google Checkout. This page shows step by step how
to set up a merchant account and link it to a developer account. A merchant account
can also be set up directly at the Google Checkout Merchant section (www.google
.com/wallet/merchants.html). While testing in-app billing in an application, an actual
credit card must be used; however, any transactions made will be refunded.

Google is currently transitioning the developer console; if the link to add a merchant account cannot be found, add a new application and the link should appear
under the Price and Distribution section.

Recipe: Installing Google's In-App Billing Service

Google provides a library named the Google Play Billing Library. This library contains
all of the classes and interfaces needed to connect to Google's in-app billing services.
It can be installed from the Android SDK under the **Extras** section of the **SDK Manager**. Figure 13.1 shows where this is located.

Installing the Google Play Billing Library adds some folders and files to the SDK
installation directory, including an in-app billing sample application that can be
used for reference. These items can be found in the ***SDKInstallationDirectory/
extras/google/play_billing/in-app-billing-v03*** or ***SDKInstallationDirectory/
google-marker-billing/in-app-billing-v03*** folder on the filesystem. The file

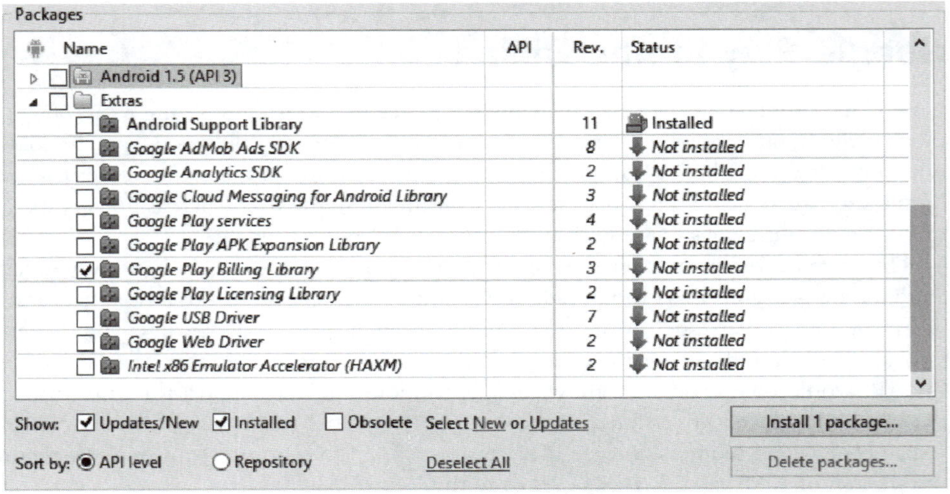

Figure 13.1   Installing the Google Play Billing Library version 3

IInAppBillingService.aidl can be found in that folder and will need to be included in any project that includes in-app billing.

After the required files are in the development environment, a public key must be generated. Log in to the developer console and create a new application. Name the application and click on the Prepare Store Listing button. On the new page that appears, there are several tabs on the left side of the screen; locate the Service & APIs tab and copy the generated public license key for the application.

To experiment with the Google-provided sample application **TrivialDrive**, create a new project (using the default options, including naming the activity **MainActivity**) and copy the assets of the sample application over the new ones. Then, perform a little maintenance on the application by refactoring the classes to the chosen package name and then modifying the application manifest XML to match the package name.

To add in-app billing to an existing application, copy the **IInAppBillingService .aidl** file into the **src** directory of the project. Note that if Eclipse is not being used as the IDE, the following path needs to be created in the **src** directory and the **IInAppBillingService.aidl** file placed into it:

```
com/android/vending/billing
```

To confirm proper installation, build the project and make sure the **gen** folder contains the **IinAppBillingService.java** file.

Recipe: Adding In-App Billing to an Activity

To provide in-app billing, an application must be able to communicate with the billing service. The `BILLING` permission needs to be added to the application manifest XML file to ensure this functionality. In addition to any of the other permissions that the app requires, add the following:

```
<uses-permission android:name="android.permission.BILLING"/>
```

To establish a connection from an activity to the Google Play in-app billing service, create an `IabHelper` object. Pass `IabHelper` the current context as well as the public key that was generated in the developer console for the application. Note that when using the public key, consider building the string at run-time. This will deter users from replacing the public key with their own and faking out the service to avoid having to pay for items in the application.

After creating the `IabHelper` object, bind the service by calling the `startSetup()` method on it. This will be passed another method, `OnIabSetupFinishedListener()`, which is called after some asynchronous setup is complete. An object will be returned to the method that can be used to determine if setup with the in-app billing servers was successful. If there is a problem, the message is passed back in the object.

When the activity is closed, remove the binding to the in-app billing service. Doing so will help with overall system resources and performance. This can be done by calling the `dispose()` method on the `IabHelper` object.

Listing 13.1 shows boilerplate code for establishing in-app billing through Google Play.

Listing 13.1   **In-App Billing Boilerplate**

```
IabHelper mHelper;

@Override
public void onCreate(Bundle savedInstanceState) {
  super.onCreate(savedInstanceState);
  setContentView(R.layout.activity_main);

  // Consider building the public key at run-time
  String base64EncodedPublicKey = "YourGeneratedPublicKey";

  mHelper = new IabHelper(this, base64EncodedPublicKey);

  mHelper.startSetup(new IabHelper.OnIabSetupFinishedListener() {
    public void onIabSetupFinished(IabResult result) {
      if (!result.isSuccess()) {
        // Replace Toast with error-handling logic
        Toast.makeText(context, "iab fail: "+result, Toast.LENGTH_LONG).show();
        return;
      }

      // iab successful, handle success logic here
    }
  });
}
@Override
public void onDestroy() {
 if (mHelper != null) mHelper.dispose();
 mHelper = null;
}
```

Recipe: Listing Items for In-App Purchase

For users to make an in-app purchase, they need to know what is available for purchase. Items that are available for purchase can be set up in the developer console. Each item is created with an item number or SKU and can cost between $0.99 and $200. Once there is at least one item for a user to buy, Google Play can be asked programmatically to list the items through the in-app billing service.

To query Google Play for the list of items for an application, use the query InventoryAsync() method and then programmatically determine the logic based on the returned object. To build on Listing 13.1, add a call to the queryInventory Async() method in the onCreate() method when the in-app billing setup is complete. The following line could be added after a successful installation:

```
mHelper.queryInventoryAsync(mCurrentInventoryListener);
```

Listing 13.2 shows how to set up a Listener that is used in the queryInventory Async() method. The listener is used to listen for the inventory transaction back from Google Play services.

Listing 13.2 **Creating a Listener for Inventory Results**

```
IabHelper.QueryInventoryFinishedListener mGotInventoryListener = new
IabHelper.QueryInventoryFinishedListener() {
  public void onQueryInventoryFinished(IabResult result, Inventory inventory) {
      if (result.isFailure()) {
        Toast.makeText(context, "inventory fail: "+result, Toast.LENGTH_LONG).show();
        return;
      }

      // Inventory has been returned, create logic with it

      // Do UI updating logic here
  }
};
```

To allow a user to purchase an item from an app, use the `launchPurchaseFlow()` method. This method takes five arguments: `Activity`, product ID (`String`), request code value (`int`), listener to notify (`OnIabPurchaseFinishedListener`), and a payload (`String`). Google recommends using the payload for storing customer-identifying information for purchase verification, although this can be any randomly generated string. The call to this method appears as follows; it can be called from inside a triggering event such as a button click:

```
mHelper.launchPurchaseFlow(this, YOUR_SKU, 12345,
    mPurchaseFinishedListener, "R4nd0mb17+0hs7r1nGz/");
```

When the order succeeds, a `Purchase` object is returned. This can be handled similarly to how the `queryInventoryAsync()` method was handled; set up logic for the returned `Purchase` object inside the `Listener`. Listing 13.3 gives an example of how this is done.

Listing 13.3 **Completing a Purchase**

```
IabHelper.OnIabPurchaseFinishedListener
    mPurchaseFinishedListener = new IabHelper.OnIabPurchaseFinishedListener() {
  public void onIabPurchaseFinished(IabResult result, Purchase purchase) {
    if (result.isFailure()) {
      Toast.makeText(context, "Purchase failed: "+result, Toast.LENGTH_LONG).show();
      return;
    }

    if (purchase.getSku().equals(YOUR_SKU)) {
      // Do something with this item
    } else if (purchase.getSku().equals(ANOTHER_SKU)) {
      // Do something with this item
    }
  }
};
```

14

Push Messages

Push messaging is a communication method in which a connected client is informed of an event in a remote system by receiving notifications from that system. As opposed to pull messages, where the client needs to query the remote system at given time intervals, pushed messages are triggered by the remote system itself without having the client ask for a status update. Android supports message push through the Google Cloud Messaging (GCM) library. GCM is available on all Android devices running API Level 8 or higher, which should include most active devices. This chapter shows how to integrate with GCM and how to send and receive messages.

Google Cloud Messaging Setup

Google Cloud Messaging relies on the presence of both the Google Play store and a logged-in Google user account on the device. For sending messages, an API key is needed. This key is tied to the Google account that will be used for publishing the application on the Google Play store later, so be sure to set up an account for this first.

Recipe: Preparing for Google Cloud Messaging

First, an API key must be obtained. To do this, log in to the Google developer account and go to https://code.google.com/apis/console. A new API project will have to be created to use GCM. If this is the first API project, click the Create Project button. Otherwise, click the drop-down at the top left and choose **Create**. In both cases, enter a name for the project, such as **cookbook**. After the project is created, a screen similar to Figure 14.1 will be shown.

Notice two things in this figure. First, there is a huge list of available APIs to work with. Finding GCM requires scrolling down quite a bit. Second, the URL has changed to something like **https://code.google.com/apis/console/b/0/?pli=1#project: 123456**. Make a note of the number behind **#project:**. It is the unique project number

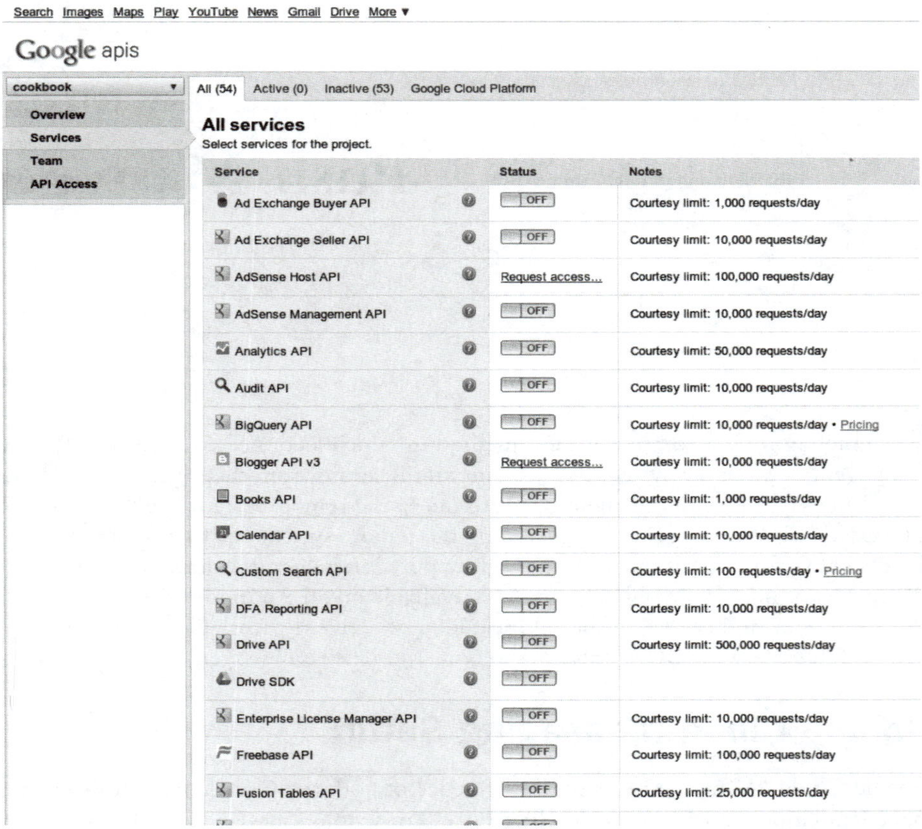

Figure 14.1 API services overview

and will act as the sender ID later on. The sender ID ensures that GCM sends messages to the correct app even if more than one application with a channel for push messages exists on the device.

Now, scroll down to Google Cloud Messaging and set the toggle to ON. Agree to the terms of service on the next page. To get the actual API key, navigate to the API Access page from the menu on the left. It should look similar to Figure 14.2.

Click the Create New Server Key... button. A window will appear where the server's IP address can be entered if needed. It is OK to leave this blank and just press Create. There will then be a newly created server key on the API Access screen. Save this number to a text file or write it down; it will be used to send messages later.

Next, the add-on library must be integrated into the project. Open the Android SKD Manager, go to the Extras section, and tick the check boxes for Google Cloud Messaging for Android Library. After installing GCM, the directory **./extras/**

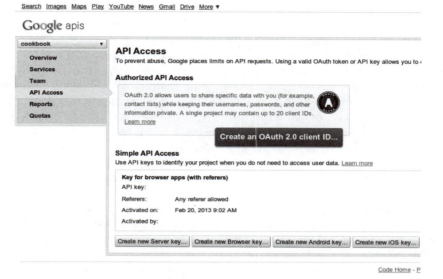

Figure 14.2   API Access page

google/gcm will be found in the Android SDK folder. Gather the **.jar** files from both the **gcm-client** and **gcm-server** subdirectories and put them in the **/libs** folder of the project.

Sending and Receiving Push Messages

In most use cases, push notifications would be sent through a server system, informing the user or the application about events happening somewhere in the backend systems. There is, however, no immediate need to send push notifications this way. Because this book is about Android, and because dealing with servers can be a complex topic on its own, this method will not be used. Instead, a short ping will be sent to the GCM endpoint from within the app itself. While sending a push notification to one's own device might seem useless, sending it from one phone to another could well be appealing. Adding this functionality to an application would be easy.

Recipe: Preparing the Manifest

A bunch of permissions are needed in order to send and receive messages. First, android.permission.INTERNET is needed for all data transfers. A WakeLock is needed to make sure messages are received even when the receiving device is turned off or in standby, so add android.permission.WAKE_LOCK. GCM relies on Google accounts, which means android.permission.GET_ACCOUNTS is required to access them. And to be able to actually receive the messages, a custom permission called com.

google.android.c2dm.permission.RECEIVE, defined by the GCM library, must be added. (Although the service is now known as GCM, the old name of C2DM still shows up from time to time, which can be confusing.)

On top of those permissions, one permission, ***your.package.name*.C2D_MESSAGE**, must be created, where ***your.package.name*** is the package name given in the manifest tag. This permission is not needed if only Android 4.1 and higher is targeted.

Next, a BroadcastReceiver class is needed to receive the messages, and an IntentService class is needed to handle them. The service is declared as <service android:name=".receive.GCMService"></service>. It is recommended that the service name be set to *your.package.name*.GCMService; doing so will make the GCM library pick up the service name automatically. Because the service name used here has an additional subpackage, the part of the BroadcastReceiver class that determines the service name must be overridden, as will be seen later.

The BroadcastReceiver class is named .receive.GCMBroadcastReceiver and requires its own permission, com.google.android.c2dm.permission.SEND. The intent filter holds two actions, RECEIVE and SEND, as well as a category of *your.app.package*.

Now all that is needed is to add the rest of the application's activities and other components. The full **AndroidManifest.xml** file for this recipe is given in Listing 14.1.

Listing 14.1   AndroidManifest.xml

```xml
<manifest xmlns:android="http://schemas.android.com/apk/res/android"
    package="cc.dividebyzero.android.cookbook.chapter14"
    android:versionCode="1"
    android:versionName="1.0">

    <uses-sdk android:minSdkVersion="8" android:targetSdkVersion="15" />

    <permission
android:name="cc.dividebyzero.android.cookbook.chapter14.permission.C2D_MESSAGE"
android:protectionLevel="signature" />
    <uses-permission
android:name="cc.dividebyzero.android.cookbook.chapter14.permission.C2D_MESSAGE"
/>

    <!-- App receives GCM messages -->
    <uses-permission android:name="com.google.android.c2dm.permission.RECEIVE" />
    <!-- GCM connects to Google Services -->
    <uses-permission android:name="android.permission.INTERNET" />
    <!-- GCM requires a Google account -->
    <uses-permission android:name="android.permission.GET_ACCOUNTS" />
    <!-- Keeps the processor from sleeping when a message is received -->
    <uses-permission android:name="android.permission.WAKE_LOCK" />
    <!-- Use this for sending out registration and other messages
         to a potential server -->
    <uses-permission android:name="android.permission.INTERNET"/>

    <application android:label="@string/app_name"
        android:icon="@drawable/ic_launcher"
        android:theme="@style/AppTheme"
        >
```

```
    <receiver
        android:name=".receive.GCMBroadcastReceiver"
        android:permission="com.google.android.c2dm.permission.SEND" >
      <intent-filter>
        <action android:name="com.google.android.c2dm.intent.RECEIVE" />
        <action android:name="com.google.android.c2dm.intent.REGISTRATION" />
        <category android:name="my_app_package" />
      </intent-filter>
    </receiver>

    <activity android:name=".Chapter14">
        <intent-filter>
            <action android:name="android.intent.action.MAIN" />

            <category android:name="android.intent.category.LAUNCHER" />
        </intent-filter>
    </activity>
    <activity android:name=".GCMPushReceiver"/>

    <service android:name=".receive.GCMService"></service>
  </application>

</manifest>
```

Receiving Messages

In order to receive messages, a few things need to be done. First, the device needs to register itself within GCM. The registration ID must then somehow be given to the custom server, so that the system knows where to send the messages. Because the message is sent from the device itself, this ID can just be saved locally. Then, the code in place that actually reacts to incoming messages needs to be in place. This leaves three things that must be added: the BroadcastReceiver class, the IntentService class, and some boilerplate registration code in the main activity.

Recipe: Adding the BroadcastReceiver Class

The BroadcastReceiver class must extend com.google.android.gcm.GCMBroadcast Receiver in order to work. The good news is that not much needs to be done here besides returning the name of the service to start; the rest of this process is handled by the superclass. Because the service is in a subpackage, GCMService.class.get CanonicalName() must return. Listing 14.2 shows the complete implementation.

Listing 14.2   GCMBroadcastReceiver.java

```
public class GCMBroadcastReceiver extends
com.google.android.gcm.GCMBroadcastReceiver {

    @Override
    protected String getGCMIntentServiceClassName(Context context)
```

```
            return GCMService.class.getCanonicalName();
    }

}
```

Recipe: Adding the IntentService Class

The IntentService class must extend GCMBaseIntentService and implement its
abstract methods. The registered and unregistered event hooks that can be used to send
the registration ID to some backend must be handled. The onError event is handled
just by logging errors to the system log. The onMessage event is given an intent that
holds the actual payload of the push message itself in the "msg" extra. Here, the device
can react to incoming messages in any way that makes sense for the application, for
instance, using the incoming push as a wake-up signal for syncing user data. Listing 14.3 provides a simple example by sending plain text messages, which are displayed
in a toast.

Listing 14.3   GCMService

```
public class GCMService extends GCMBaseIntentService {
    private static final String LOG_TAG = GCMService.class.getSimpleName();

    private Handler mToaster = new Handler(new Handler.Callback() {

        @Override
        public boolean handleMessage(Message msg) {
            Toast.makeText(
                    GCMService.this,
                    ((String) msg.obj),
                    Toast.LENGTH_SHORT
                    ).show();
            return true;
        }
    });


    @Override
    protected void onError(final Context ctx, final String errorMsg) {
        android.util.Log.v(LOG_TAG, "error registering device; " + errorMsg);

    }


    @Override
    protected void onMessage(final Context ctx, final Intent intent) {
        android.util.Log.v(LOG_TAG,
                "on Message, Intent="
                + intent.getExtras().toString()
                );
        Message msg = mToaster.obtainMessage(
                1,
                -1,
                -1,
```

```
                        intent.getStringExtra("msg")
                        );
            mToaster.sendMessage(msg);
        }

        @Override
        protected void onRegistered(Context ctx, String gcmRegistrationId) {
            android.util.Log.v(LOG_TAG,
                    "onRegistered: gcmRegistrationId>>"
                    + gcmRegistrationId + "<<"
                    );
            sendRegistrationToServer(gcmRegistrationId);
        }

        @Override
        protected void onUnregistered(Context ctx, String gcmRegistrationId) {

            sendDeregistrationToServer(gcmRegistrationId);
        }


        private void sendRegistrationToServer(String gcmRegistrationId) {
            SharedPreferences.Editor editor = getSharedPreferences(
                    AppConstants.SHARED_PREF,
                    Context.MODE_PRIVATE
                    ).edit();

            editor.putString(AppConstants.PREF_REGISTRATION_ID, gcmRegistrationId);
            editor.commit();
        }


        private void sendDeregistrationToServer(String gcmRegistrationId) {
            SharedPreferences.Editor editor = getSharedPreferences(
                    AppConstants.SHARED_PREF,
                    Context.MODE_PRIVATE
                    ).edit();

            editor.clear();
            editor.commit();
        }

}
```

Because the service was started from a different thread, the incoming message is channeled to a handler, which then displays the toast. As the handler can only ever receive one type of message, it can be created with all default values and the text put as a string into the message.obj field by calling the following:

```
mToaster.obtainMessage(1, -1, -1, intent.getStringExtra("msg"));
```

In the onRegistered method, sendRegistrationToServer(gcmRegistrationId) is called, and in the onUnregistered method, sendDeregistrationToServer (String gcmRegistrationId) is called. These two custom private methods should normally be used to make sure the backend system knows the ID of the device as well as additional information to tie it to a user account. Because the messages are sent from the same device that will receive them, there is no communication with the network here; instead, the registration ID is saved into a **sharedpreferences** file.

Recipe: Registering a Device

All that is left to do to be able to receive messages is register the device once the app is started. This is done by calling the private method `registerGCM()` in the `onCreate` method of the main activity, as shown in Listing 14.4.

Listing 14.4   **registerGCM()**

```
private void registerGCM() {

    GCMRegistrar.checkDevice(this);
    GCMRegistrar.checkManifest(this);
    final String regId = GCMRegistrar.getRegistrationId(this);
    if (regId.equals("")) {
      GCMRegistrar.register(this, getString(R.string.sender_id));
    } else {
      android.util.Log.v(LOG_TAG, "Already registered");
    }
}
```

GCM creates a device ID once and stores it safely on the device, so it is a good idea always to check if an ID already exists before calling `GCMRegistrar.register(..)`. The `sender_id` class is the one obtained at GCM registration. This ID is stored in an extra XML file in **/res/values** called **sender_id.xml**. It is declared as a string resource, so it gets added to the `R.string` class. This is shown in Listing 14.5.

The calls `checkDevice()` and `checkManifest()` are mandatory and ensure that the device and application are configured correctly to use GCM. They throw an exception if the check is not successful.

Listing 14.5   **sender_id.xml**

```
<?xml version="1.0" encoding="utf-8"?>
<resources>
    <string name="sender_id">12345678</string>
</resources>
```

Sending Messages

Sending a message to a client is done by delivering the target ID and the message payload to the GCM servers. Usually one would do that from an application's backend systems. Several libraries for common web languages are available. The Java library will be used here for connecting to the GCM servers directly from the device. A small activity will be used to read in text and hand it over to the GCM servers by using an AsyncTask for communication. The **gcm-server.jar** file obtained while installing the GCM add-on earlier will be used, so make sure it is in the **/libs** directory of the application.

Recipe: Sending Text Messages

Here, simple text messages, read from an input field in the layout, will be sent whenever the Send button is pressed. Listing 14.6 shows the very simple layout used.

Listing 14.6   gcm_acv.xml

```xml
<?xml version="1.0" encoding="utf-8"?>
<LinearLayout xmlns:android="http://schemas.android.com/apk/res/android"
    android:layout_width="match_parent"
    android:layout_height="match_parent"
    android:orientation="vertical"
    >
    <EditText
        android:id="@+id/message"
        android:layout_height="wrap_content"
        android:layout_width="match_parent"
        />
    <Button
        android:id="@+id/message"
        android:layout_height="wrap_content"
        android:layout_width="match_parent"
        android:text="send"
        android:onClick="sendGCMMessage"
        />
</LinearLayout>
```

To send the message, an `AsyncTask` class is used that gets fired in the `sendGCMMessage()` method defined as the `onClick` target in the XML layout. The message string is read from the text field and the target ID from the shared preferences, where the service stored the registered device ID. The layout gets loaded in `onCreate`. The main activity is shown in full in Listing 14.7.

Listing 14.7   Main Activity

```java
public class GCMPushReceiver extends Activity{
    private static final String LOG_TAG = GCMPushReceiver.class.getSimpleName();
    private EditText mMessage;


    public void onCreate(Bundle savedState) {
        super.onCreate(savedState);
        setContentView(R.layout.gcm_acv);
        mMessage = (EditText) findViewById(R.id.message);
```

```
        registerGCM();
    }


    private void registerGCM() {

        GCMRegistrar.checkDevice(this);
        GCMRegistrar.checkManifest(this);
        final String regId = GCMRegistrar.getRegistrationId(this);
        if (regId.equals("")) {
            GCMRegistrar.register(this, getString(R.string.sender_id));
        } else {
            android.util.Log.v(LOG_TAG, "Already registered");
        }
    }


    public void sendGCMMessage(final View view) {
        final String message = mMessage.getText().toString();
        SendGCMTask sendTask = new SendGCMTask(getApplicationContext());
        SharedPreferences sp = getSharedPreferences(
                AppConstants.SHARED_PREF,
                Context.MODE_PRIVATE
                );


        final String targetId = sp.getString(
                AppConstants.PREF_REGISTRATION_ID,
                null
                );
        sendTask.execute(message, targetId);
    }
}
```

Recipe: Sending Messages with AsyncTask

The good news about using the GCM server library is that developers don't have to deal with things like HTTP connections themselves. Instead, they can just initialize a Sender object with the API key obtained when registering for GCM. The API key is stored in an extra XML file as a string resource, just like the sender ID, as can be seen in Listing 14.8.

Listing 14.8   api_key.xml

```
<?xml version="1.0" encoding="utf-8"?>
<resources>
    <string name="api_key">12345678</string>
</resources>
```

The message itself is created by a simple builder pattern. It is then passed to the sender for processing with sender.sendNoRetry(gcmMessage, targetId). That's basically all there is to it. Some result handling and boilerplate code is needed, which is shown in Listing 14.9.

Listing 14.9   **SendGCMTask.java**

```
public class SendGCMTask extends AsyncTask<String, Void, Boolean> {

    private static final int MAX_RETRY = 5;
    private static final String LOG_TAG = SendGCMTask.class.getSimpleName();
    private Context mContext;
    private String mApiKey;


    public SendGCMTask(final Context context) {
        mContext = context;
        mApiKey = mContext.getString(R.string.api_key);
    }


    @Override
    protected Boolean doInBackground(String . . . params) {
        final String message = params[0];
        final String targetId = params[1];
        android.util.Log.v(LOG_TAG,
                "message>>" + message + "<< "
                +"targetId>>"+ targetId + "<<"
                );

        Sender sender = new Sender(mApiKey);
        Message gcmMessage = new Message.Builder()
                .addData("msg", message)
                .build();


        Result result;


        try {
            result = sender.sendNoRetry(gcmMessage, targetId);

            if (result.getMessageId() != null) {
                String canonicalRegId = result.getCanonicalRegistrationId();


                SharedPreferences.Editor editor = mContext
                        .getSharedPreferences(
                                AppConstants.SHARED_PREF,
                                Context.MODE_PRIVATE
                        ).edit();
                String error = result.getErrorCodeName();

                if (canonicalRegId != null) {
                    // Same device has more than one registration ID: update
                    // database
                    editor.putString(
```

```
                              AppConstants.PREF_REGISTRATION_ID,
                              canonicalRegId
                              );                        editor.commit();


                } else if (error != null
                        && error.equals(Constants.ERROR_NOT_REGISTERED)) {
                    // Application has been removed from device: unregister
                    // database
                    editor.clear();
                    editor.commit();
                }

            }


            return true;
        } catch (IOException e) {
            // TODO autogenerated catch block
            e.printStackTrace();
        }


        return false;
    }
}
```

Context is given in the constructor and is needed only to read the API key from the resource file. The message string and the target device ID are passed to the execute method from the activity. The corresponding callback can be seen in Listing 14.7.

The `Message.Builder.addData(..)` method is used to set the message payload. The key used for setting the string message is the same one used in the service in Listing 14.3 to retrieve the string from the incoming push message.

The result of the send method will flag errors by setting the corresponding fields, and a check is run to see if the `.getErrorCodeName()` value equals ERROR_NOT_REGISTERED. This means the device is no longer available to receive push messages (or never was), and its ID should be removed from the database. This is done by clearing the shared preferences. If `result.getCanonicalRegistrationId()` is not null, the device has been registered more than once, and the canonical ID should then be used for sending messages. In that case, the shared preferences are updated to the new device ID.

15

Android Native Development

This chapter shows two different strategies for integrating native C code into Android applications. One strategy is to use Java Native Interface (JNI) to write wrapper functions in C and then Java to access a library of C code. The other strategy is to make use of the native activity, which allows an application not to have any Java code at all.

Android Native Components

When a computationally intensive function is critical to an Android application, it might be worthwhile to move the intensive computation to native C or C++ for efficiency. The Android Native Development Kit (NDK) exists to help in the development of a native component. The NDK is a companion to the Android SDK and includes a bundle of libraries that can be used to build C/C++ libraries. Steps to set up and build an Android native component follow:

1. Download the Android NDK from http://developer.android.com/sdk/ndk/, which includes detailed documents on usage.

2. Install the Eclipse C/C++ Development Tooling (CDT).

3. Download the Eclipse NDK plugin from https://dl-ssl.google.com/android /eclipse/.

4. Set the NDK path by going to **Eclipse → Window → Preferences → Android → NDK → set path to NDK**.

5. Create an Android project through the normal means.

6. Right-click and select **Android Tools → Add Native Support**.

7. Give a name to the native library.

8. Click **Finish**. The **/jni** folder, an **Android.mk** make file, and a stub **cpp** file are created.

9. Run **Project → Build Project** to compile both C and Java files.

Using the Eclipse IDE, the native libraries are properly bundled with the application upon build.

Recipe: Using Java Native Interface

In this recipe, a C program is used to create a numerical factorial function. Then, an activity in Java calls the C library function and shows the result on the screen. First of all, the C program is shown in Listing 15.1.

Listing 15.1   **jni/cookbook.c**

```c
#include <string.h>
#include <jni.h>

jint factorial(jint n){
    if(n == 1){
      return 1;
    }
    return factorial(n-1)*n;
}

jint Java_com_cookbook_advance_ndk_ndk_factorial( JNIEnv* env,
                                              jobject this, jint n ) {
    return factorial(n);
}
```

Inside this C program, there is a special type, `jint`, which is the Java type defined in C/C++. This provides a way to pass native types to Java. If return values from Java to C are necessary, a casting can be done. Table 15.1 summarizes the type mapping between Java and native description.

There are two functions inside the C program. The first `factorial` function is used to do actual calculations. The second function, named `Java_com_cookbook_`

Table 15.1   **Type Mapping between Java and Native**

Java Type in C/C++	Native Type	Description
jboolean	unsigned char	Unsigned 8 bits
jbyte	signed char	Signed 8 bits
jchar	unsigned short	Unsigned 16 bits
jshort	short	Signed 16 bits
jint	long	Signed 32 bits
jfloat	float	32 bits
jlong	long long _int64	Signed 64 bits
jdouble	double	64 bits

advance_ndk_ndk_factorial, will be called from within a Java class. The name of the function should always be defined as the JAVA_CLASSNAME_METHOD format for interface.

There are three parameters in the second function: a JNIEnv pointer, a jobject pointer, and a Java argument the Java method declares. JNIEnv is a Java Native Interface pointer passed as an argument for each native function. These functions are mapped to a Java method that is the structure that contains the interface to the Java Virtual Machine (JVM). It includes the functions necessary to interact with the JVM and to work with Java objects. In this example, it does not use any Java functions. The only argument needed for this program is the Java argument jint n.

The make file for the builder is shown in Listing 15.2. It should be placed in the same location as the C program. It contains a definition of LOCAL_PATH for the builder and a call to CLEAR_VARS to clean up all LOCAL_* variables before each build. Then, LOCAL_MODULE is identified as the name of the custom library ndkcookbook, which is used to identify the source code files to build. After all these declarations, it includes BUILD_SHARED_LIBRARY. This is a generic make file for building a simple program. More detailed information on the make file format is provided in the **ANDROID-MK.HTML** file under the **docs/** directory of the NDK.

Listing 15.2   jni/Android.mk

```
LOCAL_PATH := $(call my-dir)

include $(CLEAR_VARS)

LOCAL_MODULE    := ndkcookbook
LOCAL_SRC_FILES := cookbook.c

include $(BUILD_SHARED_LIBRARY)
```

The next step is to build the native library. With NDK-r4 or higher, calling the provided build script ndk-build at the NDK root directory of the project builds the libraries with an associated make file. For older versions, the command make APP=NAME_OF_APPLICATION is needed. After the libraries are built, a **lib/** folder is created containing the native library **libndkcookbook.so**. In NDK-r4, it also contains two GDB files that help with debugging.

The Android activity that uses this library calls System.loadLibrary() to load the **ndkcookbook** library. Then, the native function needs to be declared. This is shown in Listing 15.3. The output is shown in Figure 15.1.

Listing 15.3   src/com/cookbook/advance/ndk/ndk.java

```
package com.cookbook.advance.ndk;

import android.app.Activity;
import android.widget.TextView;
import android.os.Bundle;
```

```
public class ndk extends Activity {
    @Override
    public void onCreate(Bundle savedInstanceState) {
        super.onCreate(savedInstanceState);
        TextView tv = new TextView(this);
        tv.setText(" native calculation on factorial :"+factorial(30));
        setContentView(tv);
    }
    public static native int factorial(int n);
    static {
        System.loadLibrary("ndkcookbook");
    }
}
```

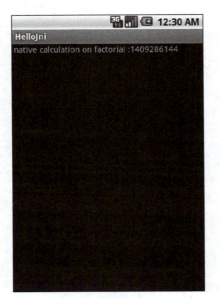

Figure 15.1   Output of the NDK application

Recipe: Using the NativeActivity

NativeActivity is a helper class that handles communication between C code and the
Android Framework. This allows applications to be written using only C. The steps to
create a project using a native activity follow:

1. Create an Android project through the normal means in Eclipse.

2. Right-click and select **Android Tools → Add NativeSupport**.

3. Give a name to the native library.

4. Press **Finish**. The **/jni** folder, an **Android.mk** make file, and a stub **cpp** file
   are created.

5. Edit the manifest to hold a reference to the native activities.

6. Edit the **Android.mk** file to add libraries if needed.

7. Run **Project → Build Project** to compile both C and Java files.

To declare a native activity, simply drop it in the **AndroidManifest.xml** file as seen in Listing 15.4.

Listing 15.4 **AndroidManifest.xml**

```xml
<manifest xmlns:android="http://schemas.android.com/apk/res/android"
    package="com.cookbook.nativeactivitydemo"
    android:versionCode="1"
    android:versionName="1.0" >

    <uses-sdk
        android:minSdkVersion="14"
        android:targetSdkVersion="17" />

    <application
        android:allowBackup="true"
        android:icon="@drawable/ic_launcher"
        android:label="@string/app_name"
        android:theme="@style/AppTheme"
        android:hasCode="true"
          >

        <activity android:name="android.app.NativeActivity"
            android:label="@string/app_name"
            android:configChanges="orientation|keyboardHidden"
            >

        <meta-data android:name="android.app.lib_name"
            android:value="native-activity"
            />
            <intent-filter>
              <action android:name="android.intent.action.MAIN" />
              <category android:name="android.intent.category.LAUNCHER" />
            </intent-filter>
        </activity>

    </application>

</manifest>
```

The android:name attribute of the activity tag must be set to android.app.Native Activity. The metadata tag tells the system which library to load. Its android:name attribute must be set to "android.app.lib_name". The android:value attribute of the metadata tag must be in the filename of the module without the **lib** prefix and **.so** suffix. Filenames must not have spaces in them and must be all lowercase. To ensure that the compiled native **libs** are exported and installed properly, set the application attribute android:hasCode="true".

There are two ways to implement a native activity. The first way is to use the `native_activity.h` header directly, which defines all structs and callbacks needed to implement the activity. The second and recommended way is to use `android_native_app_glue.h`. The app glue interface ensures that callbacks are handled in a way that does not block the UI thread. Native applications still run in their own virtual machine, and all callbacks to the activity are executed on the application's main thread. If those callbacks are handled in a way that blocks the UI thread, the app will receive Application Not Responding errors. The easiest way to solve this is by using app glue interfaces. App glue creates another thread that will handle all callbacks and input events and send them as commands into the code's main function.

To be able to compile code with app glue, it must be added as a static library to the **Android.mk** file. Here, the log library and some OpenGL libs are also added. Because a native activity is responsible for drawing its own window, EGL will most likely be used for drawing things on the screen. The **Android.mk** file is shown in Listing 15.5.

Listing 15.5   /jni/Android.mk

```
LOCAL_PATH := $(call my-dir)

include $(CLEAR_VARS)

LOCAL_MODULE      := NativeActivityDemo
LOCAL_SRC_FILES   := NativeActivityDemo.cpp
LOCAL_LDLIBS      := -landroid -llog  -lEGL -lGLESv1_CM
LOCAL_STATIC_LIBRARIES := android_native_app_glue

include $(BUILD_SHARED_LIBRARY)
$(call import-module,android/native_app_glue)
```

A native activity needs to have a void `android_main(struct android_app* androidApp)` function. This will act as the main entry point for starting the activity. It works very similarly to main functions from Java threads or other common event-based systems, meaning a main event loop of `while(1)` is needed to ensure that the code keeps running until it is stopped from the outside.

The `android_app` struct is a helper class that handles some of the boilerplate, needed for running. Its `userData` field can be used for anything. In this case code it should hold the current state information of the activity. As the same instance of the `android_app` is passed to all the following functions, the state can always be retrieved from here.

The other two things that need to be set into this struct are two function pointers: one for handling input events (such as touch or keyboard events) and one for handling the activity lifecycle. Because those are defined as static later in the code, here they can just be passed as pointers. The `android_main` function is shown in Listing 15.6.

Listing 15.6   **android_main**

```
void android_main(struct android_app* androidApp) {

    struct activity_state activity;

    // Make sure glue isn't stripped
    app_dummy();

    memset(&activity, 0, sizeof(activity));
    androidApp->userData = &activity;
    androidApp->onAppCmd = handle_lifecycle_cmd;
    androidApp->onInputEvent = handle_input;
    activity.androidApp = androidApp;

    LOGI("starting");

    if (androidApp->savedState != NULL) {
        // We are starting with a previous saved state; restore from it
        activity.savedState = *(struct saved_state*)androidApp->savedState;
    }

    // Loop waiting for stuff to do

    while (1) {
        // Read all pending events
        int ident;
        int events;
        struct android_poll_source* source;

        // Wait for events
        while ((ident=ALooper_pollAll(-1, NULL, &events,(void**)&source)) >= 0) {

            // Process this event
            if (source != NULL) {
                source->process(androidApp, source);
            }

            // Check if the app has exited
            if (androidApp->destroyRequested != 0) {
                close_display(&activity);
                return;
            }

        }

    }

}
```

Calling app_dummy() first ensures that app glue is not stripped from the library. This call should always be in a native activity. The pointers for event handling are set, the state is saved, and then the event loop is started. If the application is stopped, the `android_app->destroyRequested` flag will be set, and the loop will have to be exited.

The activity lifecycle is handled in the `handle_lifecycle_cmd` function given to app glue as a pointer. There are integer command constants for all lifecycle events of an activity, as well as some window-related commands for focus and resizing. The `handle_lifecycle_cmd` function is shown in Listing 15.7.

Listing 15.7   **handle_lifecycle_cmd**

```
static void handle_lifecycle_cmd(struct android_app* app, int32_t cmd) {
    struct activity_state* activity = (struct activity_state*)app->userData;
    switch (cmd) {
        case APP_CMD_SAVE_STATE:
            // The system has asked us to save our current state.  Do so.
            activity->androidApp->savedState = malloc(sizeof(struct saved_state));
            *((struct saved_state*)activity->androidApp->savedState) =
                activity->savedState;
            activity->androidApp->savedStateSize = sizeof(struct saved_state);
            break;
        case APP_CMD_INIT_WINDOW:
            // activity window shown, init display
            if (activity->androidApp->window != NULL) {
                init_display(activity);
                draw_frame(activity);
            }
            break;
        case APP_CMD_TERM_WINDOW:
            // activity window closed, stop EGL
            close_display(activity);
            break;
        case APP_CMD_INPUT_CHANGED:

            break;
        case APP_CMD_START:
            //activity onStart event
            LOGI("nativeActivity: onStart");
            android_app_pre_exec_cmd(app, cmd);
            break;
        case APP_CMD_RESUME:
            //activity onResume event
            LOGI("nativeActivity: onResume");
            android_app_pre_exec_cmd(app, cmd);
            break;
        case APP_CMD_PAUSE:
            //activity onPause event
            LOGI("nativeActivity: onPause");
            android_app_pre_exec_cmd(app, cmd);
            break;
        case APP_CMD_STOP:
            //activity onStop event
            LOGI("nativeActivity: onStop");
            android_app_pre_exec_cmd(app, cmd);
            break;
```

```
    case APP_CMD_DESTROY:
        //activity onDestroy event
        LOGI("nativeActivity: onDestroy");
        android_app_pre_exec_cmd(app, cmd);
        break;
    }
}
```

The init and termination events here are acted on only for initializing the EGL display. All other lifecycle events are just logged to the system log with LOGI("message"). The call to android_app_pre_exec_cmd(app, cmd); serves as the replacement for the mandatory super.onCreate, super.onPause, ..., calls in Java code.

The other function needed to react to events is handle_input. The function arguments are a pointer to the app and a pointer to the event. The event type can be extracted by calling AInputEvent_getType(event), which will return an integer constant. The coordinates of the touch event are read by calling AMotionEvent_getX(..) or AMotionEvent_getY(..), respectively. This is shown in Listing 15.8.

Listing 15.8   handle_input

```
static int32_t handle_input(struct android_app* app, AInputEvent* event) {
    struct activity_state* activity = (struct activity_state*)app->userData;
    if (AInputEvent_getType(event) == AINPUT_EVENT_TYPE_MOTION) {
        activity->savedState.x = AMotionEvent_getX(event, 0);
        activity->savedState.y = AMotionEvent_getY(event, 0);
        draw_frame(activity);
        return 1;

    }
    return 0;
}
```

It is evident that there is more boilerplate code to be written in C, even if the app glue library takes away some of it. The benefits of the native activity are that it allows a whole application to be written purely in C/C++, which makes it ideal for heavy computation or cross-platform development.

16

Debugging

Debugging software can easily take as long as or longer than the development itself. Understanding the different ways to debug common problems can save a lot of time and effort. This chapter introduces the basic approach of debugging Android applications, and it examines the many tools available. First, the common Eclipse IDE debugging tools are discussed. Then, the Android tools provided from the Android SDK are discussed. Finally, the tools available on the Android system are discussed. Each application is different, so the appropriate debugging methodology depends on the characteristics of the application itself.

Android Test Projects

The Android testing framework gives developers a set of tools that can be used for application testing. The testing suites for Android are based on JUnit. Those familiar with JUnit will take comfort in knowing that it can be used to test classes of a project that do not extend Android components. An Eclipse installation that contains Android Development Tools (ADT) will already have all of the tools needed to create test suites. Without Eclipse or ADT, tests can be created using the `android` command-line tool.

Test projects are created as stand-alone projects that use instrumentation to connect to the application that will be tested.

Recipe: Creating a Test Project

It is strongly recommended that test projects be created using Eclipse, as all of the tooling required to set up a test (including directory structure) is built in.

To get started from Eclipse, choose **File** → **New** → **Other** from the menu. In the wizard that appears, choose the **Android** section and click on **Android Test Project**, then click the Next button. Figure 16.1 shows the New Project wizard.

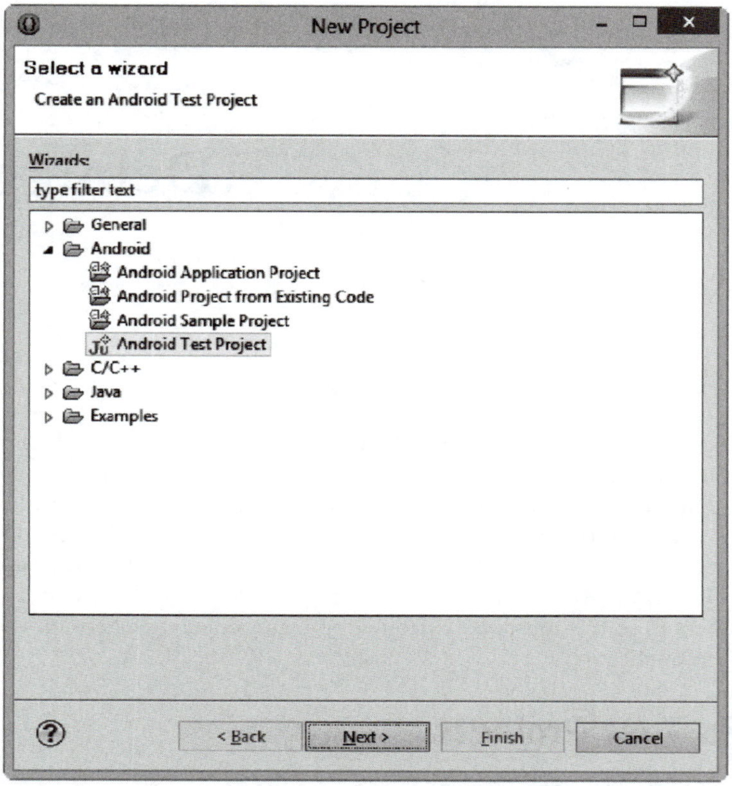

Figure 16.1   New Project wizard

In the Project Name field, choose a name that is suitable to what the test will be for. This can be as simple as the name of the application to be tested with the word *Test* appended to it, or it may be as complex as what type of testing the application will do and for what project. For this project, the name **HelloWorldTest** will be used. The location of where the project will be stored may be changed. Use the default settings and click the Next button. Figure 16.2 shows the naming step of the project.

The next step of the wizard allows a choice of the target project with which the test project will be working. If multiple projects are open, make sure to select the right one. Figure 16.3 shows an example target of **MainActivity**, which is the only project open in this Eclipse workspace.

To pick a specific build level as a target, click the Next button and choose from a list. Figure 16.4 shows the build target portion of the wizard. If there is no specific build level to test, click the Finish button.

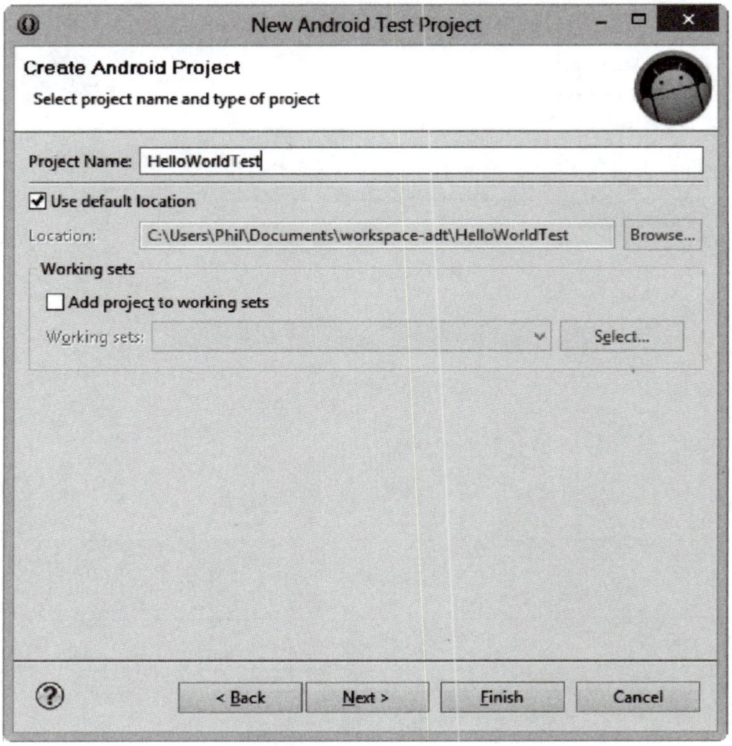

Figure 16.2   Naming the test project

Recipe: Populating Unit Tests on Android

Once a test project has been created, it is time to populate it with the tests to be run. This is done by adding classes to the test package, which is found under **src/com.yourtargetproject.projectname.test**, where **com.yourtargetproject.projectname** refers to the package name of the target project. For the superclass, put in `ActivityInstrumentationTestCase2<MainActivity>`, where *MainActivity* is the name of the activity in the target project to be used. `ActivityInstrumentation TestCase2` is a testing class that is used to test a single activity.

When the class has been created, use an import for the activity to be tested and add a test case constructor. The constructor should be set up as follows:

```
public HelloWorldTest(Class<MainActivity> activityClass) {
  super(activityClass);
}
```

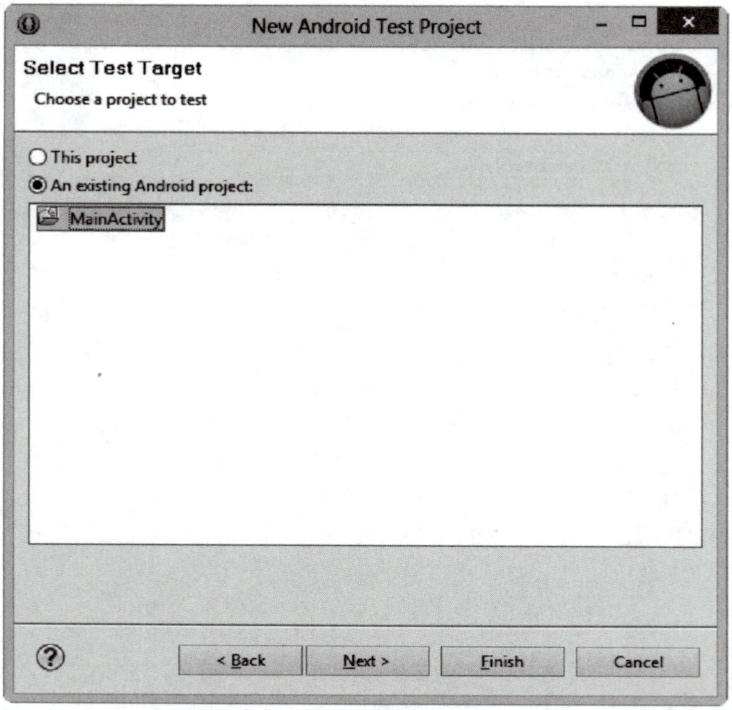

Figure 16.3   Choosing the target project

The setUp() method is used for every test and is used to set variables and run any cleanup from previous tests. For those familiar with JUnit testing, it is worth mentioning that the tearDown() method can also be used. Listing 16.1 is a skeleton that can be used to create and use the setUp() method:

Listing 16.1   **Maintenance Methods Used in Testing**

```
protected void setUp() throws Exception {
  super.setUp();

  setActivityInitialTouchMode(false);

  mActivity = getActivity();

  // Test something in the activity by using mActivity.findViewById()

}
protected void tearDown() throws Exception {
  super.tearDown();
}
```

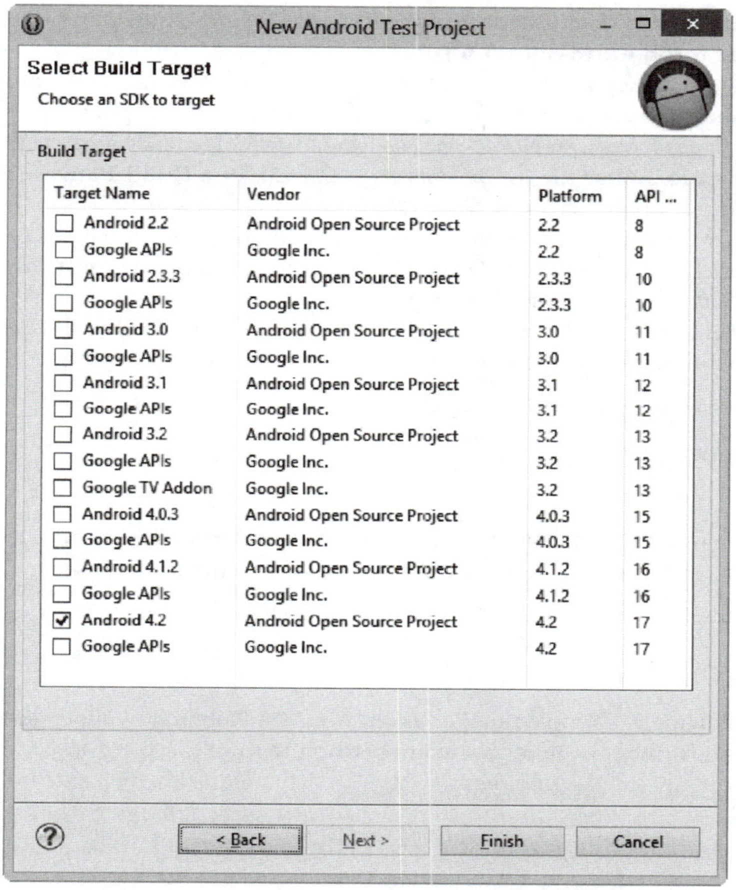

Figure 16.4   Selecting a target API level to fine-tune testing

Note that `setActivityInitialTouchMode(false)` must be used in order to use the `setUp()` method.

After the test values have been added, the test can be run by right-clicking on the test project and selecting **Run As → Android JUnit Test**. This will open up the JUnit view, which will display how the test performs, including runs, errors, failures, and a summary.

Recipe: Using Robotium

Robotium is a utility that helps developers write and execute various tests. To start using it, first download the **.jar** file from http://code.google.com/p/robotium

/downloads/list and then include it in the test project (at the time of writing, the most current **.jar** is **robotium-solo-3.6.jar**).

To include it in a project, create a folder named **libs** at the root of the project and put the **robotium-solo.3.6.jar** file there. In Eclipse, refresh the project to make sure that the changes have been picked up. Navigate to the folder and right-click on the **robotium-solo.3.6.jar** file. In the context menu, click on **Build Path** → **Add to Build Path**.

If the **.jar** file is to be stored in a separate location, open the properties of the test project and choose **Java Build Path** and then click on **Add (external) Jar**. This will allow finding the **.jar** file and including it in a project.

After the **.jar** file has been added, open the class file being used for the test project. Inside this file, add the following import:

```
import com.jayway.android.robotium.solo.Solo;
```

Then, add a new variable:

```
private Solo solo;
```

The solo object is the main way to interact with Robotium; it contains all of the methods needed for testing. Then, add the following to the `setUp()` method:

```
solo = new Solo(getInstrumentation(), getActivity());
```

Now that the solo object has been initialized, it can be used in custom functions for testing.

The following is a sample function taken from the Robotium sample test project that shows how the solo object is used to perform testing:

```
public void testMenuSave() throws Exception {

  solo.sendKey(Solo.MENU);
  solo.clickOnText("More");
  solo.clickOnText("Prefs");
  solo.clickOnText("Edit File Extensions");
  Assert.assertTrue(solo.searchText("rtf"));

  solo.clickOnText("txt");
  solo.clearEditText(2);
  solo.enterText(2, "robotium");
  solo.clickOnButton("Save");
  solo.goBack();
  solo.clickOnText("Edit File Extensions");
  Assert.assertTrue(solo.searchText("application/robotium"));

}
```

More information about Robotium and an in-depth tutorial can be found at http://code.google.com/p/robotium/wiki/RobotiumTutorials.

Eclipse Built-In Debug Tools

The Eclipse IDE included with the ADT plugin is a user-friendly development environment. It includes a what-you-see-is-what-you-get (WYSIWYG) user interface and the tools needed to convert resource layout files into the necessary ingredients to build an Android executable. A step-by-step guide to setting up the configuration is included in the following recipe. The ADT version of Eclipse (3.7 Indigo as of this writing) is assumed, although most steps are the same between Eclipse versions.

Recipe: Specifying a Run Configuration

The run configuration is a separate profile for each application. It tells Eclipse how to run the project and start the activity and whether to install the application on the emulator or a connected device. The ADT automatically creates a run configuration for each application when it is first created, but it can be customized as described in this recipe.

To create a new run configuration or edit an existing one, select **Run** → **Run Configurations...** (or **Debug Configurations...**) in Eclipse to launch the Run Configurations menu shown in Figure 16.5. Inside the run configuration, there are three tabs related to application testing, which contain settings that must be set:

- Android—Specify the project and activity to launch.
- Target—Select the virtual device upon which the application will run. For the emulator environment, the launch parameters are specified here, such as the network speed and latency. This allows for a more realistic simulation of the wireless link conditions to test how the application behaves. Developers can also choose to wipe out the persistent storage of the emulator with every launch.
- Common—Specify where the run configuration settings are saved and also whether the configuration is displayed in the Favorite menu.

After these settings are properly set, the application can be run on the target device with a single click of the Run button. If an actual Android device is not connected to the host computer or the target chosen is a virtual device, the emulator is launched to run the application.

Recipe: Using the DDMS

After the application is run on a target, the Dalvik Debug Monitoring Server (DDMS) can be opened to examine the status of the device, as shown in Figure 16.6. DDMS can be run from the command line or by selecting **Window** → **Open Perspective** → **DDMS** in Eclipse.

Inside the DDMS are three panels that provide different kinds of debugging data:

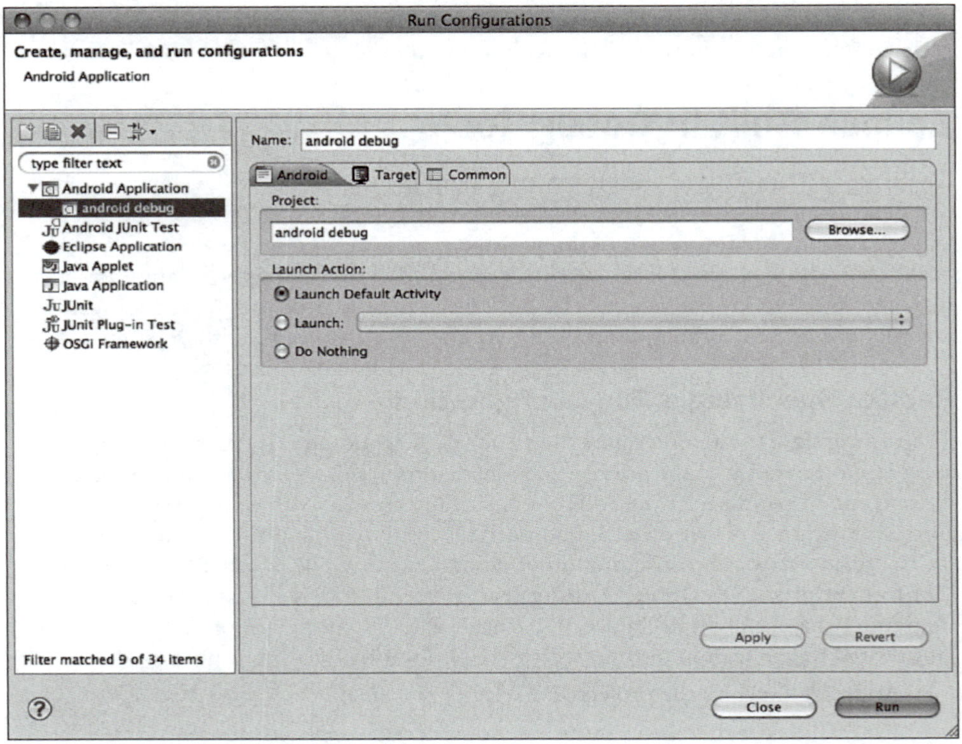

Figure 16.5   The Run Configurations menu in Eclipse

- Devices—Displays the connected Android devices, including emulators and actual Android devices.
- Bottom panel—Contains two tabs: LogCat and Console. The LogCat tab shows all the logging data from the device in real time. It includes system log messages and user-generated log messages accessed using the Log class in applications. The Console tab may be familiar to Eclipse users, as this tab displays SystemOut messages as well as some errors during compilation or run-time.
- Top right panel—Contains six tabs: Threads, Heap, Allocation Tracker, Network Statistics, File Explorer, and the Emulator Control. These are mostly used to analyze the process and network bandwidth. The Emulator Control has several options for controlling voice and data format, network speed, and latency. It also contains options for creating fake phone calls (for testing), as well as GPS spoofing options to help with testing locations in the emulator. Clicking the device in the Devices tab can cause these four tabs to reflect the currently selected device/emulator's running values, as shown in Figure 16.7.

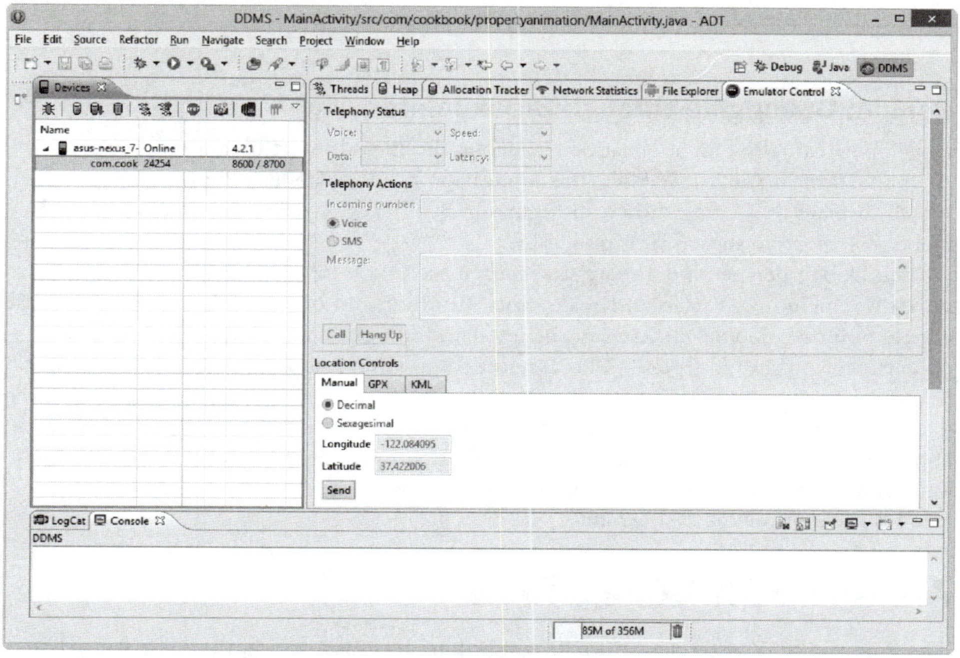

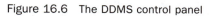

Figure 16.6   The DDMS control panel

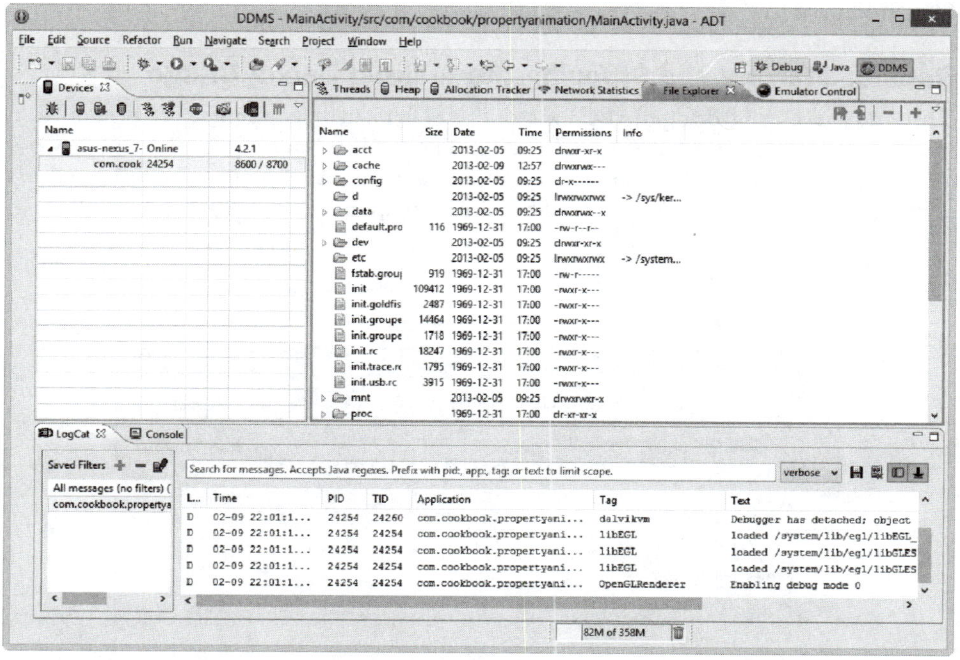

Figure 16.7   The DDMS control panel with the File Explorer, LogCat,
and Devices panels open

Recipe: Debugging through Breakpoints

Developers can also run applications in debug mode and insert breakpoints to freeze an application in run-time. First, the application needs to be launched in debug mode, which displays the dialog shown in Figure 16.8. If "Yes" is selected, it switches to the Debug perspective shown in Figure 16.9.

The Debug perspective displays the source file in a window along with some other windows, including Variables, Breakpoints, Outline, and others. Developers can toggle a breakpoint by double-clicking in the left-hand margin next to the line where the code execution should freeze. A breakpoint is set when a small blue circle is present on that line.

Using breakpoints is a standard debug method for embedded programmers. The ability to stop at an instruction, step through functions, see variable values in memory, and modify values in run-time provides a powerful method to chase down complicated bugs and unexpected behavior.

Android SDK Debug Tools

The Android SDK provides multiple stand-alone tools for debugging. The Android Debug Bridge, LogCat, Hierarchy Viewer, and TraceView tools are discussed in the following recipes. They can be found in the **tools/** directory of the Android SDK installation.

Recipe: Starting and Stopping the Android Debug Bridge

The Android Debug Bridge (ADB) provides a way to manage the state of an emulator instance or USB-connected Android device. The ADB is built of three components: a client, a server, and a daemon. The client component is initiated by the **adb** shell script on the development machine. The server component runs as a background pro-

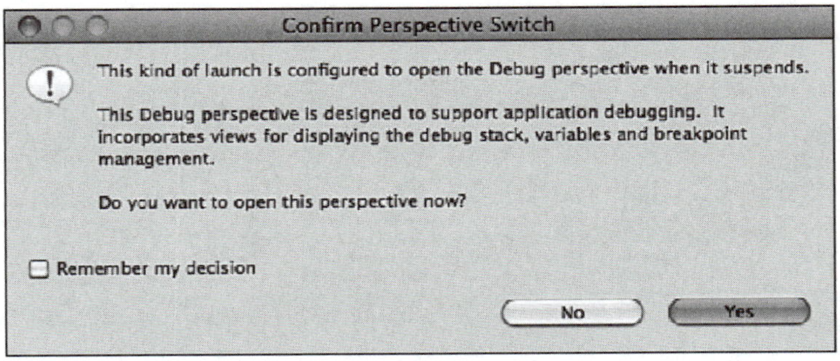

Figure 16.8   The Confirm Perspective Switch dialog box

cess on the development machine. This server can be started or stopped using one of the following commands:

```
> adb start-server
> adb kill-server
```

The daemon component is a background process that runs on the emulator or Android device.

Recipe: Using LogCat

LogCat is the real-time logging tool Android provides. It collects all system and application log data in circular buffers, which can then be viewed and filtered. It can be accessed as a stand-alone tool or as part of the DDMS tool.

LogCat can be used in the device after executing the **adb** shell to log in to the device or by using the logcat command through the **adb**:

```
> [adb] logcat [<option>] ... [<filter-spec>] ...
```

All the messages that use the android.util.Log class have an associated tag and priority. The tag should be meaningful and related to what the activity does. The tag and priority make the logging data easier to read and filter. Possible tags are:

- V—Verbose (lowest priority) displays as much information as possible in the logs.
- D—Debug displays errors, information, and variable values.
- I—Info displays information only, such as a connection status.
- W—Warning displays warning messages that are not necessarily errors but deserve attention.
- E—Error displays errors that occur during run-time.
- F—Fatal displays information only when a crash occurs.
- S—Silent is the highest priority, on which nothing is ever printed.

The logcat data has a multitude of information, and filters should be used to avoid overload by specifying the tag:priority argument to the logcat command:

```
> adb logcat ActivityManager:V *:S
```

This shows verbose (V) data on the ActivityManager while silencing (S) all other log commands.

A circular buffer system is used inside Android logging. By default, all information is logged to the main log buffer. There are two other buffers: one that contains radio/telephony-related messages and one that contains event-related messages. Different buffers can be enabled using the -b switch:

```
> adb logcat -b events
```

This buffer also shows event-related messages:

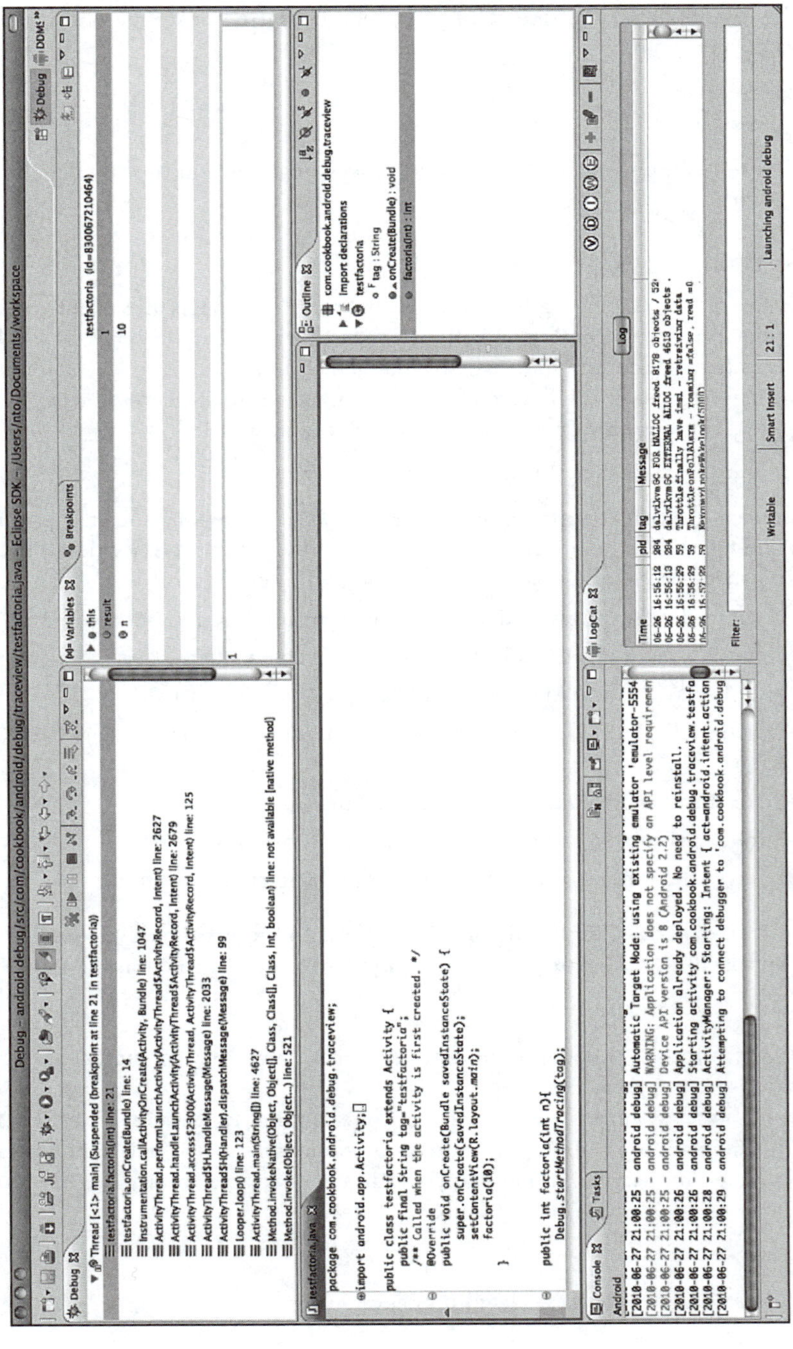

Figure 16.9   The Debug perspective in Eclipse

```
I/menu_opened(    135): 0
I/notification_cancel(    74): [com.android.phone,1,0]
I/am_finish_activity(    74):
[1128378040,38,com.android.contacts/.DialtactsActivity,app-request]
I/am_pause_activity(    74):
[1128378040,com.android.contacts/.DialtactsActivity]
I/am_on_paused_called(    135): com.android.contacts.RecentCallsListActivity
I/am_on_paused_called(    135): com.android.contacts.DialtactsActivity
I/am_resume_activity(    74): [1127710848,2,com.android.launcher/.Launcher]
I/am_on_resume_called(    135): com.android.launcher.Launcher
I/am_destroy_activity(    74):
[1128378040,38,com.android.contacts/.DialtactsActivity]
I/power_sleep_requested(    74): 0
I/power_screen_state(    74): [0,1,468,1]
I/power_screen_broadcast_send(    74): 1
I/screen_toggled(    74): 0
I/am_pause_activity(    74): [1127710848,com.android.launcher/.Launcher]
```

Another example follows:

```
> adb logcat -b radio
```

This shows radio/telephony-related messages:

```
D/RILJ (    132): [2981]< GPRS_REGISTRATION_STATE {1, null, null, 2}
D/RILJ (    132): [2982]< REGISTRATION_STATE {1, null, null, 2, null, null,
null, null, null, null, null, null, null, null}
D/RILJ (    132): [2983]< QUERY_NETWORK_SELECTION_MODE {0}
D/GSM (    132): Poll ServiceState done:  oldSS=[0 home T - Mobile T - Mo-
bile 31026  Unknown CSS not supported -1 -1RoamInd: -1DefRoamInd: -1]
newSS=[0 home T - Mobile T - Mobile 31026  Unknown CSS not supported -1 -
1RoamInd: -1DefRoamInd: -1] oldGprs=0 newGprs=0 oldType=EDGE newType=EDGE
D/RILJ (    132): [UNSL]< UNSOL_NITZ_TIME_RECEIVED 10/06/26,21:49:56-28,1
I/GSM (    132): NITZ: 10/06/26,21:49:56-28,1,237945599 start=237945602
delay=3
D/RILJ (    132): [UNSL]< UNSOL_RESPONSE_NETWORK_STATE_CHANGED
D/RILJ (    132): [2984]> OPERATOR
D/RILJ (    132): [2985]> GPRS_REGISTRATION_STATE
D/RILJ (    132): [2984]< OPERATOR {T - Mobile, T - Mobile, 31026}
D/RILJ (    132): [2986]> REGISTRATION_STATE
D/RILJ (    132): [2987]> QUERY_NETWORK_SELECTION_MODE
D/RILJ (    132): [2985]< GPRS_REGISTRATION_STATE {1, null, null, 2}
D/RILJ (    132): [2986]< REGISTRATION_STATE {1, null, null, 2, null, null,
null, null, null, null, null, null, null, null}
D/RILJ (    132): [2987]< QUERY_NETWORK_SELECTION_MODE {0}
```

LogCat is useful when using Java-based Android applications. However, when applications involve native components, it is harder to trace. In this case, the native components should log to System.out or System.err. By default, the Android system sends stdout and stderr (system.out and system.err) output to /dev/null. These can be routed to a log file with the following ADB commands:

```
> adb shell stop
> adb shell setprop log.redirect-stdio true
> adb shell start
```

This stops a running emulator/device instance; use the shell command setprop to enable the redirection of output and restart the instance.

Recipe: Using the Hierarchy Viewer

A useful way to debug and understand the user interface is by using the Hierarchy Viewer. It provides a visual representation of the layout's view hierarchy and a magnified inspector of the display (shown in the Pixel Perfect window). Please note that while the Hierarchy Viewer can still be used, many of the features it contained have been moved into the Android Debug Monitor, which also contains the DDMS.

The Hierarchy Viewer is accessed using the tool **hierarchyviewer**. Executing this program launches the interface shown in Figure 16.10. It displays a list of Android devices that are currently connected to the development machine. When a device is selected, a list of running programs on the device is shown. It is then possible to select the program intended for debug or user interface optimization.

After the program is selected, Load View Hierarchy can be selected to see the View Tree constructed by the Hierarchy Viewer. It contains four views:

- Tree View pane—A hierarchy diagram of the views on the left
- Tree Overview pane—A bird's-eye view of the hierarchy diagram
- Properties View pane—A list of the selected view's properties on the top right
- Layout View pane—A wire-frame drawing of the layout on the bottom right

This is shown in Figure 16.11.

These four views are used to display different information about the hierarchy to help optimize the UI. When one node of the view is selected, the properties view and wire-frame view are updated. In an Android system, there is a limitation on the View Tree that each application can generate. The depth of the tree cannot be deeper than 10 and the width of the tree cannot be broader than 50. In Android 1.5 or earlier, a stack overflow exception is thrown when the View Tree passes that limit. Although it is good to know the limitations, a shallow layout tree always makes applications run faster and smoother. This can be accomplished using merge or RelativeLayout instead of LinearLayout to optimize the View Tree.

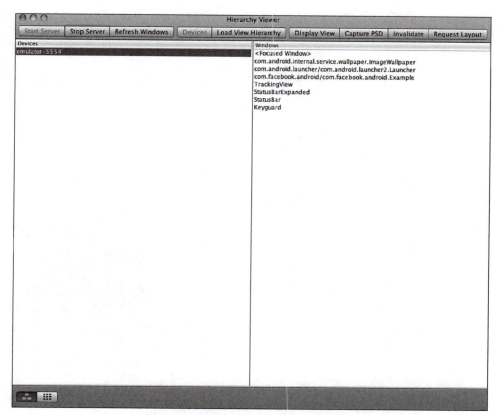

Figure 16.10   The Hierarchy Viewer tool

Recipe: Using TraceView

TraceView is a tool to optimize performance. To leverage this tool, the Debug class
needs to be implemented in the application. It creates log files containing the trace
information for analysis. This recipe specifies a factorial method and another method
that calls the factorial method. Listing 16.2 shows the main activity.

Listing 16.2   **src/com/cookbook/android/debug/traceview/TestFactorial.java**

```
package com.cookbook.android.debug.traceview;

import android.app.Activity;
import android.os.Bundle;
import android.os.Debug;
```

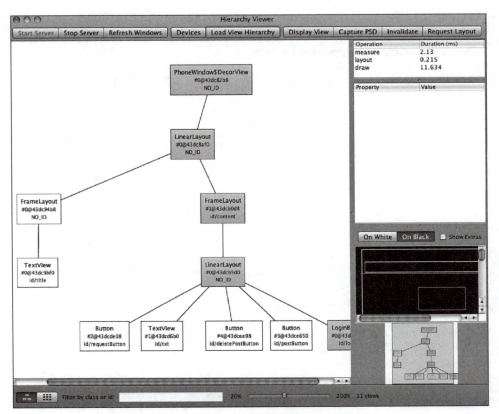

Figure 16.11   The Layout View in the Hierarchy Viewer tool

```java
public class TestFactorial extends Activity {
    public final String tag="testfactorial";
        @Override
        public void onCreate(Bundle savedInstanceState) {
            super.onCreate(savedInstanceState);
            setContentView(R.layout.main);
            factorial(10);
        }

        public int factorial(int n) {
            Debug.startMethodTracing(tag);
            int result=1;
            for(int i=1; i<=n; i++) {
                result*=i;
            }
            Debug.stopMethodTracing();
            return result;
        }
}
```

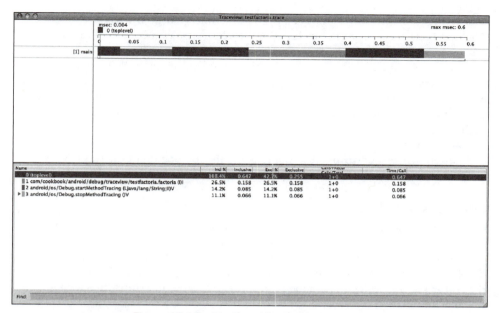

Figure 16.12   The TraceView analysis screen

The `factorial()` method contains two calls to the `Debug` class; the trace is started in a file called **testfactorial.trace** when `startMethodTracing()` is called. When the `stopMethodTracing()` method is called, the system continues buffering the generated trace data. After the method `factorial(10)` returns, the trace file should be generated and saved in **/sdcard/**. After the file is generated, it can be retrieved to the development machine using the following command:

```
> adb pull /sdcard/testfactorial.trace
```

The **traceview** tool in the Android SDK **tools** folder can then be used to analyze the trace file:

```
> traceview testfactorial.trace
```

After the script command is run, it produces an analysis screen, as shown in Figure 16.12.

The screen shows a Timeline Panel and a Profile Panel. The Timeline Panel on the top half of the screen describes when each thread and method started and stopped. The Profile Panel on the bottom half of the screen provides a summary of what happened inside the factorial method. When the cursor is moved around in the Timeline Panel, it displays the time when the tracing started, when the method was called, and when the tracing ended.

The Profile Panel shows a summary of all the time spent in the factorial method. The panel also shows both the inclusive and exclusive times (in addition to the percentage of the total time). Exclusive time is the time spent in the method. Inclusive time is the time spent in the method plus the time spent in any called functions.

The ***.trace** file is constructed by a data file and a key file. The data file is used to hold the trace data. The key file provides a mapping from binary identifiers to thread and method names. If an older version of TraceView is used, the key file and data file need to be combined into a trace file manually.

There is another way to generate a graphical call-stack diagram from trace log files in Android: **dmtracedump**. This tool requires the installation of the third-party Graphviz dot utility to create the graphical output.

Recipe: Using lint

lint is a tool that has been included with ADT from version 16 and beyond. This is run automatically inside Eclipse and is responsible for validating code by highlighting it when it may not function as expected or when it will fail upon compilation. For developers who are not using Eclipse and would prefer to run **lint** on projects from the command line, this can be done by running **lint** from the **tools** directory inside the SDK installation directory.

The following is an example of running **lint** from the command line. Note that this was done in the command line of Windows, so the slashes may need to be adjusted when running on different platforms. Also, when running from the command prompt, the lines will automatically be broken and may appear exactly as follows:

```
lint \temp\PropertyAnimation
Scanning PropertyAnimation: . . . . . . . . . . . .
Scanning PropertyAnimation (Phase 2): . . . . . . . .
src\com\cookbook\propertyanimation\MainActivity.java:32: Error: Call requires API
level 11 (current min is 8): android.animation.ObjectAnimator#ofInt [NewApi]
        ValueAnimator va = ObjectAnimator.ofInt(btnShift, "backgroundColor", start,
end);
                                 ~~~~~
src\com\cookbook\propertyanimation\MainActivity.java:32: Error: Class requires API
level 11 (current min is 8): android.animation.ValueAnimator [NewApi]
        ValueAnimator va = ObjectAnimator.ofInt(btnShift, "backgroundColor", start,
end);
        ~~~~~~~~~~~~~
src\com\cookbook\propertyanimation\MainActivity.java:33: Error: Call requires API
level 11 (current min is 8): android.animation.ValueAnimator#setDuration [NewApi]
        va.setDuration(750);
           ~~~~~~~~~~~
src\com\cookbook\propertyanimation\MainActivity.java:34: Error: Call requires API
level 11 (current min is 8): android.animation.ValueAnimator#setRepeatCount [NewApi]
        va.setRepeatCount(1);
           ~~~~~~~~~~~~~~
```

```
src\com\cookbook\propertyanimation\MainActivity.java:35: Error: Call requires API
level 11 (current min is 8): android.animation.ValueAnimator#setRepeatMode [NewApi]
        va.setRepeatMode(ValueAnimator.REVERSE);
           ~~~~~~~~~~~~~
src\com\cookbook\propertyanimation\MainActivity.java:36: Error: Call requires API
level 11 (current min is 8): android.animation.ValueAnimator#setEvaluator [NewApi]
        va.setEvaluator(new ArgbEvaluator());
           ~~~~~~~~~~~~
src\com\cookbook\propertyanimation\MainActivity.java:36: Error: Call requires API
level 11 (current min is 8): new android.animation.ArgbEvaluator [NewApi]
        va.setEvaluator(new ArgbEvaluator());
                            ~~~~~~~~~~~~~
src\com\cookbook\propertyanimation\MainActivity.java:37: Error: Call requires API
level 11 (current min is 8): android.animation.ValueAnimator#start [NewApi]
        va.start();
           ~~~~~
res\menu\activity_main.xml: Warning: The resource R.menu.activity_main appears to be
unused [UnusedResources]
res\values\strings.xml:5: Warning: The resource R.string.hello_world appears to be
unused [UnusedResources]
    <string name="hello_world">Hello world!</string>
                  ~~~~~~~~~~~~~~~~~~~
res\layout\activity_main.xml:13: Warning: [I18N] Hardcoded string "Rotate", should
use @string resource [HardcodedText]
        android:text="Rotate" />
                     ~~~~~~~~~~~~~~~~~~~~~
res\layout\activity_main.xml:21: Warning: [I18N] Hardcoded string "Shift", should use
@string resource [HardcodedText]
        android:text="Shift" />
                     ~~~~~~~~~~~~~~~~~~~~
res\layout\activity_main.xml:29: Warning: [I18N] Hardcoded string "Sling Shot",
should use @string resource [HardcodedText]
        android:text="Sling Shot" />
                     ~~~~~~~~~~~~~~~~~~~~~~~~~~
8 errors, 5 warnings
```

As you can see from this output, this particular project has several errors that will need to be corrected, as well as five warnings or suggestions for how it could better follow standards.

Developers may wish to force **lint** to skip some requirement checks by passing -disable, followed by what type of errors or warnings are to be skipped. For example, if possible unused resources, unused IDs, and hard-coded text were not concerns, the command could be changed to the following:

```
lint -disable UnusedResources,UnusedIds,HardcodedText \temp\PropertyAnimation
```

Due to all of the warnings being disabled, the only thing the command will return now is the errors that need to be fixed.

Android System Debug Tools

Android is built on top of Linux, so many Linux tools can be leveraged. For example, to show the applications currently running and the resources they are using, the `top` command can be used. The following command can be issued at the command line when a device is connected to a host computer through a USB cable or when the emulator is running:

```
> adb shell top
```

An example output from this command is shown in Figure 16.13.

The `top` command also shows the percentage of CPU and memory used in the overall system.

```
Terminal — adb — 202×56

User 2%, System 5%, IOW 0%, IRQ 0%
User 7 + Nice 0 + Sys 18 + Idle 292 + IOW 0 + IRQ 0 + SIRQ 1 = 318

  PID CPU% S  #THR     VSS      RSS PCY UID       Name
 8129   4% R     1    912K     396K fg  root      top
   40   0% S     8   7760K     300K fg  root      /sbin/adbd
  113   0% S    17 121204K   15756K fg  radio     com.android.phone
    4   0% S     1      0K       0K fg  root      events/0
    5   0% S     1      0K       0K fg  root      khelper
    6   0% S     1      0K       0K fg  root      suspend
    7   0% S     1      0K       0K fg  root      kblockd/0
    8   0% S     1      0K       0K fg  root      cqueue
    9   0% S     1      0K       0K fg  root      kseriod
   10   0% S     1      0K       0K fg  root      kmmcd
   11   0% S     1      0K       0K fg  root      pdflush
   12   0% S     1      0K       0K fg  root      pdflush
   13   0% S     1      0K       0K fg  root      kswapd0
   14   0% S     1      0K       0K fg  root      aio/0
   22   0% S     1      0K       0K fg  root      mtdblockd
   23   0% S     1      0K       0K fg  root      kstriped
   24   0% S     1      0K       0K fg  root      hid_compat
   25   0% S     1      0K       0K fg  root      rpciod/0
   26   0% S     1      0K       0K fg  root      mmcqd
   27   0% S     1    740K     316K fg  root      /system/bin/sh
   28   0% S     1    812K     292K fg  system    /system/bin/servicemanager
   29   0% S     3   3740K     396K fg  root      /system/bin/vold
   30   0% S     3   3720K     400K fg  root      /system/bin/netd
   31   0% S     1    668K     240K fg  root      /system/bin/debuggerd
   32   0% S     4   5392K     540K fg  radio     /system/bin/rild
   33   0% S     1  85100K   14192K fg  root      zygote
   34   0% S     5  21744K    1168K fg  media     /system/bin/mediaserver
   35   0% S     1    812K     340K fg  root      /system/bin/installd
   36   0% S     1   1620K     280K fg  keystore  /system/bin/keystore
   37   0% S     1    740K     328K fg  root      /system/bin/sh
   38   0% S     1    840K     344K fg  root      /system/bin/qemud
   51   0% S     1    796K     312K fg  root      /system/bin/qemu-props
   59   0% S    47 157736K   26216K fg  system    system_server
  107   0% S     9 112220K   14944K bg  app_17    com.android.inputmethod.latin
  115   0% S     6 119100K   17712K bg  app_16    com.android.launcher
    1   0% S     1    312K     220K fg  root      /init
  167   0% S     6 111600K   14576K bg  system    com.android.settings
  183   0% S     6 106268K   14096K bg  app_30    com.android.alarmclock
  198   0% S     7 107172K   14780K bg  app_14    android.process.media
  208   0% S     8 107304K   13620K bg  app_22    com.android.defcontainer
  243   0% S     6 105436K   13436K bg  app_7     com.android.protips
  256   0% S     6 106592K   14084K bg  app_12    com.android.music
  264   0% S     6 105232K   13428K bg  app_8     com.svox.pico
  284   0% S     7 106704K   15888K bg  app_41    com.facebook.android
 2918   0% S     6 105864K   15340K fg  app_43    com.cookbook.android.debug.traceview
 8128   0% S     1    740K     328K fg  root      /system/bin/sh
  141   0% S     9 121044K   19768K bg  app_0     android.process.acore
    2   0% S     1      0K       0K fg  root      kthreadd
    3   0% S     1      0K       0K fg  root      ksoftirqd/0
```

Figure 16.13   Sample output from the `top` command

```
Asset Allocations
    zip:/data/app/com.facebook.android-2.apk:/resources.arsc: 3K
nelsontos-MacBook-Pro:tools nto$ ./adb shell ps
USER      PID   PPID  VSIZE  RSS    WCHAN    PC               NAME
root      1     0     312    220    c009b74c 0000ca4c S /init
root      2     0     0      0      c004e72c 00000000 S kthreadd
root      3     2     0      0      c003fdc8 00000000 S ksoftirqd/0
root      4     2     0      0      c004b2c4 00000000 S events/0
root      5     2     0      0      c004b2c4 00000000 S khelper
root      6     2     0      0      c004b2c4 00000000 S suspend
root      7     2     0      0      c004b2c4 00000000 S kblockd/0
root      8     2     0      0      c004b2c4 00000000 S cqueue
root      9     2     0      0      c018179c 00000000 S kseriod
root      10    2     0      0      c004b2c4 00000000 S kmmcd
root      11    2     0      0      c006fc74 00000000 S pdflush
root      12    2     0      0      c006fc74 00000000 S pdflush
root      13    2     0      0      c00744e4 00000000 S kswapd0
root      14    2     0      0      c004b2c4 00000000 S aio/0
root      22    2     0      0      c017ef48 00000000 S mtdblockd
root      23    2     0      0      c004b2c4 00000000 S kstriped
root      24    2     0      0      c004b2c4 00000000 S hid_compat
root      25    2     0      0      c004b2c4 00000000 S rpciod/0
root      26    2     0      0      c019d16c 00000000 S mmcqd
root      27    1     740    316    c0158eb0 afd0d8ac S /system/bin/sh
system    28    1     812    292    c01a94a4 afd0db4c S /system/bin/servicemanager
root      29    1     3740   396    ffffffff afd0e1bc S /system/bin/vold
root      30    1     3720   400    ffffffff afd0e1bc S /system/bin/netd
root      31    1     668    240    c01b52b4 afd0e4dc S /system/bin/debuggerd
radio     32    1     5392   540    ffffffff afd0e1bc S /system/bin/rild
root      33    1     85100  14192  c009b74c afd0dc74 S zygote
media     34    1     22772  1280   ffffffff afd0db4c S /system/bin/mediaserver
root      35    1     812    340    c0218f4  afd0d8ac S /system/bin/installd
keystore  36    1     1620   280    c01b52b4 afd0e4dc S /system/bin/keystore
root      37    1     740    328    c003da38 afd0e7bc S /system/bin/sh
root      38    1     908    412    c00b8fec afd0e90c S /system/bin/qemud
root      40    1     3460   252    ffffffff 0000ecc4 S /sbin/adbd
root      51    37    796    312    c0218f4  afd0d8ac S /system/bin/qemu-props
system    59    33    157736 26712  ffffffff afd0db4c S system_server
app_17    107   33    110168 15436  ffffffff afd0eb08 S com.android.inputmethod.latin
radio     113   33    121204 16004  ffffffff afd0eb08 S com.android.phone
app_16    115   33    119100 17844  ffffffff afd0eb08 S com.android.launcher
app_0     141   33    121044 19996  ffffffff afd0eb08 S android.process.acore
system    167   33    111604 15024  ffffffff afd0eb08 S com.android.settings
app_30    183   33    106276 14432  ffffffff afd0eb08 S com.android.alarmclock
app_14    198   33    107172 15132  ffffffff afd0eb08 S android.process.media
app_22    208   33    107304 13908  ffffffff afd0eb08 S com.android.defcontainer
app_7     243   33    105440 13736  ffffffff afd0eb08 S com.android.protips
app_12    256   33    106596 14480  ffffffff afd0eb08 S com.android.music
app_8     264   33    105232 13772  ffffffff afd0eb08 S com.svox.pico
app_41    284   33    106704 16020  ffffffff afd0eb08 S com.facebook.android
app_43    2918  33    105864 15784  ffffffff afd0eb08 S com.cookbook.android.debug.traceview
root      13187 40    740    328    c003da38 afd0e7bc S /system/bin/sh
root      13188 13187 888    332    00000000 afd0d8ac R ps
nelsontos-MacBook-Pro:tools nto$ ▊
```

Figure 16.14   Sample output from the ps command

Another important tool is ps, which lists all the processes currently running on the Android system:

```
> adb shell ps
```

An example output from this command is shown in Figure 16.14.

This provides the process ID (PID) and user ID of each running process. Memory allocation can be seen by using dumpsys:

```
> adb shell dumpsys meminfo <package name>
```

An example output from this command is shown in Figure 16.15.

```
nelsontos-MacBook-Pro:tools nto$ ./adb shell dumpsys 284
Can't find service: 284
nelsontos-MacBook-Pro:tools nto$ ./adb shell dumpsys meminfo com.facebook.android
Applications Memory Usage (kB):
Uptime: 63486347 Realtime: 63486347

** MEMINFO in pid 284 [com.facebook.android] **
                     native   dalvik    other    total
            size:      3952     3719      N/A     7671
       allocated:      3325     2621      N/A     5946
            free:        42     1098      N/A     1140
           (Pss):       790     1978     1038     3806
   (shared dirty):     1532     4160     1060     6752
     (priv dirty):      684     1184      708     2576

 Objects
           Views:        0          ViewRoots:        0
     AppContexts:        0          Activities:        0
          Assets:        2       AssetManagers:        2
   Local Binders:        5       Proxy Binders:        9
 Death Recipients:       0
 OpenSSL Sockets:        0

 SQL
            heap:        0         memoryUsed:        0
 pageCacheOverflo:        0     largestMemAlloc:        0


 Asset Allocations
      zip:/data/app/com.facebook.android-2.apk:/resources.arsc: 3K
nelsontos-MacBook-Pro:tools nto$ █
```

Figure 16.15   Sample output from the dumpsys command

These commands provide information on Java and native components. This information is therefore useful for optimizing and analyzing NDK applications. In addition to memory information, it includes how many views are used in the process, how many activities are used, how many application contexts are used, and so on.

Recipe: Setting Up GDB Debugging

The GNU Project Debugger (GDB) is a common way to debug programs on Linux. In Android, a GDB tool is available to debug native libraries. In NDK-r8, every native library is generated; it also generates **gdbserver** and **gdb.setup**. The following commands can be used to install GDB:

```
> adb shell
> cd /data/
> mkdir myfolder
> exit
> adb push gdbserver /data/myfolder
```

To run GDB, the following command can be used:

```
> adb shell /data/myfolder/gdbserver host:port <native program>
```

For example, with a program named `myprogram` running on an Android device with IP address 10.0.0.1 and port number 1234, the following command starts the server:

```
> adb shell /data/myfolder/gdbserver 10.0.0.1:1234 myprogram
```

Then, open another terminal and run GDB on the program:

```
> gdb myprogram
 (gdb) set sysroot ../
 (gdb) set solib-search-path ../system/lib
 (gdb) target remote localhost:1234
```

At the GDB prompt, the first command sets the root directory of the target image, the second command sets the search path of shared libraries, and the last command sets the target. After the target remote `localhost:1234` is running, debugging in the GDB environment can begin. For more information about the GDB project, visit www.gnu .org/software/gdb/.

Using the OpenIntents Sensor Simulator

The OpenIntents Sensor Simulator is a tool that can be used with the Android emulator to help with testing applications. It allows simulation of GPS coordinates, compass directions, orientation, pressure, acceleration, and other factors. It runs as a stand-alone Java application but requires some programming to interact with a project.

Setting Up the Sensor Simulator

To get started, first download the OpenIntents Sensor Simulator from http://code .google.com/p/openintents/downloads/list?q=sensorsimulator. Once the file is down-loaded (this appendix uses the file **sensorsimulator-2.0-rc1.zip**), uncompress it and run the **sensorsimulator.jar** file from the **bin** directory.

Figure A.1 shows what the Sensor Simulator looks like when run.

The next step is to start the emulator, either by launching the AVD Manager from the console or by launching it from Eclipse. When it has been opened, launch the desired emulator and wait for it to boot.

Once the emulator has finished booting, an **.apk** file needs to be installed. This is done by using the adb command. In the same **bin** directory that was used to launch the **sensorsimulator.jar** file, there will be two **.apk** files: **SensorRecordFrom Device-2.0-rc1.apk** and **SensorSimulatorSettings-2.0-rc1.apk**. Copy the **SensorSimulatorSettings-2.0-rc1.apk** folder to the **platform-tools** directory inside the Android SDK installation folder. Once the file has been copied, open a ter-minal or command prompt and change directories until the **platform-tools** directory is reached. A sample path may be as follows:

```
/users/cookbook/Android/sdk/platform-tools/
```

Once in the correct directory, run the following command:

```
adb install SensorSimulatorSettings-2.0-rc1.apk
```

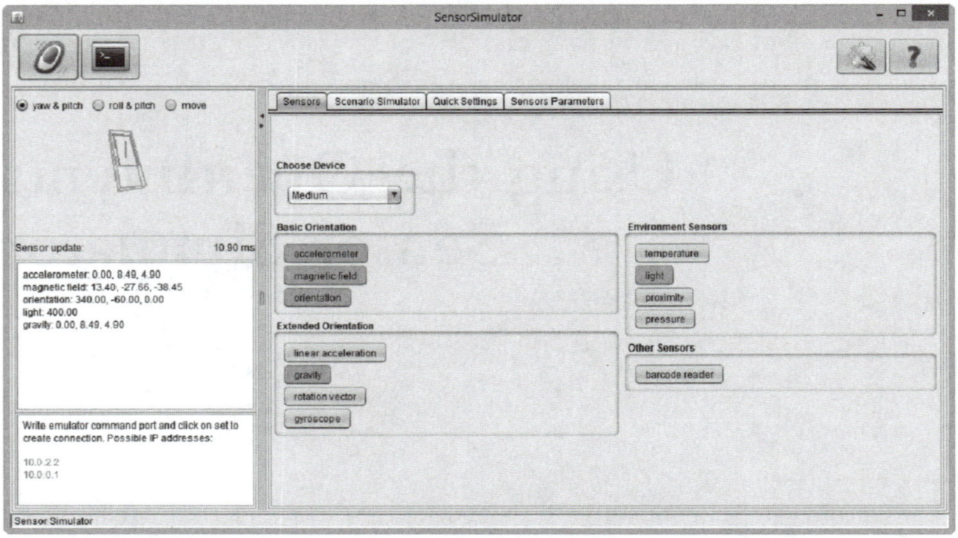

Figure A.1   Version 2.0 RC1 of OpenIntents Sensor Simulator

Note that Linux and Mac users will need to execute the command by adding ./ in front of adb.

The console or command window should roll a few lines of information by but should end with a success message. If a success message is not received, make sure that the emulator is running and try again. When the app has been successfully installed, it will show up as an installed application.

When the Android application is launched, the settings for the IP address and socket used for communication will be shown. The IP address can be found in the desktop application in the lower left corner. It is normal to have more than one IP address available and listed. Figure A.2 shows the initial settings screen on the Android application when launched.

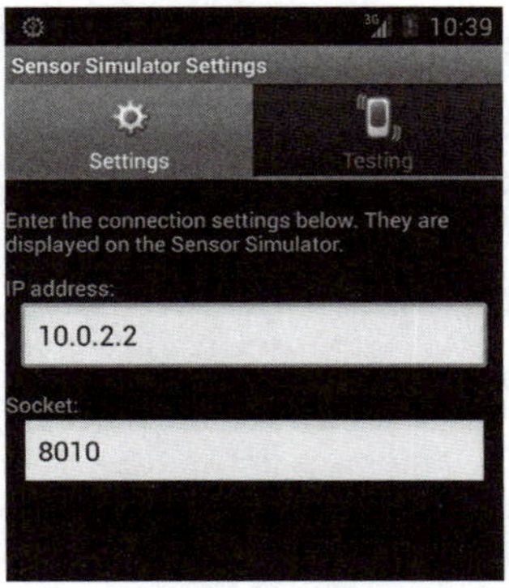

Figure A.2   Initial settings screen of the Sensor Simulator

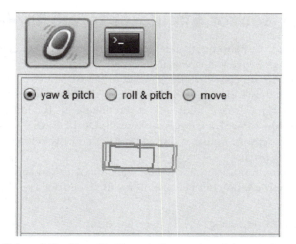

Figure A.3   Changing the rotation vector of the emulator

To test the connection, click on the Testing tab in the Android application. Next, click on the Connect button and wait while a connection is established to the desktop application. When the connection has been made, the settings on the desktop can be changed, which will change the values in the Android application. Figure A.3 shows changes made in the desktop application, and Figure A.4 shows the corresponding values in the Android application.

Figure A.4   Changed sensor data taken from values sent by the desktop application

Adding the Sensor Simulator to an Application

The Sensor Simulator can also be included in an application to help test applications when a physical device is not available. To do this, include **sensorsimulator-lib-2.0-rc1.jar** in the project. This file is found in the **lib** folder in the downloaded **sensorsimulator-2.0-rc1.zip** file. Copy the file to the **libs** folder of the project. If Eclipse is being used, refresh the folder and it should appear. Right-clicking on the **sensorsimulator-lib-2.0-rc1.jar** file and choosing **Build Path → Add to Build Path** will cause the Sensor Simulator **.jar** to be automatically referenced and added to the build path of the project.

Because of the communication needed between the Android application and the desktop application, the following permission needs to be added to the application manifest XML:

```
<uses-permission android:name="android.permission.INTERNET"/>
```

Next, set up the following imports into the class file:

```
import org.openintents.sensorsimulator.hardware.Sensor;
import org.openintents.sensorsimulator.hardware.SensorEvent;
import org.openintents.sensorsimulator.hardware.SensorEventListener;
import org.openintents.sensorsimulator.hardware.SensorManagerSimulator;
```

To access the sensors, instead of using `SensorManager` in the `onCreate()` method, use `SensorManagerSimulator`. While both use a method of `getSystemService()`, the method in `SensorManagerSimulator` has been modified to take an extra parameter. Use the following call:

```
mSensorManager = SensorManagerSimulator.getSystemService(this, SENSOR_SERVICE);
```

Now that `SensorManagerSimulator` is being used, connect it by using the `connectSimulator()` method:

```
mSensorManager.connectSimulator();
```

The application is now bound to take input from the Sensor Simulator. Please note that if the application is running on a physical device, input from it will be ignored while the application is wired to the Sensor Simulator.

The following lists the sensors that can be mapped and used with the Sensor Simulator:

- `TYPE_ACCELERATOR`—The values of movement in an x (right-side), y (top-side), and z axis (out of the screen) direction
- `TYPE_LINEAR_ACCELERATION`—The values of movement along the x, y, and z axes without the effects of gravity
- `TYPE_GRAVITY`—The direction and magnitude of gravity based on the device acceleration

- `TYPE_MAGNETIC_FIELD`—Magnetic field output in microteslas (uT)
- `TYPE_ORIENTATION`—The values of yaw (0 to 360 degrees), pitch (-90 to 90), and roll (-180 to 180)
- `TYPE_TEMPERATURE`—The ambient temperature
- `TYPE_LIGHT`—The amount of light in SI lux units
- `TYPE_PRESSURE`—The average sea-level pressure in hectopascals
- `TYPE_ROTATION_VECTOR`—The combined orientation based on both angle and axis

B

Using the Compatibility Pack

The compatibility pack, or support library, is a set of classes that have been provided to add support to legacy versions of Android (the minimum API level supported is 4).

Android Support Packages

The support library adds the following packages:

- android.support.v4.accessibilityservice
- android.support.v4.app
- android.support.v4.content
- android.support.v4.content.pm
- android.support.v4.database
- android.support.v4.net
- android.support.v4.os
- android.support.v4.util
- android.support.v4.view
- android.support.v4.view.accessibility
- android.support.v4.widget

Table B.1 shows the class that is included in the android.support.v4.accessibilityservice package.

Table B.1   android.support.v4.accessibilityservice

Type	Name	Description
Class	AccessibilityServiceInfoCompat	A helper class that allows use of AccessibilityService prior to API Level 4

Table B.2 shows the interfaces, classes, and exceptions that are included in the
`android.support.v4.app` package.

Table B.2   **android.support.v4.app**

Type	Name	Description
Interface	`FragmentManager.BackStackEntry`	Represents an entry on the fragment back stack
Interface	`FragmentManager.OnBackStackChangedListener`	Watches for changes on the back stack
Interface	`LoaderManager.LoaderCallbacks<D>`	Allows client interaction with the manager
Class	`ActivityCompat`	A helper class that accesses features in `Activity` added after API Level 4
Class	`DialogFragment`	Adds the support version of `DialogFragment`
Class	`Fragment`	Adds the support version of `Fragment`
Class	`Fragment.SavedState`	Saved state information returned from a fragment through `FragmentManager.saveFragmentInstanceState`
Class	`FragmentActivity`	A base class for activities that use `Fragment` (the support version) and `Loader` API calls
Class	`FragmentManager`	Adds the support version of `FragmentManager`
Class	`FragmentPagerAdapter`	A `PagerAdapter` that manages pages by using a fragment for each one
Class	`FragmentTabHost`	Adds a `TabHost` that allows the use of fragments for tab content
Class	`FragmentTransaction`	Adds the support version of `FragmentTransaction`
Class	`ListFragment`	Adds the support version of `ListFragment`
Class	`LoaderManager`	Adds the support version of `LoaderManager`
Class	`NavUtils`	A helper class that helps with updated Android UI navigation

(continues)

Table B.2   (*Continued*)

Type	Name	Description
Class	`NotificationCompat`	A helper class that allows access to features in `Notification` that were added after API Level 4
Class	`NotificationCompat.Action`	Support version of the `Action` used with a notification
Class	`NotificationCompat.BigPictureStyle`	A helper class that creates large-format notifications that also contain a large image
Class	`NotificationCompat.BigTextStyle`	A helper class that creates large notifications with large amounts of text content
Class	`NotificationCompat.Builder`	A builder class that creates `NotificationCompat` objects
Class	`NotificationCompat.InboxStyle`	A helper class that creates large-format notifications that also contain a list (this is limited to five strings)
Class	`NotificationCompat.Style`	Allows rich notification styles to be applied to `Notification.Builder` objects
Class	`ServiceCompat`	A helper class that accesses service features
Class	`ShareCompat`	A helper class that moves data between activities
Class	`ShareCompat.IntentBuilder`	A helper class for working with sharing intents by building `ACTION_SEND` and `ACTION_SEND_MULTIPLE` intents and starting activities
Class	`ShareCompat.IntentReader`	A helper class that reads data from the `ACTION_SEND` intent
Class	`TaskStackBuilder`	Builds back stacks used in navigation on Android 3.0+
Class	`TaskStackBuilderHoneycomb`	Allows access to the Honeycomb APIs through an implementation of `TaskStackBuilder`
Exception	`Fragment.InstantiationException`	Thrown by `instantiate(Context, String, Bundle)` during instantiation when a failure occurs

Table B.3 shows the interface and classes that are included in the `android.support.v4.content` package.

Table B.3   android.support.v4.content

Type	Name	Description
Interface	`Loader.OnLoadCompleteListener<D>`	Determines when a `Loader` has finished loading data
Class	`AsyncTaskLoader<D>`	The support version of the `AsyncTaskLoader`
Class	`ContextCompat`	A helper class for using `Context` in versions prior to API Level 4
Class	`CursorLoader`	The support version of `CursorLoader`
Class	`IntentCompat`	A helper class for using `Intent` in versions prior to API Level 4
Class	`Loader<D>`	The support version of `Loader`
Class	`Loader.ForceLoadContentObserver`	An implementation that manages connections between a `ContentObserver` and `Loader` for reloading data when data has changed
Class	`LocalBroadcastMessage`	A helper class that registers and sends broadcast intents to objects

Table B.4 shows the class included in the `android.support.v4.content.pm` package.

Table B.4   android.support.v4.content.pm

Type	Name	Description
Class	`ActivityInfoCompat`	A helper class for using `ActivityInfo` in versions prior to API Level 4

Table B.5 shows the class included in the `android.support.v4.database` package.

Table B.5   android.support.v4.database

Type	Name	Description
Class	`DatabaseUtilsCompat`	A helper class for using `Database Utils` in versions prior to API Level 4

Table B.6 shows the classes included in the `android.support.v4.net` package.

Table B.6   **android.support.v4.net**

Type	Name	Description
Class	ConnectivityManagerCompat	A helper class for using Connectivity Manager in versions prior to API Level 16
Class	TrafficStatsCompat	A helper class for using TrafficStats in versions prior to API Level 14
Class	TrafficStatsCompatIcs	An implementation version of Traffic StatsCompat for use with Ice Cream Sandwich APIs

Table B.7 shows the interface and class included in the android.support.v4.os package.

Table B.7   **android.support.v4.os**

Type	Name	Description
Interface	ParcelableCompatCreator Callbacks<T>	Support version of callbacks when using a Parcelable
Class	ParcelableCompat	A helper class for using Parcelable in versions prior to API Level 4

Table B.8 shows the classes included in the android.support.v4.util package.

Table B.8   **android.support.v4.util**

Type	Name	Description
Class	AtomicFile	The support version of AtomicFile
Class	LongSparseArray<E>	A SparseArray that maps longs to objects
Class	LruCache<K,V>	The support version of LruCache
Class	SparseArrayCompat<E>	The Honeycomb version of SparseArray that contains the removeAt() method

Table B.9 shows the interfaces and classes included in the android.support.v4.view package.

Table B.9   **android.support.v4.view**

Type	Name	Description
Interface	ViewPager.OnPageChangeListener	Interface callback that responds to changes on a page

(continues)

Table B.9   **android.support.v4.view** (*Continued*)

Type	Name	Description
Interface	ViewPager.PageTransformer	Interface that is invoked when an attached page is scrolled
Class	AccessibilityDelegateCompat	Helper class for using View. AccessibilityDelegate in versions prior to API Level 4
Class	GestureDetectorCompat	Detects gestures and events using MotionEvent
Class	KeyEventCompat	A helper class for using KeyEvent in versions prior to API Level 4
Class	MenuCompat	A helper class for using Menu in versions prior to API Level 4
Class	MenuItemCompat	A helper class for using MenuItem in versions prior to API Level 4
Class	PagerAdapter	Provides an adapter for populating pages contained in a ViewPager
Class	PagerTabStrip	Provides an interactive indicator of the current, next, and previous pages contained in a ViewPager
Class	PagerTitleStrip	Provides a noninteractive indicator of the current, next, and previous pages contained in a ViewPager
Class	VelocityTrackerCompat	A helper class for using VelocityTracking in versions prior to API Level 4
Class	ViewCompat	A helper class for using View in versions prior to API Level 4
Class	ViewCompatJB	Contains Jelly Bean-specific View API access
Class	ViewCompatJellyBeanMr1	Contains Jelly Bean MR1 View API access

(continues)

Table B.9   **android.support.v4.view** (*Continued*)

Type	Name	Description
Class	ViewConfigurationCompat	A helper class for using ViewConfiguration in versions prior to API Level 4
Class	ViewGroupCompat	A helper class for using ViewGroup in versions prior to API Level 4
Class	ViewPager	Contains a layout manager that flips through panes of data to the left and right
Class	ViewPager.LayoutParams	The parameters of the layout that are used with views added to the ViewPager
Class	ViewPager.SavedState	The saved state of ViewPager
Class	ViewPager.SimpleOnPageChangeListener	An implementation of View Pager.OnPageChange Listener that contains stub implementations of contained methods

Table B.10 shows the classes that are included in the android.support.v4.view. accessibility package.

Table B.10   **android.support.v4.view.accessibility**

Type	Name	Description
Class	AccessibilityEventCompat	A helper class for using Accessibility Event in versions prior to API Level 4
Class	AccessibilityManagerCompat	A helper class for using Accessibility Manager in versions prior to API Level 4
Class	AccessibilityManagerCompat. AccessibilityStateChange ListenerCompat	A listener for state of accessibility
Class	AccessibilityNodeInfoCompat	A helper class for using Accessibility NodeInfo in versions prior to API Level 4
Class	AccessibilityNodeProviderCompat	A helper class for using Accessibility NodeProvider in versions prior to API Level 4
Class	AccessibilityRecordCompat	A helper class for using Accessibility Record in versions prior to API Level 4

Table B.11 shows the interfaces and classes that are included in the `android.support.v4.widget` package.

Table B.11   **android.support.v4.widget**

Type	Name	Description
Interface	`SimpleCursorAdapter.CursorToStringConverter`	An interface that defines how a `Cursor` is converted to a `String` (can be used by external clients)
Interface	`SimpleCursorAdapter.ViewBinder`	An interface that binds values from the `Cursor` to views (can be used by external clients of `SimpleCursorAdapter`)
Class	`CursorAdapter`	The support version of `CursorAdapter`
Class	`EdgeEffectCompat`	A helper class for using `EdgeEffect` in versions prior to API Level 4
Class	`ResourceCursorAdapter`	The support version of `ResourceCursorAdapter`
Class	`SearchViewCompat`	A helper class for using `SearchView` in versions prior to API Level 4
Class	`SearchViewCompat.OnQueryTextListenerCompat`	A callback for changes in text in the query
Class	`SimpleCursorAdapter`	The support version of `SimpleCursorAdapter`

Adding the Support Library to a Project

Adding the support library to a project is a fairly simple and straightforward endeavor. It needs to be downloaded and installed, then added to the build path of the project.

The support library is downloaded through the Android SDK Manager. It can be found in the **Extras** folder as **Android Support Library**. When installed, the required **.jar** files can be found in the ***SDKInstallationFolder*/extras/android/support/*VersionNumber*/** directory, where ***SDKInstallationFolder*** is where the Android SDK is installed and ***VersionNumber*** is the current version of the support library (at the time of this writing, it is called **v4**).

To add the **.jar** to an application, create a folder in the project named **libs**, copy the .jar file into the folder, and add the **.jar** to the build path.

In Eclipse, refresh the project, open the **libs** folder, and right-click on the support **.jar**. From the context menu, choose **Build Path → Add to Build Path**. When finished, make sure to initiate the support library pieces needed by including them as imports and changing any required include statements to the support versions.

C

Using a Continuous Integration System

Continuous integration (CI) systems are generally used as part of the Agile or extreme programming model. The following lists the general workflow when using CI:

1. Developers check working code into a code repository.

2. The checked-in code is compiled on a build server.

3. Testing is performed (integration, unit, or both).

4. Code is then deployed to staging or production.

There are several options for the project-building process. Using a build system helps save time and reduces human error when it comes to repetitive building tasks. Table C.1 lists build tools that are available to help ease the build process.

Build tools help to manage the build process; however, several full integration systems are available. While they are not strictly necessary, they can drastically reduce integration time by performing unit and integration testing along with project deployment. They more than prove their worth when a problem is found before a deployment has rolled out to production servers by saving the developer from potential customer frustration and even possible server downtime. Table C.2 lists some common CI systems.

Table C.1 **Build Tools Commonly Used with CI in Android Development**

Tool	License	Description
Apache Ant (http://ant.apache.org/)	Apache License version 2.0	Used by the ADT team, this is a widely used Java-based build system that is highly configurable and runs from the command line.
Apache Maven (http://maven.apache.org/)	Apache License version 2.0	Maven is a sophisticated build system that is used for project management, including the ability to incorporate multiple projects into the same build system.

Table C.2   Common CI Systems

System	License	Description
Apache Continuum (http://continuum.apache.org/)	Apache License version 2.0	Continuum is an enterprise-level integration server that offers automated builds (with support for Ant and Maven); release management; support for many code repository systems, including CVS, SVN, Git, and ClearCase; and more.
Jenkins (http://jenkins-ci.org/)	MIT License	Open source and built on Java, Jenkins is a popular choice as a CI system. Jenkins is an application to help track repetitive processes such as cron jobs. It can be used for build, test, and deploy monitoring and management. It has native builds for Windows, Ubuntu/Debian, Red Hat/Fedora/CentOS, OS X, openSUSE, FreeBSD, OpenBSD, Solaris/OpenIndiana, and Gentoo. Note that Jenkins was originally part of the Hudson project.
Hudson (http://hudson-ci.org/)	MIT License	As of January 24, 2012, Hudson moved from an Oracle project to be part of the Eclipse Foundation. Hudson offers many of the same features as Jenkins, including integration with popular code repository systems such as CVS, Subversion, Git, ClearCase, and others, as well as extensibility through a plugin architecture.
CruiseControl (http://cruisecontrol.sourceforge.net/)	BSD-style	A modular build system, CruiseControl allows for integration with popular build systems such as Ant and Maven, allowing for integration and build testing.
Bamboo (www.atlassian.com/software/bamboo/overview)	Commercial; price varies depending on usage	Created by Atlassian, Bamboo is easily integrated with the JIRA project-tracking system to help push project builds, testing, and deployment. This system is offered either as a demand-based (with a scalable usage cost) or download-based system (with a yearly/monthly fee). It does feature built-in deployment configurations for Tomcat, JBoss, and SSH/SCP systems.
CircleCI (https://circleci.com/)	Commercial; price varies depending on usage and features	A new player in CI systems, CircleCI takes the management and configuration time out of the equation by providing a set of tools used to connect to a GitHub repository and run builds, tests, and deploys on it. If manually setting up tests is preferred, CircleCI provides documentation for that as well as how to overcome common integration hurdles.

D

Android OS Releases

This appendix summarizes the different OS releases and main features that are important to developers.

Cupcake: Android OS 1.5, API Level 3, Released April 30, 2009

- Linux kernel 2.6.27
- Smart virtual (soft) keyboard, support for third-party keyboards
- AppWidget framework
- LiveFolders
- Raw audio recording and playback
- Interactive MIDI playback engine
- Video recording APIs
- Stereo Bluetooth support
- Speech recognition via RecognizerIntent (cloud service)
- Faster GPS location gathering (using AGPS)

Donut: Android OS 1.6, API Level 4, Released September 15, 2009

- Linux kernel 2.6.29
- Support for multiple screen sizes
- Gesture APIs
- Text-to-speech engine
- Integrate with the Quick Search Box using the SearchManager

Eclair: Android OS 2.0, API Level 5, Released October 26, 2009

Android OS 2.0.1, API Level 6, Released December 3, 2009
Android OS 2.1, API Level 7, Released January 12, 2010

- Sync adapter APIs to connect to any backend
- Embed Quick Contact accessible in applications
- Applications can control the Bluetooth connection to devices
- HTML5 support
- Multitouch accessible through the `MotionEvent` class
- Animated wallpaper support

Froyo: Android OS 2.2, API Level 8, Released May 20, 2010

- Linux kernel 2.6.32
- Just-in-time (JIT) compilation enabled, leading to faster code execution
- Car and desk dock themes
- Better definition of multitouch events
- Cloud-to-device APIs
- Applications can request to be installed on the SD memory card
- Wi-Fi tether support on select devices
- Thumbnail utility for videos and images
- Multiple language support on keyboard input
- Application error reporting for market apps

Gingerbread: Android OS 2.3, API Level 9, Released December 6, 2010

Android OS 2.3.3, API Level 10, Released February 9, 2011

- Linux kernel 2.6.35
- Support for extra-large screen sizes and resolutions (WXGA and higher)
- Native support for SIP VoIP Internet telephony
- Keyboard improvements
- Enhanced copy/paste functionality
- NFC support
- Audio effects
- New Download Manager
- Support for multiple cameras on the device
- Support for WebM/VP8 video playback and AAC audio encoding
- Improved power management, including application management

- Switched from YAFFS to ext4 on newer devices
- Concurrent garbage collection for increased performance
- Native support for more sensors (such as gyroscopes and barometers)

Honeycomb: Android OS 3.0, API Level 11, Released February 22, 2011

Android OS 3.1, API Level 12, Released May 10, 2011
Android OS 3.2, API Level 13, Released July 15, 2011

- Linux kernel 2.6.36
- Optimized tablet support and new "holographic" user interface
- Added System Bar, with quick access to notifications, status, and soft navigation buttons
- Added ActionBar, giving access to contextual options, navigation, widgets, or other content at the top of the screen
- Simplified multitasking through use of Recent Apps in the System Bar
- Redesigned keyboard for large screens
- Simplified copy/paste interface
- Multiple browser tabs instead of new browser windows and "incognito" mode
- Hardware acceleration
- Support for multicore processors
- HTTPS stack improved with Server Name Indication (SNI)
- Connectivity for USB accessories
- Expanded Recent Apps list
- Resizable home screen widgets
- Support for external keyboards and pointing devices
- Support for FLAC audio playback
- Support for connected Wi-Fi connections when the screen is off
- Compatibility display mode for apps that have not been optimized for tablet screen resolutions
- Filesystem in Userspace (FUSE; kernel module)

Ice Cream Sandwich: Android OS 4.0, API Level 14, Released October 19, 2011

Android OS 4.0.3, API Level 15, Released December 16, 2011

- Linux kernel 3.0.1
- Soft buttons from Android 3.x now available for use on phones
- Customizable launcher

- Integrated screenshot capture
- Ability to access apps directly from lock screen
- Improved copy/paste functionality
- Better voice integration and continuous, real-time speech-to-text dictation
- Face Unlock
- New tabbed Chrome browser, allowing up to 16 tabs and automatic syncing of bookmarks with users' Chrome bookmarks
- New Roboto UI typeface family
- Data Usage section in settings to track data limits and disable data when the quota is passed
- Ability to shut down apps that are using data in the background
- Refreshed People app with social integration, status updates, and hi-res images
- Android Beam, an NFC feature for rapid short-range exchange of bookmarks, contact info, direction, YouTube videos, and other data
- Support of WebP images
- Hardware acceleration of the UI
- Wi-Fi Direct
- 1080p video recording for stock Android devices
- Android VPN Framework (AVF) and TUN (without TAP) kernel module (prior to 4.0, VPN software required a rooted device)

Jelly Bean: Android OS 4.1, API Level 16, Released July 9, 2012

Android OS 4.2, API Level 17, Released November 13, 2012

- Linux kernel 3.0.31
- Vsync timing for all drawing and animations performed by the Android Framework, as well as triple buffering in the graphics pipeline
- Enhanced accessibility
- Bidirectional text and other language support
- User-installable keyboard maps
- Expandable notifications
- Ability to turn off notifications on an app-specific basis
- Shortcuts and widgets can automatically be rearranged or resized to allow new items to fit on home screens
- Bluetooth data transfer for Android Beam
- Offline voice dictation
- Tablets with smaller screens now use an expanded version of the interface layout and home screens used by phones

- Improved voice search
- Multichannel audio
- USB audio
- Audio chaining for gapless playback
- Stock Android browser is replaced with mobile version of Google Chrome on devices with 4.1 preinstalled
- Google Now search application
- Ability for other launchers to add widgets from the app drawer without requiring root access
- Photo Sphere panorama photos
- Lock screen improvements, including widget support and swipe to camera
- Notification power controls
- "Daydream" screen saver, showing information when idle or docked
- Multiple user accounts (tablets only)
- Support for wireless display with Miracast
- Increased number of extended notifications and Actionable Notifications for more apps
- SELinux
- Always-on VPN
- Premium SMS confirmation
- Phonelike launcher for small tablets in Android 4.1 extended to larger tablets
- Added Bluetooth gamepads and joysticks as supported HID devices

Index

D

M